T0394220

Votes, Drugs, and Violence

One of the most surprising developments in Mexico's transition to democracy is the outbreak of criminal wars and large-scale criminal violence. Why did Mexican drug cartels go to war as the country transitioned away from one-party rule? And why have criminal wars proliferated as democracy has consolidated and elections have become more competitive subnationally? In *Votes, Drugs, and Violence*, Guillermo Trejo and Sandra Ley develop a political theory of criminal violence in weak democracies that elucidates how democratic politics and the fragmentation of power fundamentally shape cartels' incentives for war and peace. Drawing on in-depth case studies and statistical analysis spanning more than two decades and multiple levels of government, Trejo and Ley show that electoral competition and partisan conflict were key drivers of the outbreak of Mexico's crime wars, the intensification of violence, and the expansion of war and violence to the spheres of local politics and civil society.

Guillermo Trejo is Associate Professor of Political Science at the University of Notre Dame and Director of the Violence and Transitional Justice Lab at the Kellogg Institute for International Studies. He studies political and criminal violence, social movements, and human rights. He is the author of *Popular Movements in Autocracies: Religion, Repression, and Indigenous Collective Action in Mexico* (2012).

Sandra Ley is Assistant Professor at CIDE's Political Studies Division in Mexico City. She studies criminal violence and political behavior.

Cambridge Studies in Comparative Politics

General Editor

Kathleen Thelen *Massachusetts Institute of Technology*

Associate Editors

CATHERINE BOONE *London School of Economics*
THAD DUNNING *University of California, Berkeley*
ANNA GRZYMALA-BUSSE *Stanford University*
TORBEN IVERSEN *Harvard University*
STATHIS KALYVAS *University of Oxford*
MARGARET LEVI *Stanford University*
MELANIE MANION *Duke University*
HELEN MILNER *Princeton University*
FRANCES ROSENBLUTH *Yale University*
SUSAN STOKES *Yale University*
TARIQ THACHIL *University of Pennsylvania*
ERIK WIBBELS *Duke University*

Series Founder

Peter Lange *Duke University*

Other Books in the Series

Christopher Adolph, *Bankers, Bureaucrats, and Central Bank Politics: The Myth of Neutrality*
Michael Albertus, *Autocracy and Redistribution: The Politics of Land Reform*
Michael Albertus, *Property Without Rights: Origins and Consequences of the Property Rights Gap*
Santiago Anria, *When Movements Become Parties: The Bolivian MAS in Comparative Perspective*
Ben W. Ansell, *From the Ballot to the Blackboard: The Redistributive Political Economy of Education*
Ben W. Ansell and Johannes Lindvall, *Inward Conquest: The Political Origins of Modern Public Services*
Ben W. Ansell and David J. Samuels, *Inequality and Democratization: An Elite-Competition Approach*
Adam Michael Auerbach, *Demanding Development: The Politics of Public Goods Provision in India's Urban Slums*
Ana Arjona, *Rebelocracy: Social Order in the Colombian Civil War*
Leonardo R. Arriola, *Multi-Ethnic Coalitions in Africa: Business Financing of Opposition Election Campaigns*
David Austen-Smith, Jeffry A. Frieden, Miriam A. Golden, Karl Ove Moene, and Adam Przeworski, eds., *Selected Works of Michael Wallerstein: The Political Economy of Inequality, Unions, and Social Democracy*

Continued after the index

Votes, Drugs, and Violence

The Political Logic of Criminal Wars in Mexico

GUILLERMO TREJO
University of Notre Dame

SANDRA LEY
CIDE, Mexico

CAMBRIDGE
UNIVERSITY PRESS

CAMBRIDGE
UNIVERSITY PRESS

University Printing House, Cambridge CB2 8BS, United Kingdom

One Liberty Plaza, 20th Floor, New York, NY 10006, USA

477 Williamstown Road, Port Melbourne, VIC 3207, Australia

314–321, 3rd Floor, Plot 3, Splendor Forum, Jasola District Centre,
New Delhi – 110025, India

79 Anson Road, #06–04/06, Singapore 079906

Cambridge University Press is part of the University of Cambridge.

It furthers the University's mission by disseminating knowledge in the pursuit of
education, learning, and research at the highest international levels of excellence.

www.cambridge.org
Information on this title: www.cambridge.org/9781108841740
DOI: 10.1017/9781108894807

First published 2020

A catalogue record for this publication is available from the British Library.

Library of Congress Cataloging-in-Publication Data
NAMES: Trejo, Guillermo, (Writer on politics), author. | Ley, Sandra, (Writer on
politics), author.
TITLE: Votes, drugs, and violence : the political logic of criminal wars in Mexico /
Guillermo Trejo, Sandra Ley.
DESCRIPTION: First edition. | New York : Cambridge University Press, 2020. | Series:
Cambridge studies in comparative politics | Includes bibliographical references and
index.
IDENTIFIERS: LCCN 2020018253 (print) | LCCN 2020018254 (ebook) | ISBN
9781108841740 (hardback) | ISBN 9781108894807 (ebook)
SUBJECTS: LCSH: Democracy – Mexico – 21st century. | Democratization – Mexico –
21st century. | Mexico – Politics and government – 21st century. | Drug control –
Mexico – History – 21st century.
CLASSIFICATION: LCC JL1281 .T695 2020 (print) | LCC JL1281 (ebook) | DDC
364.40972–dc23
LC record available at https://lccn.loc.gov/2020018253
LC ebook record available at https://lccn.loc.gov/2020018254

ISBN 978-1-108-84174-0 Hardback
ISBN 978-1-108-79527-2 Paperback

Contents

Figures

Maps

Tables

Preface

In the most widely accepted minimalist definition, democracy is conceived as a governance system in which citizens select their representatives through competitive elections and resolve their differences without bloodshed. While in recent decades scholars have shown that countries transitioning from authoritarian rule to democracy tend to experience major outbreaks of political violence, and that peace prevails only after democratic rules and practices have been fully engrained in society, the association of democratic mechanisms with different forms of violence continues to be mind-boggling. It continues to be analytically surprising and morally disheartening when newly established democratic mechanisms like voting and competitive elections become catalysts of collective violence. It is even more disconcerting when democratic mechanisms become triggers of violent conflict among "non-political" actors like organized criminal groups and drug cartels, which have long been considered quintessential examples of private illicit actors that have no interest or meaningful connection with electoral politics.

This book is the result of a long intellectual shared journey aimed at making sense of an uncommonly intense wave of large-scale criminal violence in Mexico that began six years after the end of one-party rule, when President Felipe Calderón (2006–2012) declared war on the country's drug cartels, triggering multiple state–cartel and inter-cartel violent conflicts across Mexican territory. Our efforts to explain the outbreak and intensification of multiple criminal wars as the country transitioned from authoritarian rule to democracy began at Duke University, where Trejo was an Assistant Professor and Ley a Political Science PhD student; it expanded at the University of Notre Dame, to where Trejo moved in 2012 and where Ley became a post-doctoral student in 2015; and came to fruition as Ley became Assistant Professor at CIDE (Mexico City) and Trejo continued his work at Notre Dame as Associate Professor. A grant from the Trent Foundation at Duke University enabled the initial stages of data collection in 2011–2012; the Kellogg Institute for International Studies at the University of Notre Dame facilitated our collaboration in 2015–2016, when the different pieces of the book began to come together; and a Mexico City collaboration grant from Notre Dame International was key for the writing of the book manuscript and the completion of the project in 2018–2019.

Our academic institutions, the University of Notre Dame and CIDE, provided us with the supportive environment we needed to finalize the research and write the book.

Trejo is grateful to two cohorts of extraordinary political science graduate students who were and continue to be superb interlocutors in the development of a research program on criminal violence and transitional justice at the University of Notre Dame. He is particularly grateful to Juan Albarracín, Camilo Nieto Matiz, and Lucía Tiscornia and to Diana Isabel Güiza-Gómez, Joséphine Lechartre, Natán Skigin, and Jacob Turner. Trejo also recognizes the Notre Dame graduate students who have taken his PhD seminar on "The Logics of Political and Criminal Violence," and the undergraduate students who have taken his junior seminar on "Organized Crime in Latin America." The book's main findings have been presented and discussed in these seminars over the course of the past seven years. Co-teaching a graduate seminar for advanced PhD students on "Large-Scale Criminal Violence in New Democracies" with Hernán Flom, a Kellogg Institute Visiting Fellow in 2016, proved to be crucial for the development of the book. Discussions with Flom and with seminar participants, including Juan Albarracín, Leslie MacColman, Camilo Nieto Matiz, Stefanie Israel de Souza, and Lucía Tiscornia, allowed us to consolidate some of the book's main theoretical ideas.

At the University of Notre Dame, the support of Michael Desch and David Campbell at the Political Science Department and of Paolo Carozza and Sharon Schierling at the Kellogg Institute were crucial during different stages in the development of this project. Kellogg's ability to recruit some of the leading scholars of political and criminal violence as visiting fellows or as participants in lectures, seminars, and workshops was invaluable in improving some of the arguments contained in the book. The Kroc-Kellogg working group on peace, conflict, crime, and violence, which Trejo convenes with Gary Goertz and Laurie Nathan, has been a focal point of novel ideas and insightful scholarly exchanges, where several of the book's chapters were discussed. A number of Trejo's colleagues at Notre Dame's Political Science Department provided important feedback on the book's main claims and findings, including Jaimie Bleck, Michael Coppedge, Sarah Daly, Robert Dowd, Gary Goertz, Scott Mainwaring, Aníbal Pérez-Liñán, and Patrick Regan.

Ley is grateful to the Political Science Department at Duke University for providing the funds that enabled her to spend several summers conducting data collection activities related to this book while she was a PhD student. She specially thanks the Kellogg Institute at the University of Notre Dame for the fellowship that enabled her to spend an entire academic year of fruitful and close exchanges with Trejo and the entire Kellogg community and to envision the plan for this volume. At CIDE, the encouragement and support of Javier Aparicio, Guillermo Cejudo, Ivania de la Cruz, Céline González, María Inclán, Sergio López-Ayllón, Giovanni Mantilla, Hilda Melgoza, and Julio Ríos-Figueroa were essential at different stages of the research and writing processes. Ley also benefited from a growing community of scholars at CIDE interested in the study of criminal violence. She is particularly grateful to Luis de la Calle and Brian Phillips for organizing inspiring conversations with leading scholars of criminal violence invited to CIDE's Violence and Democracy Seminar, where some of the book's early findings were discussed.

Beyond our home academic institutions, we have benefited greatly from a larger intellectual community that connects many individuals from several universities and multiple countries. Presentations in these venues allowed us to discuss, err, learn, and rewrite our ideas in numerous forms and on many occasions.

We made individual or joint presentations of specific parts of the book and received invaluable feedback from seminar participants and audiences at Brown University, CIDE, Columbia University, Harvard University, Pontificia Universidad Católica de Chile (Santiago, Chile), Universidad de los Andes (Bogotá, Colombia), Universidad Loyola del Pacífico (Acapulco, Mexico), the University of Chicago, the University of Kentucky, the University of North Carolina–Greensboro, and the University of Notre Dame. We presented early versions of the entire book manuscript at Nuffield College at Oxford University, Princeton University, the University of Chicago, the University of Notre Dame, the University of Texas at Austin, and Yale University. We also presented the early scholarly findings on which the book is based at the annual meetings of the American Political Science Association, the Midwest Political

Science Association, and the Latin American Studies Association. In all these presentations we benefited greatly from the sharp and generous feedback of multiple discussants, including Peter Andreas, Francisco Cantú, Abby Córdova, Oeindrila Dube, Angélica Durán-Martínez, Todd Eisenstadt, Hernán Flom, Edward Gibson, Richard Locke, Pablo Picatto, and Verónica Zubillaga.

Some material used in this book is drawn from G. Trejo and S. Ley (2018), "Why Did Drug Cartels Go to War in Mexico? Subnational Party Alternation, the Breakdown of Criminal Protection, and the Onset of Large-Scale Violence," *Comparative Political Studies* 51(7), and from G. Trejo and S. Ley (2019), "High-Profile Criminal Violence: Why Drug Cartels Murder Government Officials and Party Candidates in Mexico," *British Journal of Political Science*, 5 September, DOI: https://doi.org/10.1017/S0007123418000637.

Our thinking about organized crime and large-scale criminal violence has been deeply influenced by a multi-generational and intellectually heterogeneous group of scholars who are creating a new field of a political science of organized crime, to which our work seeks to contribute.

We have benefited immensely from a fruitful ongoing dialogue with Desmond Arias, Ana Arjona, Abby Córdova, Alberto Díaz-Cayeros, José Miguel Cruz, Angélica Durán-Martínez, Benjamin Lessing, Beatriz Magaloni, Eduardo Moncada, Richard Snyder, Federico Varese, and Deborah Yashar. Multiple conversations with Gary Goertz proved to be crucial for the development of our theory and an ongoing dialogue with Ana Arjona and Stathis Kalyvas has been particularly instructive in identifying similarities and differences between criminal wars and civil wars. Over the years, we have received important suggestions from Nicholas Barnes, Adela Cedillo, Andreas Feldmann, Marco Fernández, Agustina Giraudy, Ezequiel González-Ocantos, Kenneth Greene, Susan Gzesh, Juan Antonio Le Clercq, Fabrice Lehoucq, Shannan Mattiace, and Vicky Murillo.

Camilo Nieto Matiz served as statistical consultant for this project and helped us conduct the quasi-experimental analyses of the book. Sebastián Garrido from CIDE also served as consultant in the initial stages of our analysis of geographic spillover effects of criminal violence. We received insightful advice on specific modeling techniques from Melina Altamirano, Javier Aparicio, Fernando Bizzarro Neto, Philippe LeMay-Boucher, and Javier Márquez.

Our work has benefited greatly from close dialogue with journalists, human rights defenders, and security analysts. We are particularly grateful to Verónica Calderón, Katherine Corcoran, Edgar Cortez, Rocío Culebro, Eduardo Guerrero, Carlos Juárez, Jean Mendieta, Fabián Sánchez Matus, and Marcela Turati.

We are deeply grateful to all the people who generously shared with us their time and experiences and answered many questions we had during multiple rounds of fieldwork in different parts of Mexico. Our conversations allowed us to better understand the political logic of criminal violence and refine our arguments. The names of some of our interviewees are listed throughout the book, but many others remained anonymous to protect our respondents' confidentiality and preserve their personal security. Whether named or not, their input proved to be crucial for our investigation.

This research would not have been possible without the superb research assistance of very talented young researchers and professionals who worked with us while they were undergraduate students at CIDE, Duke University or the University of Notre Dame. We are grateful to Magdalena Guzmán, Mario Moreno, Elizabeth Orozco, and Valeria Ramírez for their assistance in gathering large amounts of data from newspaper sources. We want to express our gratitude to the Parametría team in Mexico City for helping us transform words into numbers.

Caroline Domingo edited several iterations of the book manuscript. Caroline's rigorous professional standards and her deep commitment to our work allowed us to sharpen the book's language and clarify our ideas, concepts, and findings in truly important ways. It has been a true privilege working with her over the past seven years. We are grateful to Sarah Perkins for her excellent proofreading of the final version of the book manuscript and to Alejandra Quezada for diligently assisting us in preparing the manuscript for submission.

Sara Doskow guided us through the submission and publication process at Cambridge University Press with the intellectual commitment, efficacy, transparency, and expediency that makes publishing a truly rewarding experience. Her choice of two incredibly thoughtful reviewers helped us improve the book in fundamental ways. We want to acknowledge the reviewers' intellectual generosity and sharp suggestions; this book is significantly better as a result of their incisive requests for clarity and depth.

We are grateful for the unflinching support of our families throughout the several years of making this book. Without their love, understanding, and solidarity our intent to shed light on a complicated and sensitive subject would have been untenable.

During the long years of research and writing of this book we have always kept in mind the hundreds of thousands of civilians and their families who have become victims of criminal wars and the victims movements and the human rights defenders who are at the forefront of peace building in Mexico. May this book contribute to rethinking the drivers of criminal violence and to building a peaceful, just, and truly democratic Mexico.

Acronyms

AALMAC	Asociación de Autoridades Locales de México/ Association of Local Authorities in Mexico
BLO	Organización Beltrán Leyva/Beltrán Leyva Organization
CAPAM	Criminal Attacks against Public Authorities in Mexico Dataset
CICIG	Comisión Internacional Contra la Impunidad en Guatemala/International Commission Against Impunity in Guatemala
CISEN	Centro de Investigación y Seguridad Nacional/Center for Research and National Security
CNDH	Comisión Nacional de Derechos Humanos/Human Rights National Commission
CRAC-PC	Coordinadora Regional de Autoridades Comunitarias-Policía Comunitaria/Regional Coordinator of Community Authorities-Community Police
CVM	Criminal Violence in Mexico Dataset
DEA	Drug Enforcement Agency
DFS	Dirección Federal de Seguridad/Federal Security Directorate
DINA	Dirección de Inteligencia Nacional/National Intelligence Directorate
ENVE	Encuesta Nacional de Victimización de Empresas/ National Business Victimization Survey
FARC	Fuerzas Armadas Revolucionarias de Colombia/ Revolutionary Armed Forces of Colombia

FASP	Fondo de Aportaciones para la Seguridad Pública/Public Security Contribution Fund
FMLN	El Frente Farabundo Martí para la Liberación Nacional/Farabundo Martí National Liberation Front
FREPASO	Frente País Solidario/Country Solidarity Front
GAFES	Grupo Aeromóvil de las Fuerzas Especiales/Special Forces Airmobile Group
MC	Movimiento Ciudadano/Citizen's Movement
OGC	organized criminal group
PAN	Partido Acción Nacional/National Action Party
PGR	Procuraduría General de la República/Attorney General's Office
PRD	Partido de la Revolución Democrática/Party of the Democratic Revolution
PJ	Partido Justicialista/Justicialist Party
PRI	Partido Revolucionario Institucional/Institutional Revolutionary Party
PSV	Partido Socialista de Venezuela/Socialist Party of Venezuela
PT	Partido del Trabajo/Labor Party
SUBSEMUN	Subsidio para la Seguridad en los Municipios/Subsidy for Security in Municipalities
UCR	Unión Cívica Radical/Radical Civic Union
UNDP	Programa de las Naciones Unidas para el Desarrollo/United Nations Development Program
UNODC	Oficina de las Naciones Unidas contra la Droga y el Delito/United Nations Office on Drugs and Crime

Introduction

One of the most surprising developments in Mexico's transition from authoritarian rule to democracy is the outbreak of criminal wars and large-scale criminal violence after the demise of seven decades of one-party rule. Under the reign of the Institutional Revolutionary Party (PRI), several major drug cartels had coexisted in relative peace and pursued their criminal activities without conflict among themselves or serious confrontation with the state. But as the country moved into multiparty competition and opposition parties scored unprecedented victories across cities and states in the 1990s, eventually winning presidential power in 2000, the cartels went to bloody war over profitable drug trafficking routes. As the late journalist Jesús Blancornelas (2002) observed, the first major inter-cartel war emblematically broke out in Tijuana in the northwestern state of Baja California where, in a historic 1989 election, the PRI had lost control of a state for the first time in the century. Subsequent inter-cartel wars erupted in other central and northern states where leftist and right-wing opposition candidates unseated the PRI for the first time. In the 1990s, battle deaths reached an annual peak of 350; by 2005, the death count surpassed the threshold of 1,000 murders – this is the threshold commonly used to classify a conflict as a case of civil war.[1]

The consolidation of multiparty elections as the sole mechanism to select and remove leaders, and to allocate power through peaceful means, did not bring peace in Mexico but was associated with a dramatic increase in criminal violence. Six years into democracy,

---

[1] See Fearon and Laitin (2003).

incoming President Felipe Calderón from the right-wing National Action Party (PAN) – the party that had defeated the long-reigning PRI in 2000 – declared war on the cartels and deployed the army throughout Mexico's most conflictive regions in 2006. The War on Drugs and the outbreak of state–cartel wars intensified inter-cartel wars, and drug violence grew between five and six times throughout Calderón's six-year term in office. According to the official government count made by Calderón's successor, between 2006 and 2012, 70,000 Mexicans were murdered in inter-cartel and state–cartel conflicts. This is more than four times greater than the median death toll of all civil wars in the second half of the twentieth century.[2]

Over the course of six years of state–cartel and inter-cartel wars, Mexico's criminal underworld experienced dramatic transformations. Cartels fragmented and went from 5 to 62 organized criminal groups (OCGs), and the street gangs working for them went from dozens to hundreds (Guerrero 2010, 2011a). These groups rapidly expanded their range of illicit activities beyond drug trafficking and ventured into new criminal markets, including the illegal *extraction* of human wealth (e.g., extortion and kidnapping for ransom) and of natural resource wealth (e.g., illicit plundering of mines, forests, gas and oil refineries). As a result of these new ventures, OCGs expanded their targets of attacks from rival cartels and state institutions to unarmed civilians. But one of the most surprising transformations took place when drug lords and their criminal associates began to systematically murder mayors and municipal party candidates in their attempts to influence subnational election results and gain de facto control over municipal governments, peoples, and territories. By 2012, more than two decades after the onset of inter-cartel wars and six years after the launching of the federal War on Drugs, one-third of Mexico's population lived in municipalities where local government officials and party candidates had been victims of lethal criminal attacks and where OCGs sought to establish subnational criminal governance regimes.

Why did Mexican cartels go to war as the country transitioned from one-party rule to multiparty democracy? Why did wars become more intense as elections in Mexico's 31 states and more than 2,400 municipalities turned increasingly competitive, party alternation became widespread, and power was increasingly decentralized and fragmented along the country's federal system? Why did cartels and their criminal associates

---

[2] Sambanis (2004) estimates that the median death toll was 17,000 murders.

launch major attacks against local government officials and party candidates during election cycles, and why did they develop an interest in becoming de facto rulers over Mexico's municipal governments and local populations and territories?

The outbreak of criminal wars as countries transition from authoritarian rule to electoral democracy and the intimate association between political change and large-scale criminal violence in democracy are, to be sure, not Mexico-specific phenomena. In South America, Brazil experienced an outbreak of criminal violence after democratization in 1985 (Arias 2006a; Lessing 2017), and gang violence has intensified decade after decade as electoral competition, political plurality, and political decentralization have increased (Albarracín 2018). Drug trafficking gangs have developed criminal governance regimes in large swaths of the impoverished favelas in Rio de Janeiro and other major metropolitan centers (Arias 2006a). In Central America, after the establishment of competitive multiparty elections in the 1980s and shortly after the peace agreements that brought decades of civil war to an end in the 1990s, Guatemala and El Salvador experienced a dramatic increase in criminal violence (Cruz 2011; Yashar 2018). And gangs in El Salvador have established tight controls over local neighborhoods and their populations in the country's largest urban centers (Córdova 2019).

Explaining why OCGs go to war as countries outgrow autocracy, why democratic institutions become intimately intertwined with criminal violence, and why criminal lords develop interests in becoming de facto subnational rulers poses major challenges to dominant theories of crime and violence in the social sciences. From the sociology of crime to the economics of crime and mafia studies, students of organized crime and criminal violence have ignored or only superficially considered politics as a potential driver of criminal peace and violence.

Following Durkheim's (1893/1964) seminal work on social alienation and social control, **sociologists** have argued that broken communities and mono-parental households in impoverished urban areas provide the structural conditions for young men to join criminal gangs and engage in violent criminal behavior (Sampson and Groves 1989; Sampson 1993). More dynamic explanations emphasize the social dislocation that results from major periods of urbanization and outmigration from rural to urban areas. Both the static and dynamic approaches underscore the importance of weak social networks, the erosion of social capital, and the lack of social mobility as drivers of criminal violence. In studies that concentrate on neighborhood-level dynamics, the police appear as the only relevant state actor and scholarly research has focused mainly on police strategy (coercive engagement through incarceration versus developing police legitimate and community cooperation) and on how different forms of police engagement with the community and the use of extralegal violence are mediated by class, race, and ethnicity (Braga, Brunson and Drakulich 2019). Whether the focus is on community structures or the police or both, state and electoral politics have been conspicuously absent from dominant sociological theories of criminal violence. Criminal gangs are assumed to be *apolitical* organizations, and the sphere of policing is considered to be detached from electoral politics.

While the scholarship on the sociology of crime may be particularly useful in explaining why some Mexican communities may be predisposed to experience greater criminal violence, it fails to account for the intimate linkages between electoral politics, drug wars, and large-scale criminal violence that developed as Mexico transitioned from authoritarian rule to multiparty democracy.[3]

At least since Becker's (1968) foundational contribution to the economics of crime, **economists** have sought to explain criminal behavior and violence in terms of the incentives that encourage people to engage in criminal activities (*push factors*) and the state actions that deter them from so doing (*pull factors*). Following Becker's proposition that individuals engage in crime when their opportunity cost is low and they have little to lose, economists suggest that poverty, the lack of labor market opportunities, poor schooling and high drop-out rates from school often drive young men into committing violent crime (Neumayer 2003; Fajnzylber, Lederman and Loayza 2002). Others have looked into state capacity and effective policing as a deterrent of crime and criminal violence (Fajnzylber, Lederman and Loayza 2002; Levitt 2004). Mirroring established assumptions in the sociology of crime, economists have long assumed that organized crime is a private, illicit economic enterprise and OCGs are primarily *apolitical* groups. Influenced by the economics of interest groups, some scholars have departed from this strong initial assumption and have modeled drug cartels as a specific family of interest group in which criminal bosses rely on bribery and coercion to influence government policy in their favor (Dal Bó, Dal Bó, and Di Tella 2006).

---

[3] For an important exception, see Villarreal (2002). His work, however, focuses on ordinary crime, not necessarily on organized crime and Mexico's drug wars. Beyond Mexico, see Vargas (2016).

The *push* and *pull* factors emphasized by the economics of crime may help explain individual predispositions toward violence, but they provide no direct interpretation of the potential political foundations of Mexico's criminal wars. Becker's emphasis on the state's policing capacity may represent a bridge to politics. As students of civil war have conjectured, states in transitional regimes tend to have low governing and policing capacities (Fearon and Laitin 2003). But this claim is devoid of politics. Although elections are the key mechanism of political change in transitions from closed autocracy to electoral autocracy and into multiparty democracy, most studies assume state capacity to be a financial or a technical problem, rather than a political question in which electoral incentives may inform the development of state presence and capacities in such areas as security and policing.

Since the publication of Gambetta's (1996) path-breaking interpretation of the Sicilian Mafia, analytic sociologists and political economists have made crucial theoretical developments to explain the rise of mafias, the rationality of their strategic behavior, and the conditions under which they become violent. Focusing on periods of major structural transformation, in which the state is relatively absent, **mafia scholars** have suggested that mafias emerge as OCGs that seek to provide protection to players in the criminal underworld. This happened in Italy during the transition from feudalism to capitalism and after the reunification of the country (Gambetta 1996), and in Russia after the collapse of communism (Varese 2001). To operate successfully, mafiosi need to develop a comparative advantage in information gathering and in violent coercion. That is why members of the old order – for instance, feudal guards in nineteenth-century Italy or former KGB agents in late twentieth century Russia – have played a leading role in the development of the mafia. As Gambetta contends, mafias operate within the confines of cities or small subnational regions, because information gathering and the capacity to enforce agreements cannot be effectively exercised beyond the mafiosi's place of residence. In these limited geographic spaces, mafia bosses can aspire to have the monopoly of force in the criminal underworld and promote an environment in which the everyday operations of illicit markets are kept away from the spotlight and state authorities are kept at bay either through the secrecy of illegal activities or through bribery. It is a widely held claim in this literature that mafiosi go to war only when their monopolistic controls are challenged. Competition is the main driver of violence in the criminal underworld (Schelling 1971; Gambetta 1996; Skaperdas 2001; Varese 2010).

While mafia studies have established the theoretical foundations of our understanding of the criminal underworld and an exploration of the linkages between macro-political change and criminal violence, three problems remain that limit the power of this literature to explain the outbreak of criminal wars and large-scale criminal violence in Mexico and other new democracies. First, contrary to expectations that OCGs would operate in the criminal lord's place of residence, Mexican cartels have expanded well beyond their home cities or states and have ventured into other parts of Mexico and abroad. These are large-scale, multisite, transregional and in some cases transnational criminal organizations. Second, rather than rely on the secrecy of bribery or on targeted violence to resolve conflicts without unnecessarily attracting the attention of state authorities, drug cartels and their private militias have engaged in lethal and barbaric violence resembling that of civil war. Large-scale criminal violence of the magnitude experienced in countries such as Mexico, Brazil, Guatemala, or El Salvador is an anomaly for mafia studies. Finally, in contrast to the desire for secrecy that characterizes the criminal underworld described in mafia studies, and contrary to the presumed restriction of OCGs' activities to the criminal sphere, Mexican cartels' decision to systematically murder local government officials and party candidates and to seek to develop subnational criminal governance regimes defies theoretical assumptions from mafia studies.

Although the study of organized crime and large-scale criminal violence has been conspicuously absent from political science (Barnes 2017), in recent years scholars of Latin America have led the way in developing a new understanding of the political foundations of crime and violence. Since Arias's (2006) pioneering work, scholars have increasingly recognized that different forms of engagement between OCGs and state agents are crucial factors in defining peace and violence in the criminal underworld. This approach develops a new understanding in which the state is no longer viewed as a homogenizing organization that seeks to monopolize violence. In this emerging literature, criminal gangs, drug cartels, and armed private militias are conceived as illicit organizations that engage in some form of competitive state-building in cities, towns, and neighborhoods (Arias 2006a; Snyder and Durán-Martínez 2009; Arias and Goldstein 2010; Arias 2017; Barnes 2017; Lessing 2017; Albarracín 2018; Bergman 2018; Yashar 2018; Flom 2019; Lessing and Willis 2019). When criminal bosses develop collusive agreements with state agents and learn to coexist, peace reigns in the criminal underworld. But when OCGs compete for turf against each other or compete for state protection – or when they compete against the state – war and large-scale violence become the dominant form of interaction.

These new understandings of OCGs as political actors that compete for order and subnational territorial control provide the political basis to start thinking about the potential linkages between political change and peace and violence in the criminal underworld. However, an important theoretical limitation is that in this state-centric approach, *political regimes* and *elections* are not recognized as key mechanisms for the distribution of state power that may affect the forms of engagement between state agents and criminal organizations. To disentangle the relationship between political change and organized criminal violence we need a political approach that recognizes the role of the state, political regimes, and elections in a new explanation of the ontology of organized crime and of the conditions that lead to war and peace in the criminal underworld.

OBJECTIVES

In this book we seek to explain why Mexican cartels went to war as the country transitioned from authoritarian rule to democracy, why violence skyrocketed in democracy, and why – over the course of the War on Drugs – cartels and their criminal associates developed political interests and established de facto subnational political controls across important swaths of Mexico's territory, subverting local democracies. We seek to explain three crucial moments in the development of Mexico's drug wars: the *outbreak* of wars, the *intensification* of violence, and the *expansion* of war and violence to the spheres of local politics and civil society.

In addressing these questions, the book necessarily ventures into foundational theoretical and conceptual work. Because the leading theories of crime – most of them developed in economics and sociology – have focused mainly on (1) economic incentives and social structures that contribute to the rise of violent criminal groups; (2) law enforcement activities that deter or stimulate criminal behavior; and (3) the internal organization of criminal groups, politics has been systematically overlooked. To be sure, scholars of mafia studies and organized crime have recognized that OCGs have historically emerged during periods of major economic and political transformation (Gambetta 1996; Skaperdas 2001; Varese 2001). Moreover, cross-national studies have shown that criminal violence tends to increase as countries transition from authoritarian rule to democracy (Neumayer 2003; Fox and Hoelscher 2012; Rivera 2016). And political scientists studying organized crime in Latin America have begun to develop the theoretical foundations for understanding the political basis of criminal violence. Yet, our understanding of politics as a potential driver of large-scale criminal violence in Mexico and elsewhere remains impaired without explicitly theorizing political regimes and elections.

In taking a new theoretical approach that brings together the state, political regimes, and elections to explain the outbreak of criminal wars in new democracies, we hope to contribute to a new generation of scholarly work that seeks to develop **a political science of organized crime and large-scale criminal violence** – or what Barnes (2017) has called a subfield of criminal politics. We do this by redefining widely held assumptions and concepts, offering new theoretical formulations, and providing new data sources to rigorously test whether politics should have a central place in the field of criminology. The literatures on the micro-foundations of mafias and criminal behavior,[4] civil wars,[5] and state-centric explanations of criminal violence in Latin America[6] provide crucial analytical guidance and serve as the basis for theoretical reformulation. And a close dialogue with the sociology of crime[7] and with specific explanations of the outbreak of criminal violence in Mexico and Latin America provides invaluable inputs for considering alternative explanations.[8]

CONCEPTS AND THEORETICAL PROPOSITIONS

In building a new political understanding of organized crime and large-scale criminal violence, we first provide a new conceptualization of organized crime based on the state–criminal nexus. We then explain why different political regimes explain different forms of state–criminal association. Finally, focusing on transitions from authoritarian rule to democracy, we assess how changes in the distribution of state political power via

---

[4] See Schelling (1971), Gambetta (1996), Skaperdas (2001), Varese (2001), and Skarbek (2014).
[5] See Kalyvas (2006), Steele (2011), Arjona, Kasfir, and Mampilly (eds.) (2015), and Arjona (2016).
[6] See Astorga (2005), Arias (2006a and 2017), Bailey and Taylor (2009), Arias and Goldstein (2010), Snyder and Durán-Martínez (2009), Arias (2017), Lessing (2017), Albarracín (2018), Durán-Martínez (2018), Bergman (2018), and Yashar (2018).
[7] See Sampson (1993) and Villarreal (2002).
[8] See Astorga (2005), Astorga and Shirk (2010), Dube, Dube, and García-Ponce (2013), Calderón et al. (2015), Osorio (2015), Rios (2015), Shirk and Wallman (2015), Trejo and Ley (2016 and 2018), Durán-Martínez (2018), Flores-Macías (2018), Pansters (2018), and Cedillo (2019).

the introduction of electoral competition can upset state–criminal inter-actions, create uncertainty, and give rise to incentives for criminal wars.

Bringing the State Back in: Redefining the Relationship between the State and Crime

Unlike most studies that conceptualize OCGs as illegal economic enter-prises that operate in opposition to state authorities, we follow state-centric studies of organized crime in Latin America in the critical theoretical move of conceiving OCGs as illegal groups that are intimately related to the state.[9] We make the strong ontological assumption that organized crime cannot exist and successfully operate illicit markets without some level of informal state protection. Drug traffickers and human smugglers, for example, require some level of state complicity to transport drugs and humans across international and domestic borders; some level of protection is required in the event that they are caught and need to derail an investiga-tion, escape from prison, or simply continue operating businesses from behind bars. Absent these protections, traffickers do not go very far in becoming viable players in the smuggling industries.

Rather than picture OCGs and the state as axiomatically engaged in a zero-sum game – as criminologists have long assumed – we focus on the areas where the spheres of crime and the state intersect.[10] To be sure, not all state agents are part of informal networks of government protection for criminals and not all criminal groups seek protection from state agents. But when these two spheres intersect and state agents and criminals collude, the intersection creates *a gray zone of criminality* where the rise of organized crime is possible. The gray zone is the habitat of organized crime; the ecosystem in which OCGs can breathe, grow, reproduce, and succeed. Outside the gray zone there are common criminals but no OCGs, and state agents that do not operate in the gray zone are actually law enforcement agents – they may be repressive, particularly when they use iron-first policies to fight criminals, but they are not in collusion with organized crime.[11]

---

[9] See Arias (2006a and 2017), Snyder and Durán-Martínez (2009), Jaffe (2013), Trejo and Ley (2016 and 2018), Albarracín (2018), Durán-Martínez (2018), Yashar (2018), and Sobering and Auyero (2019).
[10] For pioneering analyses on state–criminal collusion, see Astorga (2005), Arias (2006a), Bailey and Taylor (2009), Snyder and Durán-Martínez (2009), and Arias and Goldstein (2010).
[11] The concept of the gray zone has been widely used by students of the Italian mafia (see Allum, Merlino, and Colletti 2019). Similar formulations include the concepts of

Introducing Political Regimes: The Electoral Foundations of Criminal Peace and Violence

Our central claim is that any major change in the sphere of state power or state policy that upsets the terms of engagement between the state and OCGs can destabilize the gray zone, introducing uncertainty and generating incentives for large-scale criminal violence. Because political regimes and institutions define how state power is distributed and the public policies that states adopt, politics is constitutive of organized crime. Politics is crucial in defining whether a criminal industry is dominated by a single monopolistic organization or whether there is competition for turf. And, as scholars of organized crime in economics (Buchanan 1973; Schelling 1971; Skaperdas 2001) and sociology (Gambetta 1996; Varese 2001) have long established, the prospects for peace and violence in the criminal underworld are largely dependent on whether criminal markets are monopolistic or competitive.

To understand the dynamics of peace and violence in criminal markets, we need to go beyond the state and understand how state power is distributed. This is the world of political regimes. We suggest that the gray zone of criminality often emerges in authoritarian regimes and is intimately associated with the state's repressive apparatuses.[12] Autocrats rule by means of coercion and cooptation (Svolik 2012; Trejo 2012). Although economic cooptation is a key trait of most authoritarian regimes (Magaloni 2006; Greene 2007), to stay in power autocrats rely on state specialists in violence whose chief mandate is to gather information from political dissidents and to punish them when they become a threat to regime survival. Authoritarian specialists in violence are members of special units within the armed forces (or the police), secret service agencies, and civilian forces that are subcontracted as shadow powers to keep dissidents at bay (Greitens 2016). To undertake their work effectively, these state specialists in violence enjoy impunity – they carry a state

---

"parapolitics" and the "deep state" (Cribb 2009 and Tunander 2009). In Chapter 1 we discuss the novelty of our own formulation of the gray zone and distinguish it from its more common use in the Italian literature and in studies of parapolitics and the deep state.

[12] We do not imply that the gray zone of criminality only exists in autocracies. To be sure, the gray zone also exists in young and consolidated democracies. Yet, as we explain below and in Chapter 1, because repressive state specialists in violence enjoy high levels of impunity and play such a critical role in our definition of the gray zone, their more widespread existence in autocracies renders autocracies more likely to experience wider gray zones than consolidated democracies.

license to kill, torture, or "disappear" their enemies. This uncommon power, however, turns them into a potential threat to authoritarian rulers.

To safeguard their loyalties, and to prevent palace coups, autocrats often allow state specialists in violence to regulate and profit from the criminal underworld. As we will explore in subsequent chapters, from Mexico to Russia, from Guatemala to Panama, and from Chile to Brazil, autocrats have given state specialists in violence access to the criminal underworld.[13] As long as the authoritarian regime remains stable, the criminal underworld is peacefully regulated by state specialists in violence. Contrary to the widespread assumption that criminal lords always have private armies of hit men available to protect them and their turf, we provide evidence suggesting the opposite. In authoritarian regimes criminal lords do have bodyguards and private personnel for their personal security, but they do not have private militias to defend their turf because security is informally provided by state security agents.

However, when authoritarian structures begin to crumble, the uncertainty about state protection can destabilize the criminal underworld. OCGs then have powerful incentives to militarize, develop and train their own private armies, and prepare for a world of competition and conflict in which the command of their own private militias will empower criminal lords to defend their turf and seek to conquer rival territory. When countries transition from authoritarian rule to multiparty democracy, the expansion of electoral competition, the constant rotation of parties in office, and the decentralization and fragmentation of power that characterize democratic politics can become a major source of turbulence for the gray zone of criminality. Multiparty democracy stimulates the redistribution of state power, the removal of old personnel, and the appointment of new officials in national and subnational governments who embrace new policies and develop new alliances. Thus, every new election cycle can become a major threat or an opportunity for the redefinition of criminal power and the outbreak of new cycles of criminal violence. The periodic redefinition of power, alliances, and policies affects the gray zone of criminality because OCGs can only exist and thrive when criminal groups develop collusive informal agreements with state agents.

---

[13] See Chapter 1.

Scope Conditions: Criminal Wars in New (Illiberal) Democracies

While transitions from authoritarian rule to democracy can result in major spikes of criminal violence, they can also open trajectories for, comparatively, more peaceful development. Whether countries follow peaceful or violent trajectories of postauthoritarian development largely depends on what they do with state specialists in violence. Cross-national studies of criminal violence suggest that countries that prevent the outbreak of large-scale criminal violence after democratization are those in which elites adopt major security-sector reforms (Cruz 2011; Yashar 2018; Tiscornia 2019) to dismantle the networks of state repression and criminality built during the authoritarian era (e.g., Nicaragua). Countries that prevent major outbreaks of criminal violence also include those in which postauthoritarian elites engage in major transitional justice processes (Trejo, Albarracín, and Tiscornia 2018) that expose, prosecute, and punish perpetrators of gross human rights violations (many of whom also led criminal networks; for example, in Argentina, Chile, and Peru). These are cases of transitions to democracy in which postauthoritarian politics go beyond the mere establishment of multiparty competitive elections to begin to institutionalize a democratic rule of law. In contrast, cross-national studies of criminal violence show that when elites in postauthoritarian societies fail to adopt extensive security-sector reforms or ambitious transitional justice processes, the gray zone of criminality forged under authoritarian rule persists and expands in democracy (e.g., Mexico, Brazil, or Honduras). These are countries that transition from military or one-party rule to multiparty elections without developing the foundations for a democratic rule of law.

Mexico is a conspicuous case in which postauthoritarian elites failed to adopt any meaningful security-sector reform or a meaningful transitional justice process. It is a country that experienced an "electoral" transition from one-party rule to multiparty democracy in which the policing and judicial practices from the authoritarian regime remained intact. In fact, the Mexican transition is a prominent example of the limited or "thin" transitions that Karl (1986; 2000) categorized as cases of "electoralism" and that resulted in what Zakaria (2003) called "illiberal democracies." These are postauthoritarian regimes in which multiparty electoral competition does not translate into military, policing, and judicial reforms to protect human rights and civil liberties. Brazil and Honduras, like Mexico, are quintessential cases of thin transitions that resulted in the development of illiberal democracies. And although post-conflict Guatemala and El Salvador developed truth commissions to look into a repressive past, the immediate adoption of blanket amnesties forestalled judicial action and the development of major security-sector and judicial reforms to prevent the renewal of violence. Two or three decades into the postauthoritarian era, electoral competition in all these countries has failed to endogenously generate incentives for transitioning from illiberal to liberal democracies.

Our theoretical discussion suggests that when countries with long histories of state–criminal collusion forged under authoritarian rule transition to thin, multiparty democracy, without developing a democratic rule of law and without dismantling the networks of collusion between state repressive agents and criminal groups, the electoral mechanisms by which state power is distributed are likely to become intimately intertwined with criminal violence. In these illiberal democracies, electoral competition, the democratic removal of leaders, and the fragmentation and decentralization of political power are likely to generate uncommon uncertainty in the gray zone of criminality and become a permanent stimulus to, rather than a deterrent of, criminal violence. Contrary to expectations by Schumpeter (1943), Popper (1962), and Przeworski (1991), in these illiberal democracies – where state specialists in violence from the authoritarian regime remain untouched and the gray zone of criminality remains intact – the selection of leaders by means of free and fair multiparty elections is unlikely to become a "mechanism to settle our differences without bloodshed."

EMPIRICAL TESTING

Why Mexico

Instead of comparing trajectories of criminal violence across new democracies, this book focuses on the Mexican case – a country that was most likely to experience an outbreak of criminal violence because postauthoritarian elites failed to reform the country's authoritarian security and judicial systems at the time of transition. By design, the Mexican case allows us to keep constant the military, policing and judicial institutions and practices that gave rise to the gray zone of criminality under authoritarian rule. It also allows us to explore whether, and the extent to which, the dynamics of political-electoral change in illiberal democracy became a causal driver of the outbreak, intensification, and expansion of Mexico's drug wars. We take a long-term view and assess the outbreak and evolution of drug wars and large-scale criminal violence from the 1980s to

2012. And we open our analytical lens to assess the subnational evolution of drug violence across 31 states and 2,018 municipalities.[14]

Why Mexican Subnational Regions

Unpacking criminal violence across subnational units has major theoretical advantages for the study of drug wars.[15] Because drug trafficking is *a global chain of local operations*, a focus on subnational units allows us to understand incentives for peace and violence in the most relevant geographic space where drug cartels and their criminal associates operate and forge the informal linkages with state agents that constitute the gray zone. Throughout the book we are mindful of how changes at the global and national levels can affect the drug trafficking industry. Yet subnational jurisdictions are the most meaningful space to visualize the gray zone of criminality, to shed light on the likely connections between politics and the criminal underworld, and to explain the outbreak and evolution of criminal violence. While we recognize sociologists' common practice to disaggregate even further and assess the dynamics of violence in urban neighborhoods, our emphasis on electoral politics and formal power structures compels us to use political-administrative jurisdictions (e.g., states and municipalities) as units of analysis.

Focusing on the evolution of criminal violence over time offers a unique opportunity to assess the likely impact of the dynamics of political change along Mexico's transition to electoral democracy, on the changing nature of drug cartels, and on incentives for peaceful coexistence and war. A crucial part of the story in this book is the dramatic transformation of Mexican drug cartels over the course of the transition from one-party rule to multiparty democracy and as a result of the War on Drugs. This change enabled cartels to transform themselves from business organizations operating the drug trafficking industry to armed territorial actors who sought to monopolize multiple criminal industries and become de facto rulers over local populations and territories. Taking time seriously – both through the lens of history and through time-series cross-sectional analyses – allows us to understand mutations in criminal objectives, in

---

[14] Mexico's Federal District, which had a special administrative status up until 2018, is excluded from the analysis. We also exclude 418 municipalities from Oaxaca that select their mayors through indigenous customary practices and where political parties do not participate in municipal elections.

[15] For a detailed analysis of the advantages of a subnational focus, see Giraudy, Moncada, and Snyder (eds.) (2019).

organizational structures, and in cartels' uses of violence to meet their ends. As students of civil war have demonstrated, armed groups change in fundamental ways over the course of war (Kalyvas 2006; Wood 2011; Arjona 2016).

Focusing on change across subnational jurisdictions is crucial because drug violence in Mexico varies dramatically across time and space. Cartels peacefully coexisted in the 1980s; they went to war in the 1990s and early 2000s; and these wars reached unprecedented levels of violence after the 2007 federal intervention and the launching of Mexico's War on Drugs. But violence also varied dramatically across geographic jurisdictions. During the most intense period of criminal violence (2007–2012), the most violent cities in northwestern, northeastern, and southern Mexico reached murder rates higher than in El Salvador (the most violent country in Latin America and the world during the time period under analysis), but other cities in the southeastern part of the country scored levels of violence similar to those of Chile (the least violent country in Latin America).[16] The fact that political change also varied widely across time and space facilitates our inquiry into the likely impact of electoral politics and changing power structures on the dynamics of criminal violence.

Quantitative Data

The book draws on two original datasets, which we constructed: The Criminal Violence in Mexico (CVM) Dataset and the Criminal Attacks against Public Authorities in Mexico (CAPAM) Dataset.[17]

CVM provides a count of all murders that can be attributed to organized criminal groups in Mexico in the period 1995–2012. Although the Mexican government produces reliable information about homicides, official statistics do not distinguish homicides committed by common criminals from those committed by OCGs for our entire study period. Because we are interested in isolating organized criminal violence, we relied on a systematic review of Mexico's leading newspapers to document violence that resulted from conflicts involving OCGs. To be sure, this is not a census that measures the universe of murders associated with criminal organizations, but a data collection that uses Mexico's leading national newspapers to approximate the intensity of violence. To check our statistical results based on data from CVM, we relied on alternative

---

[16] For comparative data, see United Nations Development Program, UNDP (2013).

[17] For an in-depth explanation of these two datasets, see Appendix A and B.

sources of information on organized crime violence produced by the
Mexican government for limited time periods (2007–2011).[18]

CAPAM is a dataset that records a wide variety of features related to all
murders, murder attempts, public death threats, and abductions committed by OCGs against government officials and party candidates in
Mexico for the period 1995–2012. The information is based on
a systematic review of 18 Mexican national and subnational newspapers,
and two specialized weekly magazines. Because most national and subnational newspapers provide extensive coverage of these high-profile
attacks, CAPAM is the most complete source of criminal attacks against
public authorities and politicians in Mexico.

Distinguishing homicides perpetrated by common criminals from those
committed by OCGs – and identifying different forms of violence and
different groups of victims of violence – opens a unique window of
analytical opportunity to understand the uncommon behavior of
Mexican cartels and their criminal associates. Most of our statistical
knowledge about the determinants of criminal violence is predicated on
the basis of aggregate homicide rates. Developing more specialized datasets that distinguish perpetrators (e.g., deaths that can be attributed to
state–cartel and to cartel–cartel conflicts) and victims (e.g., local government officials and party candidates) allows us to identify new patterns in
what seem to be uncharted territories.

Qualitative Data

Besides the quantitative data, we draw on extensive qualitative information from more than 40 in-depth interviews with former governors and
mayors, former federal government officials, law enforcement agents and
security officials, party leaders, religious leaders, leaders of NGOs, journalists, and families of victims conducted over the course of several waves
of fieldwork between 2014 and 2018. We conducted these interviews in
Mexico City and in cities from five Mexican states: Guerrero, Michoacán,
Nuevo León, Chihuahua, and Baja California. Sometimes we met with
our interviewees in their home states; on other occasions we met them in
different places in Mexico and the US. We also draw on some of the best
work of investigative journalism, which has flourished during the War on
Drugs, as well as on path-breaking reports from Mexican NGOs working

---

[18] For a detailed discussion of the Mexican government data on homicides that can be
attributed to OCGs, see Atuesta, Sordia, and Madrazo (2018).

in collaboration with international organizations and institutions. These sources provided crucial qualitative information to unpack the logics behind the general patterns measured through the quantitative data, explain outliers, and identify the causal mechanisms that connect changes in the distribution of electoral power and the intensity of drug violence.

A Multi-Method Approach

A Multifaceted Problem

Although our analysis focuses on the likely impact of politico-electoral change on the outbreak and escalation of drug violence, let it be clear from the outset that we are not advocating for a mono-causal explanation of large-scale criminal violence in Mexico.

At an analytical level, we do recognize that the drug trafficking industry is a global chain of local operations in which multiple actors working at multiple levels are involved in moving the illegal drugs from South America into Central America and Mexico, and then into the United States. We also recognize that multiple factors drive people from different walks of life to join drug cartels and their criminal associates, and multiple causes drive these groups to use violence to achieve their ends.

At an empirical level, we acknowledge that Mexico's drug wars take place against the backdrop of an international regulatory regime that – by prohibiting the production, commercialization and consumption of a wide variety of drugs – gives rise to illicit markets. Although not all illicit markets are violent (Gambetta 1996; Snyder and Durán-Martínez 2009; Lessing 2017; Yashar 2018), the reality is that in the absence of a common power (e.g., a mafia) or third-party protection (e.g., informal networks of state protection), organized criminal groups tend to settle disputes through war and violence. We also recognize that 80 percent of illegal drugs that pass through Mexico end up in the US and that 80 percent of the weapons used in Mexico's drug wars come from the US. We are cognizant that globalization and market-oriented reforms may exacerbate economic and social inequalities and may drive young unemployed men into the arms of street gangs and OCGs. Moreover, market-oriented reforms and the privatization of natural resources may give rise to different forms of violent conflict. We understand that broken families and intra-family abuse can drive young boys into becoming foot soldiers for the drug wars. We are also aware that changes in the international prices of drugs may stimulate important changes in criminal markets and may drive competition and violence.

While recognizing the complexities of the phenomenon and the richness of the theoretical explanations across social science disciplines, our goal is to join a growing group of political scientists in making a strong claim about a major omission in criminology: the political-electoral foundations of organized crime and large-scale criminal violence.

Multivariate Regressions and Quasi-experimental Techniques

To evaluate our key theoretical propositions about the politico-electoral drivers of drug violence in Mexico, we first test for a host of variables associated with the effects of electoral competition and the fragmentation of political power on criminal violence, while controlling for a wide variety of economic, social, and demographic factors that operate at global, national, and subnational levels. We use results from time-series cross-sectional regression models as a baseline for the viability of our arguments.

To more effectively isolate the likely *causal impact* of political variables on the dynamics of criminal violence, we rely on quasi-experimental techniques to move from correlational to causal analysis. We use synthetic control models (Abadie, Diamond, and Hainmueller 2015) and natural experiments (Dunning 2008) to measure counterfactual scenarios. While we take causal identification seriously, we do not dismiss observational techniques associated with regression analysis because we do recognize the multi-causal nature of the phenomenon and hence would want to recognize the substantive impact of alternative explanations and controls.

Using both classical techniques of regression analysis with quasi-experimental tests allows us to (1) recognize the multi-causal nature of large-scale criminal violence; (2) show how political variables improve our explanations; and (3) identify and isolate the likely causal impact of political-electoral factors on the intensity of criminal violence.

Case Studies

Following the logic of nested analysis (Lieberman 2005), we make active use of case studies to identify causal mechanisms – the concatenation of incentives that connect politics with violence. We select cities and states that we can identify on the regression models. Based on our own extensive fieldwork, local histories, and reports from investigative journalism, we then conduct process-tracing analyses (Waldern 2015) to identify how changes in state power affect the gray zone of criminality and the conditions under which this uncertainty may stimulate the outbreak of large-scale criminal violence. By identifying the causal chain of actors and events, we can also address questions of endogeneity (Goertz 2017). Throughout this book, our historical case studies will be in intimate dialogue with the observational and the quasi-experimental results.

EMPIRICAL FINDINGS

The book's main findings center on three major transformations that took place in Mexico's drug industry over the course of two decades: (1) The outbreak of inter-cartel wars during the transition from authoritarian rule to democracy; (2) the escalation of drug violence to unprecedented levels in democracy; and (3) the development of subnational criminal governance regimes after two decades of war.

Subnational Alternation and the Outbreak of Inter-cartel Wars

Although most scholars of drug violence in Mexico associate the outbreak of inter-cartel wars with the national transition to democracy in 2000 – when the PRI lost presidential power – and the escalation of violence with President Calderón's decision to launch a War on Drugs against the cartels in 2006, we present new evidence showing that cartels first went to war in the early 1990s at a time when the federal government was not pursuing a proactive anti-drug policy.[19] Rather than associate the outbreak of inter-cartel wars with national alternation or national policy changes, we show that cartels went to war during a wave of subnational party alternation, when opposition parties won several gubernatorial seats throughout the 1990s and early 2000s. Because state-level police forces and agents associated with the state attorneys' offices played a central role in the development of informal networks of government protection for the cartels in the era of one-party rule, the alternation of political parties in state gubernatorial power and the removal of top- and mid-level officials in the police and the public prosecutors' offices created an era of acute uncertainty in Mexico's gray zone of criminality. This rendered cartels vulnerable to attacks by incoming authorities and rival cartels. To cope with this uncertainty, cartels took a momentous decision that would change Mexico's drug trafficking industry forever: drug lords created

---

[19] Prior to Calderón's War on Drugs, Mexican governments under the PRI launched Plan Cóndor, a major US-backed campaign against drug cultivation and traffic that spanned from the 1970s to the mid-1980s. See Cedillo (2019). Between 1985 and 2005, the Mexican government's anti-drug policies were reactive.

their own private militias to defend themselves and their turf against their enemies. Once cartels had secured their turf, these private militias empowered drug lords to seek to conquer rival territories whenever a new rotation of political parties in state power affected competing cartels. Our findings show that in Mexico, the spread of subnational party alternations led to the proliferation of inter-cartel wars across states with drug trafficking routes.

Subnational party alternation and the incoming opposition governors' decision to name new state attorneys and new chiefs of police had a dramatic, unforeseen impact on the gray zone of criminality. Because Mexico did not adopt a major security-sector reform or any transitional justice program to dismantle the networks of criminality that state specialists in violence had forged under the PRI's long period of authoritarian rule, party alternation in gubernatorial power – one of the defining features of democracy – changed the criminal balance of power, opening a new era marked by conflict and violence. Students of Mexican democracy have long argued that the electoral and federalist nature of the transition – opposition parties first scored major electoral victories across cities, then in state gubernatorial power, and finally in presidential power – resulted in a decentralized and peaceful process of regime change from below (Becerra, Salazar, and Woldenberg 2001; Merino 2003; Magaloni 2006; Greene 2007; Lucardi 2017). Our findings reveal that the narrow nature of the transition planted the seeds of violence in Mexico's nascent democracy: subnational dynamics of political competition and the rotation of political forces would unwittingly harbor incentives for the outbreak of narco wars and large-scale violence in the criminal underworld.

When transitions from authoritarian rule to democracy are confined to the electoral arena and past repressive, criminal arrangements are not carefully dismantled through major security-sector reform or via transitional justice mechanisms,[20] democratic mechanisms rapidly become

---

[20] As Tiscornia (2019) suggests, security-sector reforms help to dismantle criminal networks and contribute to the decline in criminal violence when new elites demilitarize armed forces that have been forged in the authoritarian era, and increase internal and external mechanisms of police accountability. Trejo, Albarracín, and Tiscornia (2018) show that by adopting ambitious transitional justice programs centered on truth and justice, new democratic elites expose, prosecute, and punish authoritarian specialists in violence who committed atrocities during the authoritarian era and who were part of the gray zone of criminality. This raises the costs of impunity in democracy and deters state–criminal collusion and the use of lethal violence to defend or fight crime. See Chapter 1 for a detailed discussion.

intertwined with criminality and violence. By the time the Mexican opposition conquered the presidency in 2000 and then renewed its hold on office in 2006, Mexico's five dominant cartels had developed their own private militias and were engaged in multiple conflicts in northwestern, northeastern, and southern Mexico. Inter-cartel wars had escalated from low-intensity conflicts (350 annual battle deaths in the 1990s) to conflicts marked by large-scale violence (more than 1,000 battle deaths by 2005). Although Mexico was technically considered to be a country at peace, the country's criminal wars had surpassed the threshold of battle deaths that is typically used to define a civil war.

Intergovernmental Partisan Conflict and the Escalation of Drug Violence

There is extensive empirical evidence showing that the federal intervention in the War on Drugs and the deployment of the Mexican armed forces throughout the country's most conflictive regions between 2006 and 2012 led to a dramatic five-fold increase in the death toll of drug violence. Why violence increased, however, remains contested. One narrative suggests that the use of the military to fight the cartels provided incentives for cartels to arm themselves and fight back before they were crushed (Flores-Macías 2018). Another account suggests that the "kingpin strategy," by which federal forces killed or incarcerated the cartels' leaders, led to intra-cartel fragmentation, competition, and violence (Guerrero 2011a; Calderón et al. 2015; Phillips 2015). A third narrative argues that the use of unconditional violence to crack down on all cartels, regardless of whether they were attacking the government or not, led to a major backlash (Lessing 2017). Finally, a fourth account suggests that the federal intervention weakened the cartels and suppressed violence in subnational regions where the president was able to coordinate the government's actions with subnational co-partisan authorities, but proved to be ineffective and led to a violent backlash where authorities from different political forces failed to coordinate (Urrusti Frenk 2012; Ríos 2015).

While most explanations focus on state military strategies to crack down on the cartels, we shift the focus to the politico-electoral logics of the federal intervention and assess the extent to which partisanship informed the logic of the intervention. We argue that the uneven expansion of violence across Mexican territory between 2006 and 2012 was not a technical problem of policy coordination between the federal government and the states but one of acute intergovernmental partisan conflict.

In a context of sharp ideological polarization between Right and Left following the bitterly contested 2006 presidential election – in which the right-wing candidate defeated the leftist candidate by a razor-thin margin, without the loser admitting defeat – the president deployed the army to confront an escalating inter-cartel war (Aguilar and Castañeda 2009). Facing an immediate backlash from the cartels (Guerrero 2011b; Espinosa and Rubin 2015; Atuesta and Ponce 2017) and a sudden hike in violence that could have resulted in major electoral losses, the president devised a more comprehensive military, economic, and social intervention to contain the epidemics of violence in areas ruled by his co-partisans. At the same time, he conducted a unilateral and limited intervention in subnational regions ruled by the Left – the president's arch-enemy – and blamed the escalation of violence on the leftist officials themselves.

Intergovernmental partisan conflict and the partisan nature of the federal intervention changed the balance of power in the gray zone of criminality: it alerted the cartels to a window of opportunity to contest controls over drug trafficking routes in subnational jurisdictions where leftist subnational authorities were unprotected. These politically unprotected areas became a magnet for drug cartels and for the multiple breakaway OCGs that resulted from the kingpin strategy of cartel decapitation, by which several private militias serving the cartels became powerful independent organizations. Intense criminal competition for turf and for the expansion of the gray zone of criminality in subnational leftist states and municipalities led to a dramatic escalation of violence. The federal government reacted by blaming the escalation on its political rivals, running national smear campaigns against leftist governors and mayors, and even politicizing the national attorney's office to prosecute leftist subnational government officials.

The politicization of the federal War on Drugs was possible because Mexican postauthoritarian elites failed to transform the country's authoritarian security and judicial institutions and practices. As is the case in most authoritarian regimes, protecting authoritarian incumbents and the regime, rather than serving citizens, is the chief mandate of the military, the police, the public prosecutors' offices and the judges. As presidents during the PRI's era of authoritarian rule had done, President Calderón used the security sector and the judicial system to reward his political loyalists and punish his political enemies in the state's war against the cartels. Contrary to the Weberian ideal type, in which state leaders would seek the monopoly of violence within a given territory, the dramatic escalation of violence in Mexico during the War on Drugs reveals that electoral incentives may lead state leaders to strategically suppress violent challenges in regions that are relevant for their political ambitions, but allow the escalation of violence in areas under the control of their enemies.

Wartime Transformations: The Development of Subnational Criminal Governance Regimes

One of the most puzzling developments during Mexico's War on Drugs is the sudden outbreak of a wave of 311 lethal criminal attacks against local government officials and party candidates between 2007 and 2012. We argue that these attacks represented an inflection point in a protracted and increasingly lethal conflict, revealing a second momentous transformation in the ecosystem of the gray zone of criminality: drug cartels and their criminal associates murdered hundreds of local government officials and party candidates to take de facto control over local governments, populations, and territories. OCGs became *territorial armed actors* and developed *subnational criminal governance regimes*. This turned Mexican cartels and their criminal associates into de facto political actors.

It has been well established in the literature on Mexico's drug wars that the 2006 federal intervention led to the fragmentation of Mexico's five leading cartels into over 60 different criminal organizations by 2012 and to a fierce competition for control over the country's profitable drug trafficking routes. To finance these conflicts, several of the cartels' breakaways, particularly the private militias and the street gangs who functioned as foot soldiers of these drug wars, moved into new criminal markets. These were devoted to the extraction of human wealth – e.g., extortion, kidnapping for ransom, and human smuggling – and the looting of natural resources – e.g., forests, oil and minerals. Within this new menu of illegal sources of income for war, the cartels and other OCGs discovered the municipality as a unique source of public funding and as an institutional instrument to control local populations, natural resources, and territories. To gain control over the municipalities, OCGs found a simple method: the use of targeted lethal violence against mayors and party candidates. In this endeavor, cartels took important cues from the political environment to seize local controls.

We show that cartels and their criminal associates took advantage of the dynamics of electoral competition and intergovernmental partisan conflict to select their targets for assassination and to establish subnational criminal governance regimes. Murders and murder attempts were more likely in municipalities of states where subnational authorities were purposefully unprotected by the federal government: subnational regions ruled by leftist states – the president's main political rivals. Our analysis also reveals that lethal attacks against local government officials and party candidates more commonly took place during subnational election cycles, when new mayors were elected and when they appointed municipal cabinet members. Drawing on extensive qualitative evidence, we show that following these attacks, cartels were able to infiltrate the incoming municipal governments, taking control over the local police and key administrative positions, including such areas as finance and taxation, and public developments. Controls over formal government positions facilitated the cartels' control over coercion and taxation and allowed them to regulate local political processes and key economic activities.

During the Mexican transition to democracy, the dynamics of political change – including electoral competition and partisan alternation – undermined incentives for peaceful coexistence in the gray zone of criminality. But after the 2006 federal intervention and the War on Drugs the situation reversed, and cartels and their criminal associates increasingly began to shape local political processes. Unlike armed rebel groups who typically fight civil wars to remove national governments and establish a new political regime, drug cartels and their criminal associates did not have their eye on national power but sought to establish de facto subnational governance. Although Mexican cartels are not armed insurgent groups and the country's drug wars are not a civil war (Kalyvas 2015), recognizing OCGs as armed territorial groups and recognizing their attempt to develop subnational criminal governance regimes is crucial to understanding the power that these groups have acquired in order to reconfigure local political orders.

THE ROAD AHEAD

The book is divided into four main sections.

Part I develops the book's main theoretical claims. In Chapter 1, "The Political Foundations of Peace and War in the Gray Zone of Criminality," we outline the theoretical framework that allows us to name, conceptualize, and analyze the gray zone of criminality as the ecological space where the state and crime intersect and where state specialists in violence and criminals give rise to organized crime. We explain why the gray zone commonly emerges in authoritarian regimes and why a thin transition to electoral democracy – in which elites fail to reform the security forces and the judicial system that enabled the spread of the gray zone of criminality survives – enables the intimate association of electoral competition, political plurality, and the decentralization of political power with outbursts of large-scale criminal violence. Building on new assumptions and definitions, the chapter develops the general theoretical propositions that will serve as guidance for the formulation of specific hypotheses for testing in the empirical chapters.

Part II explains why Mexican cartels went to war as the country transitioned from authoritarian rule to electoral democracy. Chapter 2, "Why Cartels Went to War: Subnational Party Alternation, the Breakdown of Criminal Protection, and the Onset of Inter-Cartel Wars," uses information from in-depth interviews with the first opposition governments in Mexico and new data on historical patterns of government repression in Mexico to show that state-level police and judicial authorities played a key role in developing the informal network of protection for drug cartels under the PRI era of one-party rule. Based on time-series cross-sectional models, the chapter then shows that subnational party alternation in the gubernatorial seat is a key driver of the outbreak of large-scale criminal violence. Using synthetic control models, we show that this association is causal. Chapter 3, "Fighting Turf Wars: Cartels, Militias, and the Struggle for Drug Trafficking Corridors," draws on extensive interviews conducted in five Mexican states (Baja California, Chihuahua, Jalisco, Michoacán and Guerrero). It offers an in-depth analysis of how party alternation and the opposition governors' decision to appoint new personnel in the state attorneys' offices and the state judicial police led to the breakdown of protection. It also shows how cartels created their private militias in response to this political uncertainty and how the availability of these new armed organizations allowed drug lords to defend their turf and challenge rival territory. The chapter outlines the process by which sequential party alternation across states triggered an armed race among cartels, leading to dyadic conflicts in northwest, northeast, and south Mexico.

Part III focuses on the dramatic escalation of drug violence in democracy, following the federal intervention and the launching of the government's War on Drugs. Chapter 4, "Why the State's War against the Cartels Intensified Violence: Political Polarization, Intergovernmental Partisan Conflict, and the Escalation of Violence," explains why in times of acute political polarization governments may have incentives to politicize law enforcement and politicized interventions may stimulate violence. Using time-series cross-sectional models, we show that between 2007 and 2012 drug violence was more intense in municipalities of states ruled by leftist governors. This was not a problem of incompetence by leftist subnational authorities, but the result of intergovernmental partisan conflict between a right-wing federal government and leftist governors. We present a natural experiment, by which we compare the intensity of criminal violence in nearly identical municipalities located across the states of Michoacán and Jalisco, to show that the fact that Michoacán was ruled by the Left and Jalisco by the Right is a key causal driver that explains why the municipalities on the Michoacán side of the border experienced significantly higher levels of violence than their neighbors in Jalisco. Based on case studies from cities in three different states (Michoacán, Baja California, and Chihuahua), in Chapter 5, "Unpacking the War on Drugs: Presidents, Governors, and Large-Scale Narco Violence," we disaggregate the federal intervention in the War on Drugs on the military, judicial, communicative, and social policy dimensions. We show the differing trajectories depending on patterns of intergovernmental partisan cooperation or conflict. We also analyze how cartels took cues from this conflict to make decisions about contesting unprotected territories, leading to conflict escalation.

Part IV explains why, as war became more intense, cartels and their criminal associates used targeted lethal attacks against subnational government officials and party candidates to establish criminal governance regimes. Chapter 6, "Why Cartels Murder Mayors and Local Party Candidates: Subnational Political Vulnerability and Political Opportunities to Become Local Rulers," makes use of time-series cross-sectional analyses to show that cartels attacked mayors and party candidates where intergovernmental partisan conflict between Left and Right was more intense, and where mayors and local party candidates were politically vulnerable. It also shows that attacks took place disproportionately during subnational election cycles. Two natural experiments – contrasting municipalities along the Michoacán–Guerrero and Michoacán–Guanajuato borders – allow us to show that political vulnerability, afforded by intergovernmental partisan conflict and political opportunities, opened by subnational election cycles, are causally related to the probability of attacks against mayors and party candidates. Drawing on extensive interviews conducted in three different Mexican states (Michoacán, Guerrero, and Baja California), Chapter 7, "Seizing Local Power: Developing Subnational Criminal Governance Regimes," presents case studies showing how cartels used the murder of mayors and candidates to infiltrate local campaigns and municipal governments and developed controls to establish themselves as de facto local rulers.

In the Conclusion, we discuss the implications of our findings for a new understanding of the drivers of criminal violence in Mexico, for theories of criminal violence, and for security policies in new democracies. We first discuss how our theoretical focus on the politico-electoral drivers of organized crime and large-scale criminal violence offers a new interpretation of two decades of drug wars in Mexico (1990–2012). We use this lens to suggest that political and policy continuities after 2012 help explain the expansion and intensification of violence from 2012 to 2018. Beyond Mexico, we discuss how our theoretical reformulation of organized crime and our empirical findings contribute to the development of a political science of organized crime and large-scale criminal violence. We conclude the book by offering a reflection on the policy implications that follow from a political science approach to the study of crime and violence.

PART I

A POLITICAL THEORY OF CRIMINAL VIOLENCE

I

The Political Foundations of Peace and War in the Gray Zone of Criminality

The unprecedented explosion of *large-scale criminal violence* that has taken place in Mexico and other Latin American countries in the past two decades challenges major theories of crime, and organized crime, and compels us to rethink widely held assumptions and theoretical explanations. The intensity and lethality of violence produced by inter-cartel and state–cartel wars defy influential explanations that would expect organized criminal groups (OCGs) to rely on selective and low-intensity violence instead of engaging in large-scale violence, which is financially costly and could expose the criminal underworld to state intervention. Large-scale criminal violence is bad for business; therefore we need to understand why the leading players in the criminal underworld would engage in protracted wars that can be more lethal than civil wars, and why they would come out of the criminal underworld to seek to become de facto local rulers of subnational territories and populations. Understanding these transformations in the criminal underworld is crucial, because millions of citizens in countries such as Mexico now live in areas in which OCGs have established subnational criminal governance regimes and dictate the main parameters of social, economic, and political life. Life in these new criminal social orders, to quote Hobbes (1651/1968), can be "nasty, brutish, and short."

This chapter develops a new theoretical framework to rethink organized crime and to reinterpret the conditions under which OCGs coexist peacefully and those under which they go to war. The key conceptual move that we make is the recognition that organized crime is ontologically associated with the state and that the intersection of the spheres of crime and the state gives rise to an ecosystem in which OCGs emerge and that defines the incentives for peace and violence in the criminal underworld. Because political regimes define how state power is accessed and exercised, to understand this criminal ecology we need to assess how the key institutional features of autocracy and democracy are intimately associated with the constitution and transformation of the criminal underworld. We argue that a deep understanding of how state power is distributed and changes is crucial to explaining peace and violence among criminal groups. These theoretical reformulations provide us with the building blocks to develop our hypotheses for testing throughout the book and the nuts-and-bolts to explore the causal mechanisms that connect political changes with large-scale criminal violence.

The chapter is divided into five sections. We first introduce a new concept of organized crime based on different forms of engagement between criminal groups and the state. Whereas most theories of crime implicitly assume that the state and organized crime are two separate spheres in which relations between criminal actors and state agents are zero sum, we build on a new literature on the politics of crime in Latin America (Arias 2006a; Snyder and Durán-Martínez 2009; Barnes 2017; Durán-Martínez 2018; Yashar 2018) and Southern Europe (Allum, Merlino, and Colletti 2019) to argue that the joint space where both actors coexist and cooperate constitutes an ecosystem in which organized crime emerges: the *gray zone of criminality*. This conceptual move not only compels us to rethink what OCGs are but also forces us to rethink traditional conceptions of the state – to move away from the classic Weberian conception of the state as a bureaucratic organization in which leaders seek to maintain the monopoly of the legitimate use of force within a given territory (Weber 1918/1994).

In the second section we introduce political regimes – the political arrangements that define how state power is accessed and exercised. We suggest that the gray zone of criminality often emerges in authoritarian regimes, where state security agents in charge of political repression are informally allowed to regulate and operate in the criminal underworld as well. We discuss a wide variety of examples from several authoritarian regimes in Latin America where autocrats allowed authoritarian specialists in violence to regulate and profit from the drug trafficking industries, and we explain why criminal markets in autocracy tend to be relatively peaceful. These networks of state repression and criminality in authoritarian regimes represent our initial equilibrium.

In the third section we discuss transitions from authoritarian rule to democracy and suggest that when postauthoritarian elites fail to dismantle the gray zone of criminality through major security-sector reforms and/or transitional justice processes, they set the stage for the dynamics of regime change to become intertwined with organized crime and the outbreak of large-scale criminal violence. These are cases of *minimalist electoral transitions* in which countries transition from authoritarian rule to multiparty democracy without establishing the foundations for a democratic rule of law. Corrupt and authoritarian networks embedded in the military, the police, the penitentiary system and the judiciary, together with informal repressive networks, including death squads and paramilitary forces, survive the transition from authoritarian rule to (thin) illiberal democracies.

In the fourth section we explain why the survival of corrupt state specialists in violence and the state–criminal networks that dominate the gray zone of criminality in these new (thin) electoral democracies transforms the key institutional mechanisms of democratic competition into triggers of large-scale criminal violence. We discuss why, absent a democratic rule of law, multiparty electoral competition, the alternation of political parties in office, and the decentralization and fragmentation of political power become destabilizers of the criminal underworld, giving rise to incentives for criminal competition and for the outbreak of criminal wars.

In the fifth section we explain why the intensification and expansion of criminal wars in democracies transforms criminal groups in fundamental ways. To remain competitive in protracted turf wars, OCGs often become territorial actors and seek to gain de facto control over local governments, populations, and territories. We explain why war can motivate OCGs to develop local political ambitions to subvert local democracy and to become local rulers. While OCGs do not aspire to conquer national power, this section outlines the type of subnational criminal governance regimes that they develop to transform local social orders.

At the end of each section we lay out our key assumptions and definitions and use them as building blocks to outline general theoretical propositions. We offer examples from a wide variety of countries in Latin America and elsewhere to illustrate our claims. In subsequent sections of the book we will use these theoretical propositions as the general framework to develop more specific hypotheses about the outbreak and escalation of Mexico's drug wars.

THE SPHERES OF CRIME AND THE STATE: REDEFINING ORGANIZED CRIME

Extant Definitions of OCGs: Crime as an Apolitical Phenomenon

Most scholars across the social sciences define organized criminal groups as private firms that operate illicit markets (Reuter 2009). These are organizations that are assumed to operate beyond the reach of the state, in what is often referred to as the criminal *underworld*. Absent the state and law enforcement agents, OCGs develop a comparative advantage in violence and information gathering to settle disputes by means of force (Varese 2010). Most OCGs seek to become monopolists in specific criminal industries – for instance, car robberies, human smuggling, drug trafficking, or kidnapping for ransom. When they acquire sufficient coercive power and information to become a dominant force, some of them can specialize in the provision of protection and become mafias – the OCGs that provide protection in multiple criminal industries and governance in the criminal underworld (Gambetta 1996; Varese 2010; Skarbek 2014).

In the scholarly literature, OCGs are considered to be non-state actors. Because most criminologists implicitly accept Weber's (1918/1994) claim that the modern state aims to exercise the monopoly of force within a given territory, criminal studies commonly assume that OCGs and the state have a zero-sum relation: whatever one organization wins is at the cost of the rival organization. The behavioral implication is that states seek to eliminate OCGs. And because OCGs want to dominate illegal markets, they need to keep the state away from the criminal underworld. As Lessing (2015) claims, in equilibrium OCGs do not want to eliminate the state; they only want to keep state authorities – the police and the judicial system – away from their illicit activities.

The strong assumption that OCGs and states have a zero-sum relation is widespread across social science disciplines. Becker's (1968) seminal economic theory of crime, for example, suggests that a greater police presence would remove incentives for the existence of criminal groups and would deter criminal behavior. Following Becker, Skaperdas's (2001) influential economic model of organized crime explicitly claims that the existence of OCGs is the direct result of the state's absence. In this formulation, OCGs emerge in *ungoverned* spaces (Clunan and Trikunas 2010), where state security forces are either absent or ineffective. Building on Durkheim's (1893/1964) influential theories of alienation, most sociological explanations of crime implicitly assume that states and criminal groups have

opposing goals (Sampson 1993). The extensive debate about police deter-
rence in impoverished urban areas is essentially about whether policing is
effective and whether it is racially biased (Smith, Visher, and Davidson
1984); scholars seldom consider the possibility that police forces and state
agents may coexist and cooperate with organized crime and may serve some
OCGs and coordinate their actions against rival groups.

One possible explanation of this strong zero-sum assumption is that
most theory-building has been conducted by scholars observing realities
of crime and organized crime in industrial societies and advanced capitalist democracies, where the state tends to be more evenly present across
subnational regions and is more capable than in developing countries. But
even students of organized crime in the developing world – where the
state's presence and capacity can often be called into question – tend to
assume this zero-sum relation. In his seminal study of inequality and
governance, O'Donnell (1993) claimed that several developmental problems in Latin America's most marginalized communities stem from the
state's uneven presence. In his famous formulation, "brown areas" are
those subnational regions in the developing world where the state is
absent and where a wide variety of informal non-state predatory groups,
including OCGs, have become dominant players. Following O'Donnell, a
generation of scholars has associated the state's absence in Latin
America's urban peripheries with criminality and violence.[1] This, we
claim, obscures rather than facilitates a realistic understanding of organized crime and large-scale criminal violence.

Figure 1.I.a provides a visual illustration of the common claim that
OCGs and the state operate in separate spheres and that OCGs are non-
state actors (à la Becker). Figure 1.I.b illustrates the dominant claim that the
state and the criminal underworld are two independently distinct social
domains (à la O'Donnell). As this figure implies, the greater the state's
presence, the lower the space for organized crime and the less the potential
for criminal violence. Using Mann's (1984) terminology, the conclusion
would be that the size of the criminal underworld is inversely related to the
state's infrastructural power – that is, to the development of roads and the
presence of bureaucratic agencies, armed forces, and the police throughout
a country's territory. This residualistic approach represented in Figure 1.I.b
has led scholars to develop the idea of "parallel states" – social orders that
exist side-by-side in which states and OCGs rule independently.

---

[1] See Koonings and Kruijt (2004), Eaton (2010), and Fajnzylber, Lederman, and Loayza
(2002).

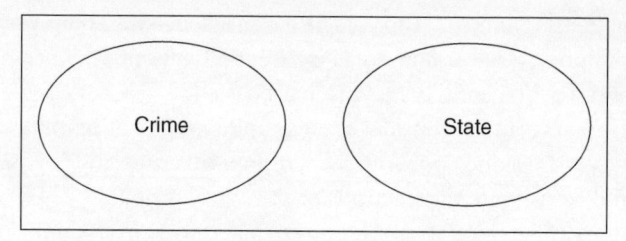

FIGURE 1.I.a Crime and the State as Separate Spheres

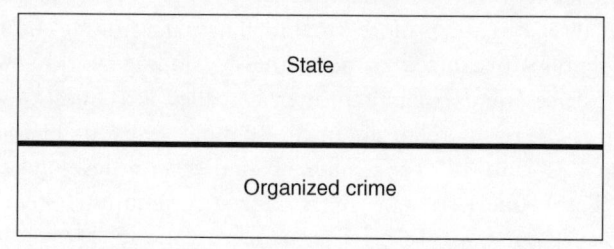

FIGURE 1.I.b Crime and the State as Parallel Social Orders

In contrast to the images portrayed in Figures 1.I.a and 1.I.b a recent generation of students of organized crime in the developing world have provided extensive empirical evidence showing that the borders between the state and organized crime can be fuzzy. Questioning the empirical accuracy of O'Donnell's concept of "brown areas," Arias's (2006a, 2009) influential studies of drug gangs in Brazil offer compelling ethnographic evidence about the prevalence of different forms of engagement between state police forces and drug gangs in the favelas of Rio de Janeiro. In her important study of organized crime in Jamaica, Jaffe (2013) uses the term the "hybrid state" to conceptualize the multiple forms of collusion between criminal gangs and police, politicians, and bureaucrats in Kingston's impoverished urban neighborhoods. In their pioneering article, Snyder and Durán-Martínez (2009) speak about "state sponsored protection rackets" to identify patterns of state protection for criminals in Mexico and Myanmar. And in her influential comparative study of criminal violence in Central America, Yashar (2018) speaks about the "complicit state." Defying the idea that street gangs and OCGs create parallel states, Arias, Jaffe, Snyder and Durán-Martínez, and Yashar describe different forms of coexistence, cooperation, and conflict between state agents and organized crime. All of them conclude that understanding criminal behavior, including peaceful coexistence and violence, requires a more refined understanding of the different forms of engagement between criminals and the state.

Rethinking Organized Crime and the State: The Political Foundations of Crime

Recognizing that the borders between the spheres of the state and crime can overlap, we take a step further and consider the intersection of crime and the state as an ontological feature of organized crime. As shown in Figure 1.1, we call the area where crime and the state overlap the gray zone of criminality. The gray zone is the area where members of the armed forces, the police, pro-government militias, public prosecutors, and directors of penitentiaries exist alongside a wide variety of criminal organizations. These are not parallel orders but *an ecosystem of coercion, corruption, and criminality* where the interactions between state agents and private economic groups give rise to organized crime.[2]

We make the strong assumption that organized crime can only exist in the gray zone in which criminal groups enjoy some level of informal

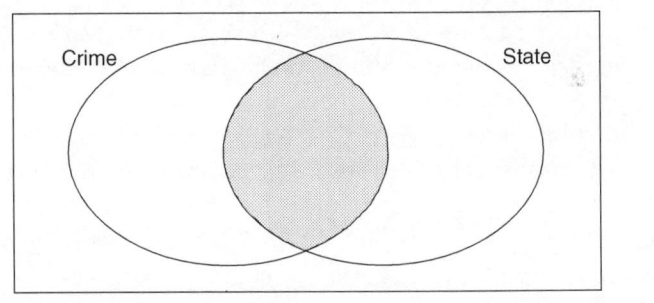

Crime   State

FIGURE 1.1 Redefining the Crime–State Nexus: The Gray Zone of Criminality

---

[2] Students of the mafia in Italy have made active use of the concept of the gray zone to conceptualize the environment where the mafia operates. Understanding the mafia as the networks of brokers who connect the illicit and the licit worlds, in this formulation the gray zone is "inhabited by professionals from the public and private sectors such as businessmen, lawyers, notaries, engineers, architects, doctors, and even people in positions of responsibility such as judges, politicians, law enforcement officers, public sector managers, accountants and solicitors, [who have an] ... invisible but vital relationship with mafia organisations ..." (Allum, Merlino, and Colletti 2019, p. 80). The main difference between this relational approach and ours is the key role that state specialists in violence – armed forces, the police, pro-government militias and members of the judicial and penitentiary systems – play in enabling the existence of organized crime in our formulation.

government protection, which is typically provided by agents from state security forces and judicial institutions. Outside the gray zone, criminal groups are simply common criminals and states are law enforcement agents. This definition recognizes two faces of crime: common criminals, for whom the state is the enemy, and organized criminal groups, for whom access to informal networks of state protection is the fuel that feeds their organism.[3] This definition also recognizes two faces of the state: state agents who do not collude with organized crime but actually fight it, and state agents who create informal networks of government protection that facilitate the existence of organized crime.

Defining the two faces of crime and the state and identifying the gray zone of criminality as the ecosystem in which organized crime can breathe, grow, and reproduce takes us away from traditional literatures of crime. Whereas the criminology literature distinguishes between common criminals and organized criminal groups on the basis of levels of organization, for us the key definitional distinction stems from the forms of engagement with the state. While common criminals do have a zero-sum relationship with state agents, *the crucial theoretical point for us is that organized crime can only exist when criminal organizations gain some level of state protection to operate illicit markets*.[4] One important implication is that defining OCGs solely as private economic groups that operate illicit markets – as the criminology literature does – becomes problematic. Because state support is ontologically constitutive of organized crime, OCGs cannot strictly be a private phenomenon. Another implication is that understanding OCGs as non-political actors may be misleading. Because state agents are elected officials or because elected officials oversee

---

[3] Common criminals are individuals or small groups of bandits whose main illicit activities pertain to the underworld of petty theft – e.g., shoplifting, pickpocketing, and home robberies. For the most part, these are illicit activities for which criminals do not require access to informal networks of state protection. Organized criminal groups, as we explain in the next few pages, are groups of bandits that engage in illicit activities for which they *must have* access to informal state protection – e.g., drug trafficking, extortion, kidnapping for ransom, and human smuggling.

[4] We do not dismiss the importance of the organizational features of criminal groups. We simply want to give conceptual priority to the crucial role state agents play in the ontological constitution of organized crime. In fact, in the empirical chapters of the book, we discuss at great length changes in the organizational structure of Mexico's drug cartels over the course of two decades of inter-cartel and state–cartel wars.

security agents, their association with organized crime implicitly connects OCGs with the sphere of politics.[5]

As a new generation of scholars of crime in Latin America have persistently recognized in their empirical work, in the gray zone the engagement between state agents and criminals can take many different forms.

The most common image we have is of OCGs capturing the state. Economists (Fiorentini and Peltzman 1995; Dal Bó, Dal Bó, and Di Tella 2006) and sociologists (Gambetta 1996; Varese 2001, 2011) studying the mafia have come to recognize some level of state capture that enables mafias to effectively operate. Scholars of organized crime in Latin America from a wide variety of social science disciplines and international institutions have identified several instances in which OCGs – particularly drug cartels – have sought to enlist informal government protection by means of bribes and coercion – *plata o plomo*, to quote Pablo Escobar's infamous dictum. Astorga's (2005) pioneering analysis of Mexico's drug industry suggests that drug cartels enlisted top-level officers from Mexico's armed forces and secret police to become key players in the international drug trafficking industry in the 1980s and 1990s. Sobering and Auyero (2019) show how Argentina's leading drug gang enlisted subnational state police forces to become the country's hegemonic criminal organization in the 2000s (also see Flom 2019). The influential UNODC (2012) report on drug trafficking operations in the Central American Northern Triangle shows how landowners and powerful local family clans in Guatemala enlisted mayors and members of the national civilian police from the southeastern part of the country to allow major cocaine operations through their administrative jurisdictions (see, also, Yashar 2018). And both Arias (2009) and Jaffe (2013) provide evidence of gangs recruiting local police forces to enable drug operations in Brazil and Jamaica.

A less common but nonetheless widespread phenomenon is that of state-elected officials becoming de facto leaders of OCGs for the operation of illicit markets, or state officials subcontracting OCGs to assist them in gaining or retaining political power. Caldeira and Holston (1999) provide evidence of Brazilian state military police becoming the leaders of street gambling networks in Brazil in the 1970s. Drawing on information from two truth commissions and research from civil society organizations, Peacock and Beltrán (2003) reveal that top officers from Guatemala's military and the

---

[5] Thus, political structures are bound to affect the workings of OCGs; moreover, as we explain in the following pages, in protracted criminal wars OCGs themselves can develop political interests, including the ambitious goal of becoming de facto local rulers.

death squads under their command played a key role in the development of the country's main criminal networks – including drug trafficking, kidnapping for ransom, and extortion – in the 1990s and 2000s. Burt (2009) also reports that in Peru, the head of the country's secret service (and his death squads) led the country's drug trafficking rings in the 1990s. Finally, Albarracín's (2018) micro-political ethnography reveals how local elected mayors from the periphery of Rio de Janeiro, Brazil, subcontracted militias to assist them in coercively removing their political rivals from electoral races and to mobilize voters through clientelistic means during Election Day.

Whether OCGs recruit state officials for protection or state officials become leaders of OCGs or subcontract criminal groups to achieve their political ends, the fact is that there are multiple possibilities of coexistence between criminals and state agents in the gray zone. A crucial factor in defining the nature of these arrangements is the structure of political power. Because political regimes define the rules of political power, we suggest that whether power is centralized or decentralized, or whether state officials are elected through multiparty elections or appointed by an authoritarian leader can play a crucial role in defining the contours and modes of operation of the gray zone.

Before turning to political regimes, however, let us present a summary of the main theoretical building blocks we have so far outlined:

Assumption 1: Organized crime needs some form of state protection to exist.

Assumption 2: Some state agents act as law enforcement agents and fight crime, but others collude with criminal organizations.

Definition 1: Organized criminal groups (OCGs) are business organizations that operate illicit markets with some level of informal state protection. Their goal is to monopolize such markets.

Definition 2: The gray zone of criminality is the ecosystem in which criminals and state agents informally coexist and in which OCGs live, grow, and reproduce.

ORGANIZED CRIME IN AUTOCRACY: STATE SPECIALISTS IN VIOLENCE AND THE PAX MAFIOSA

One of the most important – though often unnoticed – facts about authoritarian regimes is that they provide the natural political environment for the rise and orderly expansion of the criminal underworld. In autocracies there is a surprising connective line that goes from state coercion to corruption and criminality that needs to be theorized and empirically illustrated. This does not imply that organized crime and the gray zone of criminality only emerge in autocracies. Rather, it means that something specific about autocracies, which we associate with how coercion is used and the role and status of state specialists in violence, turns these types of political regimes into a germane political space where the nexus between state coercive actors and criminals is more likely to develop. Our rationale for this follows.

Authoritarian regimes are political arrangements in which leaders govern by means of cooptation and coercion. As scholars in political economy have shown, political leaders in authoritarian regimes usually seek to control the economy and make active use of public resources to reward loyalties and punish regime enemies (Magaloni 2006; Blaydes 2010; Greene 2010). Autocrats also engage in the active redistribution of assets, particularly land (Albertus 2015). Because economic resources are limited and economies can go into crisis, authoritarian leaders combine carrots and sticks and make extensive investments in developing coercive capacity to govern political dissent. To this end, they strengthen the armed forces and the police, keep tight controls over the prison system, and develop secret service agencies (Greitens 2016). When they face rebel threats or when their countries plunge into civil war, these security forces often create pro-government militias (paramilitary forces) and death squads to undertake the most brutal operations in anti-insurgency campaigns (Carey, Colaresi, and Mitchell 2015). Security-sector agents are not strictly law enforcement agents, whose main mandate should be to safeguard citizen security, but authoritarian rulers' employees, whose key mandate is to facilitate the regime's political survival. Hence, we do not refer to them as law enforcement agents but as *authoritarian specialists in violence*. Because repression can cause a backlash and alienate the people from the rulers, autocrats in general would prefer to rule by means of cooptation rather than repression (Trejo 2012). But when cooptation is not feasible, particularly in times of major economic crises when economic resources are not readily available for authoritarian rulers to co-opt potential enemies, autocrats rely on state specialists in violence to stay in power.

To fulfill their mandate, high-ranking members of the military and the police develop an expertise in information gathering and coercion and operate with impunity. In stable authoritarian regimes, these state specialists in violence have privileged access to information about the rulers and coalition members as well as about dissident groups. They also receive the best possible coercive training and have access to the most powerful weapons and the best equipment available to the government to confront anti-regime threats. Members of the military and police forces often train civilians to serve as shadow powers to keep dissidents at bay – these are the anti-riot civilian forces and the pro-government militias that so commonly play a key governance role in authoritarian regimes. Beyond information and weapons, authoritarian specialists in violence need state-guaranteed impunity to operate. They need a license to kill – to engage in extrajudicial executions, torture, and forced disappearance of the regime's political enemies, knowing that they will not be held accountable for these atrocities. Public prosecutors, judges, and directors of penitentiaries play a crucial role as agents of impunity for state specialists in violence.

Developing a comparative advantage in violence and information gathering and enjoying impunity for the lethal use of force turns authoritarian specialists in violence into powerful actors who may one day become a threat to authoritarian rulers. By empowering these repressive agents to solve the problem of *authoritarian control* of the masses (Svolik 2012), autocrats can unwittingly create incentives for a palace coup. One potential solution is to engage in *authoritarian power-sharing* (Svolik 2012) and give access to legislative seats or governorships or access to party positions to state specialists in violence (Gandhi and Przeworski 2007; Magaloni 2008).

Beyond institutional power-sharing, another possibility is to transform repressive agents' political impunity into criminal immunity and provide them with access to the criminal underworld – or, in our conceptual language, to the gray zone of criminality. Both their privileged access to information and their coercive capacity are highly valued skills in this environment (Gambetta 1996). Allowing authoritarian specialists in violence to regulate the criminal underworld or to lead specific criminal industries can provide them with valuable private benefits, increasing their stakes in the survival of the regime. To maintain a balance between private profits and regime loyalty, specialists in violence are allowed to keep a significant share of criminal profits but are expected to share the rest with the authoritarian leaders.

Authoritarian incumbents have powerful incentives to demand from state specialists in violence that they effectively keep the use of violence by OCGs to a minimum level and that the collusion between state agents and OCGs is kept in the gray shadows of the criminal underworld and away from the public view. For autocrats, regulating the use of violence and preventing OCGs from becoming powerful armed actors is crucial to avoiding the mounting of armed challenges to the regime. It is also crucial to keep state–criminal collusion away from the public eye to prevent the outbreak of any major scandal that would associate the regime not only with repressive practices but also with illicit criminal activities. Autocrats outsource repression and hide criminal corruption because they want to avoid domestic and international discredit and future punishment. And this often works. For example, truth commissions operating in the post-authoritarian period generally focus their activities on unveiling the different sources and types of state repressive violence and gross human rights violations during the authoritarian era, but the linkages that connect state specialists in violence with crime often remain unexplored.

Latin American twentieth-century autocracies provide prominent examples of the leading role that authoritarian state specialists in violence have played in the development of the gray zone of criminality. To show that this is a widespread phenomenon – and not something unique to a specific country or a particular type of authoritarian regime – we report evidence from three types of autocracies: military, personalistic, and one-party hegemony.

As Caldeira and Holston (1999) and Albarracín (2018) have documented, the Brazilian military regime allowed members of the state military police to regulate and run the street gambling industry in the 1970s – the most proximate antecedent to the country's drug trafficking rings in the favelas of Rio de Janeiro and São Paulo. Gillies (2018) developed the concept of state-narco networks to describe how Bolivia's military regimes in the 1960s and 1970s used cocaine production and traffic as a source of patronage to reward state specialists in violence and local elites. These networks enabled General Luis García Meza (1980–1981) to conduct a coup in coalition with the country's leading traffickers and to establish a "narco-state." Even the military regime of Augusto Pinochet (1973–1989), which persistently claimed to be uncorrupt, allowed members of the powerful secret service agency (DINA) to process large quantities of coca leaf into cocaine and ship them to Western European markets. Some of these resources served to keep DINA specialists in violence loyal to the regime, and they also provided unaccounted-for cash to finance anti-communist paramilitary operations in the Southern Cone and Central America (De Castro and Gasparini 2000; O'Shaughnessy 2000).[6]

[6] During the Cold War, state specialists in violence in a wide variety of authoritarian regimes, from Panama (under Noriega) and Chile (under Pinochet) to Mexico (under the

The personalistic regime of Alberto Fujimori in Peru allowed his chief of intelligence, Vladimiro Montesinos, to lead and coordinate drug trafficking operations in the 1990s. Grupo Colina, the government's leading paramilitary force in the anti-insurgency operations against the Shining Path and in suppressing any form of even non-violent dissent through mass atrocities, played a key role in drug trafficking (Beltrán 2008). The personalistic regime of Fulgencio Batista in pre-revolutionary Cuba in the 1950s allowed members of the army and Batista's personal police to run illegal operations associated with the gambling and drug industries on the island (English 2007; Sáenz-Rovner 2008). After the military coup that brought his clique to power in Panama, General Manuel Antonio Noriega allowed members of his military elite to establish a close business association with the Medellín Cartel and become key players in the transnational chain of drug smuggling from Colombia into Miami (Bagley 2011).

In Mexico's one-party regime, the government allowed special military units fighting rural and urban guerrillas during Mexico's Dirty War in the 1970s to run major drug operations (Aviña 2018). As historian Adela Cedillo (2019) demonstrates, Plan Cóndor, a major anti-drug program led by the Mexican government in cooperation with the US government in the 1970s and early 1980s, played a key role in enabling the rise of authoritarian state specialists in violence as regulators of the drug trafficking industry. Under the lead of the Federal Security Directorate (DFS) – Mexico's militarized secret service agency – elite members of the military, together with the federal police and their death squads, carried out brutal anti-insurgency operations in the southern state of Guerrero (Aviña 2018) and in the Northern Triangle of Chihuahua, Sinaloa and Durango (Cedillo 2019). They also played a key role in the anti-drug operations. In these states, which were the focal points for drug production and traffic, Mexico's state specialists in violence displaced local caciques and families of traffickers and took over the drug trafficking business (Pansters 2018). In Cedillo's formulation, the uncommon coercive power and impunity they gained during the Dirty War and the War on Drugs enabled these forces under the DFS lead to (1) regroup the country's main traffickers in the city of Guadalajara and into the Guadalajara Cartel – the grandfather of Mexico's four dominant cartels that rose to international prominence in the 1990s; and (2) regulate, protect, and profit from the drug industry (Lupsha 1991; Astorga 2005; Sierra 2012).

PRI), were able to take direct control over drug trafficking operations and used some of these profits to finance anti-communist struggles. See Cribb (2009) and Cedillo (2019).

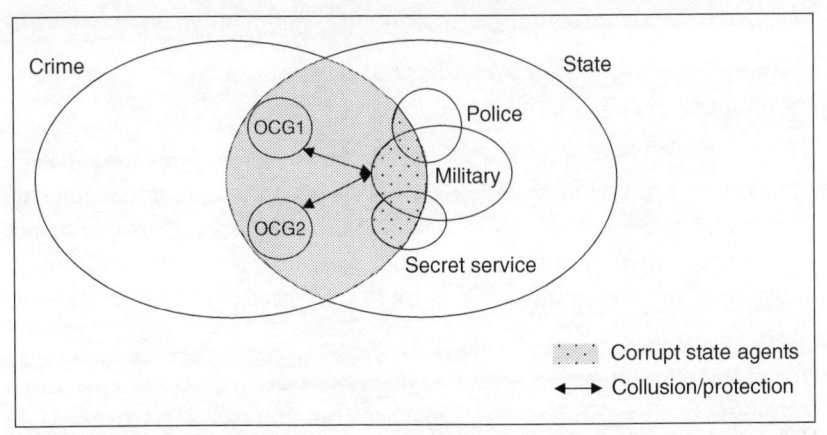

FIGURE 1.2 Informal Government Protection for Organized Criminal Groups (OCGs) in Autocracy

Finally, there is growing evidence that as Venezuela has regressed from democracy into autocracy (Mainwaring 2012), elite members of the armed forces have become key actors in drug trafficking operations from Colombia into Venezuela and then to the Central America–Mexico–United States route. By 2016, all governors from the states along the Colombia–Venezuela international border were members of the military and of the ruling Socialist Party of Venezuela (PSV), and there is growing evidence of the involvement of state security forces under their command in drug trafficking operations across international borders (InSight Crime 2018).

All these examples suggest that there is an intimate connection between authoritarian rule and the rise of the gray zone of criminality. Figure 1.2 provides a generic image of the key institutions, actors, and relationships that give rise to and characterize the gray zone of criminality. We identify the military, the police, and the secret service as key institutions involved in state repression against dissidents and in the development of networks of regulation and protection for OCGs. The figure identifies members of the military that collude with OCGs (see dotted area) and those who do not (see white area). Because the military tends to be a central institution in most authoritarian regimes and military leaders often control both the secret services and the police, the figure suggests that militarized police and secret service agents are part of these informal networks of protection for OCGs. Military agents, however, take the upper hand in protecting or colluding with OCGs and in regulating illicit industries in the gray zone of criminality (see bidirectional arrows).

Here is a summary of our new theoretical building blocks:

Assumption 3: Authoritarian leaders rely on state specialists in violence to guarantee regime survival.

Definition 3: Authoritarian state specialists in violence are special units within the armed forces and the police whose key mandate is to guarantee the regime's survival. To achieve this goal, specialists in violence have privileged access to political information, receive unique coercive training, and are granted immunity from judicial prosecution for gross human rights violations.

Proposition 1: Organized crime and the gray zone of criminality often emerge in authoritarian regimes, where autocrats allow state specialists in violence to profit from the criminal underworld as a way to keep them faithful to the regime. Networks of state repression, corruption, and criminality emerge and reinforce each other under authoritarian auspices.

TRANSITIONS FROM AUTHORITARIAN RULE TO DEMOCRACY: WHY THE NATURE OF A TRANSITION MATTERS FOR ORGANIZED CRIME

The breakdown of authoritarian regimes and transitions to democracy are likely to have a major impact on the gray zone of criminality and on criminal behavior. Cross-national quantitative studies of criminal violence have shown that, on average, murder rates tend to increase as countries transition from authoritarian rule to democracy (Neumayer 2003; Moran 2011; Fox and Hoelscher 2012; Rivera 2016; Frantz 2018). But this is a probabilistic statement rather than a causal law. In fact, the record shows that while many new democracies experience spirals of criminal violence, a few remain relatively peaceful. Explaining why countries follow different trajectories will allow us to outline the scope conditions for this study and will help us justify our focus on Mexico.

Cross-national evidence shows that countries which adopt major security-sector reforms to democratize the armed forces and the police from the authoritarian era are more likely to deflate the gray zone of criminality and to break the arrows that connect state security agents with OCGs. As Tiscornia's (2019) important work suggests, effective security-sector reforms entail the demilitarization of the security sector and the introduction of important internal and external accountability mechanisms in the police forces. When these reforms succeed, there are fewer corrupt officials available to recreate informal networks of government protection for criminals and fewer officials willing to defect to organized crime to fight turf wars. And there are more security officials who are willing to fight crime through lawful means, following due process, rather than adopting iron-fist policies, which stimulate, rather than deter, violence.

In his important work on criminal violence in Central America, Cruz (2011) shows that despite high levels of poverty and inequality and a history of civil conflict, Nicaragua's multiple waves of police reforms in the 1980s and 1990s explain the country's relatively low levels of criminality in the 2000s. Through these reforms, consecutive leftist and conservative regimes dismantled the police forces from the Somoza dictatorship, demilitarized the revolutionary police built by the Sandinistas, and created a decentralized police force accountable to local communities. Yashar's (2018) important comparative research about different trajectories of post-conflict violence in Central America provides extensive evidence of the demilitarization and professionalization of a new police force with new personnel subject to internal and external accountability mechanisms. This allowed Nicaragua to develop law enforcement institutions. In turn, these deterred transnational drug trafficking organizations from establishing the country as a transit zone of the global chain of drug trafficking operations that connects the Andes with the US – as they did in Guatemala, Honduras, and El Salvador.

Cross-national studies of criminal violence also show that countries that adopt major transitional justice processes to expose, prosecute and punish authoritarian state specialists in violence – who committed gross human rights violations during the authoritarian era – can undermine the links between state agents and OCGs, reduce the gray zone of criminality, and contain possibilities for the outbreak of criminal violence (Trejo, Albarracín, and Tiscornia 2018). When countries engage in extensive domestic prosecutions and sentence authoritarian specialists in violence to prison for gross human rights violations, they de facto remove potential business partners for criminal groups. When countries adopt robust truth commissions to expose individuals, institutions from the security sector, and clandestine illegal forces for gross human rights violations, they increase the costs for members of the military or the police to capitalize on their coercive power to serve the criminal underworld or to fight criminals through iron-fist policies. As Trejo, Albarracín, and Tiscornia

(2018) have shown, the joint adoption of truth commissions and trials in Latin America introduces an *accountability shock* to the system that reduces both the size of the gray zone of criminality and the murder rate.

Countries such as Argentina, Chile, or Peru are cases in which new democratic elites adopted some of the most ambitious transitional justice processes to deal with a repressive past. Through a combination of robust truth commissions and multiple high-profile human rights trials, they were able to deter specialists in violence – members of the armed forces and the secret police – from becoming leading actors in the gray zone of criminality. These anti-impunity programs contributed to the reduction of criminal violence. They deterred prominent members of the security forces from defecting to the criminal underworld and deterred those who stayed in government from developing informal government protection networks for criminals or using brutal anti-insurgency campaigns to fight criminals. In the absence of any meaningful transitional justice mechanism, (thin) electoral transitions to democracy in Mexico, Honduras, and Brazil facilitated the survival of state–criminal networks and of repressive practices that fueled turf wars in democracy.

When elites in new democracies fail to carry out major security-sector reforms or to adopt major transitional justice processes, the survival of authoritarian state specialists in violence and the persistence of the gray zone of criminality connect the dynamics of regime change with the criminal underworld. This means that the redistribution of power that is intrinsic to a process of regime transition and to the rise of new democratic institutions will have a major destabilizing effect on the gray zone. By removing OCGs' old allies from positions of state coercive power and introducing new rules for the allocation of power through competitive elections, transitions to democracy are likely to generate turbulence and introduce a great deal of uncertainty into the gray zone. This removes the incentives for criminals' peaceful coexistence that often characterize the criminal status quo in autocracies.

To summarize:

Assumption 4: When postauthoritarian elites fail to enact major security-sector reforms or adopt robust transitional justice processes to dismantle networks of state repression, corruption, and criminality, transitions from authoritarian rule to democracy generate major instability in the gray zone of criminality, giving rise to incentives for violence.[7]

---

[7] In this book, we present this statement as an assumption that we will not put to empirical test. If we transformed the statement into a proposition for testing, an empirical test would

Our central goal in this book is to explore theoretically (this chapter) and empirically (Parts II and III) the interaction between political change and criminal behavior in a context in which postauthoritarian elites fail to dismantle the authoritarian security apparatuses through security-sector reforms and/or transitional justice processes and thus allow the survival of the gray zone of criminality. This is the world of illiberal democracies – countries that transition from authoritarian rule to *electoral* democracy without properly developing a democratic rule of law. As we suggested in the Introduction, Mexico is a text-book case of an illiberal democracy. It is a country that experienced an electoral transition to multiparty democracy but without a corresponding development of a democratic rule of law. In Mexico, the PRI lost power after seven decades of uninterrupted hegemonic rule but postauthoritarian elites failed to introduce any meaningful reform of the military, the police, and the justice system, all of which continued to operate as authoritarian enclaves (Lawson 2000; Zepeda 2004; Davis 2006).

ORGANIZED CRIME AND THE OUTBREAK OF LARGE-SCALE CRIMINAL VIOLENCE IN ILLIBERAL DEMOCRACIES

When the actors and informal institutional networks that constitute the gray zone of criminality survive the breakdown of authoritarian regimes and become key actors in the new illiberal democratic order, the dynamics of political change quickly become intertwined with the criminal underworld, giving rise to incentives for OCGs to engage in large-scale violence to settle disputes. The outbreak of large-scale criminal violence becomes intimately associated with elections and with the distribution of political power in the polity. In fact, incentives for the use of criminal violence stem from two political sources: the removal of political leaders through competitive elections and the decentralization and vertical fragmentation of political power.

Multiparty Competition, Party Alternation, and Large-Scale Criminal Violence

To the extent that the spheres of the state and crime remain connected in illiberal democracies, any change in state power will create

require a cross-national, rather than a subnational, research design. In a parallel project, one of us is engaged in actually empirically testing the impact of transitional justice processes on criminal violence in postauthoritarian societies. See Trejo, Albarracín, and Tiscornia (2018).

instability and uncertainty in the gray zone. In one-party, dominant-party, and hegemonic-party regimes the prevalence of the same political actors in office provides some degree of stability and allows criminal actors to engage in long-term planning. In illiberal democracies, by contrast, intense electoral competition and the frequent removal of political leaders are likely to disrupt the informal networks of government protection for OCGs, affecting the balance of power in the gray zone of criminality.

The rotation of political leaders and the likely removal of top personnel in the state security apparatus will force the frequent reconstitution and renegotiation of informal government protection, which could take some time to materialize. Because OCGs cannot go one day without protection without running the risk of state crack downs or lethal attacks by their rivals (Schelling 1971), the prospect of even a short-term absence of protection will motivate criminal lords to develop their own private armies. These private armies enable them to protect their turf while at the same time seeking to conquer rival territory, and to renegotiate the terms of informal government protection with newly elected politicians through bribes *and* coercion. To illustrate the logic of criminal violence when informal state protection is no longer guaranteed in new illiberal democracies, consider the case of drug trafficking – the criminal industry under empirical investigation in this book.

The central asset in the drug trafficking industry is the control over *drug trafficking routes* – the de facto property rights over the ports, airports, highways, roads, border exit and entry points, and the people who operate them, that constitute these corridors of illicit trade. Drug traffickers are not producers or retail street sellers but wholesale distributors of illicit substances, particularly marijuana, cocaine, poppy and heroin, and synthetic drugs. These are multibillion-dollar industries. Following the popular usage, we call drug trafficking organizations *drug cartels.*[8] Cartels are criminal organizations that connect drug producers with retail distributors. Because most illicit drugs are produced in developing countries (in the Global South) and consumed in advanced capitalist democracies (in the Global North), drug trafficking is a global industry (UNDP 2013). But because trafficking routes cut through and across countries, control over these routes has a strong local component. In gaining control over the

---

[8] Note that these drug trafficking organizations do not always behave like cartels in the economic sense – that is, they do not collude to manipulate the supply of drugs and hence affect the price level.

mountains, highways, roads, and towns that constitute trafficking routes, drug cartels actively seek the informal protection of subnational authorities. We recognize both the global and local dimensions of wholesale drug operations and hence define the drug trafficking industry as *a global chain of local operations*. This conceptual move has important implications for a theory of politics: while changes in national politics do affect the operation of the gray zone of criminality, the most direct and potentially consequential sources of instability may come from subnational political change.

Drug trafficking routes are indivisible goods – that is, two rival cartels cannot be joint proprietors of a trafficking corridor (Calderón et al. 2015; Lessing 2017). This is why a third-party enforcer is a crucial actor in the drug trafficking industry. Under authoritarian rule, as we argued, state specialists in violence have the information, coercive power, and impunity to lead or regulate the criminal underworld and to define and guarantee property rights over turf. But in the absence of a third-party enforcer, cartels have to rely on private coercion to settle disputes. The uncertainty over the control of drug trafficking routes in a postauthoritarian setting invites competition and, as Schelling (1971) and Buchanan (1973) observed a long time ago, competition in criminal markets breeds violence. Violence can be waged against different targets with distinct purposes: (1) violence against rival cartels to eliminate them as competitors; (2) violence against state agents to keep them away from drug trafficking routes and to deter them from enforcing the law; and (3) violence against newly elected politicians to force them into becoming part of state protection networks or to eliminate them and replace them with cartel loyalists.

When new democratic elites fail to dismantle the authoritarian security apparatus that guaranteed authoritarian regime survival and the transition to democracy is reduced to a thin electoral transition, they unwittingly contribute to the preservation of the gray zone of criminality where the drug trafficking industry emerges and thrives. In these illiberal democracies, multiparty electoral competition becomes quickly intertwined with the drug trafficking industry because political change upsets the distribution of power within the gray zone and changes the power struggles among drug cartels and between cartels and the state. By constantly removing political leaders, their respective chiefs of the state security apparatus, and the heads of the judicial system, multiparty competitive elections unintentionally remove the third-party enforcers who regulated and safeguarded property rights over drug trafficking routes in autocracy. This gives rise to incentives for inter-cartel competition and violence.

Although the topic of electoral politics has been absent from seminal theories of crime, new findings in economics and political science have begun to identify the intimate connection between electoral competition and lethal criminal violence perpetrated by a wide variety of criminal actors, from mafias and traffickers to racketeers. For example, Albarracín (2018) finds a strong association between the dynamics of electoral competition and gang violence in postauthoritarian Brazil, particularly in Rio de Janeiro and surrounding municipalities. A number of scholars have documented a close association between the dynamics of municipal electoral competition and the outbreak and spread of inter-cartel violence in postauthoritarian Mexico (Astorga 2005; Dube, Dube, and García-Ponce 2013; Osorio 2015). Investigative journalists have provided compelling evidence of a close association between multiparty electoral competition and fluctuations in criminal violence in postauthoritarian Guatemala and Honduras (Pachico 2011; Spring 2013).[9] Relatedly, scholars have documented the surge in targeted lethal attacks against party candidates and elected officials during local election cycles in a range of cases from postauthoritarian Brazil (Albarracín 2018) and Mexico (Trejo and Ley 2015; Blume 2017) to post-Fascist Italy (Alesina, Piccolo, and Pinotti 2019).

While some studies suggest that OCGs attack their rivals (e.g., Dube, Dube, and García-Ponce 2013) or state officials to secure control over criminal markets (e.g., Trejo and Ley 2015; Alesina, Piccolo, and Pinotti 2019), others show that local politicians subcontract OCGs to secure their control over political markets (Albarracín 2018). In either case, the persistence of the gray zone of criminality as countries transition from authoritarian rule to (thin) electoral democracy facilitates the development of multiple connections between electoral competition and the alternation of parties in office – the quintessential mechanisms of political change in democracies – and the dynamics of order and violence in the criminal underworld. It is worth stressing that electoral outcomes become triggers of violence because they operate in a context in which authoritarian state

---

[9] Beyond Latin America, Daxecker and Prins's (2016) study of maritime piracy in Indonesia shows that higher levels of electoral competition are positively associated with increases in pirate violence. Anticipating that electoral competition may disrupt collusive agreements between pirate organizations and government authorities, pirates elevate their attack rates before political changes undermine their agreements.

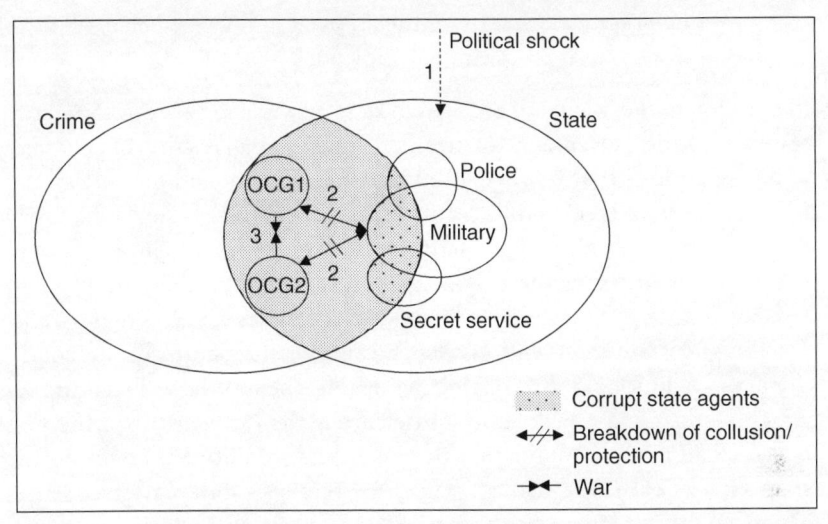

FIGURE 1.3 Partisan Alternation, the Breakdown of Informal Government Protection for Organized Criminal Groups (OCGs), and the Onset of Criminal Wars (Numbers indicate sequence of events)

specialists in violence survived the transition and reinvented themselves in the context of illiberal democracy – that is, political systems characterized by competitive elections without a democratic rule of law.

Figure 1.3 illustrates the likely impact of electoral competition and party alternation on the gray zone of criminality in a country that exclusively transitioned from authoritarian rule to illiberal democracy and hence key members in the security forces continue to use their political immunity to repress political dissidents and engage themselves in the criminal underworld. It shows that changes in electoral competition (see arrow illustrating an exogenous political shock) can temporarily weaken the informal networks of protection when corrupt officials (dotted parts) are removed (see dashed bidirectional arrows), giving rise to inter-cartel violence (see collision of unidirectional arrows between OCGs). Whereas in Figure 1.2, state specialists in violence effectively regulate OCG interactions, promoting a *pax mafiosa*, Figure 1.3 shows that peaceful coexistence can turn into criminal wars for turf when authoritarian specialists in violence are removed and informal networks of protection for criminals become temporarily ineffective.

The Fragmentation of Political Power and Large-Scale Criminal Violence

In addition to the impact of changes in state power and the rotation of top state authorities, incentives for criminal violence may result from changes in public policies that newly elected leaders sometimes adopt in response to voters' demands for public security. As Osorio (2015) suggests, newly democratic leaders may adopt active anti-criminal policies in response to voters' concerns, and these policies may result in violent backlashes. Lessing's (2015, 2017) model of state–cartel conflict suggests that cartels' reactions to state interventions depend on whether states use unconditional or conditional forms of violence against them. Whereas conditional attacks – the state attacks only those cartels that attacked it in the first place – lead to the containment of violence, unconditional attacks – the state attacks cartels regardless – lead to spirals of state–cartel violence. Tiscornia (2019) alternatively suggests that when state specialists in violence in illiberal democracies continue to use authoritarian/militaristic logics of law enforcement and rely on anti-insurgency strategies to wipe out their enemies through iron-fist policies, OCGs have incentives to preemptively attack the state, giving rise to spirals of violence (see, also, Flores-Macías 2018).

While we recognize that state strategies are crucial in defining trajectories of criminal violence, we want to underscore the political motivations that may lead to state interventions. In illiberal democracies, in which the rule of law is relatively weak and presidents can *politicize* law enforcement for electoral purposes, state interventions can be politically motivated. Postauthoritarian multiparty competition stimulates the decentralization and vertical fragmentation of power between national and subnational governments. Thus, higher-level authorities have incentives to cooperate with lower-level co-partisan authorities and confront (or simply fail to cooperate with) political challengers, as part of their efforts to secure their partisan strongholds and collect greater electoral support. Such differentiated partisan support for local governments can have important consequences for local security and development. In the case of the drug trafficking industry, when drug lords learn that law enforcement is politically motivated, they recognize in the vertical fragmentation of power a unique political opportunity to compete for turf in unprotected territories. This gives rise to spirals of violence against rival cartels and against vulnerable local opposition politicians.

Students of ethnic conflict and social movements have eloquently demonstrated the importance of electoral incentives and partisan logics in guiding policing decisions in federal democracies. In his influential study of inter-ethnic violence in India, Wilkinson (2004) shows that state-level police forces protected Muslim minorities from Hindu attacks where Muslims were pivotal voters and could cast a decisive vote in state elections but left them unattended when they were electorally insignificant. In his important study of food riots in Argentina following the 2001 economic collapse, Auyero (2006) shows that subnational police forces prevented rioters from looting supermarket stores that were associated with *peronismo* (the Partido Justicialista, PJ), but allowed them to vandalize stores that were associated with the rival national incumbent (the Unión Cívica Radical, UCR–Frente País Solidario, FREPASO, alliance).

Partisanship has been recognized as an important factor in the efficacy of federal policing interventions in Mexico. Focusing on the Mexican drug wars, Urrusti Frenk (2012), Ríos (2015), and Durán-Martínez (2018) provide important evidence showing that partisan vertical coordination allowed the Mexican president to more effectively coordinate the War on Drugs with subnational co-partisans and contain spirals of violence. Durán-Martínez extends the claim of partisan coordination to Colombia, where she finds that the national government enacted more effective anti-drug policies in regions where national officials could collaborate with co-partisan mayors (2018).

While we recognize the importance of partisanship for intergovernmental coordination, we look at the flipside of the coin to argue that there is more to this than a technical inability of politicians from opposing parties to work together. Following Wilkinson (2004) and Auyero (2006), we move beyond coordination as a technical problem and suggest that higher-level authorities may deploy security forces and effectively confront inter-cartel conflict and contain drug violence in areas ruled by co-partisans but leave their political rivals unattended – and then attribute the blame for failing to contain the violence in their areas to them. Thus, we connect partisan logics with electoral ambitions: in federations with a weak rule of law, in which presidents can politicize law enforcement, federal incumbents can reward their loyalists and punish their opponents (1) to reap electoral benefits from the intervention and (2) to transfer the political costs of violence onto their political enemies.

Figure 1.II.a illustrates the likely impact of an effective federal intervention in which the military leads a coordinated attack against OCGs – e. g., a war against drug cartels. We claim that electoral incentives may lead

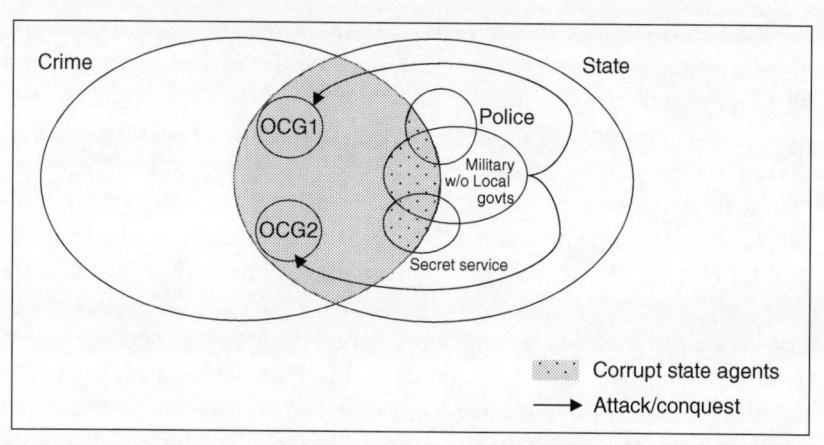

FIGURE I.II.a Effective Military Intervention against Organized Criminal Groups (OCGs) – Cooperation between Federal and Local Co-Partisan Governments Suppresses OCGs

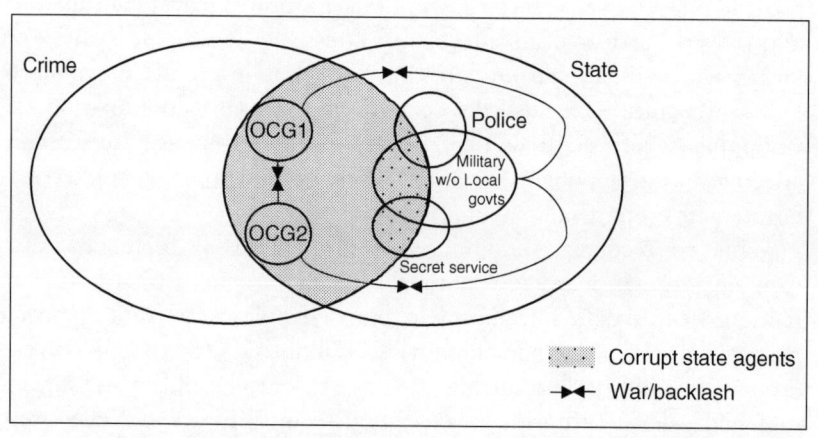

FIGURE I.II.b Ineffective Military Intervention against Organized Criminal Groups (OCGs) – Intergovernmental Partisan Conflict between Federal and Local Governments Stimulates War

the federal government to launch an effective intervention if co-partisan subnational authorities (governors and mayors) are confronting criminal threats, contributing to the suppression of OCG violence, as shown in Figure I.II.a.

Figure I.II.b shows the case of a weak federal intervention in which the lack of cooperation between the military and subnational authorities stimulates criminal wars among OCGs and between OCGs and the state. In this case, electoral incentives may lead federal authorities to adopt a weak intervention, leave subnational authorities unprotected, and blame them for the criminal backlash against the state and the intensification of criminal wars, as illustrated in Figure 1.II.b.

To summarize: when elites in illiberal democracies fail to dismantle the networks of coercion, corruption, and criminality that flourish under authoritarian rule, the gray zone of criminality, where state specialists in violence and criminals coexist, quickly becomes intimately involved with elections and political change in democracy. Electoral democracy entails multiparty competition, the rotation of political parties in office, and the decentralization and vertical fragmentation of political power – particularly in federations. When the gray zone persists, these mechanics of political change can affect the criminal balance of power in fundamental ways and generate incentives for the outbreak of criminal wars and large-scale criminal violence.

As Figures 1.3 and 1.II.b suggest, criminal wars are armed conflicts that involve (1) OCGs fighting other criminal groups over the control of illicit markets (e.g., drug trafficking routes) and (2) states fighting OCGs over the control or suppression of illicit activities (e.g., drug trafficking). In our discussion about the dynamics of conflict in the drug trafficking industry, following Lessing (2017) we will make the distinction between inter-cartel and state–cartel wars. Beyond drug trafficking conflicts, in our formulation criminal wars have four distinguishing features. First, they are militarized conflicts over the control of illicit markets. Second, these are conflicts in which OCGs develop their own private militias to defend their turf. Private militias at the service of criminal lords are hierarchical organizations led by defectors from the armed forces or the police in which militia members receive quasi-military training for combat and have access to weapons similar to those used by regular armed forces. Third, these are lethal conflicts that produce anything from small-scale violence (from 25 to 1,000 annual battle deaths) to large-scale violence (above 1,000 annual battle deaths).[10] Finally, in protracted criminal wars OCGs and private militias often seek to establish territorial controls beyond illicit markets – they seek to gain de facto control over towns and cities (plazas) and subnational territories.

---

[10] For discussions about different thresholds of violence in the civil war literature, see Gleditsch et al. (2001) and Fearon and Laitin (2003).

Because we are particularly interested in assessing how the dynamics of political change affect the prospects for peace and war in the drug trafficking industry, it is imperative to outline some definitions and use them to develop new propositions that are specific to this industry.

Definition 4: The drug trafficking industry is a global chain of illicit local operations. Control over drug trafficking routes, through which illicit drugs are smuggled across and within countries, is the main asset in this industry. Drug trafficking routes are indivisible goods – that is, two rival cartels cannot be joint proprietors of the same corridor.

Assumption 5: Gaining control over drug trafficking routes is possible only when drug cartels enjoy some level of protection from local security and judicial authorities.

Definition 5: Criminal wars are militarized conflicts over the control of illicit markets and subnational territories in which OCGs and their private militias fight rival criminal groups and/or the state. Fought by specialists in violence trained in military combat and who gain access to high-caliber weapons, these conflicts can be as lethal as civil wars.

Proposition 2: When transitions from authoritarian rule to democracy fail and result in the rise of illiberal democracies, the dynamics of subnational electoral change – competition, alternation, political decentralization, and vertical fragmentation of political power – are likely to impact the gray zone of criminality and give rise to incentives for drug cartels to actively rely on violence to settle disputes and to engage in major turf wars to conquer rival drug trafficking routes, or to protect their own.[11]

---

[11] Although electoral competition, party alternation, and the decentralization and fragmentation of political power are prevalent in consolidated democracies, they do not stimulate the outbreak of large-scale criminal violence that we tend to see in illiberal democracies for two reasons. First, because state specialists in violence in consolidated democracies face greater constraints and are subject to more effective internal and external accountability mechanisms. This means they are less likely to become involved in the gray zone of criminality than the armed forces, the police, and the illicit clandestine actors in illiberal democracies. And, second, the existence of these constraints on state specialists in violence makes the gray zone of criminality in consolidated democracies both narrower and less prone to violence than in illiberal democracies.

WARTIME TRANSFORMATIONS: THE RISE OF CRIMINAL GOVERNANCE REGIMES IN DEMOCRACY

As the experience of postauthoritarian Latin America shows, criminal wars are not short-term phenomena but protracted conflicts that often erupt during transitions from authoritarian rule to democracy and deepen when countries develop illiberal democracies. Cross-national studies of criminal violence have shown that the breakdown of authoritarian controls and the early phases of democratization are strongly associated with increases in murder rates (Neumayer 2003; Fox and Hoelscher 2012; Rivera 2016). A good share of this violence results from major conflicts among OCGs and from conflicts between states and criminal organizations. Absent any major change in the rule of law – via transitional justice processes, extensive judicial reforms or major security-sector reforms – these conflicts become increasingly violent as electoral competition becomes closely intertwined with criminality and every new rotation of parties in power stimulates, rather than deters, violence. Brazilian criminal gangs have been at war since the early years of the country's democratization in 1985, and violence has grown exponentially over time (Lessing 2017). Mexican cartels went to war as the country experienced the first alternation in state gubernatorial power in the late 1980s, and inter-cartel and state–cartel wars have become increasingly intense as the country has moved into electoral democracy (Trejo and Ley 2018; Osorio 2015). Moreover, gang violence erupted shortly after the signing of the peace agreement in El Salvador in 1992 and has continuously grown ever since (Yashar 2018).

Protracted conflicts and the intensification of violence over long periods of time can have major consequences for warring actors. This is one of the most important lessons from the micro-studies of violence in civil war. As Kalyvas (2006) suggests, rather than the irrational desire for the destruction of their enemies, one of the key objectives of armed actors in protracted civil wars is to gain the monopoly of violence within specific subnational territories. As the conflict evolves, they actively seek to control local populations and develop new local social orders that would enable them to eventually assault national power. Arjona (2016) has effectively shown that when armed actors become territorial actors in protracted civil conflicts, they seek to develop *rebel governance* regimes in towns and villages – local orders where rebels control political, economic, and social life and where they develop their own de facto institutions.

Like combatants in civil wars, criminal actors experience major transformations over the course of protracted criminal wars marked by large-scale criminal violence. As we have argued, criminal wars are violent conflicts in which OCGs use their private armies to fight rival criminal groups and the state for the control of criminal markets and territories. In the case of the drug trafficking industry, cartels engage in wars over the control of drug trafficking routes. Yet, as turf wars become more intense, cartels are compelled to find access to new resources to finance ongoing disputes over drug trafficking routes. The experiences of Colombia, Guatemala, Honduras, and Mexico show that to remain competitive in these drug wars cartels often expand their range of actions to new illicit industries (Garzón 2012; UNODC 2012; Calderón et al. 2015; Flores-Macías 2018), particularly those that specialize in the extraction of human wealth (extortion, kidnapping for ransom, and human smuggling) and natural resources wealth (the looting of forests, mines, and oil). Scholars of organized crime have begun to document (Trejo and Ley 2015 and 2019; Arias 2017) that drug cartels and other OCGs often infiltrate local governments, obtaining access to information (e.g., tax records), to their public resources (e.g., tax revenues and federal transfers), and to local regulatory agencies as a shortcut to establish de facto subnational governance.

When cartels and their criminal associates seek to gain control over local governments, populations, and natural resources, they enter the sphere of territorial politics. Whereas armed actors that develop territorial ambitions often construct subnational rebel governance regimes in civil war (Arjona 2016), criminal actors that develop politico-territorial ambitions often move on to develop *criminal governance* regimes in criminal wars (Trejo and Ley 2019). The decision to become de facto local rulers represents a crucial inflection point in criminal wars that brings OCGs closer to armed actors in civil wars. It entails major transformations in OCGs' objectives, their form of engagement with the state, and their use and targets of violence.

The first and most important transformation is that when drug cartels become interested in extractivist industries of human and natural wealth, the control of civilian populations becomes a primary objective. Civilians become the new victims of organized crime; they become targets of kidnapping for ransom and extortion, and they are also victimized in their capacity as property holders of natural resources – either as private citizens or as collective owners of forestry or other natural resources.[12] Because local governments have privileged information about civilian property and regulate local economic activity, gaining access to local governments becomes a primary target in the effort to control households and local businesses. In sum, when conflicts over the control of drug trafficking routes become particularly intense and cartels extend their ambitions to dominance over local governments and entire populations, civilians become unwillingly involved.

A second important transformation is that their new criminal objectives lead cartels to change their conception of territorial controls. Whereas in the past they were primarily interested in controlling the highways, roads, local airports, ports, bus stations, train stations – and the people who operate them – that constitute drug trafficking routes, their interest in the extraction of human and natural wealth leads them to become interested in controlling politico-administrative jurisdictions, particularly municipalities, cities, or counties. Gaining control over local governments and local populations, which are bounded by politico-administrative jurisdictions, has major implications for conflict. By redefining the geographical boundaries of conflict into established politico-administrative jurisdictions, cartels become political actors who develop de facto (subnational) governance ambitions.

A third important transformation is that when cartels aim to take over local governments, rather than simply bribe or threaten individual local officials, they are no longer violent interest groups but become *local rulers.* In our initial definition of organized crime (see Definition 1), we conceptualized OCGs as business organizations that require some level of informal state protection to maintain control over illicit markets. In this definition the collaboration of state specialists in violence is what allows OCGs to operate. They operate like interest groups – criminal lords seek to influence local government officials into looking the other way or refraining from enforcing the law. But when cartels seek to take direct control over local governments and directly administer policing functions and the distribution of public resources, they are no longer interest groups but become de facto local rulers.

---

[12] Note that private firms, including multinational corporations, can also become key participants in the gray zone of criminality when they subcontract OCGs to repress local social movement leaders who oppose the exploitation of natural resources, including mining, forestry, gas, and oil. See Correa-Cabrera (2017).

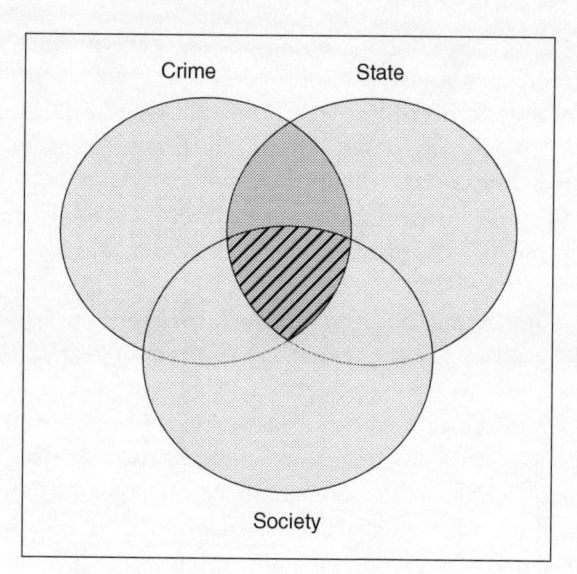

FIGURE I.4 Expanding the Gray Zone of Criminality to Civil Society

Figure 1.4 recognizes this important transformation in the criminal underworld by adding the role of society to the gray zone of criminality and identifying civilians as potential victims of the state–criminal nexus.[13] Because populations are territorially bounded in politico-administrative jurisdictions, by introducing the sphere of society we are introducing a new territorial dimension to the gray zone of criminality. While in Figures I.1–1.II.b the gray zone represented an ecosystem that characterized the interaction between criminal groups and the state in the operation of illicit industries, Figure 1.4 adds the societal and politico-administrative dimensions. To the extent that OCGs move into illicit extractivist industries of human and natural resource wealth, the attempt to control populations and territories is of paramount interest. This entails a fundamental change: OCGs become more like rebels and states. In this new world, OCGs are no longer merely business organizations interested in shaping public policies to favor their illicit industries by means of bribes and coercion, but armed criminal-territorial actors that seek to take control over and reconstitute local social orders through the development of subnational criminal governance regimes.

---

[13] We could add to this figure the role of private companies and multinational corporations operating in the extraction of natural resources. However, a focus on these private-sector actors falls outside the domain of our research.

A crucial difference between OCGs and armed rebel groups, however, is that drug cartels (one type of OCG) cannot become national rulers.[14] While rebel groups such as the Revolutionary Armed Forces of Colombia, FARC, in Colombia or the Farabundo Martí National Liberation Front (FMLN) in El Salvador knew that they could become lawful political parties after a peace negotiation, the leaders of the Sinaloa Cartel (Mexico) or the Medellín Cartel (Colombia) knew well that they could not transform their organizations into lawful political parties and become public representatives or heads of state. Moreover, while rebel groups and states fighting civil wars are subject to international norms of war, cartels and other OCGs are not subject to any international legislation when they engage in criminal wars. Even states' international responsibilities become fuzzy when they fight groups that operate and dominate the gray zone – drug cartels and their criminal associates. In the past 50 years, international norms have been established to regulate war between states and non-state actors with putative political goals and ideologies. But there are no similar international norms to regulate criminal wars that take place in the gray zone of criminality, where state agents often fight on both sides of the conflict – on the criminal and state sides.

Absent any real possibility of transforming their criminal organizations into lawful political organizations, drug lords and their criminal associates become de facto local rulers with short-term horizons. This means that they are more likely to engage in the predatory behavior that characterizes roving bandits, rather than the developmental behavior that characterizes stationary bandits who can become public goods providers (Olson 2000). Building on Olson, in her influential study of rebel governance Arjona (2016) argues that armed groups with local controls and long-term horizons tend to be less repressive, engage in public-good provision, and develop institutions for conflict resolution. The fact that these groups can aspire to become lawful political actors contributes to extending their time horizons and incentives to behave like benevolent local subnational dictators. In contrast, the short-term horizons and the

---

[14] Another important difference is that OCGs and drug cartels do not have explicit ideological views. While in some exceptional cases drug lords have expressed a pro-poor/anti-oligarchic agenda (e.g., Pablo Escobar, the leader of Colombia's Medellín Cartel) and others have used religious language to justify their actions (e.g., La Familia Michoacana in Mexico), unlike rebel groups, drug cartels and OCGs generally do not have explicit ideologies.

uncertainty over local controls that characterize subnational criminal governance regimes lead drug lords to adopt more predatory practices than rebel groups. Coercive and predatory practices become more acute in contexts marked by intense competition for turf.

While we recognize that the emerging literature on criminal governance in Latin America identifies contexts in which OCGs develop local controls through a combination of clientelistic engagements and coercion,[15] here we emphasize OCGs' more coercive and predatory practices in contexts marked by intense competition for territory. In our case, we underscore how intense competition over the control of drug trafficking routes leads cartels and their criminal associates to find alternative sources of income, particularly in illicit extractivist activities of human and natural resource wealth. In seeking to gain control over these extractivist activities that involve civilian populations, we claim OCGs tend to develop more coercive forms of local governance in which civilians become victims of gross human rights violations, rather than beneficiaries of armed clientelism.

To summarize:

Definition 6: Subnational criminal governance regimes are de facto local arrangements by which organized criminal groups, including drug cartels, take control over local populations, governments, and territories; they control local taxation, gain the monopoly of violence, influence subnational electoral processes, and regulate local economic activities and the criminal underworld.

Proposition 3: As turf wars for the control of drug trafficking routes become more intense, cartels are likely to expand beyond the drug business and venture into the extraction of human wealth, public wealth, and natural resource wealth in order to remain competitive. To control local populations, governments, and territories, cartels and their criminal associates develop subnational criminal governance regimes through the use of force.

---

[15] Arias (2006a; 2006b; 2017) reports important evidence of clientelistic engagements between civilians and gangs in Brazilian favelas. There is little systematic evidence of these engagements in Mexico's drug wars, where civilian victimization has been widely documented (Open Society Justice Initiative 2016), although Magaloni et al.'s (2019) survey evidence suggests the existence of clientelistic engagements between civilians and Mexican cartels.

CONCLUSION

By questioning some of the key assumptions that have guided the study of crime and violence in the social sciences, this chapter has developed a new framework for the study of organized crime and large-scale criminal violence. Our central assumption that organized crime can only exist when criminal lords enjoy some level of informal state protection opened the door for the study of political power. Unlike traditional studies in criminology, which see OCGs as illicit economic groups that seek to operate without any state interference, we follow students of the mafia in Italy and students of the politics of criminal violence in Latin America in placing the informal intersection between state agents and crime – the gray zone of criminality – at the center of our analysis. We discussed why this gray zone often emerges in autocracies and how transitions to electoral democracy may introduce turbulence in the gray zone, change the internal balance of power, and give rise to incentives for the widespread use of violence to settle disputes and redefine criminal power.

In the remainder of this volume we use the new assumptions, definitions, and propositions laid out in this chapter to develop new hypotheses for testing, using the Mexican case. While this chapter has made extensive use of historical examples to probe the explanatory potential of our theoretical conjectures, let us stress that state coercion, power, and electoral politics as important drivers of criminal peace and violence is a hypothetical statement that needs to be tested and explained. In the next three parts of the book we make use of original quantitative and qualitative data and of a wide variety of methodological tools to test and explain to the best of our abilities the political foundations of the outbreak and intensification of criminal violence in Mexico's drug wars.

PART II

THE OUTBREAK OF INTER-CARTEL WARS

Why Cartels Went to War

Subnational Party Alternation, the Breakdown of Criminal Protection, and the Onset of Inter-Cartel Wars

Mexico's contemporary history has been intimately intertwined with the production and smuggling of illicit drugs to satisfy the demand of US consumers. In the 1960s and 1970s local caciques, family clans, and bands of smugglers were actively involved in the cultivation and shipment of marijuana across the US–Mexico border (Enciso 2015; Cedillo 2019). In the 1980s and 1990s, however, as cocaine became the primary illicit drug of consumption in the US (Grillo 2011), a select group of these family clans and local small groups of bandits created powerful cartels that became part of a global chain of local operations. They connected coca leaf producers from the Andes with Colombian cartels, who processed the leaf into cocaine and moved the drugs from South America into Mexico, where a new generation of Mexican cartels smuggled huge shipments of cocaine through the US–Mexico border. After the 2000s, as heroin became a highly demanded drug among US consumers (Quiñones 2015), the cultivation of poppy and its transformation into heroin gained prominence among Mexican cartels, in addition to the increasing shipments into the US that enlarged their business menu.

One of the most surprising features about the Mexican drug trafficking industry in the 1980s was the relatively peaceful coexistence of drug cartels. After Mexican security forces had defeated rebel groups in the 1970s through a lethal Dirty War, the federal government appointed the leading actors of the anti-insurgency campaign to lead a major program intended to eradicate drug production and traffic in Mexico, the Plan Cóndor. Through this program, members of the Federal Security Directorate (DFS), the country's militarized secret police, conducted a major reorganization of the drug trafficking industry. As historian Adela Cedillo (2019) has shown, rather than eradicate drug cultivation and traffic, they were able to violently seize control of the drug industry and regroup drug activities under a select group of family clans from the northwest who created an umbrella organization, the Guadalajara Cartel.[1] Another umbrella organization, the Gulf Cartel, also regrouped family clans in the northeast and the Gulf. These regroupings and the rise of powerful cartels took place after the 1982 US crackdown on the Caribbean drug trafficking route that connected the Andes with Miami through air and sea (Bagley 2012). As cocaine shipments shifted from sea to land, Mexico became a key corridor. While the Guadalajara Cartel made a strategic alliance with Pablo Escobar and the Medellín Cartel, the Gulf Cartel worked with Escobar's enemies, the Cali Cartel. Under the centralized control of the DFS, Mexican cartels rose to international prominence without bloodshed. Relative peace persisted, even after the dissolution of the DFS in 1985 and the arrest of the leadership of the Guadalajara Cartel in the late 1980s, when associates of the Guadalajara organization created three new cartels shown in Map 2.1: the Tijuana

MAP 2.1 Mexican Cartels and Drug Trafficking Zones in the 1980s

[1] For a discussion about this process of transition from family clans to cartels – or the *cartelization* of the drug industry – see Mendoza Rockwell (2012) and Pansters (2018).

Cartel, the Juárez Cartel, and the Sinaloa Cartel. As historians have noted, the rise of Mexico's four leading cartels – Tijuana, Juárez, Sinaloa, and Gulf – as key players in the international drug trafficking industry took place in a remarkably peaceful context under the tight grip of the Institutional Revolutionary Party (the PRI). This is what Astorga (2005) aptly called the *pax mafiosa*.

But after a decade of relatively peaceful coexistence, inter-cartel wars broke out in Mexico. Cartels surprisingly went to war in the 1990s at a time when the Mexican government was no longer pursuing any significant anti-drug policies. In a remarkable move that would change Mexico's drug trafficking industry and the criminal underworld, over the course of the 1990s drug lords from all four major cartels created their own private militias to defend their turf and to conquer rival drug trafficking routes. Conflicts first broke out in the northwestern part of Mexico, then in the northeast, and subsequently spread to other parts of the country. In the second half of the 1990s Mexico experienced an average of 350 annual battle deaths; by 2006 inter-cartel wars had become particularly intense, reaching 1,281 annual battle deaths (Trejo and Ley 2018).

As security scholars have long noted, cartels went to war as Mexico transitioned from authoritarian rule to democracy (Astorga 2005; Astorga and Shirk 2010; Dube, Dube, and García-Ponce 2013; Trejo and Ley 2018). After six decades under the PRI reign, Mexico experienced a federalist electoral transition from one-party rule (in which the government was in charge of organizing elections and election fraud was widespread) to multiparty democracy (with relatively free and fair elections organized by an independent election-management body). Opposition parties experienced their first major electoral victory in the 1989 gubernatorial election of the northwestern state of Baja California. A wave of gubernatorial and municipal opposition victories in northern, western, and southern states followed in the 1990s, paving the way for the opposition victory in the 2000 presidential election (Magaloni 2006; Greene 2007).

A prevalent scholarly view suggests that inter-cartel violence in Mexico broke out after 2000, when the main networks of informal government protection for the cartels, associated with the high echelons of the PRI and the federal government, allegedly broke down (O'Neil 2009). An alternative view suggests that inter-cartel wars broke out in the 1990s, when hundreds of opposition mayors displaced the PRI from municipal power, where the informal protection networks for the cartels had operated at the local level (Dube, Dube, and García-Ponce 2013; Ríos 2015). While the breakdown of informal networks of government protection has been used as the leading mechanism to explain the outbreak of criminal wars, there is no agreement as to the level of government where criminal protection was offered.

Unlike scholars who focus on party alternation at the national level and emphasize the causal impact of the defeat of the PRI in the 2000 presidential election on the outbreak of inter-cartel wars, and unlike studies that focus on municipal democratization in the 1990s, in this chapter we focus on changes in *state gubernatorial power*. Our focus on state-level politics rests on new evidence about the dynamics of state repression and corruption in Mexico's authoritarian regime. We draw on a hitherto unexplored dataset of political repression and human rights violations against dissidents under the PRI (Centro de Derechos Humanos Fray Francisco de Vitoria, 1989–1998) and on in-depth interviews with the first opposition governors in multiple states. This enables us to identify the *state judicial police* – under the command of the states' attorney generals – as the most important repressive arm of the Mexican government and the central institution in which corrupt police chiefs and their agents developed the informal networks of protection that allowed the cartels to thrive in the 1980s and 1990s. While we recognize that the modern drug trafficking industry emerged after a period of centralization of coercion following the Dirty War and the Plan Cóndor in the 1970s and 1980s (Cedillo 2019), these new sources of information reveal that after the closure of the DFS in 1985, state coercion became decentralized and state-level police forces became the leading actors in the informal provision of protection for cartels.

We suggest that Mexican cartels went to war when they lost access to informal networks of *subnational* government protection in the 1990s – one decade before the 2000 defeat of the PRI in national elections.[2] Because drug trafficking is a global chain of *local* operations, in which subnational judicial and police authorities play a crucial role in the provision of protection for drug trafficking operations, our focus is on subnational political actors rather than on national authorities. We argue that, after six decades of one-party rule, subnational electoral democratization and the alternation of political parties in *state gubernatorial power* led to the breakdown of informal government protection networks. This

---

[2] For pioneering studies of informal government protection networks for drug cartels in Mexico, see Astorga (2005), Bailey and Taylor (2009), Snyder and Durán-Martínez (2009), and Astorga and Shirk (2010).

motivated drug lords to create their own private militias to protect themselves against potential attacks from rival cartels and from incoming
opposition authorities.[3] Cartels recruited security forces from the authoritarian era – members of the police and the military – to train young males
from street gangs to defend the cartels' drug trafficking routes. The development of private militias marked a major transformation in Mexico's
drug trafficking industry. It allowed cartels to defend their turf, renegotiate informal protection with incoming opposition authorities by means of
bribes and coercion, and venture beyond their own turf to conquer drug
trafficking routes under their rivals' control. The spread of party alternations in states with drug trafficking routes led to the proliferation of
private militias and to the outbreak of large-scale criminal wars.

Unlike scholars who suggest that the anti-narcotics policies launched
by incoming opposition authorities against the cartels explain the outbreak of drug violence (Osorio 2015), we argue that by simply *removing*
top- and mid-level personnel in the state attorney's office and the state
judicial police – the institutions that had provided informal protection for
drug cartels under one-party rule in the 1980s – incoming opposition
governors unwittingly created turbulence and a great degree of uncertainty in the gray zone of criminality. This provided incentives for drug
lords to create their own private armies to defend their multibillion-dollar
illegal businesses.

We test our claim about the impact of party alternation in gubernatorial power on inter-cartel violence using data from the Criminal Violence
in Mexico (CVM) Dataset, an original newspaper-based databank of
inter-cartel murders that we created. We recognize that multiple factors
associated with subnational socioeconomic structures, drug markets conditions, and the state's capacity for law enforcement can be driving factors
of inter-cartel wars; therefore, we test our main proposition – that subnational party alternation and the breakdown of protection motivated cartels to go to war – against several alternative explanations.

Our analyses from multivariate regression models show that inter-
cartel violence in municipalities from states that underwent party alternation in gubernatorial power was 79.1 *percent greater* than in those where
the PRI remained in the gubernatorial palace. Our results also show that
the most significant increase in violence took place during an opposition

---

[3] Prior to the defeat of Mexico's ruling party in the 2000 presidential election, several states
experienced a process of subnational party alternation (Beer 2003; Díaz-Cayeros 2006).

governor's first year in office, when old personnel had been removed and new security policies had not yet been implemented.

To explore whether the rotation of political parties in gubernatorial power after six decades of one-party rule actually had a causal impact on the onset of inter-cartel wars in Mexico, we rely on the synthetic control method (SCM). The SCM allows us to test a counterfactual scenario in which we assess the evolution of inter-cartel violence in state x – which experienced party alternation in state gubernatorial power – against a hypothetical case x'. This is a weighted average of a number of Mexican states that had not experienced gubernatorial party alternation prior to x experiencing alternation. We use the cases of Michoacán and Guerrero to demonstrate the independent causal impact of party alternation on the outbreak of inter-cartel wars.

The chapter is divided into five parts. Drawing on the theoretical tools developed in Chapter 1 and on new evidence about the role that members of state-level judicial police played in the development of informal government protection networks for the cartels, we first develop our own hypotheses about subnational political alternation, the breakdown of informal government protection, and the onset of criminal wars. In the second part we discuss alternative explanations. In the third section we present the statistical tests and the robustness checks, and in the fourth part we report the results from the synthetic control method. In the conclusion we discuss why our findings about party alternation in gubernatorial power, triggering the rise of private militias and the proliferation of inter-cartel wars, constitute a novel explanation of Mexico's drug violence. We explore why these findings contribute in important ways to a more appropriate understanding of the political drivers of large-scale criminal violence in new democracies – particularly in cases of "thin" electoral transitions, in which countries adopt multiparty electoral democracy without reforming corrupt, repressive, and politicized security and judicial systems.

A POLITICAL EXPLANATION OF THE ONSET OF INTER-CARTEL WARS

To explain why cartels went to war in Mexico after a period of peaceful coexistence and whether and the extent to which the breakdown of one-party rule in Mexico and the alternation of political parties triggered these conflicts, we need to go beyond traditional conceptualizations of the state and organized crime as separate spheres. It is therefore necessary to explore the ecosystem in which state agents and criminals come together to constitute what we called in Chapter 1 the *gray zone of criminality*. We proceed in two steps: we first discuss new quantitative and qualitative evidence that helps us historically identify the authoritarian state specialists in violence who developed the informal networks of government protection and facilitated the rise of Mexican cartels to international prominence. We subsequently use this factual evidence and the key theoretical propositions developed in Chapter 1 to outline an explanation for why cartels went to war. We set out the hypotheses and the mechanisms that constitute our explanation and that formed the bases for the empirical testing described later in this chapter.

Authoritarian Rule and Organized Crime: Constituting the Gray Zone of Criminality in Mexico

In Chapter 1 we argued that security forces in authoritarian regimes often play a key role in the development of criminal markets because they have the skills and enjoy the political impunity to operate illegal markets. To fulfill their mandate of suppressing political dissidents, military and police personnel and members of paramilitary forces typically develop special skills in extrajudicial violence and in illegal information gathering. While these two skills prepare authoritarian specialists in violence to repress political dissidents, they also empower them to regulate or protect the criminal underworld.[4] We argued that because authoritarian specialists in violence could also use their skills to rebel against the regime, authoritarian leaders often seek to appease them by extending their political immunity into criminal impunity and allowing them to profit from regulating, running, or protecting criminal industries. Through these egregious arrangements, autocrats secure the loyalty of state specialists in violence and at the same time secure the stability of criminal markets.

There is a consensus in the literature on drug trafficking in Mexico that government and security officials under the PRI's long one-party reign regulated drug operations in and out of the country (Astorga 2005) and developed informal networks of protection for drug cartels (Snyder and Durán-Martínez 2009). But there is little agreement about the actors who provided this protection and about the structure of these informal

---

[4] Information gathering and violence are precisely the two skills most crucial to success in the criminal underworld (Gambetta 1996).

networks. While some scholars underscore the role of national authorities and the armed forces in the creation of these informal networks of protection, many others highlight the protective role of the municipal police. The problem is that these studies have a static view of state coercion and corruption in Mexico. In fact, between 1970 and 2000, despite continuities in repressive practices, the state specialists in violence and the security institutions charged with repressing political dissidents experienced important transformations. Although they often go unnoticed, these changes in state coercion had a dramatic impact on the operation of the gray zone of criminality.

National protection networks. In Mexico's post-revolutionary regime, the military was the key actor charged with repression of political dissidents from 1929 up until 1982. Although the federal and the state police, local caciques, and white guards in the haciendas played an important role in keeping political dissidents at bay, the military had the upper hand in suppressing dissent (Trejo 2012). Created in 1947 and led by military personnel, the Federal Security Directorate (DFS) became the security agency charged with political policing and anti-insurgency operations until it was disbanded in 1985 (Sierra 2012). Although it was part of the Ministry of the Interior, nine out of ten DFS directors between 1947 and 1985 were members of the military. During the Dirty War, when the Mexican government launched a brutal anti-insurgency campaign to fight urban and rural guerrilla movements, the DFS gained uncommon power and became what historians and security analysts have referred to as the Mexican "deep state" (Scott 2009; Cedillo 2019). It was the leading agency that coordinated military and police forces and pro-government militias and death squads in conducting the government's most egregious repressive actions and gross human rights violations to eliminate dissent and keep the PRI in power.

Information from declassified documents and testimonies by protected witnesses in two military trials have now clearly established that top Mexican officials linked to the DFS regulated the criminal underworld in Mexico and developed the first informal networks of protection that enabled the rise of Mexican cartels to world prominence in the 1980s (Aranda 2002; Astorga 2005; Sierra 2012; Aviña 2018). As Cedillo (2019) documents, some of the key DFS agents fighting rebels were assigned to lead the Plan Cóndor – the US-backed anti-drug campaign led by the Mexican government from 1975 to 1983. DFS agents capitalized on their comparative advantage in violence and their impunity acquired in the Dirty War to become key players and remake the gray zone of criminality – to centralize, regulate and profit from the drug trafficking industry. For example, officers in charge of the Dirty War in the southern state of Guerrero used the same aircraft they utilized to dump hundreds of bodies of political dissidents in the Pacific Ocean to transport illicit drugs to the US–Mexico border (Castillo García 2002). The fact that high-ranking military officers knew about these actions has led Cedillo (2019) to conclude that the Mexican government had a payoff system to reward authoritarian state specialists in violence for their work in the Dirty War to keep the PRI in power.

The authoritarian state specialists in violence from the DFS were able to dominate Mexico's gray zone of criminality in the 1970s and 1980s. However, the end of the Dirty War, the partial liberalization of authoritarian controls in 1977, and pressure from the US government led to the dissolution of the DFS in 1985 and to the decentralization of political repression from the military to civilian authorities and the police in Mexico's 31 states. US pressure came after leaders of the Guadalajara Cartel ordered the assassination of a Drug Enforcement Agency (DEA) agent who had infiltrated the cartel. This was a major transformation in Mexico's coercive institution that has surprisingly gone unnoticed by students of drug violence.

Subnational protection networks. After 1985, many DFS agents were relocated to the state-level delegations of the national attorney's office (PGR) and were able to influence federal police operations in the states.[5] But the upper hand and the know-how of political repression were transferred from the DFS and the armed forces to the state-level judicial police under the control of state governors and the state attorney generals (the state public prosecutors). Many of the new techniques of repression developed during the Dirty War, including the systematic use of extrajudicial executions, clandestine massacres, forced disappearances, torture, and sexual violence, were transferred to the state judicial police. This transfer of power and know-how had huge implications, not only for who used state coercion to repress political dissidents but also for who used the information, the ability to repress, and political impunity to profit from the criminal underworld.

---

[5] Anonymous interview with former opposition state official.

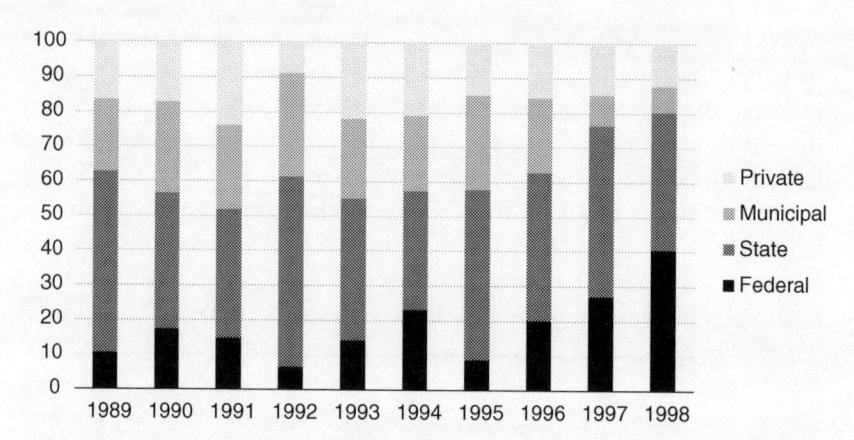

FIGURE 2.1 Repression of Political Dissidents by Perpetrator in Mexico, 1989–
1998 (%) *Source: Centro de Derechos Humanos Fray Francisco de
Vitoria Private = private guards; Municipal = municipal police; State: state
judicial police; Federal: army and federal police.*

Drawing on the most extensive dataset on repression and human rights
violations in the last quarter of the twentieth century in Mexico, Figure
2.1 shows the breakdown of repressive actions by perpetrator. It reveals
that in the late 1980s and throughout the 1990s, the state judicial police
force was indeed the main repressive force against political dissidents in
Mexico. While the army was an important actor, mainly in response to the
outbreak of armed insurgency in the mid-1990s, the evidence shows that
subnational security forces, particularly officers from the state judicial
police, gained the coercive upper hand at a time when cartels were
expanding. As unlawful detentions became the main tool of repression
of political dissidents, the judicial police actively used many of the techniques of torture and sexual violence developed during the Dirty War to
interrogate and produce evidence to incriminate these dissidents in crimes
they had not committed (see Trejo 2012).

    While we have strong theoretical reasons to suggest that state judicial
police in their new role as authoritarian specialists in violence would
become the new leaders in the provision of informal government protection
for cartels, the evidence for this cannot be deduced from the time-series of
government repression in Figure 2.1. To substantiate this point, we rely on a
series of in-depth interviews with former opposition governors and their
cabinet members, in which they consistently identified the state judicial
police as the leading player in the development of informal networks of
government protection for drug cartels from the mid-1980s onwards.

Ernesto Ruffo (PAN),[6] the first opposition mayor of Ensenada (1986–1989) in the northwestern state of Baja California, reports that during his tenure "when municipal police forces [under his command] found any drugs, state judicial police and members of the federal police would dismantle any operation." In his recollection, commanders from the state judicial police were simultaneously "in charge of political repression" and of "establishing connections with drug traffickers." When Ruffo became the first opposition governor in Baja California (1989–1995), he quickly recognized the state judicial police, the state-level delegation of the national attorney's office, and the federal police as the key institutional nodes from which officers provided informal protection for drug trafficking operations and ensured drug lords had impunity to thrive in illegal markets.

Alberto Cárdenas (PAN),[7] the first opposition governor in the western state of Jalisco (1995–2001), describes the previous government under the PRI as a case of "narco power." His first public prosecutor, Jorge López,[8] is explicit about the importance of informal government protection networks for the development of the drug trafficking industry: "The narco industry can only flourish through the corruption of the state judicial police, the state attorney, and the public prosecutors' offices."

Zeferino Torreblanca, from the leftist Party of the Democratic Revolution (PRD) and the first opposition governor in the southern state of Guerrero (2005–2012),[9] is equally explicit about the political–criminal nexus under one-party rule: "Prior [PRI] governments regulated organized crime" and "there were no inter-cartel conflicts because one cartel dominated the business." For Torreblanca, "the central actors" in the provision of criminal protection were "state judicial police officers who colluded with the state attorney's office." Lázaro Cárdenas Batel (PRD),[10] the first opposition governor in the western state of Michoacán (2001–2007), likewise underscores the central role that "commanders from the state judicial police" played in the informal provision of government protection for cartels under the PRI. In both governors' accounts, municipal police officers were *informants* for state-level judicial police who enabled criminal operations and, in collusion with officers from the state

---

[6] Interview with Governor Ernesto Ruffo, Mexico City, July 2014.
[7] Interview with Governor Alberto Cárdenas, Guadalajara, July 2014.
[8] Interview with Jorge López, Guadalajara, July 2014.
[9] Interview with Governor Zeferino Torreblanca, Mexico City, July 2014.
[10] Interview with Governor Lázaro Cárdenas Batel, Washington, DC, September 2014.

attorneys' offices, derailed investigations to avoid criminal punishment for narcos.

Based on interviews with this group of first opposition governors, Figure 2.2 provides a visual image of the key institutional actors in the informal networks of protection that enabled drug trafficking operations in the 1985–2006 period. The central players in these networks were top- and mid-level officials from the state judicial police who recruited officers from the state public prosecutors' offices and directors of the prison system. They also enlisted municipal police officers and federal police officers from the state-level delegations of the national attorney to work as informants. While national and municipal actors were part of these multilayered networks, their role was dependent on state-level officials. Without jurisdiction to deal with criminal cases and with limited weaponry, municipal police forces were too weak to play a central role in these networks. And although drug-related crimes were the sole jurisdiction of federal judicial and police institutions, state-level police forces played a key mediating role in determining whether a criminal would be prosecuted and whether the case would be scaled up to the federation.[11]

In sum, while federal forces linked to the DFS and the high echelons of the military played a key role in providing protection for the early development of Mexico's drug trafficking industry in the late 1970s and early 1980s, the data on government repression and the interviews with the first generation of opposition governors strongly suggest that state-level judicial police officers, linked to the state attorney general offices, became the key players that enabled the transformation of Mexico's drug cartels from powerful domestic actors to key international players in the global drug trafficking industry in the mid-1980s. This means that to the extent that political change had any substantive impact in eroding the informal networks of government protection for drug cartels in the 1990s, it was subnational political change, particularly changes in the governors' seats and in the state government judicial and police institutions, the catalyst of major transformations in Mexico's drug trafficking industry.

---

[11] Although state-level judicial and police forces became the leading actors in the provision of protection for drug cartels, some elite members of the military continued to provide protection to drug lords, as attested by the prominent case of Mexico's top anti-drug boss, General Jesús Gutiérrez Rebollo, who was found to be on the payroll of the Juárez Cartel and was sentenced to prison in 1997.

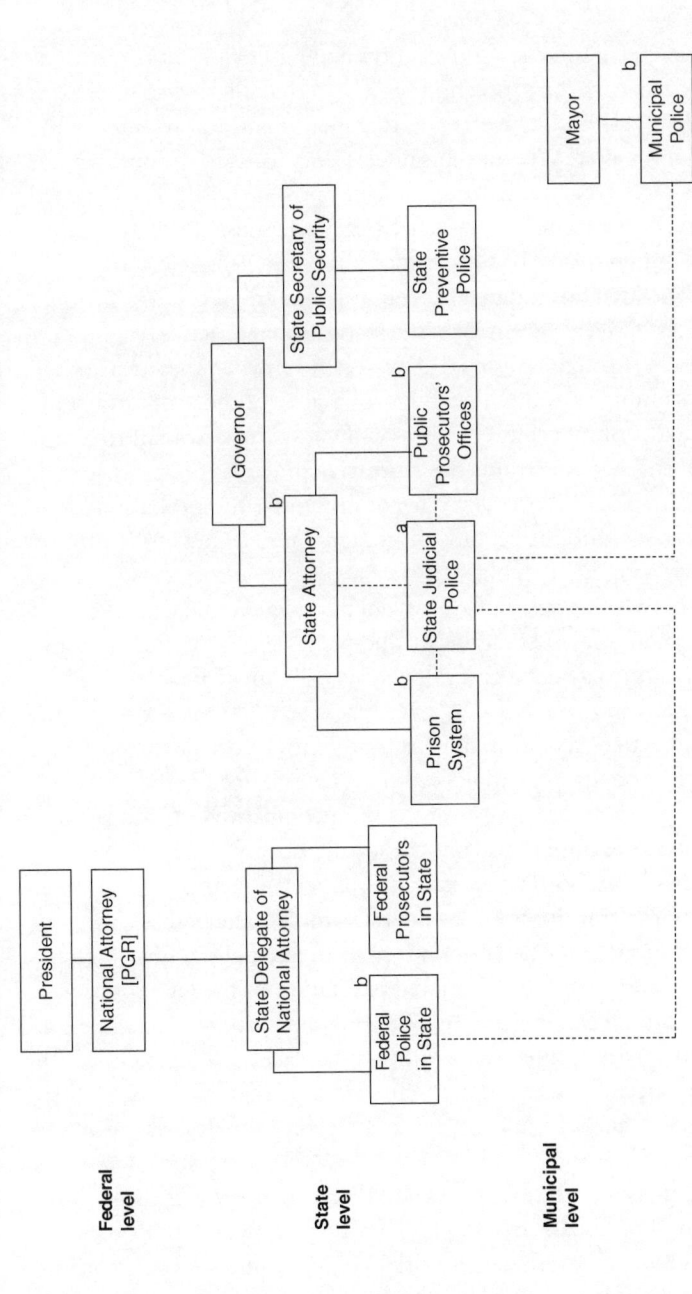

Federal level

President

National Attorney [PGR]

State Delegate of National Attorney

Federal Prosecutors in State

Federal Police in State (b)

State level

Governor

State Secretary of Public Security

State Preventive Police

State Attorney (b)

State Judicial Police (a)

Public Prosecutors' Offices (b)

Prison System (b)

Municipal level

Mayor

Municipal Police (b)

a   Primary role
b   Secondary role
...... Informal network connections

FIGURE 2.2 Government Institutions with Agents Involved in Informal Networks of Protection for Drug Cartels in Mexico, 1985–2006

THE SUBNATIONAL TRANSITION TO MULTIPARTY DEMOCRACY
AND THE ONSET OF CRIMINAL VIOLENCE

As we discussed in Chapter 1, the breakdown of authoritarian regimes has the potential to disrupt the protection networks that allow illegal markets to operate effectively and hence create turbulence and uncertainty in the gray zone of criminality. Whether this uncertainty leads to the outbreak of criminal wars or not partly depends on what postauthoritarian elites do with authoritarian specialists in violence – the protectors or regulators of the criminal underworld. If they expose these repressive actors and remove them through fair judicial procedures that are part of transitional justice processes, or if they transform the institutional practices of military and police forces through major security-sector reforms, they restrict the gray zone of criminality and reduce the probability of the postauthoritarian violent expansion of crime. But if new democratic elites fail to adopt any major reform that constrains the repressive practices of authoritarian specialists in violence and breaks cycles of impunity, the probability that new democratic institutions become intimately intertwined with criminal markets is correspondingly high.

We highlight two features that are crucial to understanding whether and the extent to which the breakdown of one-party rule in Mexico and the transition to a multiparty democracy opened possibilities for violence. First, postauthoritarian elites in Mexico gave up on any transitional justice process and failed to enact any major security-sector reform after the defeat of the PRI in the 2000 presidential election. As we claimed in the introduction, Mexico experienced a transition from uncompetitive to competitive elections without developing a democratic rule of law – that is, Mexico transitioned from authoritarian rule to illiberal democracy. Second, Mexico's electoral transition to democracy took a federalist path, by which opposition victories first took place in municipalities and states in the early 1990s and then in the national legislature in the late 1990s and eventually the presidency in 2000. Electoral competition and the alternation of political parties in subnational office took place in a context in which the judicial and security institutions that served to repress political dissidents – and to create informal networks of protection for the cartels – remained unreformed.

Our first claim is that the breakdown of PRI hegemony in the states and the alternation of political parties in gubernatorial power in the 1990s led to the breakdown of informal networks of government protection for drug cartels and motivated drug lords to develop their own private militias to defend their drug trafficking routes. Because organized crime *cannot go one day without protection* (Schelling 1971), only the development of a private army would allow cartels to defend themselves from two threats: incoming state opposition authorities and rival cartels. After an alternation in state power, drug lords did not have the option of simply waiting until things settled down and they could then work on reestablishing protection networks among the new police and judicial officials. The delay would leave them vulnerable to incursions from state authorities and rivals. Hence the need for private militias to protect them from this major disruption in the gray zone of criminality.

The election of opposition authorities and the appointment of new personnel in the state attorney's office and the state judicial police introduced a great degree of uncertainty for the home cartel. While drug lords could renegotiate informal protection with incoming authorities – as they actually did – penetrating opposition networks to corrupt new officers would take some time. As new opposition governors would initially seek to differentiate themselves from previous PRI governments by emphasizing anti-corruption and pro-human rights agendas, a private army would allow cartels to defend themselves in the event of a sudden government attack and would also empower them to renegotiate protection with incoming authorities using bullets – rather than only bribes, as they had done in the past.

The election of opposition authorities and the breakdown of informal government protection networks not only created a great degree of uncertainty about the incoming government but also made the home cartel vulnerable to rival attacks. Attacks from rival cartels would be imminent because cartels cannot easily divide up prized drug trafficking routes. More importantly, after subnational political alternation and the removal of state security agents who regulated and protected the criminal underworld, cartels would be unable to credibly commit themselves to honoring an agreement.[12] In the absence of a third-party enforcer, the rapid development of a private security apparatus would allow cartels to safeguard property rights over drug trafficking routes.

Thus we would expect that in Mexico's formerly one-party regime:

H.1. Subnational party alternation in gubernatorial power (*a*) contributed to the breakdown of informal government protection

---

[12] In Fearon's (1995) seminal formulation, war is the result of bargaining indivisibility and commitment problems. For a discussion of rationalist theories of war in the context of Mexican Drug Wars, see Calderón et al. (2015) and Lessing (2015).

networks for drug cartels and (*b*) motivated drug lords to develop their own private militias to protect their drug trafficking routes.

Our second claim is that the spread of subnational party alternation in states with drug trafficking routes and the proliferation of private militias led to the outbreak of inter-cartel wars. Besides providing immediate protection to cartels in states experiencing political alternation and allowing them to renegotiate protection with incoming authorities, the development of private militias would also empower drug lords to contest their rivals' control over drug trafficking territories. When a cartel survives the alternation of political parties in office, and the removal of their former protectors, and is able to create a powerful private army to defend its domain, the cartel's leaders can take advantage of subsequent party alternation experiences in other states to send their private armies to try to conquer rivals' territories. As Lessing (2015) puts it, inter-cartel wars are "wars of conquest."

Thus we would expect that in Mexico:

H.2. The spread of subnational party alternations in state governments led to the outbreak of multiple inter-cartel wars and to large-scale criminal violence.

Figure 2.3 summarizes our central argument and outlines our research strategy. As the Figure illustrates, in the remainder of this chapter we subject to statistical tests the likely association between the alternation of political parties in gubernatorial power and inter-cartel violence (H.2). In Chapter 3, we use case studies to assess whether political alternation and the removal of key personnel in

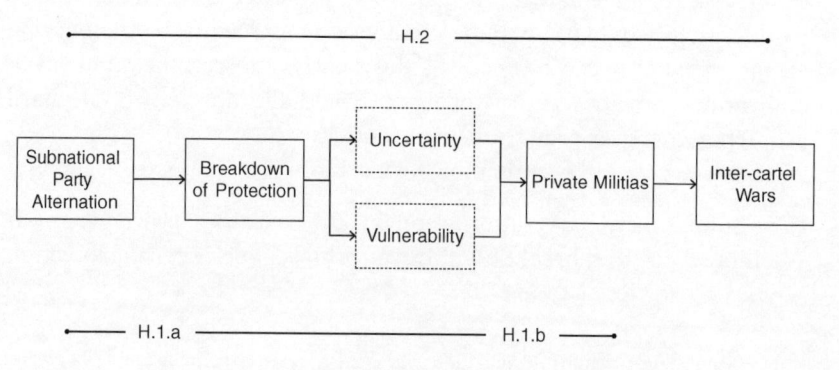

FIGURE 2.3 Explanatory Model of Inter-Cartel Wars

the states' judicial and police institutions led to the breakdown of informal government protection networks (H.1.a), to the rise of private militias (H.1.b), and to the outbreak of war.

ALTERNATIVE EXPLANATIONS

While subnational party alternation and the breakdown of protection may lead to the outbreak of inter-cartel wars and the onset of large-scale criminal violence, students of crime and violence have identified a number of alternative factors that we cannot overlook. Drawing on classical theories of the economics and sociology of crime, three influential theoretical propositions have framed most empirical studies: (1) competition in criminal markets stimulates criminal violence (Schelling 1971; Buchanan 1973); (2) criminal groups engage in violence when they have access to guns (Dube, Dube, and García-Ponce 2013) and to foot soldiers (Sampson 1993); and (3) organized criminal groups emerge where the state is weak (Gambetta 1996; Skaperdas 2001) and become violent when it represses poorly (Lessing 2015). This wide variety of factors speaks to the potentially multi-causal nature of inter-cartel wars, but it also opens the possibility for confusion. To more effectively assess these factors, we group different explanations using a simple framework in which we assume that drug cartels are OCGs that maximize drug profits and seek to have monopolistic control over drug trafficking corridors. They go to war when they are confronted with exogenous *threats* that jeopardize their turf, or when they perceive *opportunities* to expand their reign, and when they have access to *organizational resources* to fight.[13]

Threats

Scholars of drug wars in Mexico have primarily focused on changes in government policies and informal practices to explain variation in drug violence. Focusing on informal government protection for cartels – as we do – they have suggested that the breakdown and loss of protection leads to competition and war. Focusing on federal policies to combat drug trafficking, another influential argument suggests that the adoption of poor strategies of state repression against the cartels may cause a backlash and lead to state–cartel and inter-cartel wars.

---

[13] We take inspiration for this framework from the social movement literature. See Tarrow (1998) and Trejo (2012).

Protection loss. Assuming that federal authorities were the leading
actors in the provision of protection for drug cartels, one account suggests
that the defeat of the PRI at the national level in 2000 opened a new era of
violent turf wars (O'Neil 2009). A second account assumes that municipal
police forces were key in the provision of protection for cartels and
suggests that municipal electoral competition jeopardized the cartels'
access to informal protection networks (Dube, Dube, and García-Ponce
2013).[14] A third account suggests that alternation at all levels of government (federal, state, and municipal) undermined the state's role in drug
trafficking operations and left cartels on their own to autonomously
regulate the drug industry through violence (Astorga and Shirk 2010;
Ríos 2015).

The first account's claim that the defeat of the PRI in the 2000 presidential election led to the onset of inter-cartel violence fails to explain the
turf wars of the northwest, northeast, and Pacific coast that broke out in
the 1990s (see Maps 2.I.a and 2.I.b below). Due to this time inconsistency,
the only plausible case to make is that national alternation may have
stimulated, but did not originate, inter-cartel wars. Accounts of the second
type based on municipal electoral competition do not face this time
inconsistency problem, because Mexico experienced a major surge of
municipal multiparty competition in the 1990s. The main problem here
is that municipal authorities cannot provide extensive protection for
cartels because they have very limited weaponry (Sabet 2012) and because
they have no jurisdiction over drug trafficking operations (these are the
responsibility of federal and/or state-level authorities). Although the
approach that points at alternation at all levels of government does not
suffer from the limitations of the first two approaches, we show below
that it overestimates the federal and municipal effects while underestimat-
ing the impact of state-level politics.

State repression. Focusing on the major escalation of drug violence
after the Mexican federal government declared war on the cartels in
2007 and deployed the military throughout the country's main conflictive regions, scholars suggest that the policy of leadership decapitation – arresting or killing cartel leaders – led to intra-cartel
succession crises, fragmentation and competition, and a dramatic
increase in violence (Guerrero 2011a; Calderón et al. 2015; Phillips

---

[14] We do not explicitly discuss Villarreal's (2002) pioneering analysis of the impact of
    municipal electoral competition on homicide rates in Mexico, because his article does
    not deal with OCGs and inter-cartel violence.

2015). Scholars also suggest that after Mexico's democratization in 2000, incoming federal and municipal opposition authorities, responding to an electoral mandate to confront drug cartels, seized drugs and weapons from the cartels, triggering a violent backlash (Osorio 2015). An alternative formulation argues that when national governments adopt conditional repression and target only those cartels who attack them, violence does not substantially increase; but when governments follow strategies of unconditional repression and attack all cartels, violence becomes particularly intense. According to Lessing (2017), the state's adoption of a strategy of unconditional repression, initially in 2005 and more decisively since 2007, explains the dramatic increase of violence in Mexico.

Arguments that focus on state repression can explain the intensification of cartel violence – and we will address them in subsequent parts of this book – but not why cartels went to war in the first place in Mexico. The main limitation is that cartels went to war a decade before national democratization in 2000 and in a context in which federal authorities had taken a merely reactive anti-narcotic stance, as opposed to the proactive policies that they adopted after 2006.[15]

Opportunities

The literature on organized crime and drug violence has focused on changes in drug markets and state presence/absence to explain competition in criminal markets and the onset of violence as a result of rising opportunities.

Change in international drug prices. Scholars have suggested that exogenous business shocks in the drug trafficking global industry provided powerful economic incentives for cartels to fight for control over drug trafficking corridors. An important account suggests that the crackdown on Colombian cartels in the 1990s and the potential

---

[15] In Chapter 4 we use partisanship and assess intergovernmental partisan conflict between the federal government and governors as predictors of violence. We do not test for these variables for two reasons. First, as we explained above, the federal government did not pursue an active anti-drug policy in the 1990s and early 2000s. While the federal government may have been at odds with opposition governors on other policy realms (e.g., federal transfers or social policy), the absence of a proactive drug policy made this area relatively unimportant for center–periphery conflict. Second, as we discuss in Chapter 4, the study of partisanship in explaining intergovernmental conflict is particularly relevant in contexts of sharp ideological polarization, such as the one Mexico experienced after the 2006 Mexican presidential election.

for a major *business expansion* led Mexican cartels to fight for control over the production of cocaine and the shipment of this valuable illegal drug from South America into the US (Bagley 2012; Shirk and Wallman 2015).

If changes in international drug prices due to the crackdown on Colombian cartels provided an incentive for turf wars, we should expect that the expansion of the drug trafficking business would lead to the simultaneous outbreak of inter-cartel wars across drug trafficking routes in Mexico. Yet inter-cartel wars broke out unevenly and sequentially over the course of the 16 years from 1990 to 2006. This punctuated pattern suggests that exogenous business shocks may not have initiated inter-cartel wars but only contributed to the escalation of ongoing conflicts.

State absence. Students of organized crime – like students of armed rebellion and civil war (Fearon and Laitin 2003) – have long argued that OCGs and mafias emerge in countries with weak state presence, where criminal lords take advantage of ungoverned spaces (Gambetta 1996; Skaperdas 2001). In these ungoverned territories, criminals rely on violence to settle disputes over criminal markets, and the outbreak of criminal competition leads to violence.

Although a state-centric explanation could help us understand the uneven geographic spread of large-scale violence in Mexico, this account faces an important empirical challenge: inter-cartel wars in the 1990s and 2000s initially broke out in prosperous cities where the state had more presence, not where it was relatively absent. This unusual pattern in which criminality is associated with greater state presence suggests, following our discussion of the state–criminal nexus in Chapter 1, that we need to move beyond the prevailing zero-sum conception of the relationship between states and armed groups in the political violence and organized crime literatures and develop a different understanding of the relationship between drug cartels and the state.

Organizational Resources

Whether cartels decide to go to war in search of profits or protection or to seize opportunities to enlarge their turf, they need soldiers and weapons to fight these conflicts.

Soldiers. One of the most consistent findings in the sociology of crime shows that young men from mono-parental families in impoverished US urban areas are attracted to street gangs and criminal organizations, and often engage in lethal criminal violence (Sampson 1993). Sociologists analyzing criminal wars in Latin America have documented that a desire for rapid economic mobility, status, and social respect has led large numbers of young men from marginalized urban communities to become foot soldiers in the drug wars (Brenneman 2013; Wolf 2018).

While the structural availability of young men to fight criminal wars can explain a crucial aspect of Mexico's inter-cartel violence, it cannot by itself explain why cartels went to war in the first place. Young men from impoverished areas or members of street gangs may be available to fight turf wars in exchange for economic rewards, but if cartels have no incentives to fight, drug lords will not develop private militias and young males will not become foot soldiers. Hence, the availability of willing soldiers may explain the duration of criminal wars but not the cartels' initial motivation to wage them.

Weapons. Because most of the assault weapons in Mexico's inter-cartel wars come from the US, Dube, Dube, and García-Ponce (2013) assess the impact of the 2004 expiration of the US ban on assault weapons on criminal violence in Mexican municipalities located along the US–Mexico border. Using California – the state where a local ban remained in effect – as a point of comparison, they show that Mexican municipalities along border states where the ban was lifted, and cartels had access to assault weapons, experienced a significant increase in criminal violence after 2004.

Although the availability of weapons can explain the evolution of inter-cartel wars, it cannot explain the cartels' initial incentives to fight. In fact, cartels in northwestern Mexico – the Tijuana Cartel, the Sinaloa Cartel, and the Juárez Cartel – created private militias and went to war as the US ban on assault weapons went into effect in 1994. Dube, Dube, and García-Ponce (2013) recognize this point and supplement their central claim about the relation between the availability of US assault weapons and Mexican inter-cartel violence. They argue that the cartels' *initial* motivation to fight came from the breakdown of informal government protection networks in municipalities along the US–Mexico border, led by municipal electoral competition in the 1990s.

In the next section we use multivariate regression models to test our claim about the impact of subnational partisan alternation on the onset of inter-cartel wars alongside alternative explanations. Subsequently, using quasi-experimental techniques, we zoom in on the impact of partisan alternation on drug violence to assess whether the breakdown of one-party rule and the transition to multiparty competition had a *causal* impact on inter-cartel violence.

Inter-cartel Violence

In the 1990s, after a decade of peaceful coexistence in which they rose to world prominence in the drug trafficking industry, Mexican cartels went to war. Drawing on the CVM Dataset, we analyze 4,257 murders perpetrated by drug cartels and their criminal associates between 1995 and 2006. The CVM reports murders resulting from inter-cartel conflicts; these are not homicides committed by common criminals.[16]

Inter-cartel wars first broke out in northern Mexico in the early 1990s, but violence quickly spread to other parts of the country. As Map 2.I.a shows, the first major inter-cartel conflicts broke out in the states of Baja California, Chihuahua, and Sinaloa in *northwestern* Mexico, where the Tijuana, Juárez, and Sinaloa cartels engaged in major turf wars (Blancornelas 2002). Inter-cartel conflicts spread throughout the 1990s to states under the control of the Sinaloa Cartel, including the *western* state of Jalisco along the Pacific coast (Grillo 2011). As Map 2.I.b shows, violence first appeared in the late 1990s in the *northeastern* states of Tamaulipas and Nuevo León, two strongholds of the Gulf Cartel, where the Sinaloa Cartel sought to take control over the Gulf's territories (Grillo 2011). As Map 2.I.c reveals, inter-cartel violence broke out in the 2000s in the *western* state of Michoacán and the *southwestern* state of Guerrero along the Pacific coast, where the Gulf Cartel and their private militia, the Zetas, sought to displace the Sinaloans (Maldonado 2012). As Map

---

[16] The CVM contains information on drug-related violent events reported in three Mexican daily newspapers: *Reforma* (1995–2006), *El Universal* (1995–2006), and *El Financiero* (1997–2006). Based in Mexico City and Monterrey, and with extensive coverage of central and northern Mexico, *Reforma* is the most specialized source of daily information on drug trafficking in Mexico (Shirk and Wallman 2015). *El Universal* offers good coverage of central Mexico and the Pacific and Gulf coasts, and *El Financiero* covers the central region. The three newspapers together provide a fair coverage of the south. While the CVM does not provide a census of drug-related violence, it minimizes any significant geographic bias. For a more detailed explanation of CVM and our data generation process, see Appendix A.

2.I.d shows, by 2006 Mexico was experiencing multiple inter-cartel wars.

The intensity of inter-cartel violence in the municipality i and in year t is our dependent variable. We use a municipal count of narco murders covering all Mexican municipalities (N = 2,018) between 1995 and 2006 as the indicator of inter-cartel violence.[17] Note that whereas homicide data often include all deaths reported by judicial authorities, here we only analyze murders that can be attributed directly to drug cartels.[18]

Subnational Party Alternation and the Loss of Protection

Party alternation in state gubernatorial power is our key explanatory variable. We use a dummy variable, *State alternation*, to identify all municipalities in states where the political party in gubernatorial power changed.[19] We assign a value of 0 to municipalities where the PRI remained in gubernatorial power and 1 where a governor from a different party was elected to office. Governors rule for six-year terms, so we assign a value of 1 to every year in which a party other than the PRI governed during a six-year term. Because we associate the rotation of political parties in gubernatorial power with the breakdown of informal networks of protection, when the same opposition party is re-elected (e.g., the PAN in Baja California) we no longer consider it to be a case of power rotation and code the second or third term in office as 0 until a new party comes to office. This specification assumes (1) that the most significant rotations in top- and mid-level personnel in the state attorney's office and police forces took place when parties alternated in office; and (2) that drug cartels were able to reconstitute subnational networks of protection with opposition governors and that a subsequent rotation of power could lead to the outbreak of violence.[20]

---

[17] We exclude 418 municipalities from Oaxaca where political parties do not compete for office because communities select mayors through indigenous customary practices. We also exclude Mexico City because the city had a special status during the time period under analysis here.
[18] When news reports did not include the names of the cartels involved, we relied on three indicators to decide whether to include a murder in the dataset: the use of assault weapons; signs of torture and brutal violence; and written messages left on the bodies.
[19] Electoral data come from CIDAC: http://cidac.org/base-de-datos-electoral/. Accessed May 10, 2017.
[20] We draw on interviews with the first opposition governor and their cabinet members to substantiate these assumptions. They all reported new appointments in their judicial and

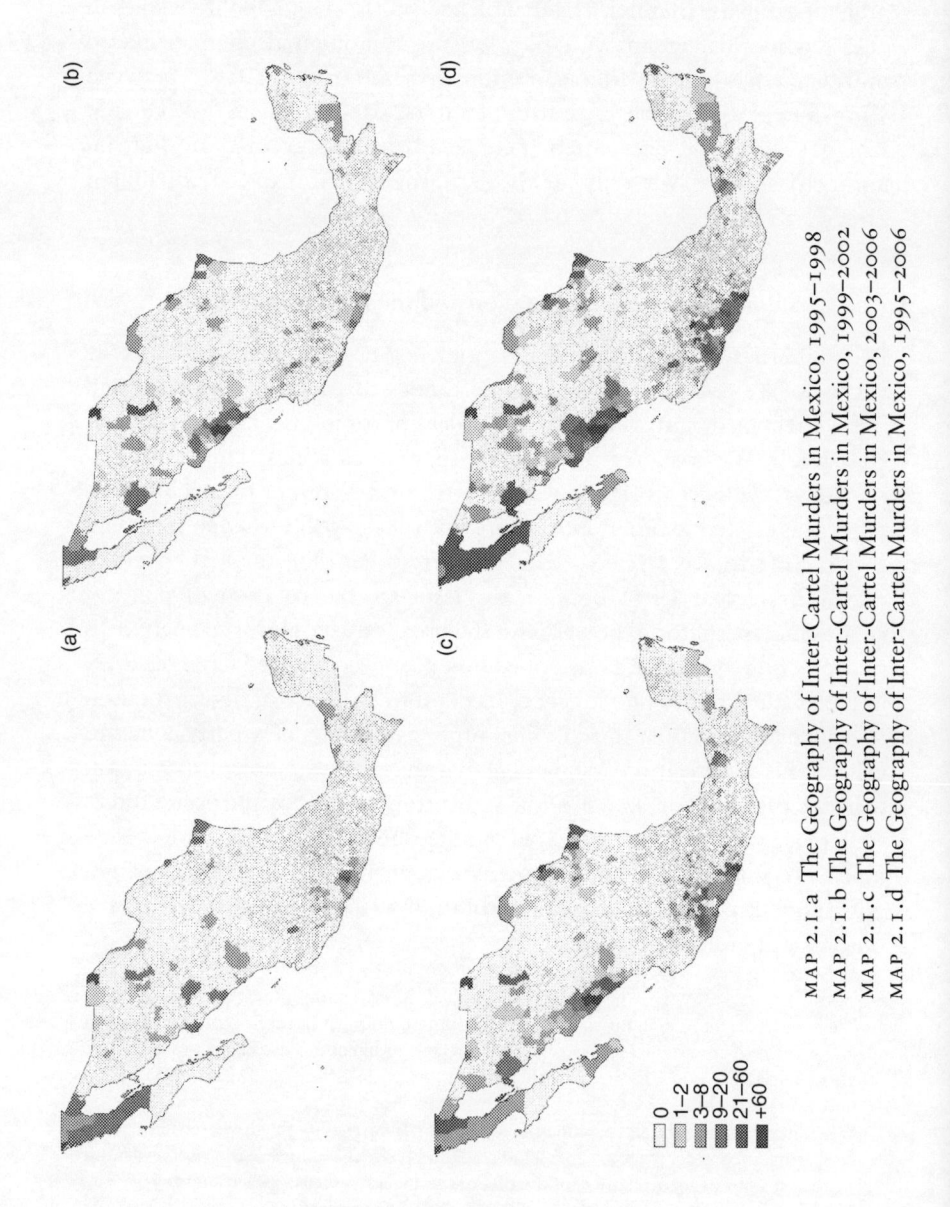

(a) (b) (c) (d)

Legend: 0, 1–2, 3–8, 9–20, 21–60, +60

MAP 2.1.a The Geography of Inter-Cartel Murders in Mexico, 1995–1998
MAP 2.1.b The Geography of Inter-Cartel Murders in Mexico, 1999–2002
MAP 2.1.c The Geography of Inter-Cartel Murders in Mexico, 2003–2006
MAP 2.1.d The Geography of Inter-Cartel Murders in Mexico, 1995–2006

As an alternative indicator, we create an ordinal index of subnational alternation, *Subnational alternation index*, which identifies municipalities experiencing simultaneous rotation in parties in gubernatorial and municipal powers.[21] The index takes values from 0 to 3. We consider four combinations of alternation. Municipalities with no alternation in gubernatorial or municipal power, where the PRI ruled at both levels, receive a 0 score. Municipalities where a new mayor but not a new governor came to power receive a score of 1, and municipalities where a new party won the governorship but the PRI remained in control of the municipality receive a score of 2. And municipalities with dual alternation receive a 3 score. This specification assumes that party alternation at the gubernatorial and municipal level can have an impact on inter-cartel violence because officials at both levels play important roles in the provision of protection for cartels.

Maps 2.II.a–2.II.d show the geographic evolution of state and municipal alternation in Mexico at different points in time: 1991, 1996, 2001, and 2006. Up to 1988 the PRI had won every gubernatorial election in Mexico's 31 states and nearly all municipal races since its foundation in 1929. But, as the maps show, between 1989 and 2006 Mexico experienced a subnational democratic revolution (Beer 2003; Díaz-Cayeros 2006): the center-Right PAN won nine governorships, the center-Left PRD won six, and two-thirds of Mexican municipalities experienced a rotation of political parties in office.[22] We explore whether the uneven spread of party alternation trajectories had an impact on the outbreak of inter-cartel wars.

---

police institutions and complained that after a few months some of these institutions actively sought to co-opt the new authorities (and often succeeded). See Chapter 3.

[21] Table C.2 in Appendix C shows the regression results using this independent variable.

[22] Even though subnational alternation began in 1989, our statistical testing covers the 1995–2006 period. We began the analysis in 1995 because the sources of information on cartel murders are not sufficiently systematic for earlier periods. *Reforma*, the most specialized newspaper on drug violence, and our key information source, was not launched until 1994–1995. This should not bias our results in any meaningful way. Between 1989 and 1994 there were two gubernatorial party rotations: Baja California (1989) and Chihuahua (1992). Starting in 1995, our panel covers most of the gubernatorial term of Chihuahua but only the last year of Baja California. To address this omission, we include Baja California as one of our case studies.

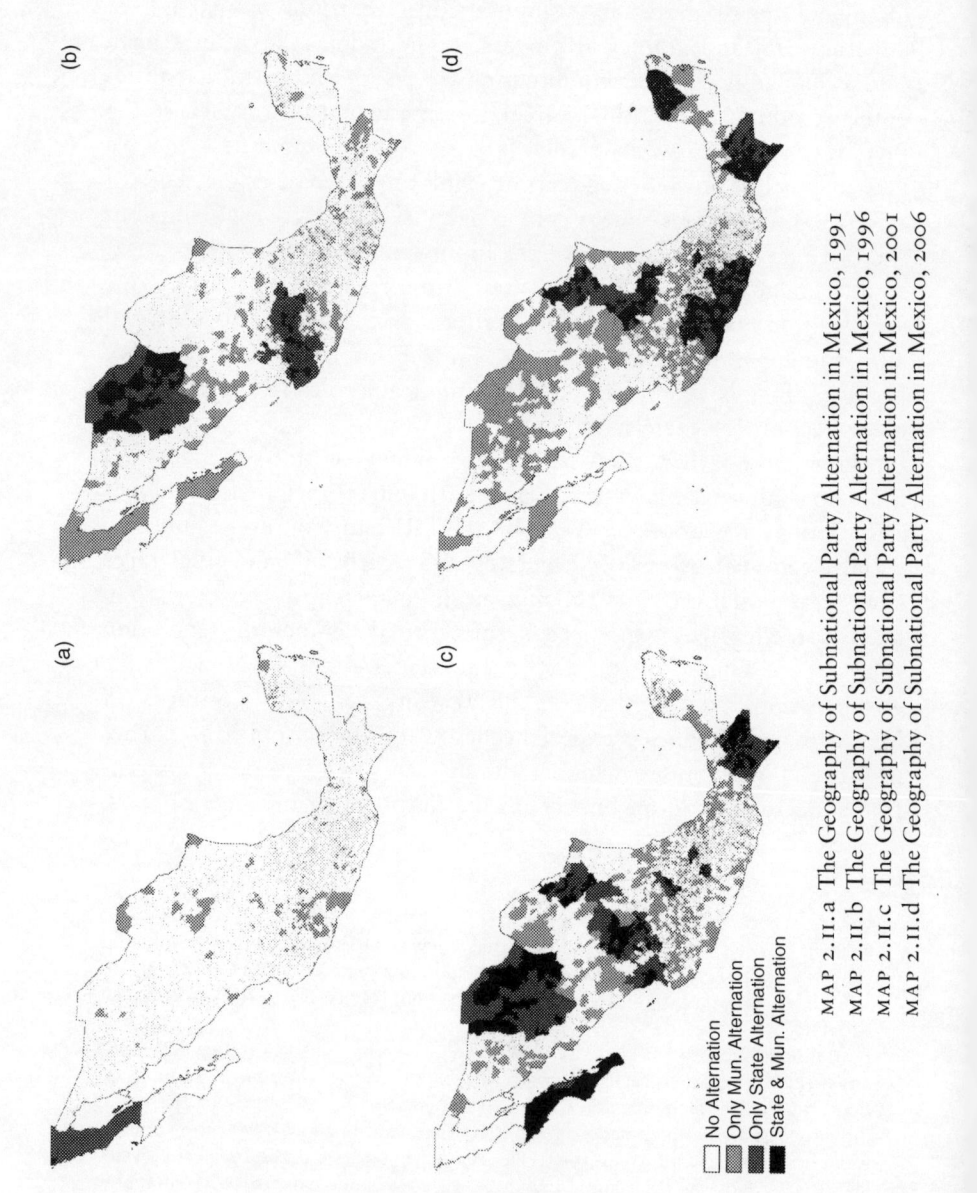

(a)

(b)

(c)

(d)

☐ No Alternation
▨ Only Mun. Alternation
▨ Only State Alternation
■ State & Mun. Alternation

MAP 2.II.a The Geography of Subnational Party Alternation in Mexico, 1991
MAP 2.II.b The Geography of Subnational Party Alternation in Mexico, 1996
MAP 2.II.c The Geography of Subnational Party Alternation in Mexico, 2001
MAP 2.II.d The Geography of Subnational Party Alternation in Mexico, 2006

Alternative Explanations and Controls

We test for alternative motivations to go to war and control for a number of factors associated with organizational resources and threats and opportunities.

Threats I: Protection. To assess the likely role of municipal and national alternation in the breakdown of government protection networks, we include a dummy variable, *Municipal alternation*, which identifies municipalities that experienced a rotation in the party in office. We also include a dummy variable, *National alternation*, to identify the years following the PRI's presidential defeat.

Threats II: State repression. To test for arguments about state repressive activities against the cartels, we draw on the CVM dataset to include a count of cartel bosses who were imprisoned or killed – *Leadership decapitation*. For every boss eliminated, we assign a value of 1 to all the municipalities from the cartel's home state.

Opportunities I: Change in international drug prices. To address the formulation that cartels went to war in response to exogenous shocks in international drug markets, we test for the percentage change of the *International retail price of cocaine* in the previous five years (UNODC 2008).

Opportunities II: State absence. To test for the state presence, we use the number of *public Prosecutors per 10,000 population*[23] per municipality.[24]

Organizational resources I: Soldiers. To test for the claim that lack of social cohesion in impoverished urban communities leads young males into violent criminal activities, we control for the municipal share of the population *Ages 15 to 34*, the municipal proportion of *Mono-parental households*, and the municipal *Sex ratio*.[25] We also control for the municipal Gini index of *Income inequality* (Jensen and Rosas 2007) to assess claims about aspirational crime.

---

[23] Note that for larger units of analysis such as states we use a population base of 100,000 inhabitants, but for municipalities, which range from 2,000 to hundreds of thousands in the population, for convenience we use a base of 10,000.

[24] INEGI judicial statistics 1990, 2000, and 2005: http://sc.inegi.org.mx/cobdem/. Accessed February 2, 2017.

[25] INEGI 1990, 2000, and 2005 censuses: http://sc.inegi.org.mx/cobdem/. Accessed February 2, 2017. Note that because in most of the cases women are in charge of mono-parental households, our measure actually codes female-headed households. We decided to keep the generic category of "mono-parental" family, however, because we do not want to contribute to stereotyping.

Organizational resources II: Weapons. Finally, to test for the availability of weapons, we use a dummy variable to identify the years after the
2004 *Expiration of the US ban on assault weapons.*

We control for seven geographic regions – *North, North-center,
Center, Gulf, Pacific, Southwest,* and *Southeast* (reference category) –
and use the natural log of population as the models' offset variable.

For statistical testing we use negative binomial (NB) models – the most
appropriate modeling technique for count data when observations are
non-independent and over-dispersed. We fitted random effects models,
because some of the key independent variables do not vary for several
consecutive years, rendering fixed effects inappropriate. We transform
coefficients into incidence rate ratios (IRR) to facilitate substantive
interpretation.

Results

The results, summarized in Table 2.1, strongly suggest that the alternation
of political parties in gubernatorial power is a powerful predictor of inter-
cartel violence in Mexico during the 1995–2006 period.

Model 1 presents our baseline results. Controlling only for subnational
geographic regions, our findings show that inter-cartel violence in municipalities from states that experienced party alternation in gubernatorial
power was 55.3 percent greater than in municipalities from states that
remained under PRI hegemony (IRR = 1.553). These are places where
cartels presumably lost protection as a result of the rotation of parties in
gubernatorial power.

But cartels may find themselves without protection and nonetheless fail
to create an army if they do not have access to fighters and weapons – that
is, to the organizational resources required to go to war. The results in
Model 2 show that after controlling for these factors, the rotation of
political parties in gubernatorial power remains a strong predictor of
narco violence: municipalities from states experiencing party alternation
on average had 63.2 percent more inter-cartel violence (IRR = 1.632) than
those that remained under PRI hegemony.

Considering all potential threats and the organizational resources to go
to war, the results in Model 3 show the effect of party alternation at the
state level in the presence of municipal and national alternation.[26] To

---

[26] These models do not include the expiration of the US ban on assault weapons because this
variable is collinear with national alternation.

TABLE 2.1 *Subnational Party Alternation and Inter-Cartel Violence in Mexico, 1995–2006 (Random Effects Negative Binomial Models with Logged Population as Offset Variable)*

	Model 1		Model 2		Model 3		Model 4	
	Coefficient	IRR	Coefficient	IRR	Coefficient	IRR	Coefficient	IRR
Threats								
State alternation	0.440*** [0.083]	1.553	0.490*** [0.082]	1.632	0.487*** [0.083]	1.627	0.583*** [0.082]	1.791
Municipal alternation					0.094 [0.069]	1.098	0.062 [0.069]	1.064
National alternation					0.532*** [0.079]	1.702	0.740*** [0.079]	2.096
Leadership decapitation					−0.188*** [0.067]	0.828	−0.077 [0.070]	0.926
Opportunities								
△International retail price of cocaine							0.045*** [0.003]	1.046
Prosecutors per 10,000 pop							0.143*** [0.047]	1.154
Organizational resources								
Ages 16–34			0.045*** [0.014]	1.046	0.064*** [0.016]	1.066	0.013 [0.016]	1.013
Mono-parental households			0.105*** [0.014]	1.111	0.126*** [0.014]	1.134	0.093*** [0.014]	1.098
Sex ratio			0.091*** [0.012]	1.096	0.099*** [0.013]	1.104	0.090*** [0.012]	1.094
Income inequality			1.496*	4.465	2.297***	9.943	0.851	2.342

TABLE 2.1 *(continued)*

	Model 1		Model 2		Model 3		Model 4	
	Coefficient	IRR	Coefficient	IRR	Coefficient	IRR	Coefficient	IRR
			[0.810]		[0.845]		[0.828]	
Expiration of US ban on assault weapons			0.882*** [0.070]	2.416				
Geographic controls								
North	1.715*** [0.322]	5.559	1.852*** [0.341]	6.374	1.868*** [0.343]	6.473	1.746*** [0.343]	5.734
North-center	−0.628 [0.384]	0.534	−0.029 [0.410]	0.971	0.042 [0.413]	1.042	−0.124 [0.412]	0.883
Center	0.07 [0.335]	1.072	0.527 [0.358]	1.694	0.58 [0.361]	1.787	0.537 [0.360]	1.710
Gulf	0.808** [0.335]	2.244	1.011*** [0.355]	2.749	1.004*** [0.357]	2.730	1.034*** [0.357]	2.813
Pacific	1.573*** [0.325]	4.820	1.962*** [0.352]	7.114	2.011*** [0.356]	7.470	1.912*** [0.355]	6.770
Southwest	1.182*** [0.329]	3.261	1.412*** [0.352]	4.103	1.410*** [0.355]	4.097	1.336*** [0.354]	3.804
Constant	−15.104*** [0.318]		−28.855*** [1.715]		−31.074*** [1.810]		−25.819*** [1.768]	
Observations	24,023		23,830		23,830		23,830	
Log-likelihood	−4323.363		−4161.406		−4212.754		−4111.013	
BIC	8747.594		8473.992		8596.846		8413.52	

Standard errors in brackets

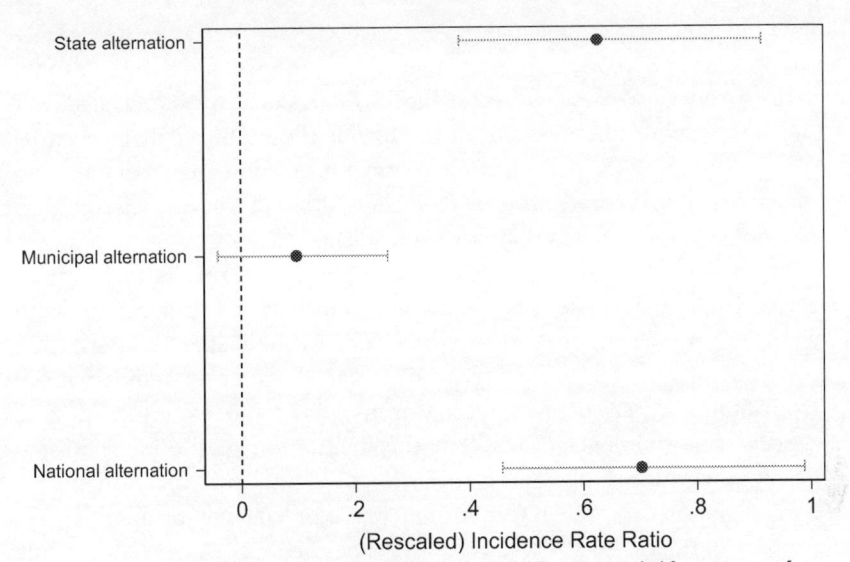

Incidence Rate Ratios (IRR) from Model 3 were rescaled for purposes of interpretation.
Original IRRs were subtracted one unit to show the direct impact of each variable on violence.

FIGURE 2.4 Impact of Party Alternation on Inter-Cartel Violence in Mexico, 1995–2006

facilitate the substantive interpretation of these results, Figure 2.4 provides a graphic representation of the model's main findings. It shows incidence rate ratios of violence for party alternation at different levels. Note that variables are not statistically significant when the confidence intervals cross the zero line. Three main findings stand out. First, the rotation of political parties at the state level continues to be a strong predictor of inter-cartel violence: violence in municipalities from states that experienced party alternation in the governor's office was 62.7 percent greater than municipalities from states that remained under the control of the PRI (IRR = 1.627). Second, municipal alternation is not statistically significant.[27] Third, national alternation is a significant predictor of violence and has a strong substantive effect: compared to pre-2000 municipalities, post-

[27] We ran additional tests (Appendix C, Table C.1) to test for municipal electoral competition instead of municipal alternation. The results reveal that electoral competition is not statistically significant. While these findings do not contradict Dube, Dube, and García-Ponce's (2013) claim that electoral competition in municipalities along the US–Mexico border is associated with more narco violence, they do show that when we look beyond Mexico's northern border and consider *all* of Mexico's municipalities, municipal electoral competition is no longer statistically significant.

national alternation municipalities experienced 70.2 percent more violence (IRR = 1.702). Note, however, that since national alternation cannot explain the 1995–2000 violence, the PRI's defeat in presidential power can only explain the intensification but not the outbreak of inter-cartel violence. Shifting the focus from the loss of protection after party alternation toward direct state attacks, the results show that leadership removal had no consistent effect on inter-cartel violence.[28]

If we include opportunities in the analysis, the results in Model 4 reveal that when we add economic motivations associated with changes in the international price of cocaine, party alternation becomes a stronger predictor of inter-cartel violence: municipalities from states experiencing gubernatorial alternation experienced 79.1 percent more violence. Note that the fluctuation of the international price of cocaine had a large net effect: a one unit increase in the percent change of the international price of cocaine resulted in 4.6 percent more violence (IRR = 1.046). These results suggest that while the rotation of parties and the loss of government protection gave cartels an incentive to create private militias to defend their turf, increases in the price of cocaine possibly motivated them to use these private armies to conquer new territories.

Considering other sources of opportunities yields surprising findings. The results in Model 4 show that municipalities with more public prosecutors were more, not less, likely to experience inter-cartel violence. The fact that greater state judicial presence is associated with more criminal violence is consistent with the theoretical assumption about different forms of collusion between OCGs and state agents. What this finding suggests is that in widely corrupt judicial systems, in which law enforcement agents often collude with organized crime – as in the Mexican system – the presence of public prosecutors or police agents is often associated with more criminality and violence.

The results across models reported in Table 2.1 suggest that, consistent with the vast sociological literature on criminal violence, organizational factors matter: inter-cartel violence was more intense in municipalities where young males from mono-parental households

---

[28] This result does not contradict findings from scholars analyzing the impact of decapitation policies during the 2006–2012 period. Our analysis focuses on a time period in which the state was not pursuing a systematic attack on the cartels. See more on this in Chapters 4 and 5.

were available to fight and when cartels had access to US assault weapons.[29]

Time Trends

If it is the case that by removing key personnel in the judicial and police system, incoming opposition governors unwittingly dismantled the informal networks of government protection for drug cartels, then we should observe a major uptick of inter-cartel violence during opposition governors' first year in office. To assess time trends, we created a count variable to identify each of the six years of a governor in office, *State govt cycle*. For convenience, we code the first year in office as 0. We then assess the evolution of violence after a rotation of political parties in gubernatorial office through the interaction *State alternation* × *State govt cycle*.[30]

The results in Table 2.2 reveal a conspicuous hike in inter-cartel violence during the first postauthoritarian year. Model 1 shows an important increase in violence immediately after the rotation of political parties in a state governorship. In this interaction model, the coefficient of the *State alternation* variable shows that when *State govt cycle* is equal to 0 – that is, during an opposition governor's initial year in office – violence increases by 53.5 percent (IRR = 1.535). The interaction *State alternation* × *State govt cycle* shows that after the significant increase of violence during the first year of an opposition governor in office, violence increases slightly at an annual rate of 6.6 percent (IRR = 1.066) for the remainder of the six-year term in office. This result strongly suggests that drug cartels

---

[29] In Appendix C, we show that our key findings are robust to different specifications of subnational alternation (Table C.2), as well as to a number of additional controls, including poverty and a municipality's physical proximity to global markets (Table C.3). Our main finding also remains unchanged when we use fixed effects models to capture unobserved characteristics of the municipalities (see Table C.4); when we split the sample by geographic region (see Table C.5) and test our models using only municipalities from the two regions with the greatest impact on inter-cartel violence (North and Pacific, as shown in Table 2.1); and when we address potential biases due to a large number of zero counts and test all our models using a dichotomous measure of the dependent variable (1 = non-zero counts of inter-cartel murders; 0 = otherwise) (Table C.6) and subsequently retest the models only using positive counts (Table C.7). In Table C.7 we include a lag of murders in neighboring municipalities to test for spatial effects, and the results continue to suggest that party rotation in gubernatorial power remains an important predictor of inter-cartel violence.

[30] We follow a similar procedure to control for municipal time trends.

TABLE 2.2 *Assessing the Evolution of Violence Following Party Alternation, 1995–2006 (Random Effects Negative Binomial Model with Logged Population as Offset Variable)*

| | Model 1 | |
	Coefficient	IRR
Threats		
State alternation	0.428***	1.535
	[0.129]	
State government cycle	−0.029	0.972
	[0.024]	
State alternation × State govt cycle	0.064*	1.066
	[0.038]	
Municipal alternation	−0.01	0.990
	[0.105]	
Municipal government cycle	−0.123**	0.885
	[0.051]	
Municipal alternation × Mun govt cycle	0.061	1.063
	[0.078]	
National alternation	0.744***	2.104
	[0.079]	
Leadership decapitation	−0.096	0.908
	[0.071]	
Opportunities		
△International retail price of cocaine	0.046***	1.047
	[0.003]	
Prosecutors per 10,000 pop	0.142***	1.153
	[0.048]	
Organizational resources		
Ages 16–34	0.015	1.015
	[0.016]	
Mono-parental households	0.095***	1.100
	[0.014]	
Sex ratio	0.092***	1.097
	[0.012]	
Income inequality	0.812	2.253
	[0.829]	
Geographic controls	YES	

(continued)

TABLE 2.2 *(continued)*

	Model 1	
	Coefficient	IRR
Constant	−25.905***	
	[1.782]	
Observations	23,830	
Log-likelihood	−4,105.512	
BIC	8,442.835	

Standard errors in brackets
*** p<0.01, ** p<0.05, * p<0.10

went to war during the first year after a rotation of parties in gubernatorial office. We used this finding to guide our qualitative interviews with the first opposition governors. As we report in the next chapter, all newly elected governors independently confirmed this unusual hike in violence during the first weeks and months in office.

QUANTITATIVE EVIDENCE II: SYNTHETIC CONTROL MODELS

While our different multivariate statistical models have shown a substantively strong association between party alternation in Mexico's gubernatorial offices and the intensity of inter-cartel violence, two challenges remain before we can actually claim that this is a causal effect. It could be the case that criminal violence leads to party alternation (rather than the other way around, as we claim) and that a number of unknown covariates (which we are unable to measure) may explain both party alternation and inter-cartel wars. To address these challenges, we rely on the synthetic control method (Abadie, Diamond, and Hainmueller 2015) – a quasi-experimental technique that helps us isolate the impact of party alternation on the outbreak and evolution of inter-cartel violence in a state that experienced alternation and compare it against violence in a counterfactual case. We first explain the logic of the model and then report our results using two cases: Michoacán and Guerrero.

The Synthetic Control Method

The synthetic control method (SCM) is a quasi-experimental technique developed for small-N analysis that is best suited for the study of the likely causal effect of major policy changes on a specific unit. Using a counterfactual framework, SCM enables the study of a "treated unit" against a "synthetic unit" (or an artificially constructed untreated case that serves as a counterfactual). A synthetic unit is constructed using a "donor pool" of similar cases to the untreated unit. In our study a treated unit would be a Mexican state x that has experienced party alternation in gubernatorial power, and an untreated unit would be any state that has not yet experienced party alternation and that shares a number of important features with x that are associated with the outbreak of violence. Through SCM we construct *synthetic* x using the weighted average of the cases from the donor pool that most closely resemble state x. The main output of the SCM is a graphical representation that compares the evolution of the outcome variable (i.e., the temporal evolution of inter-cartel violence over a significant period of time) for state x against *synthetic* x. If there is a gap between the two cases after the introduction of the political shock (i.e., party alternation in gubernatorial power), we can conclude that the political change actually had a causal impact on the outcome variable.

To test for the likely causal impact of party alternation in state gubernatorial power on the intensity of inter-cartel violence, we use the cases of the western state of Michoacán and the southern state of Guerrero. These are two cases of leftist alternation. Although the outbreak of inter-cartel wars following party alternation affected leftist and right-wing opposition parties alike (see Chapter 3), we use these cases of leftist states because right-wing party alternations happened mostly in the early 1990s and leftist alternations in the 2000s. The SCM works better when there is a relatively long time series prior to the treatment. Because our dataset begins in 1995, we had little choice but to select the leftist cases. An in-depth analysis of cases of right- and left-wing party alternation in Chapter 3 will present a more balanced analysis. In any case, the SCM models that we discuss below do allow us to isolate the likely causal effect of alternation on criminal violence.

Michoacán

After nearly seven decades of uninterrupted PRI rule in gubernatorial power, Michoacán experienced its first party alternation in 2002, when the leftist PRD candidate, Lázaro Cárdenas Batel, won the governorship. We use 2002 as our treatment year and compare the evolution of inter-cartel violence in Michoacán against *synthetic* Michoacán. We construct the latter using a donor pool of 14 states that had not previously experienced party alternation in the governor's office.[31] These states resembled Michoacán on the following dimensions: sex ratio, the state proportion of mono-parental households, the state proportion of population aged 15–34, Gini coefficient, effective number of parties,[32] prosecutors per 100,000, the number of public prosecutor agencies and agents, total population, and a one-year lag of inter-cartel violence.

Table 2.3 displays the weights of each of the states in the donor pool for *synthetic* Michoacán. A higher weight means that the state more closely resembled Michoacán in terms of the pre-treatment characteristics that are more closely associated with the dynamics of inter-cartel violence. As the results in Table 2.3 show, Guerrero and the State of Mexico are the two states that most closely resembled Michoacán and thus provided the input to create the *synthetic* case. The weights for the rest of the states in the donor pool are equal to 0.

Table 2.4 provides a comparison of the pre-treatment characteristics of Michoacán with those of *synthetic* Michoacán. Overall, the output shows a great affinity between Michoacán and its synthetic counterpart. This means that, prior to the treatment (the 2002 party alternation in the

---

[31] We exclude from the analysis states that also experienced alternation in 2002. We also exclude Tamaulipas and Sinaloa. Although Tamaulipas did not experience alternation and in principle could be part of the donor pool, the 1997 party alternation in state gubernatorial power in the neighboring state of Nuevo León had a dramatic effect on Tamaulipas's gray zone of criminality because the families of the drug lords of the Gulf Cartel (which had its headquarters in Tamaulipas) had their residence in Nuevo León's state capital, Monterrey (see Chapter 3 for a detailed explanation of the de facto integration of Nuevo León and Tamaulipas for the narcos). Similarly, although Sinaloa did not experience party alternation in the government's office in this time period, alternation in the nearby state of Jalisco, where the families of the drug lords of the Sinaloa Cartel had their residence, had a major impact on Sinaloa's gray zone of criminality (see Chapter 3 for an extended discussion of this point). Abadie, Diamond, and Hainmuller (2015) suggest that a key criterion for inclusion of cases in the donor pool is that "they must not have been subject to structural shocks that may have affected the outcome variable during the sample period of study." For the reasons explained above, Tamaulipas and Sinaloa clearly were not free of the alternation shock and hence should not be included in the donor pool.

[32] The effective number of parties is used as a measure of the fragmentation of the party system and in dominant-party systems it is taken to be a measure of electoral competition. The ENP = $1/\Sigma p_i^2$, where p_i is the percentage of votes received by party i.

TABLE 2.3 *Synthetic Weights for the Donor Pool of States Used to Create* Synthetic *Michoacán*

State	Synthetic Control Weight
Campeche	0
Coahuila	0
Colima	0
Durango	0
Guerrero	0.65
Hidalgo	0
Mexico	0.349
Oaxaca	0
Puebla	0
Quintana Roo	0
San Luis Potosí	0
Sonora	0
Tabasco	0
Veracruz	0

governor's office), there was a great degree of resemblance between Michoacán and the artificial counterfactual case.

Figure 2.5 displays the trajectory of inter-cartel violence in Michoacán (the solid line) and *synthetic* Michoacán (the dashed line) for the 1995–2006 period. As the figure shows, during the pre-treatment period, from 1995 to 2002 when the PRI was in power, inter-cartel violence in *synthetic* Michoacán closely tracks the trajectory of violence in Michoacán. This suggests that *synthetic* Michoacán is a reasonable predictor of the number of inter-cartel murders that actually took place in Michoacán prior to the opposition victory in the state gubernatorial election. However, as Figure 2.5 reveals, following the 2002 defeat of the PRI and the rotation of parties in office the two lines begin to diverge: following an initial gap in 2002 and 2003, starting in 2004, *synthetic* Michoacán had a consistently low level of inter-cartel violence and violence in Michoacán skyrocketed. By 2006, four years after party alternation, inter-cartel violence in Michoacán was twice greater than in the counterfactual scenario.[33]

---

[33] Note that the regression results reported earlier provide average estimated effects across 2,018 Mexican municipalities, while the results from this analysis provide estimates about internal processes within each state under analysis.

TABLE 2.4 *Inter-Cartel Violence Predictor Means before Party Alternation for Michoacán (Treated) and* Synthetic *Michoacán*

	Treated	Synthetic
Sex ratio	92.993	95.299
Mono-parental households (%)	20.882	21.841
Population aged 16–34 (%)	34.116	34.326
Gini coefficient	0.496	0.454
Effective number of parties (mean)	2.09	1.922
Prosecutors per 100,000	1.115	1.068
Prosecutor agencies (count)	94.5	81.49
Prosecutor agents (count)	218.833	332.244
Total population	3,946,433	6,389,384
One-year lag of inter-cartel violence	19	18.09

Note: We report the donor pool sample mean.

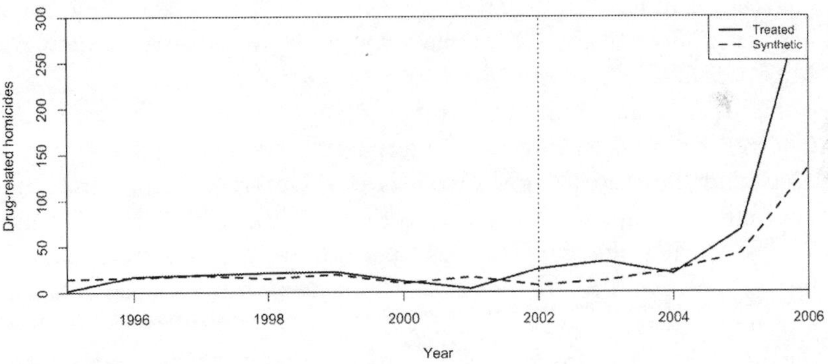

FIGURE 2.5 Trends in Inter-Cartel Violence: Michoacán versus *Synthetic* Michoacán

In a context in which postauthoritarian Mexican elites did not engage in a major transitional justice process or launch a major security-sector reform that would have reduced and brought under control the gray zone of criminality, any democratic political change resulted in a major change in the balance of power in the criminal underworld, giving rise to incentives to settle disputes through war.[34] As we will explain in Chapter 3, the alternation of parties in the governor's office in Michoacán – and the new governor's decision to remove top- and mid-level officials in the state attorney's office and the state judicial police – undermined traditional networks of government protection for the Sinaloa Cartel, making the Sinaloans vulnerable to attacks by rival cartels. Without a third-party enforcer, Michoacán – a key place for the cultivation of marijuana and for the production and trafficking of heroin and synthetic drugs – was quickly immersed in lethal turf wars.

Guerrero

The southern state of Guerrero experienced its first party alternation in gubernatorial office in 2005 when Zeferino Torreblanca, from the leftist PRD, defeated the PRI after more than seven decades of uninterrupted one-party rule in the state. We use 2005 as our treatment year. The donor pool to create *synthetic* Guerrero includes 12 states that had not previously experienced party alternation in the governor's office[35] and that resembled Guerrero on the same number of dimensions as the ones we used to construct *synthetic* Michoacán.

Figure 2.6 shows the trajectories of inter-cartel violence in both Guerrero and its *synthetic* counterpart for the 1995–2006 period. The solid line depicts the treated case – Guerrero before and after alternation – and the dashed line the *synthetic* case. As the figure shows, during the pre-treatment period, from 1995 to 2005, the lines follow similar trends and do not depart from each other in any major way. However, after the defeat of the PRI in 2005 and the arrival of the opposition in the governor's office, inter-cartel violence experienced an exponential growth in Guerrero, while

---

[34] To be sure, as we explained in Chapter 1, a major transitional justice process or a major security-sector reform would have had a major impact on the gray zone of criminality. However, the accountability shocks entailed in these processes would deter state specialists in violence from colluding or serving organized crime or from using iron-fist policies to fight them. For specifics about how these processes actually reduce the gray zone of criminality and prospects for criminal violence, see Trejo, Albarracín, and Tiscornia (2018) and Tiscornia (2019).

[35] We exclude from the analysis states that experienced alternation in 2005 and Tamaulipas and Sinaloa for the reasons stated above.

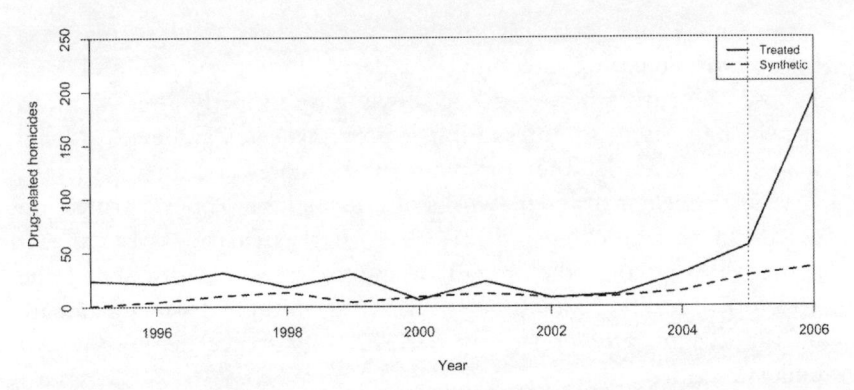

FIGURE 2.6 Trends in Inter-Cartel Violence: Guerrero versus *Synthetic* Guerrero

murders remain relatively stable at historical levels in *synthetic* Guerrero. We do not assess inter-cartel violence beyond 2006 because on December 10, 2006, President Felipe Calderón launched a major War on Drugs and the drivers of drug violence in Mexico changed in important ways – as we will show in Part III of the book. At any rate, the dramatic spike of violence immediately following the arrival of an opposition party in Guerrero's state government provides strong support for our claim that, in the absence of any major reform of the authoritarian security apparatus that had provided protection to cartels for decades, party alternation in state gubernatorial power had a significant causal impact on inter-cartel violence.

In Chapter 3 we will explore in detail how party alternation changed the balance of power in Guerrero's gray zone of criminality. We will demonstrate how the Gulf Cartel and its private army, the Zetas, seized this unique opportunity to contest the Sinaloa Cartel's hegemony over the state's cultivation of marijuana and poppy and over the profitable drug trafficking routes connecting the Pacific Ocean with central Mexico and the United States.

CONCLUSION

In this chapter we have suggested that Mexican cartels went to war in the 1990s because they lost access to the informal networks of government protection they had enjoyed under one-party rule.

Although national security forces under military tutelage played a key role in regulating the criminal underworld in the 1970s and early 1980s, we provide new evidence showing that shortly after Mexican cartels had risen to international prominence, state-level judicial police forces, under the command of the states' attorney generals, were at the center of the networks of informal government protection for the drug trafficking industry. We offer extensive statistical evidence showing that the spread of multiparty competition and the breakdown of PRI controls across Mexican states had a major impact on the dynamics of previously peaceful coexistence in the criminal underworld.

Our statistical findings unambiguously show that party alternation in state gubernatorial power in the 1990s and 2000s was a key motivating factor for the outbreak of inter-cartel wars and a crucial explanatory factor of the intensity of violence across Mexican municipalities. Our evidence shows that, after controlling for a wide variety of alternative explanations, partisan alternation in the state governor's office had a large independent effect on inter-cartel violence. Political factors in our analysis do not trump sociodemographic factors and factors related to changes in international drug markets as drivers of violence. But one of the key takeaway messages from our findings is that any analysis that overlooks politico-electoral dynamics as a key determinant of large-scale criminal violence is likely to suffer from a major omitted variable bias. Using quasi-experimental techniques, our results reveal that the end of one-party rule and the rotation of parties in gubernatorial power in Mexico did have an independent causal effect on the outbreak and intensity of inter-cartel wars.

Our analysis differs from dominant accounts of Mexico's drug violence in important ways. Highlighting these differences has crucial implications not only for our understanding of inter-cartel wars in Mexico but also for the study of large-scale criminal violence more generally.

Whereas leading explanations of drug violence in Mexico suggest that uncertainty associated with municipal electoral competition led to the breakdown of informal government protection networks and to inter-cartel wars, we show a causal path involving a different mechanism – party alternation – operating at a different geographic level – state jurisdictions. Our evidence reveals that, rather than electoral competition and the mere presence of opposition parties waging electoral campaigns, it was the actual *rotation of parties* in state gubernatorial power and the *removal* of top- and mid-level officials from the state attorney's office and the state judicial police that triggered the breakdown of protection. In our account, municipal actors were not the central players in the provision of criminal protection; instead, officers from the *state-level* judicial police were the central organizing actors of these networks. Whether municipal or state-level actors are the central suppliers of criminal protection is not simply a scholastic quarrel. If policymakers intent on undermining criminal protection networks focus on dismantling municipal police forces and empowering state police forces – as Mexican lawmakers have advocated for years – they may very well be strengthening state–criminal networks and inadvertently establishing the institutional basis for greater criminal violence.

The important theoretical implication is that party alternation – one of the defining features of representative democracy – can be a trigger of large-scale violence in societies where the spheres of organized crime and state authority intersect. Scholars of organized crime in economics and sociology have long assumed that government authorities and OCGs operate in separate, opposing spheres. However, in this chapter we have provided extensive empirical evidence of the existence of a gray zone of state and criminal interaction that has enabled the rise and development of Mexico's drug trafficking industry. Whether these linkages are forged at the national, state, or municipal levels is largely a contextual matter that varies from one time period to another and from one country to another. What is more general, however, is the impact that party alternation can have on unraveling state–criminal arrangements and triggering violence in countries in which there is a significant gray zone of criminality.

Although in this chapter we have argued that changes in gubernatorial power led to the breakdown of protection and motivated drug lords to create their own private militias to defend their turf against potential attacks from incoming opposition governments and from rival cartels, we have not yet provided any evidence of the existence of these private militias. Because the militias were the central military player in Mexico's inter-cartel wars – they empowered cartels to renegotiate informal protection with opposition authorities and allowed them to conquer rival territories in other states where the breakdown of PRI hegemony made home cartels vulnerable – a thorough explanation of the outbreak of inter-cartel wars needs an in-depth exploration of these private armies. In Chapter 3, we assess the intimate connection between party alternation and the rise and proliferation of private militias in Mexico's main drug trafficking corridors, together with its implications for the dynamics of criminal peace and war in the gray zone of criminality.

3

Fighting Turf Wars

Cartels, Militias, and the Struggle for Drug Trafficking Corridors

Students of comparative democratization have long viewed the Mexican transition to democracy as a quintessential example of a federalist transition in which voters first elected opposition parties to municipal governments, then to state gubernatorial office, and eventually to the presidency (Beer 2003; Díaz-Cayeros 2006; Lucardi 2017). Unlike other transitions marked by elite pacts from above or armed revolutionary action from below, in the Mexican case there is a consensus that voters – not elites or armed rebel groups[1] – peacefully removed the PRI from the presidency without bloodshed. In Chapter 2, however, we argued that a narrow transition to electoral democracy, in which elites failed to reform a corrupt security and judicial system that had played a key role protecting the drug trafficking industry, meant that Mexico's illiberal democracy became intimately intertwined with drug violence from birth. We showed that the decentralized nature of the transition – by which the opposition conquered power from the periphery to the center – was intimately associated with the outbreak of inter-cartel wars. Using a wide range of multivariate and quasi-experimental statistical models, our results unambiguously showed that in subnational regions with drug trafficking corridors every party alternation in state gubernatorial power became a trigger of inter-cartel violence.

This chapter seeks to disentangle the causal chain that goes from party alternation in gubernatorial office to the outbreak of inter-cartel wars over the control of drug trafficking routes. Drawing on a series

[1] For a dissenting view, see Trejo (2012: Chapter 8).

of in-depth interviews with the first opposition governors and some of their cabinet members, the chapter reconstructs the historical sequence that led from party alternation, to changes in the new governor's security and judicial teams, to the breakdown of informal government protection, the rise of private militias, and the onset of inter-cartel wars. Following principles of process tracing (Waldern 2015), our goal is to uncover the concatenation of actors and mechanisms that led from one event to another along the chain that connects the rotation of parties in gubernatorial power (after six decades of one-party rule) and the proliferation of turf wars.

We focus on the six states that experienced party alternation in gubernatorial power, that had major cartel presence, and that were part of major drug trafficking corridors: Baja California (northwest), Chihuahua (north), Jalisco (west), Nuevo León (north), Michoacán (west) and Guerrero (south). In the first four cases party alternation was led by candidates from the center-Right National Action Party (PAN) and in the last two cases by candidates from the center-Left Party of the Democratic Revolution (PRD).[2] We sequentially assess party alternations that began with Baja California in 1989 and ended with Guerrero in 2005 because we want to show how every new rotation of parties in office led to the rise of new private militias and to the outbreak of new violent conflicts. We focus only on positive cases – that is, on states that experienced both party alternation and the outbreak of inter-cartel wars – because we are interested in fleshing out the causal mechanisms that undergird the process that goes from political change to the outbreak of violence.[3] Because we have already extensively assessed positive and negative cases through the statistical analyses reported in Chapter 2, here we conduct a historical study of positive cases to identify the actors and mechanics of this process.

Our case studies reveal that after assuming office, new opposition governors systematically removed top- and mid-level officials in the state attorneys' offices and in the state judicial police. The simple removal of these officials – who were at the center of informal networks of protection – created a great degree of uncertainty for drug

---

[2] By expanding the analysis to states experiencing right-wing alternation, we seek to complement the analysis from the synthetic control models presented in Chapter 2.

[3] For a discussion about the adequacy of focusing on positive cases for purposes of process tracing and the identification of causal mechanisms, see Goertz (2017).

cartels. We provide detailed information about the private militias that drug lords created in every state to face potential threats and to defend their turf from rival cartels and from incoming opposition authorities. Through the sequential analysis we were able to identify an arms race that led to the development of increasingly more lethal private armies. As part of this race, the Gulf Cartel – the last major cartel to experience a party alternation in its home state – took the bold decision to recruit elite members of the Mexican military to lead their private militia. The creation of the Zetas – Mexico's most lethal private militia – was a strategic decision taken by the Gulf Cartel after seeing that all the other cartels had already constituted their own armies and were ready to conquer the Gulf's drug trafficking routes leading into Texas.[4]

On the basis of the analysis of the outbreak of inter-cartel wars in these six Mexican states, we are able to illustrate the major transformation that the development of private militias entailed for the balance of power in Mexico's gray zone of criminality. Cartels would never be the same after they took the step of creating their own private armies. They delegated the security of their families and of their drug trafficking corridors to defectors from the federal and state judicial police. These, in turn, recruited and trained young males from impoverished areas and members of street gangs as foot soldiers to fight the cartel's turf wars. Maintaining control over these new powerful actors that had been vertically integrated into the cartels' organizational structure became an extraordinary challenge for drug lords, particularly after the Mexican federal government launched a War on Drugs in 2007 with the goal of dismantling the leadership of the cartels.

The chapter is structured in five sections. We first discuss how cartels were organized and how they coexisted during the period of the *pax mafiosa*, when they all enjoyed protection from subnational PRI authorities. Drawing on in-depth interviews with former

[4] We use the terms "private militia" and "private army" interchangeably. We stress the private character of these groups, because unlike pro-government militias identified in the civil war literature (Carey, Colaresi, and Mitchell 2015), these militias are created to defend private actors such as the cartels. And, as we discuss below, the military nature of these groups stems from their members and training – the high-echelons of these private militias are defectors of police and military forces; that is, they are former state specialists in violence who lead and train young men and gang members in combat techniques. In the Mexican case, they transferred the techniques first developed during the Dirty War in the 1970s, which prevailed and were transferred from the DFS, the military and the federal police, to state-level police forces, and then to the cartels' private militias.

opposition governors, in the second section we provide a detailed explanation of the breakdown of protection, the rise of private militias, and the onset of criminal wars state by state. In the third section we analyze the spread of dyadic inter-cartel conflicts in three Mexican subnational regions following subnational party alternations, and in the fourth section we assess how two decades of inter-cartel wars and the emergence of private armies under the cartels' command transformed forever the internal organizational structure of drug trafficking organizations. We conclude with a discussion about similarities and differences between criminal wars and civil wars, and about the armed actors that engage in both types of conflict.

THE PAX MAFIOSA: THE INITIAL EQUILIBRIUM

After the US government's crackdown on the Caribbean drug trafficking route that connected South America with Miami in the early 1980s, cocaine operations moved from sea to land and Mexico became a key geographic region in the global chain of drug trafficking operations (Bagley 2012). Two cartels initially dominated operations in Mexico: the Guadalajara Cartel, which controlled the Pacific Coast and western Mexico, and the Gulf Cartel, which dominated the Gulf of Mexico and the eastern states. But in 1985, when the drug lords of the Guadalajara Cartel ordered the murder of Enrique Camarena, a US undercover agent, the entire drug industry was shaken. Under unusual pressure from the US government, the Mexican administration of President Miguel de la Madrid (1982–1988) was forced to arrest the top leaders of the Guadalajara Cartel and to shut down the powerful Federal Security Directorate (DFS) – the military-led secret service charged with repression of political dissidents, many of whose agents had become protectors and/or regulators of Mexico's drug trafficking industry (Astorga and Shirk 2010; Cedillo 2019).

The arrest of the leadership of the Guadalajara Cartel and the transformation of the DFS into a civilian agency (Astorga 2005) had two major consequences for the gray zone of criminality and the drug trafficking industry. On the criminal front, the Guadalajara Cartel split into three major cartels – Tijuana, Juárez, and Sinaloa – led by close family members and childhood neighbors of the Guadalajara leaders. After some initial internal struggles, the Tijuana Cartel came under the control of the Arellano Félix siblings (Blancornelas 2002). The Juárez Cartel came under the control of the Carrillo Fuentes brothers (Grillo 2011), and the

Sinaloa Cartel was controlled by a group of close acquaintances and neighbors from different parts of the state of Sinaloa – Joaquín Guzmán (El Chapo), Ismael Zambada (El Mayo), Juan José Esparragoza (El Azul), and Héctor (El Güero) Palma (Grillo 2011). On the government front, after the disappearance of the DFS the federal government delegated political repression to state governors, particularly to the state judicial police under the command of the state attorneys general. DFS veterans moved to the states to head and train state judicial police forces in the art of political repression.[5]

This dual decentralization of the drug trafficking industry and of political repression constituted a new equilibrium. State judicial police forces, which now had the upper hand for political repression and political impunity from the regime for gross human rights violations, would use their comparative advantage in violence, access to privileged information, and political immunity to develop an informal network of protection for the emerging cartels. As we showed in Chapter 2, top- and mid-level officials from the state judicial police developed a dense network of protection for the cartels, which connected the police with top- and mid-level officials from the state attorney's office, the state penitentiary systems, state agents of the federal police, and municipal police forces.

In exchange for handsome fees, these subnational security forces would safeguard the cartel's property rights over drug trafficking routes from encroachment by rival cartels or from sudden attacks from the federal governments. Although PRI governors only ruled for six years and could not be re-elected, there was a continuity of personnel and standard operating procedures in the state attorney general offices and in the state judicial police that were handed from one administration to another, providing stability and a long-term horizon for the cartels.

Enjoying protection from subnational security actors, the cartels in the 1980s operated like family businesses. As illustrated in Figure 3.1, drug lords centralized the cartel's main business and financial decisions into their own hands and would entrust siblings, close family members, and childhood friends and neighbors with logistics operations associated with the transhipment of drugs from South America into Mexico. The logistics of the shipment of drugs into the US were carried out by carefully selected young neighbors or people from the drug lords' home towns known as

---

[5] Anonymous interview with former state government official.

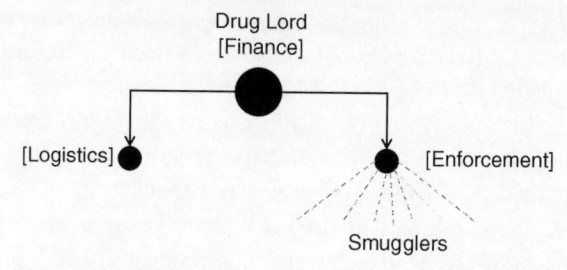

FIGURE 3.1 Organizational Structure of Mexican Cartels under One-Party Rule, 1980s

"burros" (donkeys) or "mulas" (mules) (Grillo 2011). And enforcers would serve simultaneously as bodyguards of the drug lords and as the unit charged with overseeing that the "burros" would not cheat their bosses in the delivery of drugs into the US. Because agents associated with the state judicial police and other subnational units provided informal networks of protection, cartels in the 1980s did not have access to a private professional army. As we will discuss in the next section, the centralized kinship network shown in Figure 3.1 would undergo a dramatic transformation after Mexico began experiencing partisan alternation in the gubernatorial office and incoming governors removed top- and mid-level officials from the state attorney's office and the state judicial police.

THE END OF THE PAX MAFIOSA: PARTY ALTERNATION, THE BREAKDOWN OF PROTECTION, AND THE RISE OF PRIVATE MILITIAS

After six decades of uninterrupted PRI rule in Mexico's 31 states, the country experienced a series of party alternations in gubernatorial power beginning in 1989. Over the course of nearly two decades, between 1989 and 2006, the center-Right PAN won nine governorships (mostly in the early 1990s) and the center-Left PRD won four governorships (in the late 1990s and in the 2000s). In this section we assess the main opposition victories in the six states with major drug trafficking corridors. We proceed in chronological order, starting with the first alternation in Baja California. Our focus is on opposition election campaigns, the first year in office of opposition governors, and the unintended consequences that their cabinet appointments had in redefining the balance of power in the gray zone of criminality and the drug trafficking industry.

Baja California

Ernesto Ruffo, the former PANista mayor of Ensenada who became the first opposition governor to defeat the PRI in 1989, learned about the extent of the collusion between the state judicial police and the federal police with the Tijuana Cartel during his term as municipal president (1986–1989). It was during the PRI administration of Xicoténcatl Leyva (1983–1989) – a governor notorious for widespread corruption, who was removed by the federal government before the end of his term in office – that the Arellano Félix brothers rose to international prominence in the drug trafficking world, with the protection of high-ranking government officials and judicial and police authorities directly under the governor's control (Blancornelas 2002).

Ruffo campaigned under a business-oriented anti-corruption program and promised to clean up the government, but organized crime and drug trafficking were not part of his campaign rhetoric (García and Figueiras 2006). He did not accept any federal or state protection and instead recruited 15 police members from his municipal administration to work with him.

After his victory, the new governor immediately removed the top- and several mid-level officials from the state attorney's office and from the state judicial police – he named a military zone commander as police chief and appointed his 15 loyalists to replace mid-level officials within the attorney general's office to oversee police operations.[6] In hindsight, Governor Ruffo is clear about the consequences of his initial actions: "There was a status quo between corrupt bad elements in the police and the good ones. But when the new opposition government came to power in 1989, the connections between the bad guys and the police began to crumble and violence broke out." The breakdown of protection over drug trafficking corridors under the new opposition government introduced a great degree of uncertainty in the gray zone of criminality, rendering the Tijuana Cartel vulnerable to rival attacks. A few weeks into his government, Ruffo recalls, there were several murders associated with the drug business:

---

[6] Interview with Governor Ruffo, July 2014.

"The Tijuana and the Mexicali drug trafficking corridors were very important to the Arellano Félix brothers [the leaders of the Tijuana Cartel]. After our victory, we saw rival gangs coming into the state, and conflicts over the control of the plazas broke out."

To safeguard their turf against potential government attacks and against rival cartels, the Arellano Félix reacted immediately and recruited defectors from the state judicial police, young males from the Tijuana elite (the so-called "narcojuniors"), and street gangs operating on the US–Mexico border to develop a private militia under the command of Ramón Arellano Félix (Blancornelas 2002: 207–212).[7] This was the first private militia in Mexico's drug wars (Grillo 2011: 79).[8] It enabled the Tijuana Cartel to signal to other cartels that they were not unprotected and were ready to defend their control over the profitable route into California. For the Sinaloa Cartel, which had no direct control over any city along the US–Mexico border, gaining access to such important entry points into the United States as the Tijuana–San Diego border, was a high priority. The Arellano Félix private army not only allowed the Tijuana Cartel to defend itself against the latent threat posed by the Sinaloans but also enabled them to corrupt or kill key members of the new opposition administration and renegotiate the terms of protection. As Ruffo reports, his police chief was corrupted by the Tijuana Cartel and several of his 15 police loyalists were murdered.

After the Tijuana Cartel secured its turf, the Arellano Félix brothers used their private army to venture into territory traditionally under the control of the Juárez and the Sinaloa cartels, triggering the outbreak of Mexico's first major inter-cartel war.[9] They attacked their rivals when they were most vulnerable, following the defeat of the PRI, the rotation of political parties in gubernatorial power, and the breakdown of government protections forged under the PRI in Chihuahua and Jalisco.

---

[7] The "narcojuniors" were children of well-off families involved in drug consumption and illegal activities. They represent an uncommon case. For the most part, the cartels' private armies recruited young men from impoverished urban areas and members of street gangs (mainly operating in underprivileged areas) to serve as foot soldiers.

[8] Note that levels of professionalization of the cartels' private armies varied with time. The first armies (e.g., the Arellano Félix private army, the Tijuana Cartel's private army) were less professional than subsequent ones (e.g., the Zetas, the Gulf's private army). They are nonetheless constituted by former state specialists in violence who train young men under their command as foot soldiers to defend their turf.

[9] Interview with Jalisco's former state attorney Jorge López, Guadalajara, July 2014.

Chihuahua

Francisco Barrio, the former PANista mayor of Ciudad Juárez and a leading voice in Mexico's anti-fraud movement – after he was denied victory in the 1986 gubernatorial campaign in the northern state of Chihuahua through a massive fraud – was elected first opposition governor of his home state in 1992. The election took place against the backdrop of two consecutive PRI administrations marked by widespread corruption (Proceso 1992b and 2004) in which a group of top officials from the state judicial police used their political impunity to repress political dissidents and to develop a dense network of protection for the Guadalajara Cartel and later for the Juárez Cartel (Proceso 2004).

During his election campaign, Barrio did acknowledge the rise of drug trafficking in the state and pledged to cooperate with the federal government in anti-drug activities. But his campaign centered mainly on administrative reforms – to make government bureaucracies less corrupt and more efficient and transparent – and on the adoption of market-oriented reforms – to turn Chihuahua into a focal point of foreign direct investment, particularly in the *maquiladora* sector (Mizrahi 1996).

To address problems of government corruption and inefficiency and rising insecurity in the state, Barrio appointed Francisco Molina – a schoolmate from the MBA program at the Universidad Autónoma de Chihuahua and a PAN loyalist – as state attorney and charged him with overhauling the attorney's office and the entire state judicial police. Barrio did not trust the state police because, as documented by human rights NGOs, they had brutally repressed PANista opposition candidates since the early 1980s, when Barrio became mayor of Juárez (Proceso 2004). Upon assuming office, Molina led a purge of members of the state judicial police with criminal records and announced a major anti-corruption campaign that entailed the creation of a police academy (charged with the recruitment and training of police officers) and the introduction of clear and transparent rules for promotion within the police ranks (Mizrahi 1996). These reforms did not clean up the state judicial police and criminal lords eventually recreated their networks of protection (Proceso 2004). However, the removal of top- and mid-level police personnel who had played a key role in repressing political dissidents and in developing informal networks of protection for drug trafficking operations introduced a great degree of uncertainty in Chihuahua's gray zone of criminality.

The surprising PAN victory in the 1992 gubernatorial election in Chihuahua, and the breakdown of informal government protection networks, motivated Amado Carrillo Fuentes, head of the Juárez Cartel, to appoint his brother Vicente to create a private army to protect the cartel from government raids and from growing threats from the Tijuana Cartel. The Carrillo Fuentes brothers recruited defectors from the federal, state judicial, and municipal police, and members of local and transnational street gangs, to create a powerful private army which would be known as "La Línea." As José Luis Santiago Vasconcelos, a veteran police officer in Mexico's anti-crime special units, confided to journalists Alfredo Corchado and Ricardo Sandoval, La Línea was the rogue enforcement branch of the Juárez Cartel, mainly led by defectors from the state judicial police, particularly those operating in Ciudad Juárez (Corchado and Sandoval 2004). La Línea was a more sophisticated, better equipped and trained, and more lethal militia than the Arellano Félix private army.

Initially allied with the Sinaloa Cartel, the Juárez Cartel fought a full-scale turf war against the Tijuana Cartel for over a decade. Not only did inter-cartel murders increase dramatically after 1992, but a brutal history of hundreds of femicides began in 1993 in Ciudad Juárez.[10] Having a private army enabled the Juárez Cartel to deter the expansionist ambitions of rival cartels and also empowered them to try to expand their domain into rival territory, including Sonora (to contest the Tijuana's peripheral territory), Jalisco (to contest one of two homes of the Sinaloa Cartel), and Quintana Roo in the Caribbean (to contest the Gulf's southern tail of their drug corridors). It also enabled them to explore new territory (Morelos in Central Mexico).

Jalisco

Alberto Cárdenas, the former PANista mayor of Ciudad Guzmán in the western state of Jalisco, became the first opposition governor of his home state in 1995. The election took place after a decade of mounting evidence of government corruption and the expansion of drug cartels in the state. PRI Governor Guillermo Cosío Vidaurri (1989–1992) had presented his resignation in the midst of major corruption scandals and after mishandling

---

[10] We do not delve into the tragic development of femicides in Mexico. For in-depth studies of this form of victimization, see Monarrez (2000, 2013).

a situation that resulted in a series of major gas explosions in Guadalajara which killed hundreds of residents in the state's capital in 1992 (Proceso 1992a, 1994). In the 1980s Guadalajara had become the place of residence of the Guadalajara Cartel and subsequently of the Sinaloa Cartel (Astorga 2005). Under two consecutive PRI administrations, the narcos lived peacefully and enjoyed state protection while the drug lords became intimately involved with the local political elite, as became evident with the love affair between the head of the Guadalajara Cartel and Governor Cosío Vidaurri's niece (García 2013). In the early 1990s, however, Guadalajara experienced a glimpse of inter-cartel violence between the Arellano Félix Brothers and the Sinaloa Cartel. In one of these recurring battles Guadalajara's Cardinal Juan Jesús Posadas Ocampo was killed in crossfire between the cartels' hit men (Golden 1993).

Despite this context of corruption and increasing cartel presence in Jalisco, Cárdenas's campaign did not address drug trafficking issues (Arellano 2011: 147) and instead ran a pro-business and anti-corruption campaign. Rather than focus on state–cartel collusion, the protection that petty crime received from the Guadalajara police and the widespread use of torture by members of the state judicial police were key campaign issues.[11]

To address these problems of corruption and police repression, once in government Cárdenas appointed a prominent lawyer and civilian leader, Jorge López, as his new attorney general and placed the judicial police under the command of a military zone commander, Cap. Montenegro. As López reports, at the outset of the new administration they changed every top- and mid-level official in the attorney's office and introduced a new agenda of human rights to train police officers.[12]

In hindsight, Governor Cárdenas reflects on the consequences of his team's initial actions: "If you change the rules of the game and remove some of the key pieces from the chess board, you are going to face a major counterattack." López recalls the outbreak of major inter-cartel wars: "Cartels fiercely fought to control Jalisco. The Sinaloa Cartel initially dominated this plaza. But they were first challenged by the Tijuana Cartel. Things got worse when the Juárez Cartel [from the northern state of Chihuahua] entered the dispute." Amado Carrillo, leader of the Juárez Cartel, and his private militia, La Línea, were able to corrupt Cap. Montenegro, and they became a major threat to the Sinaloans. López

[11] Interview with Governor Cárdenas, Guadalajara, July 2014.
[12] Interview with Jorge López, Guadalajara, July 2014.

eloquently recollects: "It was the outbreak of war – the dance of the machine guns!"

After the rotation of parties in Jalisco and other key states of the Sinaloa Empire – including Nayarit, Michoacán, and Guerrero – the leaders of the Sinaloa Cartel developed two private militias: one led by the Beltrán Leyva brothers to defend their turf in Sinaloa, Nayarit, and Guerrero, and a second led by Ignacio Coronel and his brothers to defend Jalisco and Michoacán (Grillo 2011). The Beltrán Leyvas and the Coronels recruited defectors from federal and state judicial police forces to operate as hit men in their new powerful armies. After Cap. Montenegro was removed from office and eventually imprisoned for providing protection to the Juárez Cartel, the Sinaloans secured their turf and used their private armies to venture into the northeast to contest the Gulf Cartel's turf in Nuevo León and Tamaulipas. As the lead private army charged with the conquest of the Gulf Cartel's empire, the Beltrán Leyva organization became particularly lethal through the recruitment of powerful gangs operating on the US–Mexico border, including Edgar Valdez ("La Barbie"), the leader of the enforcement squad, Los Negros.

Nuevo León

Fernando Canales Clariond, a member of a prominent business family from the northern state of Nuevo León, became the first opposition governor of his home state in 1997. He was elected on a PAN ticket. Canales had unsuccessfully made a first attempt in 1985 but was defeated by the PRI candidate in an election marred by fraud (Medellín 2006). Canales's campaign was launched shortly after the PRI governor, Sócrates Rizzo, had been de facto removed from office before the end of his constitutional term by President Zedillo. This occurred in the midst of major accusations of corruption, and after the brutal assassination of a local attorney who had accused Governor Rizzo, his attorney and top security officials of protecting the Gulf Cartel (Carrizales 1996).

Canales campaigned under a pro-business and anti-corruption program, promising to handle the state's mounting public debt and start a new era of honesty. As Cobis Lobo, the opposition campaign's spokeswoman, put it: The new government will "help the electorate forget about [Governor] Rizzo – as if the state had never experienced an era of unprecedented corruption" (Proceso 1997, n.p.).

After assuming office at the end of 1997, Canales appointed prominent members of the business community as key cabinet members and named José S. González Suárez, one of the state's most prominent tax lawyers, as state attorney (*El Norte* 1997a, 1997b). Surprisingly, the new governor, named Américo Meléndez, a longtime member of the federal attorney general's office, to head the state judicial police. Meléndez had participated as a young lawyer in the deposition of alleged guerrilla members during the Dirty War in the 1970s and had reportedly relied on torture to get testimonies (Plascencia 2013). Although González Suárez and Meléndez did not launch any immediate major reforms in the state's judicial and police institutions, their appointment displaced veterans who had served in the last three PRI administrations in top-level positions in the attorney's office and in the state judicial police, and they had long been suspected of providing protection to the Gulf Cartel (Proceso 2006).

The 1997 PRI gubernatorial defeat in Nuevo León was a major shock to the criminal underworld, because the Gulf Cartel leaders had traditionally had their residence in Monterrey, the state's capital (Ramírez 2002). Having no immediate protection was a major threat, not only because their families lived there but also because Monterrey was the front door to the Gulf's headquarters in the neighboring state of Tamaulipas. The breakdown of protection came at a difficult time because the Gulf's leader, Juan García Abregó, had been arrested in 1996 and the cartel was undergoing a succession struggle (Grillo 2011).

In 1998 Osiel Cárdenas, one of several leaders vying to become the Gulf Cartel's new boss, took the bold step of recruiting defectors from Mexican elite military forces – the Special Forces Airmobile Group, or GAFES – to serve as members of the Gulf's private army. This step would facilitate his rise to power within the cartel's ranks and enable it to confront the multiple sources of external threat that followed Nuevo León's party alternation in the fall of 1997. This group of specialists in violence, the Zetas, recruited hundreds of elite military members, police defectors, and *Kaibiles* (former Guatemalan Army Special Forces soldiers, the deadliest forces in Guatemala's civil war) to rapidly become the most lethal private army in Mexico and helped Cárdenas consolidate his grip as the Gulf's new drug lord (Grillo 2011). The configuration of the Zetas clearly reflected the arms race in which cartels had engaged in response to the initial creation of private armies in the early 1990s. Each new private militia was more sophisticated in terms of its recruitment and membership, as well as in its firepower and lethality.

The Zetas played a key role in defending the Gulf Cartel's drug trafficking routes from 1997 onwards. The Juárez and Sinaloa cartels had already made important inroads into Monterrey and its surrounding areas, and by 2001 the Sinaloans launched a major assault over Tamaulipas. The move was led by the Beltrán Leyva brothers, who recruited members of lethal street gangs operating along the US–Texas border to serve as foot soldiers in their conquest attempt. The Sinaloans and the Gulf Cartel and their private militias engaged in bloody battles over the control of northern Tamaulipas from 2001 to 2006. These were wars between professional armies fighting for territorial control using sophisticated guerrilla warfare techniques and the type of artillery used in civil wars (Grillo 2011). In the midst of this major conflict for the control of the northeast of Mexico, and in an attempt to weaken their enemy in their own home, the Gulf Cartel took advantage of party alternation in several states in the Sinaloa Empire and sent Zeta troops to the western state of Michoacán and the southern state of Guerrero to conquer rival territory. This would be the beginning of one of the most brutal and protracted wars in Mexico's contemporary history.

Michoacán

Lázaro Cárdenas Batel, grandson of Mexico's revered President Lázaro Cárdenas (1934–1940) and son of Cuauhtémoc Cárdenas, three-time presidential candidate (1988, 1994, and 2000) and founder of the leftist PRD, became the first opposition governor of Michoacán in 1992. He was elected on a PRD ticket. Cárdenas Batel's election came after a decade of bitter political rivalries between the PRI and the PRD in which hundreds of leftist party activists had been assassinated (Schatz 2011). Members of the state judicial police in the 1990s, who had been actively involved in repressing political dissent, also played a key role in developing the informal networks of protection that enabled the Valencia Brothers Cartel, the local allies of the Sinaloa Cartel, to become the state's dominant player in the drug trafficking industry (Maldonado 2012).

Although Cárdenas Batel reports that he was aware of marijuana production and drug trafficking in the state, and of occasional narco shootouts, these were not prominent issues during his 2001 election campaign.[13] He was more concerned about the economy, immigration,

---

[13] Crónica's (2002) report of Cárdenas Batel's inaugural address confirms this point.

establishing a good relationship with the powerful teachers' union, and overcoming a repressive past.[14] That is why he appointed new personnel with "social sensitivity" to security and police positions. Out of concern for human rights, rather than security and drug trafficking, Cárdenas Batel removed all top- and mid-level officials from the state attorney's office and the secretary of public security – everyone from "secretaries, undersecretaries, and police regional commanders" who had been implicated in repressing leftist dissidents throughout the 1990s.

The sudden outbreak of narco violence in 2002 was "a shocking surprise" to Governor Cárdenas Batel. He bitterly recalls: "I had been in office for two days when one of the Valencia brothers was brutally murdered." It was the beginning of a protracted conflict for the state's drug trafficking corridors. After the 2002 political alternation the Zetas, the powerful private militia of the Gulf Cartel, made a rapid and surprising entry into Michoacán. In collaboration with La Familia Michoacana, a self-defense group that protected citizens against the Sinaloa Cartel and its local allies, the Zetas removed the Valencias and the Sinaloans from Michoacán (Maldonado 2012). They sought to reconstitute protection networks by bribing mid-level officials and assassinating some of Cárdenas Batel's closest collaborators. By 2005, however, the alliance between La Familia and the Zetas broke down over differences in the allocation of drug trafficking routes, and the state plunged into a major new conflict (Grillo 2011). However, the Zetas' objective was not only to gain control over Michoacán's drug trafficking routes but also to take control over the routes in the neighboring state of Guerrero, at the southern tip of the Sinaloa drug empire.

Guerrero

Zeferino Torreblanca, a businessman who became the first opposition mayor of the tourist resort of Acapulco in the southern state of Guerrero, was elected the state's first opposition governor under a leftist PRD ticket in 2005. In the 1990s and early 2000s, Guerrero experienced a period of brutal repression against social movement leaders and leftist opposition leaders and party activists, including the infamous massacre of Aguas Blancas in 1995 (in which Governor Rubén Figueroa Alcocer ordered members of the state judicial police to violently crack down on a major rural mobilization, which resulted in the murder of 17 Indian peasants).

---

[14] Interview with Governor Cárdenas Batel, Washington, DC, September 2014.

Although the governor resigned, the interim governor and his successor continued with Figueroa's iron-fist policies, de facto providing police forces with political impunity.[15] It was in these years that members of the state judicial police developed a dense network of protection that facilitated prominent members of the Sinaloa Cartel to take direct control of drug operations in the state – the Beltrán Leyva brothers in Acapulco and "El Mayo" Zambada in the western coast of the state (Flores 2018).[16]

Zeferino Torreblanca ran a pro-business and anti-corruption campaign. Like most opposition candidates in the 1990s and 2000s he developed a government program marked by good governance, honesty and transparency. Although he did not directly address questions of drug trafficking, he did acknowledge mounting security issues and homicides in the state and promised to reform the state judicial institutions and the police.

After assuming office, Governor Torreblanca introduced important changes in Guerrero's police structure. As he explained to us: "When I took office I appointed an army commander from one of the state's military regions as secretary of public security. I asked him to appoint his own team and said that he would be accountable to me. He changed the entire preventive police; we developed a new police from scratch."[17] But, he confides, "changes in the attorney's office were a little slower. I reduced the size and the budget of the state judicial police but I could not fire them all ... we only changed some of the old timers and the special commissioners. It was in the state judicial police that officers were colluding with organized crime ... it was the old elements of the state judicial police."[18] Torreblanca was aware of the immediate impact of his actions: "I came into office with no previous commitments with anyone. As soon as we began our

---

[15] A path-breaking investigation from the Mexican Supreme Court found Governor Figueroa (1993–1996) directly responsible for the massacre, but he was never brought to justice. Instead, a few low-ranking police officials were prosecuted, but most cases ended up in acquittals or short sentences of no more than two years (Gutiérrez 1997).

[16] Governor Rubén Figueroa Alcocer is the son of former Governor Rubén Figueroa who presided over the Dirty War in Guerrero in the 1970s and whose close military allies, including Generals Acosta Chaparro and Hermosillo, led the counterinsurgency operations in Guerrero and were deeply involved in the drug trafficking industry from the 1970s until the 2000s. See Aviña (2018).

[17] Interview with Governor Torreblanca, Mexico City, August 2014.

[18] Note that since the 2000s, most states had two state-level police forces: the judicial police (under the command of the state attorney) and the security police (under the command of the secretary of public security).

changes, criminal groups began losing protection ... there was fragmentation ... and they started killing police officers."

The election victory of the leftist PRD, the governor's appointment of
new personnel in the state security apparatus, and the subsequent weak-
ening of traditional networks of protection for the Sinaloa Cartel in
Guerrero did not go unnoticed by the Sinaloans' enemies. The Gulf
Cartel, which was immersed in a major battle against the Sinaloa Cartel
over the control of drug trafficking routes in Tamaulipas and Michoacán,
seized this opportunity and sent Zeta troops to the tourist port of
Acapulco to try to conquer the southern tip of the Sinaloa drug empire.
By then, this area was under the control of the Sinaloans' most powerful
private militia – the Beltrán Leyva brothers. Over the course of 2005 and
2006 the Zetas and the Beltrán Leyva brothers turned Acapulco into a
bloody battleground in which combat resembled the fighting context of a
deadly civil war.

THE OUTBREAK OF MULTIPLE INTER-CARTEL WARS

The spread of subnational political alternation and the breakdown of
informal government protection networks for drug cartels led to the
proliferation of private militias throughout Mexico. As the narratives of
Baja California, Chihuahua, Jalisco, Nuevo León, Michoacán, and
Guerrero reveal, the cartels used these militias not only to defend their
turf but also to seek to conquer enemy territory. This sequence of events,
following party alternation in the gubernatorial seat, took place in other
states with less prominent drug presence, particularly the states of
Morelos (center) and Zacatecas (north-center).

Figure 3.2 shows the timeline of rotation in state gubernatorial power
in Mexico and the rise of private militias from 1989 to 2006. It identifies
with a downward arrow the timing of alternation in gubernatorial power
in states with drug trafficking routes and with an upward arrow the timing
of the rise of the cartels' private militias. The figure underscores the close
association between the actual timing of political changes and changes in
the balance of power in the gray zone of criminality leading to the rise of
private militias. It highlights the fact that private militias emerged shortly
after party alternation, not before.

Maps 3.1.a–3.3.c identify the dyads of violent conflict that broke out
throughout the 1990s and 2000s, following the spread of party alternation in gubernatorial power and the rise of private militias. For the most
part, cartels were contesting control over their rivals' headquarters or

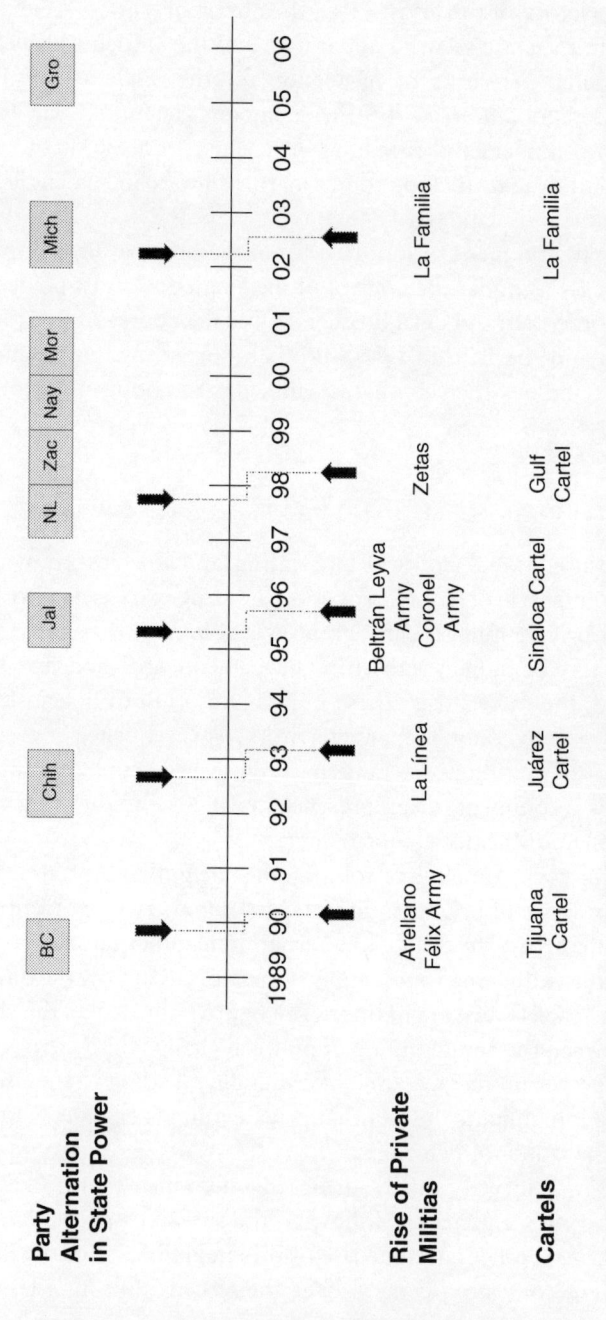

FIGURE 3.2 Timeline of Party Alternation in State Power and the Rise of Private Militias in Mexico, 1989–2006

Note: Downward arrows indicate dates of opposition governments taking office. Upward arrows indicate approximate dates of the rise of private militias. BC = Baja California, Chih = Chihuahua, Jal = Jalisco, NL = Nuevo León, Zac = Zacatecas, Nay = Nayarit, Mor = Morelos, Mich = Michoacán, Gro = Guerrero.

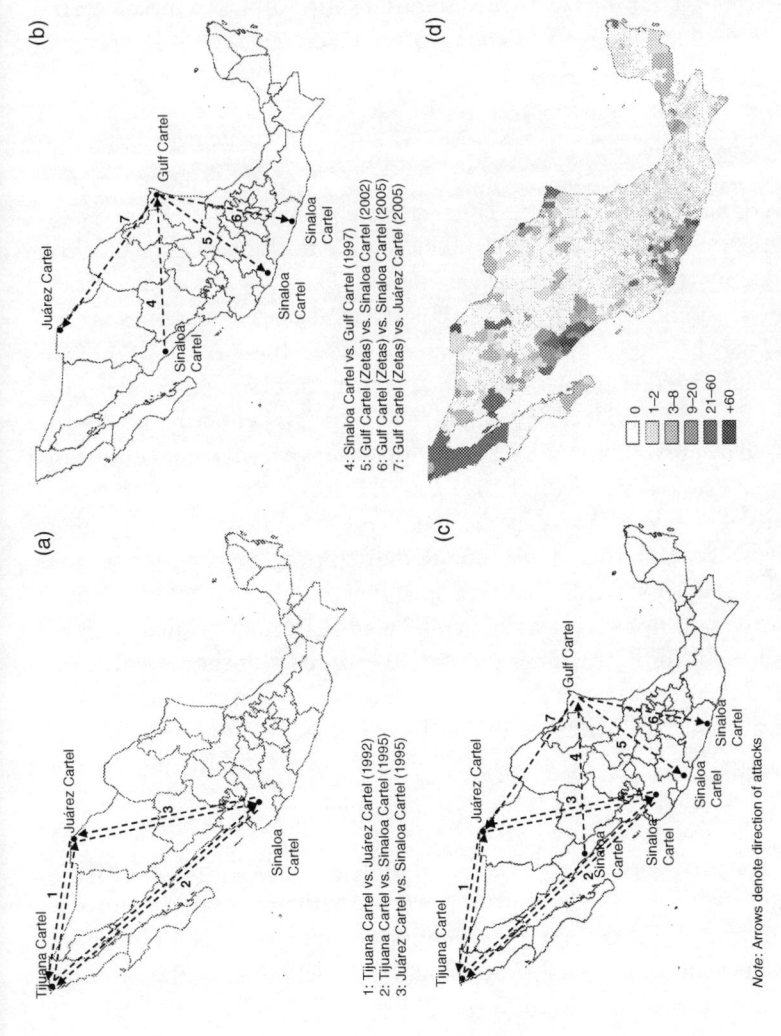

(a)

Tijuana Cartel

Juárez Cartel

1

3

2

Sinaloa
Cartel

1: Tijuana Cartel vs. Juárez Cartel (1992)
2: Tijuana Cartel vs. Sinaloa Cartel (1995)
3: Juárez Cartel vs. Sinaloa Cartel (1995)

(b)

Juárez Cartel

Gulf Cartel

7

5

4

6

Sinaloa
Cartel

Sinaloa
Cartel

Sinaloa
Cartel

4: Sinaloa Cartel vs. Gulf Cartel (1997)
5: Gulf Cartel (Zetas) vs. Sinaloa Cartel (2002)
6: Gulf Cartel (Zetas) vs. Sinaloa Cartel (2005)
7: Gulf Cartel (Zetas) vs. Juárez Cartel (2005)

(c)

Tijuana Cartel

Juárez Cartel

Gulf Cartel

7

1

3

4

5

2

6

Sinaloa
Cartel

Sinaloa
Cartel

Sinaloa
Cartel

Note: Arrows denote direction of attacks

(d)

0
1–2
3–8
9–20
21–60
+60

MAP 3.1.a Dyads of Inter-Cartel Conflict in Mexico, 1990–1996
MAP 3.1.b Dyads of Inter-Cartel Conflict in Mexico, 1997–2006
MAP 3.1.c Dyads of Inter-Cartel Conflict in Mexico, 1990–2006
MAP 3.1.d Inter-Cartel murders, 1995–2006

places of residence. Sometimes these were the same (as for the Tijuana and Juárez Cartels) but in other cartels they were different (the Sinaloa Cartel had its headquarters in Culiacán, Sinaloa, but its place of residence in Guadalajara, Jalisco; the Gulf Cartel had its headquarters in Tamaulipas but its place of residence in Monterrey, Nuevo León). Perhaps the only major exception to this rule is when the Gulf Cartel attacked the southern tip of the Sinaloa Empire in Michoacán and Guerrero.

Map 3.I.a identifies a triangle of dyadic conflicts that first emerged in northwestern Mexico after the wave of party alternation in state gubernatorial office that brought the PAN to power in several states in the region in the early 1990s. This is Mexico's "wild west." The first major violent conflict began when the Tijuana Cartel used their private army to contest the Juárez Cartel's turf in Chihuahua and the Juárez Cartel quickly responded by creating its own private militia. The conflict involved cities in Baja California (Tijuana), Chihuahua (Ciudad Juárez) and the state of Sonora, which is geographically located between these two states. The second major conflict erupted when the Tijuana Cartel sought to challenge the Sinaloans in their place of residence in Guadalajara and the Sinaloans responded by moving the conflict into Tijuana. The third major conflict in this region erupted when the Juárez Cartel also sought to challenge the Sinaloans in Guadalajara and the Sinaloans retaliated by challenging the Juárez's headquarters. Even though the actors have changed over the years, this conflict structure has remained remarkably resilient over time. Major urban centers such as Tijuana, Ciudad Juárez, and Culiacán have been dubbed at different times the "murder capitals of the world," and semi-urban and rural cities that connect these cities through corridors of drug cultivation, trafficking, and war have become killing fields. This is particularly the case for the Golden Triangle, an area that connects the mountainous terrains of the states of Chihuahua, Durango, and Sinaloa.[19]

Map 3.I.b highlights the second structure of dyadic conflicts that took place between the Sinaloa Cartel and the Gulf Cartel, following party alternations in gubernatorial power in the late 1990s and the early 2000s. By the time these conflicts emerged, some of these militias had become quasi-professional and lethal irregular armies, particularly those linked to the Sinaloa Cartel. The fourth major conflict broke out in the northeast, when the Sinaloa Cartel decided

[19] As Cedillo's (2019) work shows, the Golden Triangle was a major site of the Dirty War (the government's anti-insurgency campaign against rural and urban guerrillas) and of the Plan Cóndor (the government's anti-drug war) in the 1970s.

to use its private militias to attack Monterrey – the place of residence of the Gulf families – and use it as a springboard to launch a major assault on the Tamaulipas–US border, where the Gulf Cartel had its headquarters. The conflict between the Sinaloans, the Gulf, and the Zetas reached unprecedented levels of violence.

But the nature of this conflict became particularly complex when the Gulf deployed Zeta units to attack the southern tip of Sinaloa's Empire in Michoacán (the fifth conflict) and Guerrero (the sixth conflict) on the Pacific coast. Given the Zetas' military training in anti-insurgency operations and the access that both cartels had to high-caliber weapons – following the 2004 expiration of the US ten-year ban on assault weapons that President Clinton had imposed in 1994 – the intensity of these inter-cartel wars began to more closely resemble deadly civil wars. As most security analysts have acknowledged, the entry of the Zetas into these war dyads increased both the professionalization and lethality of these conflicts (Osorno 2012; Valdés 2013; Correa-Cabrera 2017). The transformation of inter-cartel conflict – from three (Map 3.I.a) to multiple territorial disputes (Map 3.I.b) – contributed to the rapid escalation of violence, moving the death toll from low levels of intensity to large-scale violence. By 2006, with 1,281 casualties, the death toll of these conflicts had already surpassed the 1,000 annual battle deaths that is customarily used as a threshold to define a conflict as a civil war. The structure of conflicts in Mexico's northeast and the Pacific coast has also remained remarkably constant. Over the next decade, cities that were sites of these bloody turf wars – Reynosa and Matamoros in Tamaulipas, Apatzingán in Michoacán, and Acapulco in Guerrero – would also join the ranks of "murder capitals of the world" like those in Mexico's "wild west."

Map 3.I.b also identifies the seventh major conflict that broke out when the Gulf Cartel and the Zetas ventured into the territorial domain of the Juárez Cartel. The Juárez Cartel, which by then enjoyed protection from the highest echelons of the military and the federal government, had become the world's number one smuggler of cocaine into the US in the late 1990s. However, the death of Amado Carrillo, Juárez's main kingpin, and the arrest of General Jesús Gutiérrez Rebollo, Mexico's anti-drug czar who was on Carrillo's payroll, opened opportunities for multiple challenges by rival cartels. In confronting these challenges, the Amado Carrillo family and their private army, La Línea, made extraordinary efforts to recruit a number of street gangs operating on both sides of the US–Mexico border. These new foot soldiers would be at the forefront of major deadly battles against the Zetas in years to come.

Map 3.I.c summarizes the multiple conflicts that erupted in Mexico between 1990 and 2006. The map shows that by 2006, the country experienced three major inter-cartel conflicts in three distinct geographic regions: northwest, northeast, and the Pacific coast. Map 3.I.d shows the cumulative death toll of these inter-cartel wars. A visual comparison of Maps 3.I.c and 3.I.d reveals a close correspondence between the multiple dyads of conflict and the level of intensity of inter-cartel murders. As Map 3.I.d shows, these were not conflicts that only affected municipalities and states along the US–Mexico border but were also prevalent in other Mexican regions. Moreover, the potential for spillover effects into other states was evident if we look closely at the states that the cartels had to cross on their way to attack their rivals – some of which had no drug cultivation tradition or had not been major drug trafficking corridors. Consider the case of the Zetas. On their way from Tamaulipas to Michoacán, Zeta troops had to cross Zacatecas and Guanajuato in central Mexico. Although these states had no histories of drug cultivation, nor had they been crucial corridors of drug smuggling, they quickly became valuable territories for the Zetas.[20] Similarly, the northern state of Coahuila, which stands between Chihuahua and Nuevo León along the US–Mexico border, became a crucial site for the Zetas. Over the course of the next decade, these states would slowly become sites where some of the deadliest conflicts and gross human rights violations would take place.[21]

THE NEW INDUSTRIAL ORGANIZATION OF CARTELS: DRUG LORDS, PRIVATE MILITIAS, AND STREET GANGS

War changed Mexican cartels in fundamental ways. As we explained at the beginning of this chapter, during the era of one-party rule – when

---

[20] Breakaway groups from the Zetas eventually became leading figures in the clandestine illegal tapping of the oil pipes of Mexico's state-owned petroleum company, PEMEX, in Guanajuato in the 2010s.

[21] Zeta units also became actively involved in the clandestine tapping of oil pipes and the extraction of other natural resources in these northeastern states (see Correa-Cabrera 2017). The Zetas would also gain de facto control over the prison system in Coahuila, where they committed some of the most severe mass atrocities in Mexico's drug wars. See Aguayo et al. (2016).

subnational police and judicial authorities provided protection for the drug trafficking business – cartels were organized as family businesses in which the drug lords and their closest family members centralized the businesses' key financial and logistical tasks. Drug lords were comfortable dealing with corrupt government authorities – paying fees in exchange for protection or simply bribing new authorities to defend their territory. The stability of one-party rule provided them with a long-term horizon to invest in the business without becoming specialists in violence. However, when the breakdown of one-party rule made state protection uncertain, their decision to delegate their security to private militias would transform Mexico's criminal landscape forever.

Privatizing coercion is never an easy decision, because the development of a militia generates major agency challenges. The leaders of these private armies and their foot soldiers would need to become powerful forces to defend the cartels against potential attacks from the government and from rival cartels, but if these new military leaders become too strong and independent they could eventually turn against their own bosses.[22] In the immediate aftermath of party alternation in state gubernatorial power, when governors were appointing new personnel in the state judicial and police institutions, and thus inadvertently undermining traditional networks of protection of cartels, drug lords had a choice: create a private army that could eventually turn against them or risk immediate annihilation.

Figure 3.3 provides an illustration of the multilayered organizations that cartels became after they took the historic decision to delegate their security to private militias. As the figure shows, the militias were vertically integrated into the cartels. Army chiefs, under the direct control of the cartel leaders, were charged with creating these armies from scratch and leading war operations. Because drug lords were perfectly aware of the major agency challenges involved in the development of an armed branch within their organizations, they typically entrusted the privatization of their security to their siblings (as in the Tijuana and the Juárez cartels) or to their lifelong neighbors and friends (as in the Sinaloa Cartel). It was only in the case of the Gulf Cartel – the last cartel to develop a private army after nearly a decade of inter-cartel wars – that a cartel's leadership delegated security functions to professionals in violence (defectors from elite military forces).

---

[22] This is a parallel problem to the one faced by autocrats who rely on state specialists in violence to stay in power. See Chapter 1.

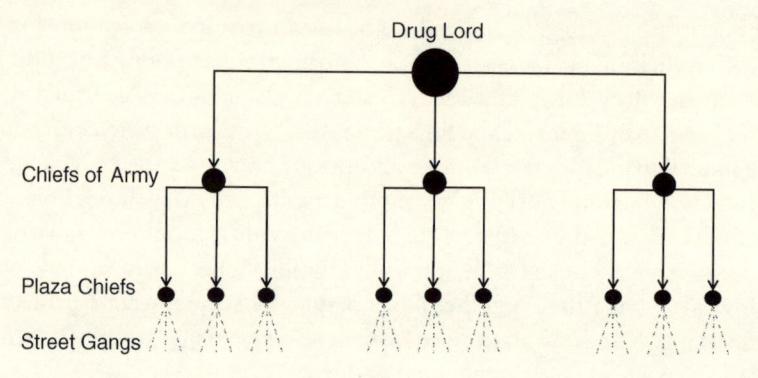

FIGURE 3.3 Organizational Structure of Mexican Cartels after Subnational Party Alternation, 1990s and 2000s

As Figure 3.3 shows, army chiefs were directly responsible for recruiting regional army bosses and foot soldiers to fight turf wars. For the most part, army chiefs recruited defectors from state judicial police forces and police forces from major metropolitan areas to serve as plaza chiefs. Mirroring the territorial organization of Mexico's police forces (Davis 2006; Grillo 2011; Sabet 2012), the private militias granted these plaza chiefs a great degree of power. Not only would they be responsible for developing new networks of protection with incoming opposition authorities, but they also became responsible for securing the safe transit of illicit drugs through their territory. When conflict broke out, they were responsible for the military defense of their turf. As inter-cartel wars became more intense, cartels increasingly sought to recruit more specialized and more lethal state specialists in violence – as the emblematic case of the Zetas, the defectors from the elite forces of the Mexican army, shows.

Plaza chiefs also played the crucial role of recruiting and training foot soldiers for war, mostly young males from impoverished urban areas and members of street gangs operating in the urban margins and shanty towns. As our statistical findings reported in Chapter 2 suggest, these were young males from mono-parental families. Extensive research on youth gangs shows that these young men, often victims themselves of intra-household violence, find bonds of belonging and solidarity in the street gangs (Brenneman 2013; Wolf 2018). Note, however, that gangs should not necessarily be equated with organized crime. It is only when gangs and their members are vertically integrated as hit men into drug cartels and other criminal organizations that they become prominent members of the criminal underworld. While young men living in violent and impoverished environments are likely to voluntarily find refuge in gangs that are eventually integrated into the criminal underworld, there is evidence that many young men are actually abducted and coerced into becoming hit men – particularly after 2006 (Torres 2019).

Although there were differences in the internal organization of cartels – for example, the Juárez and the Tijuana cartels were led by single individuals and their families, but Sinaloa had three visible leaders who coexisted in a type of federal arrangement (Grillo 2011) – all drug lords developed private militias to defend their turf.[23] And these private militias were organized into a layered structure, such as that exemplified in Figure 3.3. By 2006, after more than a decade of inter-cartel wars, Mexico's criminal landscape had five major drug cartels – Tijuana, Juárez, Sinaloa, Gulf, and La Familia Michoacana – but each one of them had at least one private army at their service, composed of multiple layers of specialists in violence. Ignoring the role of these private militias and their complex structure, as Mexican President Felipe Calderón did when he launched a major War on Drugs against the cartels in December 2016, would lead to major policy blunders and to deadly consequences.

CONCLUSION

We have suggested that Mexican cartels went to war in the 1990s because they lost access to the informal state protection they had enjoyed under one-party rule. The evidence from the six case studies confirms that in the late 1980s and throughout the 1990s, high-ranking officials in the states' judicial police forces played a key role in repressing political dissidents and providing informal protection for the drug trafficking industry. The evidence from the election campaigns of the six successful opposition candidates shows that drug trafficking was not a major policy concern for any of them and that once they came to office, they systematically removed top- and mid-level officials in their state's attorney's office and the judicial police. This was not because they knew they were colluding

---

[23] Cartels can adopt centralized and hierarchical structures (e.g., Tijuana and Juárez), or a federalist and decentralized system with multiple leaders (e.g., Sinaloa), or a franchise system (e.g., the Zetas after they broke out from the Gulf Cartel). For a discussion of different network structures of criminal organizations, see Garzón (2012). For the Zetas, see Correa-Cabrera (2017).

with the narcos, but because they had been at the forefront of repressing opposition activists. To be sure, opposition governors did not necessarily democratize their police forces and their judicial systems; they simply appointed their loyalists to the new positions. Our case studies show that after opposition governors unwittingly dismantled the complex networks of protection that facilitated the drug trafficking industry, drug lords did not hesitate to cope with the uncertainty generated by the breakdown of protection by creating their own private armies. Because cartels cannot go one day without protection, as the narratives show, these armies emerged within the first few weeks of the new opposition administrations. Access to their own private militias empowered cartels to renegotiate informal protection with opposition authorities and allowed them to conquer rival territories in other states where the breakdown of PRI hegemony made home cartels vulnerable.

The concatenation of mechanisms that led to the breakdown of protection and to the rise of private militias and war has important implications for the development of a new explanation of the outbreak of inter-cartel wars in Mexico and for a new understanding of the mechanics of criminal wars more generally.

First, most accounts view large-scale criminal violence either as a response to state attacks against organized criminal groups or as a result of market competition among criminals. In this chapter, however, we have suggested that by simply removing top- and mid-level officials who had traditionally provided protection for Mexican cartels, incoming opposition governors unintentionally created turbulence in the criminal underworld. This provided incentives for drug lords to preventively equip themselves with the organizational means to fight deadly turf wars. The proliferation of these processes in drug trafficking areas opened opportunities for cartels equipped for war to seek to conquer new territories, thus impelling home cartels to get armed to defend their turf. In this story, it was not that incoming democratically elected authorities caused a backlash by implementing policy actions to suppress the drug trafficking industry. Rather, it was the simple removal of state judicial and police authorities who had protected the criminal underworld that caused a major change in the balance of power in the gray zone of criminality, leading to war. This intimate association between changes in political and criminal power is more likely in countries that transition to democracy without developing a democratic rule of law.

Second, whereas dominant explanations of drug violence in Mexico take the existence of private militias for granted and assume that cartels were de facto equipped to fight turf wars, in this chapter we have assessed the incentives that led cartels to create their own private militias, the different groups that constitute these militias, their place within the organizational hierarchies of cartels, and the role they played to help cartels safeguard their turf and conquer new territories. Subsuming private militias under the broad conception of a cartel – as most analyses of drug violence in Mexico implicitly do – is historically inaccurate. Under one-party rule in the 1980s, Mexican drug lords only had their bodyguards to protect themselves and their families, and they subcontracted authoritarian state specialists in violence to safeguard their businesses. It was only after the onset of subnational party alternation in gubernatorial power that cartels created their own militias and de facto privatized security in the criminal underworld. The failure to identify, conceptualize, and assess the crucial role that private militias have played in Mexico's turf wars distorts the account of the outbreak and early development of criminal wars (1990–2006).

Students of civil war have recognized the importance of pro-government militias (paramilitary forces) in the production of violence, in the duration and termination of conflict, and in the transformation of local orders in civil war (Carey, Colaresi, and Mitchell 2015; Jentzsch, Kalyvas, and Schubiger 2015). While we should be mindful of the differences between paramilitaries and the cartels' private militias – the former are sponsored by the state and/or civilians to fight rebels whereas the latter are created by drug lords to fight the state and rival cartels – students of organized crime should follow the civil war literature in recognizing private militias as crucial players in Latin America's criminal wars, from Mexico to Guatemala to Brazil. Contrary to scholarly predictions that OCGs and mafias would only operate in their places of residence (Gambetta 1996), the rise of private militias has provided criminal groups with greater mobility and unprecedented fighting power to engage in large-scale violence and to seek to control criminal markets and territories beyond their home towns.

Against the backdrop of nearly two decades of inter-cartel wars, in the next part of the book we will devote two chapters to assessing why the launch of the War on Drugs after the 2006 presidential election resulted in a major escalation of violence. Detailed explanation of the actors, political institutions, and motivations that led to the outbreak and escalation of inter-cartel wars between 1990 and

2006 is crucial to understanding why the deployment of the Mexican armed forces to fight cartels in the six conflict zones between 2007 and 2012 resulted in a dramatic escalation of violence from an annual battle death of 1,281 murders per year to up to tens of thousands of casualties per year.

PART III

THE STATE'S WAR AGAINST THE CARTELS

4

Why the State's War against the Cartels Intensified Violence

Political Polarization, Intergovernmental Partisan Conflict, and the Escalation of Violence

After nearly two decades of inter-cartel wars in which the Mexican federal government failed to adopt any proactive policy strategy to confront growing drug violence, incoming President Felipe Calderón (2006–2012) declared war on the cartels and deployed the military to the country's most conflictive regions in December 2006. The federal intervention triggered a major criminal backlash against the state and stimulated the explosion of inter-cartel wars. The outbreak of state–cartel conflicts and the escalation of inter-cartel wars led Mexico into a period of unprecedented violence.[1] The year prior to the federal intervention the death toll of inter-cartel wars had reached nearly 1,300 annual battle deaths, but five years after the intervention the count of murders associated with inter-cartel and state–cartel wars had increased by a factor of five. Even though Mexico was not experiencing a civil war, the death toll of drug-related violence between 2006 and 2012 was four times greater than the death toll of the typical civil war of the twentieth century.[2]

President Calderón declared a War on Drugs after Mexico's most competitive presidential election and in the context of acute political polarization between Right and Left. The presidential candidate of the conservative National Action Party (PAN), Calderón had won by a razor-thin 0.6 percent margin over the leftist candidate of the Party of the

---

[1] For the important distinction between cartel–cartel and state–cartel conflicts, see Lessing (2017).
[2] Sambanis (2004) estimates that the median death toll for all civil wars of the second half of the twentieth century was 17,000 battle deaths. The Mexican government officially acknowledged 70,000 murders associated with state–cartel and inter-cartel conflicts between 2006 and 2012. See Heinle, Rodríguez, and Shirk (2014).

Democratic Revolution (PRD), Andrés Manuel López Obrador, who did not accept defeat and denounced a major fraud. In the midst of a major post-electoral crisis, the incoming president announced to the country his decision to go to war against the cartels and sought to rally all Mexicans behind what he called the country's true enemy – the drug cartels.[3] His attempt to distract attention from López Obrador's continuing challenges and unify the country behind the PAN presidency led Calderón to rush to war with neither a proper diagnosis of the problem nor a well-developed strategy.

Following an initial slowdown of inter-cartel violence in the months following the deployment of the army, the federal government experienced a major backlash from the cartels and Mexico entered into an unprecedented period of violence. Murders associated with drug conflicts skyrocketed in the second half of 2007 and after 2008 grew exponentially as the government launched 16 military campaigns[4] across the country's most conflictive regions (Merino 2011; Espinosa and Rubin 2015; Atuesta 2017; Flores-Macías 2018). The intensification of violence, however, varied widely across subnational regions.

Focusing on the federal government intervention, scholars of Mexico's drug violence have offered three general explanations of the dramatic increase in violence. One explanation suggests that by deploying the army – instead of the police – to attack the cartels, the federal intervention led to the intensification of violence through two channels: (1) the cartels were forced to acquire high-caliber weapons to defend themselves against the anti-insurgency military campaigns and these weapons were used to challenge rival cartels; and (2) unprepared to deal with criminal violence and conduct policing activities, the army adopted anti-insurgency campaigns that resulted in higher murder rates of civilians (Flores-Macías 2018). A second explanation focuses on the "kingpin strategy," by which the military sought to decapitate the cartels' leadership. The removal of cartel leaders led to the fragmentation of the cartels, to intense competition over the control of drug trafficking routes among breakaway organizations, and to the intensification of violence (Guerrero 2011b; Calderón et al. 2015; Phillips 2015; Atuesta and Ponce 2017). Focusing

---

[3] On Calderón's campaign, see Sánchez and Aceves (2008). For the national message, see Presidencia de la República (2006).

[4] The Mexican federal government deployed members of the armed forces and of federal security agencies in 16 states, eight of which had large scale "joint operations" (*operativos conjuntos*). See Guerrero (2011b).

on intergovernmental coordination, a third explanation suggests that in subnational regions where President Calderón was able to successfully coordinate the logistics of the federal intervention with co-partisan local authorities, the federal intervention succeeded in containing violence, but it failed where coordination broke down with opposition authorities (Urrusti Frenk 2012; Ríos 2015; Durán-Martínez 2018).

While recognizing the importance of these three explanations, in this chapter we move the discussion beyond questions about military strategy and government logistics to explore the *politicization* of the intervention, in the context of acute ideological polarization between Right and Left. A number of scholars of social conflict have recently shown that in contexts of acute political polarization in which incumbent federal authorities have unchecked control over their countries' police forces, electoral incentives often drive police interventions to suppress violence (Wilkinson 2004; Auyero 2006). Because postauthoritarian elites in Mexico did not transform the armed forces, the authoritarian security apparatus, and the politicized judicial system, democratically elected presidents continued to have tight controls over the military, the police, and the judiciary. As in Mexico's authoritarian past, in the era of illiberal democracy presidents Fox and Calderón were able to use the security forces and the judicial system for partisan electoral purposes.

In this chapter we argue that President Calderón's War on Drugs and the federal intervention followed a partisan logic by which federal authorities developed cooperative military and policing interventions in regions where the president's conservative co-partisans ruled. However, they deliberately withheld effective assistance from his main political rivals and then blamed the violence on them. The coordination argument suggests that the president developed uncooperative relations with *all opposition forces*. But we contend that the lack of military and police cooperation and the strategic decision to prosecute subnational authorities and politicians for alleged collusion with the cartels, or to launch smear campaigns to taint governors and mayors as allies of organized crime, were used *primarily against the Left*. This was the political force that had challenged the results of the 2006 presidential election, refused to recognize the president's government as legitimate, and bitterly opposed the president's market-oriented agenda. Whereas close cooperation between conservative federal and subnational authorities contained the cartel backlash and the epidemics of violence, the lack of cooperation and the federal attacks against the Left weakened leftist subnational authorities and turned their municipalities into an open field for any cartel to contest controls over drug trafficking corridors and other criminal markets. Intergovernmental partisan conflict, we argue, changed the balance of power in the gray zone of criminality: the political vulnerability of mayors in leftist states opened opportunities for cartels to contest rival territory, increased criminal competition, and stimulated the expansion of turf wars.

Drawing on the Criminal Violence in Mexico (CVM) Dataset, in this chapter we show that municipalities in states ruled by either of the main opposition parties did experience greater levels of violence than those in states ruled by the president's co-partisans. The most intense levels of violence, however, took place in Mexican cities located in states ruled by leftist PRD governors. Our results show that drug violence in municipalities in states ruled by leftist governors was 134.6 percent greater than in those ruled by conservative (PAN) governors from the president's party. While violence in municipalities ruled by the other main opposition party, the PRI, was 36 percent greater than in municipalities in conservative states, violence in leftist states was *four times* greater than in PRI-dominated states. To be sure, partisan vertical fragmentation and intergovernmental political conflict do not trump other variables that have proven to be important drivers of drug violence, including the coordination and the decapitation hypotheses and a number of sociodemographic factors. Our analysis reveals, however, that omitting intergovernmental partisan conflict between Right and Left in the explanation of drug violence during President Calderón's War on Drugs yields biased results.

To test whether intergovernmental partisan conflict had an independent causal effect on the intensification of drug violence, we present a natural experiment that compares the evolution of drug violence among a number of municipalities from the Michoacán–Jalisco state border in the western part of Mexico. This is a homogeneous group of municipalities that were separated by state borders in the nineteenth century for reasons entirely unrelated to drug trafficking activities in the twenty-first century. Despite sharing multiple geographic, sociodemographic, and cultural similarities and similar histories of criminal activity, they experienced different trajectories of violence between 2006 and 2012. A major difference is that Jalisco was ruled by a conservative (PAN) governor and Michoacán by a leftist (PRD) governor. We attribute the differing abilities of subnational authorities from either side of the border to contain the explosion of drug violence after the federal intervention to the fact that they "happened" to be located in states with governors from different political parties. In Jalisco, the governor was from the president's party and in Michoacán the governor was from the party of his main political rivals.

The chapter is structured in six sections. We first discuss the dominant explanations of drug violence in Mexico centered on the military intervention, the "kingpin" strategy, and the government coordination hypothesis. Drawing on the literature on the impact of partisanship in policymaking in federations, in the second section we develop our own explanation about partisan intergovernmental conflict and electoral incentives driving the federal intervention in the Mexican War on Drugs. Before testing our hypotheses, in the third section we provide a detailed analysis of the political polarization between Right and Left that was the background to the intervention. In the fourth section we present the findings of our multivariate statistical models and in the fifth section the findings of the natural experiment. In the conclusion we discuss how partisanship can guide security interventions in federations and how the politicization of the state's war on crime can stimulate spirals of violence.

DOMINANT EXPLANATIONS OF DRUG VIOLENCE IN MEXICO

The scholarly literature on the major outbreak of drug violence in Mexico has focused mainly on the state – on the federal intervention in the War on Drugs and the deployment of the military, across the country's most conflictive regions, to crush the cartels. While scholars have also looked at subnational political conditions associated with cartel collusion with local authorities (Snyder and Durán-Martínez 2009; Dube, Dube, and García-Ponce 2013; Osorio 2015) and at the socioeconomic structures that allowed cartels to recruit young males to serve as foot soldiers for war (Brenneman 2013; Merino, Zarkin, and Fierro 2013), the dominant narratives about the major escalation of violence during the administration of President Calderón have centered on state policy.

Three explanations have dominated the debate: (1) the use of the military for the intervention; (2) the adoption of the "kingpin" strategy to decapitate the cartels; and (3) the differential ability of the federal government to coordinate its actions with subnational authorities.

Military intervention. Lessing's (2017) influential explanation of drug violence in Latin America suggests that state interventions lead to state–cartel wars when state authorities use unconditional attacks – that is, when they attack all cartels, regardless of whether cartels were attacking the government in the first place. In this view, cartels retaliate against the state and engage in major spirals of violence motivated by self-defense.

Several scholars have produced extensive evidence showing that the Mexican federal government's decision to unilaterally launch war against all cartels led to a sudden escalation of violence. Using states as units of analysis, Merino (2011) shows that eight military joint operations resulted in approximately 10,000 additional deaths between 2007 and 2010. Using municipalities as units of analysis, Espinosa and Rubin (2015) show that military interventions resulted in up to a ten-unit increase on the *average* homicide rate within municipalities experiencing joint operations. In an influential article, Flores-Macías (2018) shows that states that experienced militarization experienced an average murder rate that was 17 percent higher than those where there was no military intervention. In his account, the deployment of the army to conflictive regions provided incentives for cartels to invest in high-caliber weaponry and military training to confront the state's anti-insurgency operations. This led to spirals of state–cartel violence but also empowered cartels to seek to conquer rival territory or expand into new illegal markets through violence. At the same time, unprepared for policing tasks, the army's anti-insurgency operations resulted in higher murder rates and in the victimization of civilians.

Kingpin strategy. Beyond a state's decision to attack cartels, scholars of Mexican drug wars have shown that the strategic goals of military intervention can be of paramount importance. Influenced by the Colombian experience and by US military strategy, the elimination of cartel bosses – arresting them and having them extradited to the US or simply murdering them – became the military intervention's chief goal. A number of scholars have shown that the kingpin strategy backfired in Mexico. The decapitation of the cartels led to violent internal succession struggles (Ríos 2013), the fragmentation of cartels (Calderón et al. 2015; Phillips 2015; Atuesta and Ponce 2017), and the onset of fierce competition between the old cartels and the emerging criminal organizations (Guerrero 2011b). As Calderón et al. (2015) show, the rapid spread of criminal organizations and the fierce competition for turf led to the dramatic escalation of violence. To put it in the conceptual language introduced in Chapter 1, the federal intervention led to a major reconfiguration of the number of criminal players and of the balance of power of Mexico's gray zone of criminality, giving rise to new incentives for violence.

While there is extensive evidence showing that the federal government's unconditional war against all cartels led to a sudden escalation of violence, and although it has been firmly established that the kingpin strategy was a major stimulus for violent conflict, a state-centric approach narrowly focused on military strategy may be biased because it views the intervention exclusively through a military lens in which politics is absent. The argument simply ignores the fact that partisanship may have affected the levels of cooperation and conflict among federal, state, and municipal authorities in the War on Drugs. In a context marked by acute political polarization, this may be an important omission.

Government coordination. In separate works, Urrusti Frenk (2012), Ríos (2015), and Durán-Martínez (2018) have suggested that partisanship mattered for the federal intervention on the War on Drugs. According to Urrusti Frenk, vertical partisan alignment allowed authorities to have more effective territorial controls. Federal, state, and municipal law enforcement agents could act in coordination to secure subnational territories, and their fluid communication and exchange of information facilitated the implementation of effective attacks against drug cartels. Thus, criminal violence was less intense under vertically integrated governments, because cartels did not try to contest drug trafficking routes where political power was coherently aligned. Under Ríos's alternative interpretation, partisan vertical alignment empowered the president to discipline his subnational co-partisans, producing coherent and consistent security policies that dissuaded drug cartels from competing for territorial controls. In Durán-Martínez's view, partisan vertical alignment contributes to state cohesion, which deters cartels from making public displays of violence against the state or rival cartels. For example, under the PRI hegemony, vertical alignment allowed PRI subnational authorities to contain violence by providing protection to the cartels. In the post-PRI era, vertical alignment under the PAN allowed subnational authorities to fight the narcos. In both cases, intergovernmental coordination dissuaded cartels from using violence against state authorities or against rival competitors.

Even though the coordination argument introduces partisan politics into the analysis of the federal intervention on the War on Drugs, distinguishing only between the federal government and the subnational opposition (regardless of party affiliation) misses a fundamental point. In a context of acute political polarization in which a conservative federal government was immersed in a major political conflict with one of the two opposition parties – the Left – the president could have used the federal intervention to punish his chief political enemies but not other less vociferous opposition forces. In Mexico's context – marked by acute political polarization between Right and Left – failing to distinguish between different opposition parties can be a major source of omitted variable bias. Beyond the view of partisan alignment in terms of policy coordination, we explore the partisan basis for cooperation and conflict.

POLICING CRIME AND VIOLENCE IN FEDERATIONS: THE POLITICS OF INTERGOVERNMENTAL COOPERATION AND CONFLICT

Although countries with federal systems vary in their degree of decentralization, a federalist design necessarily entails a division of power and responsibilities between national and subnational governments (Riker 1975; Eleazar 1997). In the field of security, most federal countries have national authorities with jurisdiction over national defense and organized crime, while subnational police forces are mainly responsible for common crime. This division of labor results in different policing capacities. Whereas national authorities have access to military forces as well as federal police forces – which have the best available weaponry to fight foreign threats or drug cartels – subnational authorities command local police forces with less sophisticated equipment and training. These differences imply that when subnational governments face particularly violent situations, they have to rely on national authorities for defense and protection. In this *asymmetric* relationship, intergovernmental cooperation is crucial for local security and for the survival of subnational authorities in violent federations.

The drug trafficking industry is a global chain of local operations, in which subnational authorities confront criminal realities for which they have neither policing capacity nor jurisdiction. The conditions under which intergovernmental cooperation takes place to confront the cartels and contain drug violence is therefore a crucial issue in federal countries such as Mexico.

Scholars of federalism long viewed intergovernmental cooperation as a question of efficiency – if responsibilities were properly assigned among different government layers, they presumed, voters at each level of government would induce elected authorities to engage in intergovernmental cooperation (Oates 1972; Petersen 1995). This approach viewed politics as the efficient result of voters' demands and elected officials' automatic responses. But there was no room for political parties and for party strategy.

By introducing partisanship to the study of federalism, Riker (1964) challenged the efficiency approach. Intergovernmental cooperation, he famously posited, depended on partisan vertical integration in the federal and subnational governments. Shared partisanship across levels of government facilitates intergovernmental cooperation and policy coherence, largely induced through party discipline mechanisms that national-level authorities can exert over subnational co-partisan incumbents. In contrast, under conditions of vertical partisan fragmentation, when subnational units are controlled by a different party from the one that governs at the national level, differences in ideology and policy interests are likely to lead to uncooperative relations and policy incoherence. As a result, vertically integrated political systems generate "harmony," produce logically coordinated policies, and facilitate intergovernmental cooperation, while vertically divided governance creates "disharmony," yields contradictory policies in federations, and is characterized by intergovernmental conflict (Riker and Schaps 1957). Advocates of the government coordination approach to the study of Mexico's War on Drugs have adopted this view.

One important limitation in Riker's study of intergovernmental relations – and by extension in the coordination hypothesis of the Mexican War on Drugs – is that it does not take into account the potential asymmetries of power in vertically divided governments and the possibility that higher-level authorities may use various policy mechanisms to reward subnational co-partisans and punish their political enemies. This approach, in fact, dismisses *electoral incentives*. As Weingast (2014, p. 20) argues, in a weak democratic regime national incumbents may "have incentives to prevent [subnational opposition] governments from succeeding" in their policy goals and "use their powers to reduce or remove the authority of local governments." Encroaching on decentralization is a means for national authorities to ultimately gain a larger electoral support base and to threaten subnational opposition forces. Various studies of distributive politics have found supporting evidence for this strategic behavior, showing that national governments can provide transfers, subsidies, tariff protections, or pork-barrel projects to core supporters or to swing voters. In their influential core-voter model Cox and McCubbins (1986) explicitly propose that governments can reward their co-partisan supporters and punish voters from rival political parties.[5]

Building on models of "distributive politics," scholars of political violence have also examined how electoral incentives can shape *policing decisions* in federations. Given the distinct policing capacities across levels of government, they analyze national authorities' deployment of police forces to confront subnational outbreaks of violence as a strategic cooperation problem, instead of regarding it as an efficiency or technical decision. Consistent with the literature on distributive politics, these studies of political violence propose that higher-level authorities may order security forces to suppress violence in co-partisan lower-level regions but tolerate or even instigate violence in lower-level areas governed by the opposition.

Scholars of political violence have shown that, under conditions of acute social or political polarization, government authorities can strategically manipulate law enforcement to reward their political allies and punish their enemies. From ethnic violence in India (Wilkinson 2004) to urban riots in Argentina (Auyero 2006), a variety of studies have shown that electoral incentives drive policing interventions to contain major outbursts of violence. Similarly, students of Colombia's civil conflict have shown that electoral incentives drove national elites to allow paramilitary violence against their political rivals (Steele 2011; Acemoglu, Robinson, and Santos 2013). This evidence challenges the classic Weberian assumption according to which state elites would axiomatically seek the monopoly on violence and would suppress any form of non-state organized violence (Weber 1918/1994). In fact, these studies show that in countries with a weak rule of law, state leaders operating in polarized political environments can use their discretionary power to tolerate or even stimulate violence against their political enemies.

We use Riker's partisan approach to intergovernmental relations as our first building block to develop our hypotheses about the impact of the state intervention on violence in the War on Drugs in Mexico. Beyond Riker, however, we draw on the literature on distributive politics and on political violence to assess how *power asymmetries* across different levels of government *and electoral incentives* may affect intergovernmental cooperation. We contend that under conditions of acute political polarization, federal authorities in a country with a weak rule of law can adopt

---

[5] For a pioneering test of the core-voter model in the allocation of anti-poverty resources in Mexico, see Magaloni (2006).

a strategic approach to policing criminal violence by which they effectively deploy security forces to protect subnational regions where their co-partisans rule but tolerate criminal violence in areas dominated by their main political rivals. We suggest that federal incumbents can adopt a "punishment" regime by which they deliberately leave their subnational political rivals unprotected in conflictive regions, in an effort to undermine their credibility and electoral base.

As we suggested in Chapter 1, major changes in state power can affect the gray zone of criminality. While the literature on drug violence in Mexico has paid special attention to assessing how state intervention in the War on Drugs – geared toward decapitating the cartels – resulted in a major reconfiguration of Mexico's drug trafficking organizations, here we focus on how patterns of intergovernmental partisan cooperation and conflict transformed incentives for criminal violence across Mexico's subnational regions.

Figure 4.1 illustrates our argument. The left-hand bar of the figure shows a country that experienced a thin electoral transition to democracy in which the security apparatus and the judicial system were not reformed. Thus, the president keeps direct authoritarian controls over the military, the police, and the public prosecutor's office. In this illiberal democracy, the president launches a major military attack against drug cartels to curb inter-cartel violence and recover territorial controls. As the figure illustrates, whether the federal intervention helps in containing violence or

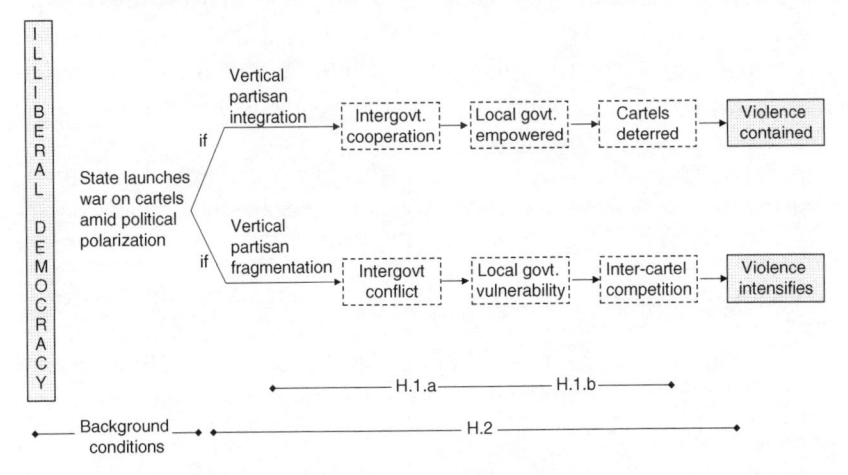

FIGURE 4.1 Explanatory Model of the Political Fragmentation Hypothesis

contributes to the intensification of violence across subnational units depends on the degree of partisan vertical fragmentation.

In vertically integrated political regions national and subnational co-partisan authorities are likely to cooperate – the military, different police forces, and the judiciary and prison system are likely to share information, plan the intervention in joint consultation, and implement the intervention through joint actions. Enjoying full subnational support, local government officials, particularly mayors, will be empowered to confront the drug cartels. Intergovernmental cooperation and cohesion will send a powerful signal that is likely to deter competing cartels from attempting to use the intervention as an opportunity to challenge the home cartel. While the intervention is likely to increase state–cartel conflict, a cohesive and coordinated response is likely to prevent other cartels from taking advantage of the attack to enter the competition to conquer this turf.

In contrast, in a context of acute political polarization, partisan vertical fragmentation is more likely to lead to intergovernmental conflict. Presidents will have incentives not to cooperate with subnational authorities and to tolerate an increase in violence and then blame it on their subnational political rivals. In vertically fragmented regions, local authorities are politically unprotected and therefore vulnerable to violence, as criminal groups take advantage of the municipal governments' political weakness to compete for the territorial control of these regions. When cartels and other organized criminal groups perceive that local authorities are politically unprotected by the center, criminal lords are likely to engage in major turf wars. They seek not only control over drug trafficking routes but control over new criminal markets, including the extraction of human wealth and natural resource wealth. As cartels and other criminal groups try to widen the gray zone of criminality, turf wars multiply, giving rise to the exponential growth of violence.

To put it formally, we would expect that in a context of acute political polarization in which the federal government engages in a major conflict against drug trafficking organizations:

H.1. Partisan vertical fragmentation and intergovernmental partisan conflict will *(a)* render subnational regions vulnerable to encroachment by drug cartels and *(b)* open opportunities for multiple cartels to fight for the control over drug trafficking routes and new criminal markets.

H.2. Inter-cartel violence will be more intense in subnational regions where political power is vertically fragmented – particularly where subnational officials belong to a party that is an ideological rival of the president's – than where power is unified.

Using Figure 4.1 as a reference, in the remainder of this chapter we use the Mexican federal intervention in the War on Drugs to assess the statistical association between partisan vertical fragmentation and criminal violence (H.2). In Chapter 5, we present qualitative evidence from three cities in three different Mexican states that explains how political *vulnerability* opened *opportunities* for cartels and other organized criminal groups to compete over territory (H.1.a) and how this competition stimulated the intensification of violence (H.1.b). Before conducting our statistical testing, however, we need to dig a little deeper into two background conditions: (1) the extent, nature, and key players of political polarization prior to the federal intervention and the launching of the War on Drugs; and (2) the history of inter-cartel violence that preceded the intervention.

MEXICO'S WAR ON DRUGS AMID POLITICAL POLARIZATION

The Road to Polarization and Partisan Conflict: The 2006 Presidential Election

The Institutional Revolutionary Party (PRI) controlled the Mexican presidency uninterruptedly for seven decades (Magaloni 2006; Greene 2007; Langston 2018). During this period of authoritarian rule, particularly after the 1968 student movement, a pro-regime/anti-regime ideological cleavage dominated the Mexican party system (Klesner 2005). The conservative PAN and the leftist PRD – the country's leading opposition forces in the 1990s – never succeeded in creating a unified anti-regime front and they followed disparate and uncoordinated strategies to dismantle the PRI's authoritarian rule – with the PAN even forming a strategic coalition with the PRI to enact major market-oriented economic reforms. However, democratization was a common goal shared by Right and Left. As Figure 4.I.a illustrates, despite their differences in economic policy along the Right–Left dimension, the opposition's shared desire for free and fair elections created a space for cooperation between the PAN and the PRD.

The 2000 presidential victory of the PAN and the concurrent victory of the PRD in Mexico City, however, led Mexico into an era of bitter postauthoritarian partisan conflict between Right and Left. In the absence

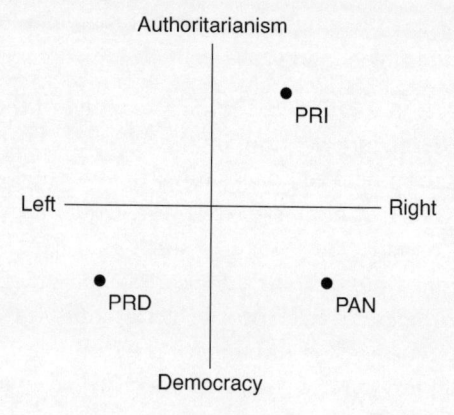

FIGURE 4.1.a Ideological Position of Mexican Parties under Authoritarian Rule, 1990s

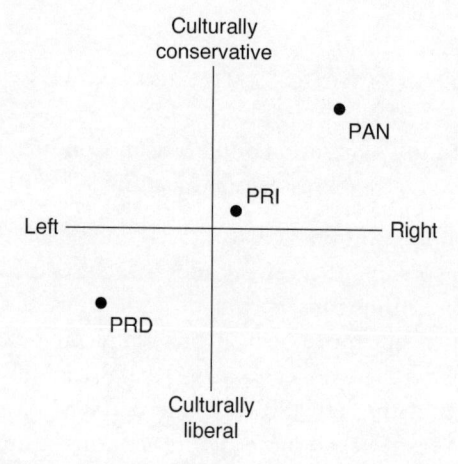

FIGURE 4.1.b Ideological Position of Mexican Parties under Democracy, 2000s

of a visible PRI leader, President Vicente Fox of the PAN and the leftist mayor Andrés Manuel López Obrador – two charismatic leaders – rapidly became Mexico's leading political figures and personified the country's political polarization.

As Figure 4.I.b illustrates, in the postauthoritarian period the economic and sociocultural dimensions became the battleground for the confrontation between Left and Right. On the economic front the PRD forcefully opposed the ambitious program of second-generation market-oriented reforms that President Fox and the PAN sought to enact from their first year in office. The PRD opposed the PAN's labor, fiscal, and energy reform initiatives in the street (Hidalgo 2001) and in Congress (Méndez 2002), contributing to the failure of the three reforms. On the socio-cultural dimension, the PAN and the PRD had an open confrontation over the legalization of abortion and same-sex marriage (Salazar and Fuentes 2002). The Mexico City government and PRD activists stood at the forefront of these issues, while Fox and his party steadfastly rejected them (Melgar 2002; Reforma 2004).

After the 2003 midterm elections – in which the PAN lost 71 congressional seats, while the PRD won 32 seats – the conflict between the federal government and the Mexico City government expanded beyond their differences over economic and sociocultural issues. The PAN–PRD rivalry became more evident and polarizing once Fox and López Obrador took these ideological battles to the mass media. An initial personal confrontation took place when a local PAN legislator showed videotapes of López Obrador's closest collaborators accepting bribes on national television. The leftist mayor argued that the federal government had intervened in the release of such recordings to damage his image and administration (Alegre 2004). In retaliation, the PRD's national council encouraged all leftist governors and legislators to "redefine their relationship with Fox" and to consider banning the presence of the president in their own states (Pensamiento, Salazar, and Pacón 2004).

Partisan conflict and political polarization reached a peak when President Fox's attorney general, General Rafael Macedo de la Concha, accused López Obrador of violating a court order to halt the construction of a hospital access road over private property. While Fox claimed that this case showed his administration's will to fight corruption and impunity, López Obrador and fellow PRD leaders argued that the president was politicizing justice. The confrontation escalated. López Obrador became subject to impeachment by the Mexican Congress, and in April 2005 – just one year before the presidential election – he was stripped of his immunity from prosecution. This meant that the Mexico City mayor had to face trial and would no longer be eligible to run for presidential office in the upcoming 2006 election, despite leading the polls on electoral preferences.[6] After an unprecedented wave of mass protest against the

---

[6] In May 2005 López Obrador had 36 percent of vote intentions, Roberto Madrazo (PRI) had 25 percent, and Santiago Creel (PAN) had 24 percent. See Moreno and Gutiérrez (2005).

impeachment of López Obrador[7] and increasingly negative public opinion, both domestically[8] and internationally,[9] President Fox dropped all charges and enabled his leftist rival to run for president in 2006. This was a political rather than a judicial decision. The case crystallized a new political reality: a few years after the PRI's loss of presidential power, the PAN and the PRD had become antithetical forces.

The 2006 presidential campaign took place in a political environment highly polarized between Left and Right (Langston 2007), and the election largely became a plebiscite on López Obrador (Schedler 2007). Both parties relied on negative campaign strategies targeted against the personal and moral character of the opposing contender.[10] The PAN candidate, Felipe Calderón, ran a series of attack ads that compared López Obrador with Hugo Chávez, portraying him as an "authoritarian populist" leader who represented a major "threat to Mexico." President Fox also launched his own campaign, urging Mexicans not to change the country's market-oriented trajectory and "not be fooled by populists and demagogues." In response, López Obrador accused Felipe Calderón of corruption and called the PAN's private sector allies a group of "white-collar criminals" (Rangel 2009). In the face of such relentless negativity, the Federal Electoral Institute ordered all parties to remove their attack ads and requested President Fox and other public authorities to abstain from intervening in the presidential campaign. However, all parties sidestepped the law and continued their bitter media confrontations.

The victory of the conservative candidate by a razor-thin margin of 0.6 percent took elite polarization to unprecedented levels.[11] López Obrador did not concede defeat, denounced the result as a major electoral fraud, and contested the election both in the courts and in the street. He demanded that the Federal Electoral Tribunal review all the

---

[7] Approximately one million citizens marched in downtown Mexico City to contest the impeachment of López Obrador. See Reforma (2005).

[8] National polls revealed that 50 percent of Mexicans considered the impeachment process was unfair. See Parametría (2005).

[9] Shortly after the Congress's verdict that stripped López Obrador of his immunity, three major international newspapers published editorials that criticized this decision. See the *Financial Times* (2005), the *New York Times* (2005), and Meyerson (2005).

[10] For a detailed account of the evolution and content of the presidential campaign, see Sánchez and Aceves (2008).

[11] On the basis of elite and general population surveys, Bruhn and Greene (2007) show that political elites became bitterly polarized during Mexico's 2006 election, but voters did not.

irregularities that occurred throughout the campaign – from the president's intervention to Calderón's campaign finance – and asked for a manual recount of the 41 million ballots. The leftist candidate also called on his followers to join a campaign of non-violent resistance and set up camps in downtown Mexico City. The barricades lasted for three months, with the participation of up to two million people. When electoral authorities confirmed the victory of the PAN candidate,[12] López Obrador refused to recognize Calderón as Mexico's president. A few days before Calderón's inauguration ceremony, López Obrador launched a "parallel government" and was sworn in as Mexico's "legitimate president"(Schedler 2007).

Protests continued both in the streets and in Congress, where PRD legislators took hold of the national legislature's tribune for three days. Concerned about the feasibility of holding Calderón's inauguration ceremony before Congress, Vicente Fox held an unusual closed-door military ceremony at the presidential residence, where Felipe Calderón was sworn into office. On the next day, with the endorsement of his party and the PRI,[13] President Calderón went to Congress to officially take his oath of office, but the inauguration ceremony only lasted a few minutes, as leftist legislators continually attempted to violently remove him from the tribune.

Facing a major post-electoral crisis and a conspicuous rise of inter-cartel violence in central and northern states, President Calderón began his administration with a radical policy announcement intended to overcome the political crisis. Immediately after his inauguration ceremony, in a separate nationally televised event, he called upon all Mexicans to transcend political rivalries and work together in the "battle" against the country's true enemy: the drug cartels. Security issues were largely absent during the campaign, but the incoming president declared that the fight against the drug cartels, crime, and insecurity was his administration's top priority (Presidencia de la República 2006). Ten days later, he deployed the first of 16 military operations throughout the country's territory to quell growing inter-cartel violence.

---

[12] Although President Fox and all political parties consistently violated Mexico's electoral laws during the electoral campaign, there was *no* compelling evidence of fraud in the counting of the votes. For a thorough analysis of the quality of the election count, see Aparicio (2009).

[13] The PRI's presence in Congress was crucial to achieve the quorum needed for Calderón's inauguration ceremony.

Inter-cartel Wars and the Evolution of Violence, 2007–2012

By the time President Calderón declared a War on Drugs, Mexico's five major cartels – Tijuana, Juárez, Sinaloa, Gulf, and La Familia Michoacana – had been at war for more than a decade, as we showed in Chapter 2. Subnational party alternation in gubernatorial power in the 1990s and early 2000s had led to the breakdown of informal networks of government protection forged under the PRI. To avoid the encroachment of rival cartels and potential attacks by incoming opposition authorities, drug lords created their own private militias. Once their turf was secure, they used their militias to seek to conquer rival territory. As we argued in Chapters 2 and 3, the spread of subnational party alternation in gubernatorial power led to the proliferation of private militias and to the outbreak of multiple inter-cartel wars in the northwest, northeast, and southwest of the country. When Calderón took power, drug-related violence had reached a historical peak and inter-cartel wars had surpassed the 1,000 annual battle death threshold, which is commonly used to define a civil war (Fearon and Laitin 2003). Calderón expected that his federal intervention would yield an easy military victory that would reunite the country and help his government overcome a major post-electoral crisis.

But the president's hope for an easy military victory in the War on Drugs never materialized. Between 2007 and 2012, inter-cartel violence increased by a factor of five. By the end of the Calderón administration 70,000 people had died in conflicts associated with inter-cartel and state–cartel wars (Heinle, Rodríguez, and Shirk 2014); more than 13,000 people were missing (DataCívica 2017); and over 300 local government officials, political candidates, and party activists had been victims of assassination attempts or had been murdered.[14] In addition, the cartels had expanded their activities from drug trafficking into new criminal markets specializing in the extraction of human wealth (e.g., extortion, kidnapping for ransom, and human smuggling) and natural wealth extraction (e.g., looting of natural resources) (Guerrero 2011b; Grillo 2011). These multiple forms of violence, however, did not spread evenly; they became more intense in some regions than in others.

Maps 4.II.a and b show the dramatic increase and the spread of violence associated with the federal intervention and inter-cartel wars.

---

[14] See Chapter 6.

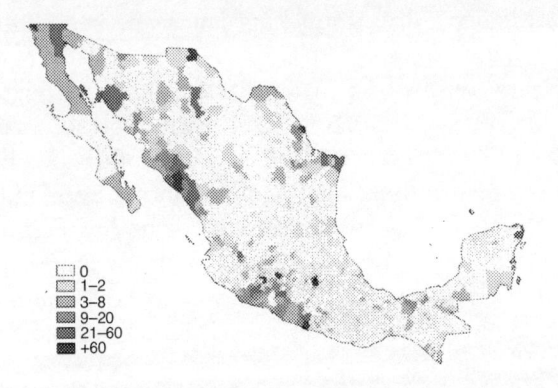

MAP 4.II.a Geography of Inter-Cartel Murders in Mexico, 2000–2006

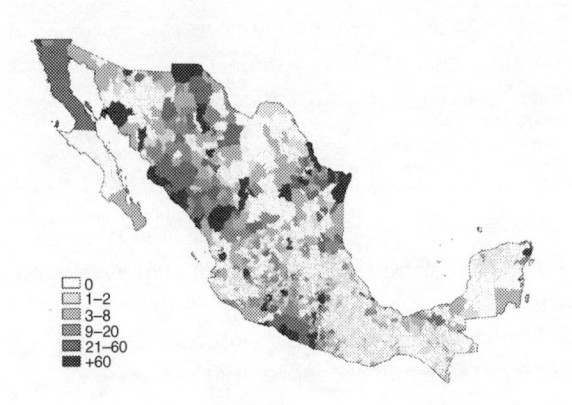

MAP 4.II.b Geography of Inter-Cartel Murders in Mexico, 2007–2012

Map 4.II.a shows the baseline of inter-cartel violence between 2000 and 2006, prior to the federal intervention. Although the overall homicide rate in Mexico had been falling since the early 1990s and by 2006 had reached a historical low, murders associated with organized crime had been on the rise, and prior to the intervention the country had three focal points of inter-cartel violence. But the federal intervention had a dramatic effect: As Map 4.II.b shows, state–cartel and inter-cartel conflicts led to an explosion of violence between 2007 and 2012. The map reveals the intensification of violence at the three focal points that already existed prior to the intervention and the rise of three new focal points: Gulf, center-north, and center.

By 2012 Mexico's drug trafficking landscape had shifted from an industry dominated by five cartels to one in which over 60 organizations were actively involved in drug trafficking and related criminal activities (Guerrero 2011a). Over the course of six years of Drug Wars, inter-cartel violence had evolved into conflicts involving numerous criminal organizations fighting for control over cities, villages, and neighborhoods. These were no longer wars for the transshipment of drugs, but conflicts over control of multiple criminal markets – including the extraction of human wealth and natural resource wealth – and administrative-territorial jurisdictions – particularly municipal governments.

Against the backdrop of acute political polarization during the 2006 presidential election and the intensification of violence after the federal intervention, we now test whether partisan vertical fragmentation of power and bitter political conflict between the president and his leftist subnational political rivals had any impact on the uneven spread of inter-cartel violence between 2007 and 2012.

QUANTITATIVE EVIDENCE I: MULTIVARIATE REGRESSION MODELS

To test whether partisan vertical fragmentation of power and intergovernmental partisan conflict had any impact on the intensity of violence in Mexico's subnational regions, we use information from the CVM database and analyze the temporal and spatial evolution of 22,000 murders and executions perpetrated by drug cartels and their criminal associates[15] across 2,019 Mexican municipalities from 2007 to 2012.[16] We use a count of murders in municipality i and year t as an indicator of our dependent variable. We retest all our models using information from a dataset collected by the Office of the President in Mexico on drug-related

---

[15] Due to the high volume of news reports on drug-related violence for this period, we rely only on the newspaper *Reforma* – the most reliable source for coverage on homicides that can be attributed to OCGs. However, because reliance on a single source can be problematic, we retest all our analyses using a dataset on drug-related violence developed by the Office of the President. For a discussion on CVM and our use of *Reforma* and the Office of the President's dataset, see Appendix D.

[16] We exclude Mexico City, which at the time had a special status, and two-thirds of Oaxaca's municipalities because local government officials are elected by means of indigenous customary laws and parties are not allowed to compete for office.

homicides, available from 2007 to 2011, and the main results remain unchanged.[17]

Partisan Vertical Fragmentation and Intergovernmental Conflict

To test our argument on the positive effect of partisan vertical fragmentation and intergovernmental conflict on inter-cartel violence, we use information on the partisan affiliation of governors and mayors.[18] Until 2012, Mexico's party system had three major political parties (PAN, PRI, and PRD) competing for office at the three levels of government (federal, state, and municipal). During the 2007–2012 period, the conservative PAN held the presidency, but gubernatorial and municipal powers were dispersed across the three major parties, including the center opposition (PRI)[19] and the Left opposition (PRD). As illustrated in Table 4.1, we identify nine different combinations of partisan vertical fragmentation, where the party identified on the first row in the triads is the party in presidential power, the second is the party in the state gubernatorial office, and the third is the party ruling the municipality.[20] As the information on the table's right-hand column shows, political power in Mexico's federation was considerably fragmented vertically. After six decades of monopolistic unified governance under the PRI, Mexico's "federalist" transition to democracy in the 1990s – by which the PRI began losing power in cities, then in states, and finally at the national level – yielded a complex mosaic of territorial power diffusion and pluralistic intergovernmental relations that continued to develop in the postauthoritarian era under the PAN in the 2000s.

On the basis of the information in Table 4.1, we create three sets of variables that distinguish between the ideological orientations of the different opposition parties in government.

First, we create a *Juxtaposition index* in which we rank the different combinations in one single metric, from zero (PAN-PAN-PAN) to eight

---

[17] See Appendix D, Table D.1.

[18] Data on governors' and mayors' partisan affiliation were collected from state electoral commissions and CIDAC.

[19] Note that during the 2000s, as an opposition party the PRI adopted a centrist agenda on most policy discussions. This would change after 2012, when the PRI returned to power, and opted for a center-right program during the administration of Enrique Peña Nieto (2012–2018). See Flores-Macías (2016).

[20] Because small parties fielded candidates for office in coalition with the three big parties, we subsumed the small parties into the three major ones. For example, we subsumed the Green Party under the PRI and the Workers' Party under the PRD. We subsumed into the PAN any party that coalesced with the federal incumbent.

TABLE 4.1 *Layering of Parties in Mexico's Three Levels of Government, 2007–2012*

Party Labels	Percentage of Municipalities
PAN-PAN-PAN	11.30
PAN-PAN-PRI	9.92
PAN-PAN-PRD	2.34
PAN-PRI-PAN	14.26
PAN-PRI-PRI	36.24
PAN-PRI-PRD	8.29
PAN-PRD-PAN	3.29
PAN-PRD-PRI	8.27
PAN-PRD-PRD	6.11

Notes: The party in the first cell is the president's; the second is the governor's; and the third is the mayor's. PAN-PAN-PAN is the reference category. PAN = national incumbent (conservative); PRI = opposition (center); PRD = opposition (Left).

(PAN-PRD-PRD).[21] This aggregate index reflects the polarization between Right and Left.

Second, we generate a set of disaggregated dichotomous variables to identify the layering of vertical distribution of parties at all levels of government. For purposes of statistical analysis, we use unified governance (PAN-PAN-PAN) as the reference category.

Third, because the findings from the second measure show that the state governors' partisan affiliation is the crucial differentiating factor of varying levels of drug violence across municipalities, we create a specific measure of intergovernmental partisan conflict focusing on the governor's party, regardless of who rules at the municipal level. *Confl1* identifies with a dummy variable all cases in which the governor belongs to the president's party (PAN, PAN, regardless); *Confl2* are cases of centrist opposition governors (PAN, PRI, regardless); and *Confl3* are cases of leftist opposition governors (PAN, PRD, regardless). We use *Confl1* as the reference category.

Alternative Explanations and Controls

Recognizing that inter-cartel violence is a multi-causal phenomenon, we control for a series of factors that have been tested in studies of drug violence in Mexico.

---

[21] For a pioneering analysis on juxtaposition in Mexico, see Remes (1999).

State security policy. One of the most significant arguments about the intensification of violence in Mexico after the federal intervention in 2007 suggests that the government's policy of eliminating the top leaders of the drug cartels fueled an escalation of inter-cartel violence (Guerrero 2011b; Dickenson 2014; Calderón et al. 2015; Phillips 2015). We control for the count of cartel chiefs and their deputies arrested or killed, *Leadership decapitation*, as a result of government operations or inter-cartel conflicts and assign the count to all of the state's municipalities where the event took place.[22]

Besides the military intervention and the policy of decapitation of cartels, the Calderón administration adopted a program of fiscal transfers to strengthen state and municipal police forces. Through the Public Security Contributions Fund or FASP (Fondo de Aportaciones para la Seguridad Pública), the federal government transferred financial resources to the states that complied with the national public security strategy. Given that these transfers took place in the midst of a highly polarized political environment, it may be the case that our predicted effect of vertical fragmentation in fact occurs through these transfers. In other words, co-partisan states may have received more generous funds than those governed by the opposition, rendering opposition subnational authorities less capable of confronting inter-cartel violence. To control for these fiscal transfers, we calculate the natural log of *Federal security funds*.[23]

State presence. Consistent with the political violence (Fearon and Laitin 2003) and organized crime (Skaperdas 2001) literatures, scholars have argued that the state's presence can be a powerful deterrent of criminal violence. We distinguish two areas of state presence: security and socioeconomic development. We control for the state's security presence using the number of *Prosecutors per 10,000 population*,[24] and we

---

[22] This information is based on a systematic keyword search in four Mexican national newspapers (*Reforma*, *El Universal*, *El Financiero*, and *Excelsior*) and 16 local dailies available through the news database ISI Emerging Markets.

[23] In 2008 the Calderón administration created another program, Subsidy for Municipal Public Security or SUBSEMUN (Subsidio para la Seguridad en los Municipios), which transferred financial resources to municipalities to strengthen municipal security institutions. Less than 10 percent of Mexican municipalities received funds from this program. We did not include SUBSEMUN because the time-series is shorter. Additional robustness tests using a dummy for SUBSEMUN recipients show that our main results for vertical fragmentation remain unchanged. See Appendix D, Table D.2.

[24] We rely on the Government, Public Security, and Justice Censuses conducted by INEGI, available since 1994, through Simbad: http://sc.inegi.org.mx/cobdem/. Accessed

use a *Poverty index* as an aggregate measure of the state's developmental presence. This is a composite index of access to public goods and services at the municipal level, including education, health, roads, sewage and clean water.[25]

Party alternation and electoral competition. As we discussed in Chapter 2, scholars of drug violence have associated the intensification of inter-cartel violence with political change and the breakdown of informal subnational government protection networks. Consistent with our results reported in Chapter 2, we include a dummy variable, *State alternation*, which identifies the rotation in the party in gubernatorial office, and a dummy variable for *Municipal alternation*, which identifies the rotation of parties in municipal power. Alternatively, other scholars have identified the breakdown of protection with electoral competition. We control for *State* and *Municipal electoral competition*, using the effective number of parties in gubernatorial and mayoral elections.

Sociodemographic controls. As we discussed in Chapter 2, cartels recruit young men from impoverished urban areas to serve as foot soldiers in turf wars. Therefore, following the extensive literature on the sociology of crime, we control for the municipal *Sex ratio*, the proportion of population *Ages 15–34*, and the proportion of *Mono-parental households*.

Spatial and geographic controls. We include a one-year lag of *Violence in neighboring municipalities* to control for the spatial dispersion of violence and to test for spatial effects.[26]

We control for seven geographic regions – *North*, *North-Center*, *Center*, *Pacific*, *Gulf*, *South*, and *Southeast*, where *Southeast* is the reference category, and we use the natural log of population as the models' offset variable.

As in Chapter 2, we use negative binomial (NB) models – the most appropriate technique for over-dispersed count data. We assume random effects because some of our key variables – for instance, the juxtaposition index and the party fragmentation variables – do not change for a number of years. We transform random effects coefficients into incidence rate ratios (IRR) to facilitate substantive interpretation.

February 11, 2017. We use prosecutors because the data series on police agents per municipality is incomplete.

[25] We use Conapo's marginality index and rescale it to a 0 to 100 range.

[26] We define neighboring municipalities as the most immediate adjacent neighbors that share geographic borders.

Results

The results summarized in Table 4.2 show that, consistent with our argument, intergovernmental partisan rivalry between the president and the leftist opposition party was an important predictor of the intensity of inter-cartel violence between 2007 and 2012. While there is evidence that partisan vertical alignment between President Calderón and his conservative subnational co-partisans resulted in lower levels of drug violence, results from the three different measures of partisan vertical fragmentation show that patterns of intergovernmental cooperation and conflict were dramatically different between the centrist PRI opposition and the leftist opposition party – the president's main political rival. Our results suggest the existence of a punishment regime by which leftist governors were left unsupported by the federal government. Our findings reveal that by failing to distinguish between different opposition parties, the coordination argument yields biased estimators and underpredicts overall variance in inter-cartel violence.

Model 1 uses the ordinal index of juxtaposition and shows that, holding all else constant, as a municipality moves away from a situation of unified conservative governance (PAN-PAN-PAN) in the direction of leftist subnational governance (PAN-PRD-PRD), the intensity of violence is likely to increase by 11.6 percent (IRR = 1.116). The cumulative effect means that a leftist municipality in a leftist state experienced 92.8 percent (11.6 × 8 layers) more violence than one under unified PAN governance.

The results in Model 2 introduce important nuances about the nature of intergovernmental partisan cooperation and conflict and allow us to distinguish between different structures of opposition power. To facilitate the substantive interpretation of these results, Figure 4.2 provides a graphic representation of the model's main findings. It shows incidence rate ratios of violence for every party layering. Note that variables are not statistically significant when the confidence intervals cross the zero line. Four findings are worth stressing.

First, the null statistical significance associated with the PAN-PAN-PRI and PAN-PAN-PRD cases shows that municipalities in PAN-dominated states experienced lower levels of violence than the rest of the country regardless of the party in control of the municipality. This suggests that coordination between the president and his co-partisan governors was crucial for keeping criminal violence under control – as the case of Baja California emblematically shows (see Chapter 5).

TABLE 4.2 *Vertical Fragmentation of Power, Partisan Conflict, and Inter-Cartel Violence in Mexico, 2007–2012 (Random Effects Negative Binomial Models with Logged Population as Offset Variable)*

	Model 1		Model 2		Model 3	
	Coeff.	IRR	Coeff.	IRR	Coeff.	IRR
Vertical fragmentation and partisan conflict						
Juxtaposition index	0.110***	1.116				
	[0.015]					
PAN-PAN-PRI			−0.089	0.915		
			[0.102]			
PAN-PAN-PRD			0.069	1.072		
			[0.211]			
PAN-PRI-PAN			0.16	1.173		
			[0.111]			
PAN-PRI-PRI			0.271***	1.312		
			[0.097]			
PAN-PRI-PRD			0.128	1.136		
			[0.143]			
PAN-PRD-PAN			0.242	1.273		
			[0.189]			
PAN-PRD-PRI			0.960***	2.612		
			[0.134]			
PAN-PRD-PRD			0.740***	2.097		
			[0.135]			

Confl2 (PAN-PRI-regardless)					0.308*** [0.083]	1.360
Confl3 (PAN-PRD-regardless)					0.853*** [0.114]	2.346

State security policy

Leadership decapitation	0.144*** [0.015]	1.155	0.143*** [0.015]	1.154	0.143*** [0.015]	1.154
Federal security funds	−0.169** [0.080]	0.844	−0.135* [0.081]	0.874	−0.140* [0.080]	0.869

State presence

Prosecutors per 10,000 pop	0.068*** [0.020]	1.071	0.066*** [0.020]	1.068	0.064*** [0.020]	1.066
Poverty index	0.018*** [0.002]	1.019	0.018*** [0.002]	1.018	0.019*** [0.002]	1.019

Party alternation and electoral competition

State alternation	−0.127** [0.061]	0.880	−0.149** [0.063]	0.861	−0.147** [0.062]	0.863
Municipal alternation	0.026 [0.050]	1.026	0.048 [0.050]	1.050	0.025 [0.050]	1.025
State electoral competition	0.422*** [0.100]	1.524	0.372*** [0.106]	1.450	0.362*** [0.105]	1.436
Municipal electoral competition	−0.107*** [0.041]	0.899	−0.095** [0.041]	0.909	−0.099** [0.041]	0.905

(continued)

TABLE 4.2 *(continued)*

	Model 1		Model 2		Model 3	
	Coeff.	IRR	Coeff.	IRR	Coeff.	IRR
Sociodemographic controls						
Sex ratio	0.077***	1.080	0.076***	1.079	0.078***	1.081
	[0.007]		[0.007]		[0.007]	
Ages 15–34	−0.021***	0.979	−0.022***	0.978	−0.022***	0.979
	[0.003]		[0.003]		[0.003]	
Mono-parental households	0.083***	1.087	0.084***	1.088	0.086***	1.090
	[0.008]		[0.008]		[0.008]	
Spatial controls						
Violence in neighboring mun. $(t-1)$	0.006***	1.006	0.006***	1.006	0.006***	1.006
	[0.001]		[0.001]		[0.001]	
Geographic controls	YES		YES		YES	
Constant	−22.181***		−22.289***		−22.469***	
	[1.459]		[1.479]		[1.475]	
Observations	11,908		12,080		12,080	
Log-likelihood	−8244.965		−8319.991		−8329.707	
BIC	16696.4		16912.56		16875.6	

Standard errors in brackets. *** p<0.01, ** p<0.05, * p<0.10. Clustered standard errors in brackets.
The party in the first cell is the president's; the second is the governor's; and the third is the mayor's. PAN-PAN-PAN is the reference category. PAN = national incumbent (conservative); PRI = opposition (center); PRD = opposition (Left).

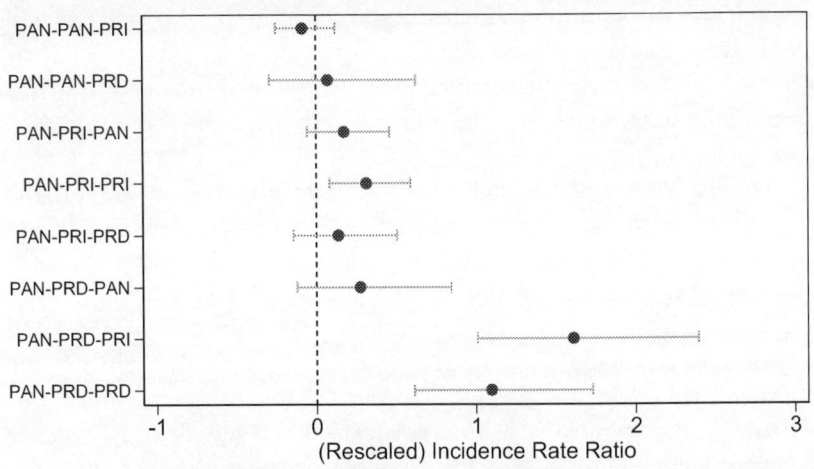

Incidence Rate Ratios (IRR) from Model 2 were rescaled for purposes of interpretation.
Original IRRs were subtracted one unit to show the direct impact of juxtaposition on violence.
PAN = incumbent party in presidential power (conservative);
PRI = opposition (center); PRD = opposition (Left).
The party in the first cell is the president's, the second one is the governor's, and the third is the mayor's. PAN-PAN-PAN is the reference category.

FIGURE 4.2 Impact of Vertical Fragmentation of Power on Criminal Violence in Mexico, 2007–2012

Second, compared to states ruled by PANista governors, municipalities in states under the PRI did not always experience higher levels of violence. It was only in cases with the PAN-PRI-PRI structure that violence was slightly higher. Compared to a case of unified governance under the PAN, PRI municipalities in states with PRI governors experienced 31 percent more criminal violence (IRR = 1.312). This suggests that President Calderón was able to reach some level of contingent cooperation with PRI governors to fight criminal violence – as the case of Chihuahua attests (see Chapter 5).

Third, results unambiguously show that municipalities in states ruled under the leftist PRD experienced significantly higher levels of criminal violence than the rest of the country. PRI and PRD municipalities in leftist states (PAN-PRD-PRI and PAN-PRD-PRD) experienced between 161 and 109 percent (IRR = 2.612 and 2.097) more violence than municipalities under PAN unified governance. As Figure 4.2 strikingly shows, the most violent municipalities were opposition municipalities in leftist states. These results suggest that President Calderón did not reach any significant cooperation agreement with leftist governors and that his conflicts with leftist subnational authorities and the strategic abandonment of leftist governors in confronting major waves of criminal attacks resulted in more intense criminal violence – as the case of Michoacán exemplifies (see Chapter 5).

Finally, results in Model 2 (Table 4.2) and Figure 4.2 provide straightforward evidence on the partisan conflict between the federal PAN government and the PRD governors. Despite having the same degree of vertical fragmentation, the PAN-PRD-PRI layering (IRR = 2. 612) yields nearly *12 times* more criminal violence than the PAN-PRI-PRD layering (IRR = 1.136). This comparison strongly suggests that in the War on Drugs, President Calderón's relations with Mexico's two major opposition parties differed significantly: whereas the president might have achieved some degree of cooperation with the PRI, the party that did not contest the president's electoral victory and that was a likely legislative ally for his economic agenda, the relationship with the Left, the president's main political rivals, was marked by confrontation, conflict, and lack of intergovernmental cooperation.

Since one of the most compelling findings in Model 2 (Table 4.2) is that the governor's partisan affiliation is a crucial factor in accounting for differing levels of inter-cartel violence, we decided to drill a little deeper into federal–state intergovernmental relations. Focusing on the governors' partisanship, Model 3 in Table 4.2 provides valuable confirmatory evidence of the existence of a major political conflict between President Calderón and leftist governors. Compared to municipalities in states ruled by the president's party, results in Model 3 show that municipalities in states ruled by PRI governors (*Confl2*) experienced 31.8 percent more violence (IRR = 1.360), but municipalities in states ruled by leftist PRD governors (*Confl3*) experienced 134.6 percent more violence (IRR = 2.346). This striking *fourfold difference* between the PRI and PRD states suggests that, contrary to the coordination argument, in the War on Drugs President Calderón established a very different relationship with the PRI (the party that supported his accession to power) and the PRD (the party that denied the president's constitutional legitimacy). As these findings strongly suggest, something unique was taking place in leftist subnational regions.

The results from the control variables reveal that other factors beyond vertical fragmentation and intergovernmental partisan conflict also mattered.

State strategy mattered in ways consistent with the literature. We find that the federal government's success in removing narco leaders stimulated, rather than deterred, inter-cartel violence. In contrast, the increased availability of federal transfers labeled for public safety became a deterrent of inter-cartel violence.[27] This means that these funds probably increased subnational authorities' capacity to prevent or contain inter-cartel violence. However, the fact that our measures of vertical fragmentation remain significant in the presence of these controls indicates that the relationship between the federal government and subnational authorities had an independent impact on violence beyond mere distributive politics.

Contrary to the Weberian (1918/1994) view, endorsed by students of civil wars (Fearon and Laitin 2003), that a greater state presence reduces violence, our findings show that municipalities with more state judicial presence – more public prosecutors – tend to be more violent. This potentially speaks of the collusion between local judicial authorities and crime – that is, that members of the public prosecutors' offices are active participants in the gray zone of criminality.

Contrary to our results for the pre-2006 period, in which party alternation in state gubernatorial power was a stimulant of inter-cartel violence, our findings for the 2007–2012 period show that party alternation had a negative effect on inter-cartel violence. However, consistent with our argument about intergovernmental partisan conflict between the federal government and the Left, further analysis reveals that the effect of party alternation on violence is conditional on the new party in government.[28] While new PAN and PRI governors were, on average, able to reduce levels of drug-related homicides, incoming PRD governors faced rising levels of inter-cartel violence. This means that, due to bitter intergovernmental partisan conflict between Right and Left, the accession of

---

[27] A more disaggregated analysis reveals that federal funds are negatively associated with violence in municipalities with PANista governors, but positively associated in municipalities with PRD governors (see Appendix D, Table D.3). Given our main results – showing higher levels of violence in municipalities from leftist states – this is a reasonable outcome because according to FASP's distribution formula, the most violent states received greater funds. We cannot disregard the potential political use of these funds, but an analysis of the assignment of federal security funds is beyond the scope of this book. For purpose of our analysis, however, it is important to note that the inclusion of federal funds in the model does not alter the impact of our main explanatory variables, indicating that the effect of partisan conflict does not (exclusively) run through the assignment of security funds.

[28] See Appendix D, Table D.3.

leftist candidates to state gubernatorial power during the presidency of President Calderón was associated with rising levels of violence.

Consistent with the scholarly finding that associates subnational electoral competition with more intense violence, results show that increasing state electoral competition has a positive impact on inter-cartel violence. Surprisingly, municipal electoral competition has a negative association with inter-cartel violence. According to Ponce (2016), drug-related violence during President Calderón's War on Drugs reduced the competitiveness of municipal elections. The negative coefficient of municipal electoral competition is thus a likely indication of reverse causality – violence reduces municipal electoral competition, rather than the other way around. Finally, the results show the existence of spillover effects of violence – inter-cartel violence increased the probability of future criminal violence in neighboring municipalities.

In summary, controlling for state security policy, state presence, subnational political structures, sociodemographic factors, and geographic factors, our results unambiguously show that after the 2007 federal intervention, criminal violence was more intense in cities from states ruled by leftist governors – the main political rivals of the conservative president.

QUANTITATIVE EVIDENCE II: A NATURAL EXPERIMENT

Although our statistical models show that partisan vertical fragmentation and intergovernmental partisan conflict were strongly associated with the intensity of inter-cartel violence in the War on Drugs, we cannot yet claim that this association is causal. It could be the case that inter-cartel violence shapes the vertical fragmentation of power rather than the other way around. In other words, cartels could be using violence to stimulate vertical fragmentation of power and subsequently take advantage of the partisan conflict between the federal PAN government and the PRD governors to conquer new territories. It could also be the case that there are unobservable factors that explain both vertical fragmentation of power and inter-cartel violence. To the extent that we cannot observe these factors, we may be erroneously attributing the intensification of violence to intergovernmental partisan conflict between Left and Right.

To address these challenges, we conduct a natural experiment and compare the evolution of inter-cartel violence across a number of municipalities located along the state borders of the western states of Michoacán and Jalisco. As Map 4.1 shows, these are municipalities from western

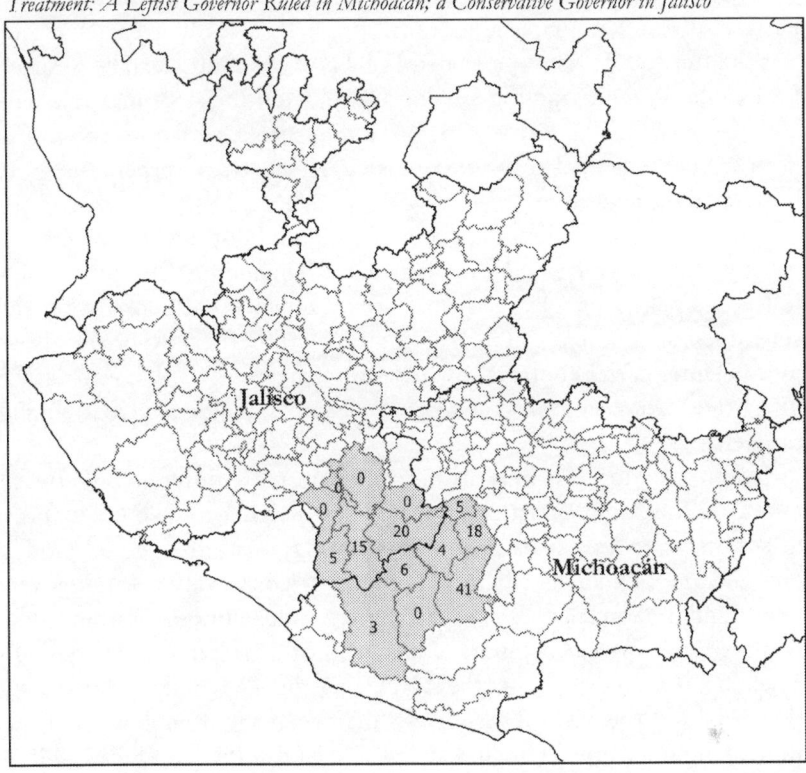

MAP 4.1 Drug-Related Murders in Neighboring Municipalities of Tierra Caliente in Michoacán and Jalisco, 2008–2011

Michoacán (Tierra Caliente) and the southeast of Jalisco.[29] Although separated by state borders, which were drawn in the nineteenth century in a process that was entirely unrelated to twenty-first-century inter-cartel wars, these municipalities share many geographic, sociodemographic, cultural, and economic features and constitute a homogeneous region (see Appendix E for detailed information and an extensive discussion of the relevance and validity of this comparison).[30]

---

[29] We use a two-degree neighborhood criterion; that is, we include a municipality's most immediate neighbors and the most immediate neighbors of the municipality's neighbors.

[30] In Appendix E we address four potential challenges: (1) imbalance of predictors and contextual factors between groups of municipalities; (2) lack of independent effect of treatment; (3) unidentified intervening variables; and (4) 'self-selection' of municipalities across states.

In terms of criminal markets, Tierra Caliente in Michoacán was the bastion of La Familia Michoacana, the state's leading cartel in the 2000s after the Zetas – the armed branch of the Gulf Cartel – assisted La Familia in removing the Sinaloa Cartel from the state in 2002. The alliance between the Zetas and La Familia broke down in 2005, and both groups engaged in a six-year deadly war that turned the state into a killing field.

From the 1980s, Jalisco had been a stronghold of the Sinaloa Cartel, but it was first challenged by the Juárez and Tijuana Cartels in the 1990s followed by challenges by the Zetas and La Familia in the 2000s, when the state, including the area along the southeastern border, experienced significant inter-cartel conflicts. By 2006 three cartels had strong presence along the Michoacán/Jalisco border: La Familia, the Sinaloa Cartel, and the Zetas.

Despite multiple similarities, an important difference between municipalities in western Michoacán and neighboring municipalities in southeastern Jalisco is that a leftist PRD governor, Leonel Godoy (2008–2011), ruled in Michoacán while a conservative PAN governor, Emilio González (2007–2013), ruled in Jalisco. Within these regions, the overwhelming majority of the municipalities in Michoacán were ruled by the PRD and the PRI and in Jalisco by the PAN and the PRI. Whereas in Michoacán the dominant distribution of political power included the PAN-PRD-PRD and PAN-PRD-PRI layers, the predominant layering in Jalisco was PAN-PAN-PAN and PAN-PAN-PRI. As a result, patterns of intergovernmental cooperation and conflict between the federal, state, and local authorities were dramatically different across the two states.

In confronting the escalation of drug violence that followed the federal intervention, President Calderón worked closely with his PAN co-partisan in Jalisco. The federal and the state governments set up "security coordination meetings," in which federal authorities, the Mexican army, and state- and municipal-level authorities discussed and agreed on security strategies to contain turf wars in the state. By 2010 these meetings were taking place on a weekly basis (Mural 2010). The coordination of the federal, state, and municipal authorities led to the detention of four drug lords from the Sinaloa Cartel[31] and, most importantly, it helped contain the subsequent rise in violence that followed the arrests (Gil and Pérez

---

[31] Oscar Nava Valencia, Juan Carlos Nava Valencia, Ignacio Coronel, and Erick Valencia Salazar.

2012). As shown in Map 4.1, between 2008 and 2011[32] the southeastern municipalities of Jalisco experienced 40 drug-related murders (28.09 murders per 100,000 of the population).

In contrast, as we explain in detail in Chapter 5, the federal intervention in Michoacán was unilateral and there was no dialogue between the military and the state security forces. Instead of cooperation, the federal government launched a large-scale ("mega") arrest against leftist security officials and mayors and ran a smear campaign to discredit the Left as corrupt and inept. These attacks weakened local political authorities and made municipalities in regions such as western Michoacán vulnerable to contestation by different cartels. As shown in Map 4.1, between 2008 and 2011 the municipalities from the western edge of Tierra Caliente Michoacán experienced 77 murders associated with inter-cartel conflicts (36.27 murders per 100,000 of the population).

We attribute the *two-fold* difference in the absolute number of attacks between these two border regions to partisan intergovernmental conflict between Left and Right. Conflicts over the control of drug trafficking routes and over new criminal markets, including extortion and kidnapping for ransom, were more severe in Michoacán than in Jalisco.[33] This was because subnational authorities in the leftist states were not only militarily unprotected but were under serious political and judicial attacks from the federal government, which rendered them vulnerable to attacks by competing cartels and OCGs.

The Left came to power in Michoacán and the Right in Jalisco for reasons unrelated to the drug violence – a fact that is crucial for our claim. The governor of Jalisco was elected prior to the War on Drugs (2006) and the governor of Michoacán was elected as the War was just starting (2007). This should dispel concerns about reverse causality. Within the states, both the western part of Tierra Caliente in Michoacán and southeastern Jalisco are small enough to render it unlikely that voting in these municipalities might have determined the outcome of the gubernatorial elections. It is therefore safe to consider the fact that one region had a leftist governor and another a conservative governor as an exogenous

[32] This is the time period in which a left- and a right-wing governor ruled in Michoacán and Jalisco.
[33] According to government data, by the end of the Calderón administration in 2012, Michoacán had a kidnapping rate of 2.34 per 100,000 inhabitants, while the figure for Jalisco was 0.42. Similarly, the extortion rate per 100,000 in Michoacán was 7.61, compared to a rate of 6.36 in Jalisco (SESNP 2016).

factor that led the two regions into different trajectories of inter-cartel violence.

CONCLUSION

After nearly two decades of inter-cartel wars in which the federal government had failed to develop any proactive policy response, in December 2006 President Felipe Calderón declared war on the cartels and deployed the military to the country's most conflictive regions. This intervention led to a major criminal backlash, to the intensification of inter-cartel wars, and to a dramatic increase in violence. But the intensification of violence varied widely across subnational regions.

In this chapter we have shown that the uneven spread of inter-cartel violence after the federal intervention was intimately associated with patterns of intergovernmental cooperation and conflict between the federal government and subnational authorities. The common view suggests that in the War on Drugs and the military intervention, President Calderón could not work with any opposition governor at all. Contrary to this, however, we have shown that it was only *leftists* with whom President Calderón could not – or would not – work. As our evidence reveals, the intervention succeeded in containing drug violence where the president had electoral incentives to work with his co-partisan subnational peers, partially worked in subnational regions ruled by the PRI, but failed in states ruled by the Left, where violence became more intense. By disaggregating the opposition, we are able to show that the most dramatic intensification of violence affected towns and cities in leftist states. In the context of a bitter partisan conflict between Left and Right, we take these findings as a strong indication that, in the War on Drugs, the federal government devised relatively successful interventions to contain the escalation of violence in municipalities from conservative states but purposefully devised poor interventions in states dominated by the Left. Our empirical findings have three important theoretical implications for the study of governance of large-scale violence in federations.

First, by introducing partisanship and partisan conflict into our understanding of intergovernmental relations, we have shown that political incentives can define security policy outcomes in federations. While students of distributive politics have long recognized the important role of political incentives in the allocation of public spending, scholars of security and policing have only recently begun to recognize the partisan use of law enforcement. Consistent with theories of distributive politics and with

Wilkinson's (2004) important finding of the partisan use of police forces to control inter-religious violence in India, we have provided evidence of the partisan use of law enforcement in Mexico's War on Drugs. We have also underlined the political incentives that led Mexico's president to protect his subnational co-partisans facing major surges in inter-cartel violence but to abandon his political enemies facing similar conditions.

Second, our findings challenge the widely held Weberian assumption that government officials will always want to adopt policies that maximize the state's monopoly of violence. Our results show that under conditions of acute political polarization between Left and Right, conservative federal authorities in Mexico sought to "manage" criminal violence, protecting the president's subnational co-partisans but deliberately leaving the president's political enemies unprotected. This finding strongly suggests that the generalized assumption that state agents will always seek to monopolize violence is unwarranted: under conditions of acute political polarization state agents can reward their allies but tolerate private violence to punish their political enemies.[34]

Finally, our findings point to the crucial need for effective checks and balances to constrain the discretionary use of the military, police forces, and law enforcement agencies by national executives in federations. As the federal intervention in the War on Drugs in Mexico shows, absent effective checks and balances President Calderón was able to devise a politicized intervention that signaled to the criminal underworld that cities and towns in states ruled by the Left were unprotected. Mexico's bitter partisan intergovernmental conflict between Left and Right, in fact, changed the balance of power in the gray zone of criminality. It made local governments and municipalities in drug trafficking regions with leftist governors vulnerable to criminal encroachment and opened opportunities for multiple cartels and new criminal organizations to fight over the control of drug trafficking routes and new criminal markets.

While in this chapter we have shown that partisan vertical fragmentation and intergovernmental partisan conflict had a causal impact on the uneven spread of inter-cartel violence during the War on Drugs, the mechanics of this process remain historically unexplained. Drawing on three case studies, the following chapter explains *how* partisanship shaped the federal intervention in the Mexican War on Drugs and *why* these varied interventions contributed to containing or intensifying inter-cartel violence.

---

[34] For a similar conclusion in the context of political violence, see Staniland (2012).

5

Unpacking the War on Drugs

Presidents, Governors, and Large-Scale Narco Violence

One of the most surprising findings in the study of federalism in recent years is that, in violent societies marked by acute political polarization, electoral incentives can shape law enforcement activities. The deployment of police forces to contain violence is not always a technical decision but may be a political one. In such federal systems violence varies widely across subnational regions partly as a result of electoral politics: higher-level authorities assist, or refrain from assisting, lower-level governments and victims when it is politically convenient (Wilkinson 2004; Auyero 2006; Trejo and Ley 2016).

In Chapter 4 we showed that the War on Drugs in Mexico, launched in a context of acute political polarization between a conservative federal government and a leftist opposition, was politically biased – that is, electoral incentives played a key role as a determinant of intergovernmental cooperation or conflict. Using multivariate statistical models and a natural experiment, we showed that the intensity of violence during the Mexican War on Drugs was disproportionately greater in municipalities of states ruled by the Left – the president's main political rival. This presented a stark contrast to municipalities in states ruled by the president's own conservative party, where drug violence was contained or even reduced.

Although our statistical analyses show that the relationship between partisan vertical fragmentation and inter-cartel violence is causal, many questions remain unanswered about the ability of co-partisan authorities to contain violence and about the linkages between intergovernmental partisan conflict and the intensification of inter-cartel violence. To explain these connections, we need to have a deeper understanding of the objectives and multiple dimensions of the federal intervention, how inter-governmental partisan conflict shaped the federal government's actions in the War on Drugs, and the cartels' responses to intergovernmental coop-eration and conflict. In this chapter we present evidence on how partisan-ship shaped the federal government interventions in the Mexican War on Drugs and why these varied interventions reduced or stimulated criminal violence.

Building on the statistical results from Chapter 4, we draw on multiple in-depth personal interviews with key national and sub-national political and social actors during President Felipe Calderón's administration (2006–2012), as well as on secondary sources, to disaggregate the federal intervention along four dimen-sions: (1) the deployment of the military and the federal police and their cooperation with subnational police forces; (2) the judicial inves-tigation and prosecution of subnational authorities suspected of collu-sion with organized crime; (3) the federal government's communication strategy to expose and denounce such corruption; and (4) the crisis management assistance – for instance, targeted social policies – to help subnational authorities confront the spiral of vio-lence that resulted from the federal government's military intervention. Our goal is to assess whether variation along these four dimensions helped to quell or stimulate criminal violence across several major urban areas in Mexico.

We focus our assessment of the federal intervention on three cities that share many relevant characteristics except for the vertical distri-bution of power: (1) Tijuana (PAN) in the state of Baja California (PAN); (2) Apatzingán (PRD) in the state of Michoacán (PRD); and (3) Ciudad Juárez (PRI) in the state of Chihuahua (PRI). These cities are urban centers that are both major drug trafficking hubs and home to powerful drug cartels. In all three cases the federal government launched a military intervention to quell inter-cartel wars. Note that each case represents a different party layering. Using the notation introduced in Chapter 4, in which the first cell represents the presi-dent's party, the second the governor's party, and the third the mayor's party, we are analyzing three cases: PAN-**PAN**-PAN (Tijuana); PAN-**PRD**-PRD (Apatzingán); and PAN-**PRI**-PRI (Juárez). Recall that the PAN was the federal conservative incumbent, the PRD was the leftist opposition, and the PRI was the centrist opposition. Map 5.1 identifies the geographic location of these three cities, together with the following cities that serve to extend the analysis:

MAP 5.1 Selected Mexican Cities Experiencing Major Outbreaks of Criminal Violence, 2006–2012

Guadalajara and Coroneo (PAN-PAN-PAN); Acapulco and Zacatecas (PAN-PRD-PRD); and Monterrey (PAN-PRI-PRI).

Because the statistical findings reported in Chapter 4 unambiguously showed that governors were the key defining actors for the success or failure of the federal intervention, our analysis pays particular attention to how the relationship between the federal government and state governors affected the dynamics of narco violence in the cities.

On the basis of the analysis of the federal intervention in these cities, we show that the federal government followed differentiated strategies across states, depending on the partisan affiliation of state authorities.

In Baja California and other PAN-led conservative states, shared electoral incentives motivated the federal government to work together with the president's co-partisan governors and mayors. They aimed to coordinate the deployment of the military and the federal police in their cities, avoid judicial prosecution of local co-partisans who colluded with organized crime, purge corrupt police forces while avoiding any media scandal, and design targeted social policy interventions to prevent the youth from joining the cartels and their private militias. These coordinated actions empowered subnational authorities to contain epidemics of violence.

In contrast, in states governed by the PRD, such as Michoacán, the federal government conducted a unilateral military intervention without consulting subnational authorities. They also withheld federal assistance, adopted a punishment strategy against leftist subnational authorities – by which the federal government publicly prosecuted and exposed through smear campaigns those whom it accused of collusion with organized crime – and failed to design any shared social policy intervention with local authorities. This hostile strategy weakened subnational authorities in leftist states and opened the way for drug cartels and their criminal associates to compete for control over drug trafficking corridors and new criminal markets, contributing to the outbreak of violence epidemics.

Unlike in leftist states, in states ruled by the PRI, such as Chihuahua, cooperation between federal and "loyal" opposition subnational authorities was contingent on local circumstances. It was largely motivated by the federal government's need of the PRI's legislative support for the success of the president's agenda of market-oriented reforms, and on pressure from civil society to achieve cooperative agreements to halt the spread of violence epidemics. This contingent cooperation partially contributed to the containment of violence.

The case studies reveal that a politicized and militaristic strategy to quell drug violence can have devastating consequences. Unilateral federal intervention becomes ineffective due to the lack of appropriate local information. Moreover, the politicization of judicial prosecution to dismantle alleged networks of local government protection for cartels, and the launching of smear campaigns against subnational government authorities, opens opportunities for rival cartels to compete for politically contested and unprotected territories. Consistent with the statistical findings reported in Chapter 4, the narratives in this chapter show that violence became more intense in municipalities in leftist states. This was not the result of leftist incompetence, but of a political strategy by which a conservative president tried to divert the political costs of a faulty federal intervention onto his political enemies. The politicization of the federal intervention in the War on Drugs was possible – as we explained from the outset of this book – because Mexico transitioned from authoritarian rule to democracy without reforming the unchecked presidential control of the armed forces and the judicial system.[1]

---

[1] For the Mexican president's control over the military, see Camp (2005) and Díez (2008, 2012). For the president's and the governors' control over the police, see Sabet (2012). For

The chapter is structured in six sections. We first discuss the general features of the federal intervention, beginning in 2006, and its transformation throughout the Calderón administration. Focusing on the case of Tijuana in Baja California, in the second section we describe how partisan alignment facilitated intergovernmental cooperation. In the third section we examine the case of Apatzingán in Michoacán and provide a detailed analysis of how partisan fragmentation in leftist states resulted in bitter intergovernmental conflict, leaving local PRD authorities unprotected. This made them vulnerable to criminal attacks, and opened opportunities for cartels to compete for control over drug trafficking routes and new criminal markets. In the fourth section we address the case of Ciudad Juárez in Chihuahua and show how partisan fragmentation in PRI-led states resulted in contingent intergovernmental cooperation. In the fifth section we illustrate the dramatic transformation of the criminal underworld as a result of federal intervention through the War on Drugs. In the conclusion we discuss the theoretical and practical implications of the joint findings presented in Chapters 4 and 5 on the politicization of militarized law enforcement actions.

THE WAR ON DRUGS: MOTIVATION AND STRATEGY FOR THE FEDERAL INTERVENTION

President Calderón's War on Drugs and the federal intervention can be divided into two phases. First, from December 2006 to mid-2008 the federal government deployed the armed forces – the military and the navy – and the federal police to the country's most conflictive regions. Second, from mid-2008 until 2012 federal authorities developed more comprehensive security interventions – including local police reform, judicial activities to dismantle state–criminal collusion, and preventive social and economic policy measures – to respond to the virulent backlash from cartels against the initial military deployment.

The initial deployment of the armed forces in December 2006 resulted from a governance imperative. By declaring war on the country's drug cartels, the president was hoping to shift public opinion away from the polarizing post-election crisis toward the country's rising security crisis. Rallying the nation behind the armed forces and their commander-in-chief to destroy the country's powerful drug cartels seemed to be a "valence

the president's control over the judiciary under the PRI and then in the post-PRI era, see Cornelius and Shirk (2007) and Ríos-Figueroa and Aguilar (2018).

issue" that would help the president to reunify the nation behind him and his administration. Hence, the initial deployment of the armed forces did not discriminate along partisan lines. In fact, it began in the leftist state of Michoacán – the president's home state – and then spread to the rest of the country's most conflictive regions. President Calderón believed that the War on Drugs would be an easy fix to an acute political crisis (Aguilar and Castañeda 2009).

Aimed at curtailing the cartels, suppressing inter-cartel violence, and recovering territories under the cartels' command, military and federal police interventions resulted in an unexpected major criminal backlash and in the dramatic escalation of violence (Espinosa and Rubin 2015; Flores-Macías 2018). The federal government's decapitation strategy, focused on arresting or killing the leaders of the country's main cartels, led to the outbreak of major spirals of intra- and inter-cartel competition and violence (Guerrero 2011b; Calderón et al. 2015; Phillips 2015). As violence skyrocketed and several cities and regions experienced the outbreak of "violence epidemics" (Guerrero 2012), the War on Drugs was no longer a valence issue; over the course of the next few years, in fact, it would become an issue that would divide the country and that would result in major electoral losses, particularly among PAN local governments (Ley 2017).

By the end of 2008, "managing violence," rather than suppressing it, became the government's new objective (Bravo 2011). President Calderón and his team were no longer Weberian state officials trying to establish the monopoly of coercion within a given territory, but opportunistic politicians trying to adopt a new strategy of damage control. They accepted responsibility for the violence in areas where President Calderón could persuade his subnational co-partisans to follow him in confronting the cartels, while elsewhere blaming the violence on his political rivals. The accusation was particularly focused on leftist subnational authorities who did not recognize him as a legitimate president, bitterly opposed his economic agenda, and were poised to become his main electoral challengers in the 2009 midterm legislative election.[2]

---

[2] Ley (2017) notes that in 2012, 45 percent of the Mexican public blamed the ongoing violence on government authorities, among whom 71 percent blamed it specifically on President Calderón. In subnational races PAN candidates sided with the president and emphasized the long-term benefits of his security policies, while opposition candidates highlighted the short-term failure of the president's militarized strategy.

The key question is whether the *partisan turn* in the War on Drugs affected the federal intervention and whether intergovernmental partisan conflict stimulated criminal violence. We address these questions by comparing the dynamics of violence in cities that are part of three different structures of partisan vertical integration: PAN-PAN-PAN, PAN-PRD-PRD, and PAN-PRI-PRI. By focusing on these three prototypical structures, we are able to explore positive cases of intergovernmental co-partisan cooperation (PAN-PAN-PAN); negative cases of intergovernmental partisan conflict between Right and Left (PAN-PRD-PRD); and uncommon cases of contingent cooperation between Right and Center (PAN-PRI-PRI). We use these case studies to compare the differentiated logics and developments of the federal interventions and assess the causal chain that connects intergovernmental cooperation and conflict to the swelling of criminal violence.

PARTISAN ALIGNMENT AND INTERGOVERNMENTAL COORDINATION

Baja California – Tijuana

The federal (PAN) intervention in the northwestern state of Baja California (PAN) in the city of Tijuana (PAN) illustrates how effective intergovernmental cooperation between federal and subnational co-partisans resulted in law enforcement actions that enabled the authorities to contain an unprecedented spiral of inter-cartel violence.[3] The intervention in Baja California also shows that intergovernmental cooperation is not an automatic or unproblematic process; it reveals, however, that shared electoral incentives can motivate co-partisans from different levels of government to work together effectively and to recover the state's authority over territories that have fallen under the control of drug cartels.

As noted in Chapter 3, the state of Baja California is the home of the Tijuana Cartel, and it was under the control of the PAN from Ernesto Ruffo's 1989 electoral victory until 2019. Following the first alternation in gubernatorial power, the state experienced the outbreak of the first major inter-cartel war in Mexico. Since then the Sinaloa Cartel has fought a protracted war against the leaders of the Tijuana Cartel, the Arellano Félix siblings, for the control of Tijuana – the main entry point into California.

---

[3] For more information on intergovernmental cooperation in Tijuana, see Sabet (2012) and Durán-Martínez (2018).

In the face of growing levels of inter-cartel wars and criminal violence in the city, President Calderón ordered the deployment of the army to Tijuana in January 2007. In line with the kingpin strategy, the army intervention's main goal was to arrest the leaders of the Tijuana Cartel in order to restore peace. After an initial slowdown, violence skyrocketed in 2008 when the Sinaloa Cartel took advantage of the arrest of Eduardo Arellano Félix, then Tijuana's criminal boss, to launch a major attack to dispute the Arellano Félix's traditional control of the city's profitable drug trafficking corridors (Guerrero 2011a, 2012). Besides a surge in inter-cartel executions, Tijuana and other major cities in Baja California experienced a major wave of kidnappings (Jones 2013) and criminal attacks against state and local police officers.

In line with the federal government's militaristic approach, the incoming PAN Governor, José G. Millán (2007–2013), approached General Sergio Aponte, the chief of the second military zone who was stationed in Baja California, for additional assistance in confronting the state's new security crisis. Aponte agreed and worked closely with high-ranking members of the army who were appointed to serve as state-level and municipal-level police chiefs (Cervantes 2007). As noted by Durán-Martínez (2018), this implied a high degree of cohesion across security forces at all government levels. Moreover, the Tijuana PAN mayor, Jorge Ramos, collaborated closely with Governor Millán, and key activities of the Tijuana police were merged with the state-level command (Zamarripa 2007).

Intergovernmental cooperation between PAN officials and security personnel faced its first major challenge when General Aponte published a surprising manifesto in the state's leading news outlets denouncing widespread corruption and collusion in organized crime in the state attorney's office, the state judicial police, the secretariat of public security, and the police forces of Tijuana and other major cities. The manifesto named over 40 high- and mid-ranking officials, mostly from PAN administrations.[4] Despite direct accusations, Governor Millán stood by his state prosecutor, Rommel Moreno, and refused to ask for his resignation (Reforma 2008a).

Facing the potential of a major political scandal in a PAN stronghold, the federal government developed a comprehensive security intervention for Baja California. First, President Calderón's federal interior minister met with General Aponte, Governor Millán, and the state prosecutor and

---

[4] The letter was reproduced by the national and local press. See Martínez (2008).

agreed to undertake a purge of the state's police forces, exchange information, and reinforce coordination among security authorities (Jiménez and Cervantes 2008). However, confrontations and tensions between state authorities and General Aponte continued (Reforma 2008b). To protect his co-partisans, President Calderón took a radical measure and transferred General Aponte to a new military station outside of Baja California and appointed General Alfonso Duarte as the new military zone commander. Governor Millán, in turn, appointed General Duarte as coordinator of all of the state's police forces and, with the support of the federal government, removed corrupt state-level officials but strategically decided *not to prosecute* any of them in order to prevent any major media scandal.[5] Jorge Ramos, the PANista mayor of Tijuana, and his secretary of public security, Colonel Julián Leyzaola, followed a similar strategy when they purged the city police. Cooperation in these cases meant the strategic and selective management of corruption and the silent removal of corrupt officers linked to PAN administrations. This would help avoid voters' punishment for corruption and signal to the Tijuana and Sinaloa cartels that the authorities were unified in their actions. As privileged beneficiaries of federal transfers, mayors in Tijuana and Mexicali – the state's capital – launched crime prevention programs.

With resolute federal support, General Duarte and Colonel Leyzaola adopted a coordinated iron-fist policy involving (1) the arrest or extrajudicial execution of drug lords and the leaders of private militias, (2) major seizures of drug shipments, and (3) the confiscation of weapons. As various human rights NGOs and the Human Rights National Commission (CNDH) reported, Baja California's militarized police systematically relied on torture and violated due process in conducting many of these arrests and investigations (Sabet 2012). Despite accusations of systematic and generalized human rights violations, the federal government supported Duarte's and Leyzaola's actions and provided renewed military assistance when their civilian bosses became the targets of criminal attacks.

With full federal assistance, including generous economic transfers, Governor Millán and successive Tijuana mayors from the PAN and the PRI launched a series of economic and social investment programs, mainly

---

[5] Such was the case of Sonia Patricia Navarro, control and security director in the state prosecutor's office, who was accused of protecting the Tijuana Cartel but was never investigated for such accusations. Instead, she resigned a few days after Aponte's letter and left her position in the state government without prosecution. See Corpus (2008).

targeted at the city's youth in impoverished areas.[6] The goal was to restore economic activity in Tijuana, to rebuild the city's public image, to open new business opportunities for the youth, and to prevent young men from continuing to join the gangs that were eventually absorbed by drug cartels to fight turf wars.

The federal intervention in Baja California and Tijuana succeeded in containing a major spiral of criminal violence and bringing drug-related murders to pre-crisis levels[7] because federal, state, and local authorities were able to engage in coordinated action to implement a broad security agenda (Durán-Martínez 2018). The military intervention was effective because a new and relatively cleaner Tijuana police force provided crucial information to military and federal police officers that facilitated multiple arrests and drug seizures. The federal protection the Tijuana mayor received when his administration had to confront a major criminal backlash prevented cartels from capturing the local government and empowered the mayor to conduct additional police purges. Finally, the coordinated social policy actions provided opportunities for economic and social mobility to young males whose only attractive option previously had been to join the cartels' private militias.

Without widespread local police protection, the Tijuana Cartel became weaker. Without extensive access to the local youth, the cartel's private militias became less effective. Moreover, the renovation and coordination of police forces in Baja California limited the opportunities for the Sinaloa Cartel to effectively contest the control of Tijuana. Aligned partisan authorities working together encouraged rival cartels to leave the city and the state and avoid further turf wars. Between 2009 and 2011, drug-related murders in Tijuana decreased by 24 percent (Guerrero 2012).

Although this coordinated strategy deactivated an epidemic of violence, Tijuana continued to be a very violent city. A few years later, it returned to the top of Mexico's ranking of violent cities because the drug smuggling business into the United States remained profitable, assault weapons from the United States continued to flow into Mexico (Dube, Dube, and García-Ponce 2013), and the Tijuana Cartel continued to enjoy some amount of state-level and municipal protection from units that the

---

[6] For examples of programs and crime prevention efforts, see Prado (2011), Rea (2011), and SESNSP (2011).

[7] By 2011 Tijuana was among the top ten Mexican cities with the largest reduction of drug-related murders (Guerrero 2011a, 2012).

federal and state governments left unpurged to avoid a major political scandal. The PAN's strategic decision not to dismantle the gray zone of criminality – to avoid a major public scandal that involved many of their prominent local officials – enabled the prevalence of the subnational linkages of state–criminal collusion that facilitate drug operations and violence.

Additional Cases

Baja California is not an isolated case of partisan alignment and inter-governmental coordination. PAN governors in other states were similarly able to work closely with the PAN federal government in containing crime epidemics, jointly dismissing cases of police corruption, and keeping potential scandals about state protection networks away from media attention. We offer evidence from two regions in PAN-controlled states: (1) Guadalajara and its metropolitan area (PAN mayor: 2007–2009; PRI mayor: 2010–2012) in the state of Jalisco; and (2) Coroneo and the southern region (PAN mayor: 2007–2009; PAN mayor: 2010–2012) in the state of Guanajuato.

Jalisco – Guadalajara and Its Metropolitan Area

As we discussed in Chapter 3, in the 1980s and 1990s Guadalajara, Jalisco's state capital, was the home of the families of the Sinaloa Cartel's bosses, where the Sinaloans had enjoyed protection from PRI state authorities. The PAN's victory in 1995 and the breakdown of traditional protections forged under the PRI allowed the Sinaloans to develop two private armies led by the Beltrán Leyva brothers and Ignacio Coronel to defend their turf. Under subsequent PAN administrations the state experienced a decade of intermittent inter-cartel conflicts between the Sinaloans, the Tijuana, and the Juárez cartels up until 2006 when President Calderón declared the War on Drugs.

Although President Calderón did not officially launch a full-blown military campaign in Jalisco to fight the cartels, between 2009 and 2010 his administration did strategically deploy the army and the federal police to arrest major drug lords and leaders of the cartel's private militias in the state, including Ignacio Coronel.[8] Such leadership decapitations resulted

---

[8] For specific military operations, see Sedena (2009), De Loza (2010), Patiño (2010), Mural (2010), and Proceso (2010c). For quantitative data on military combat, see Atuesta et al. (2018).

in the fragmentation of cartels and their private militias, which led to a sudden rise in competition for drug trafficking routes and to a considerable rise in violence. This included public displays of corpses and a wave of narco-blockades – narco-affiliated street gangs blocking major city roads and avenues – previously unheard of in the Guadalajara metropolitan area (Guerrero 2012).

Facing a major security crisis in Jalisco, President Calderón worked closely with Governor Emilio González Márquez, his PAN co-partisan, to contain a violence epidemic in the making. Starting in 2010, federal, state, and municipal government authorities held weekly "security coordination meetings" to align their goals and policy actions and to share security information (Mural 2010). These joint efforts continued through 2012, when another arrest of a major criminal actor – the leader of Cartel Jalisco Nueva Generación, Erick Valencia Salazar – took place. All three levels of government collaborated closely, including the PRI mayor of Guadalajara, Aristóteles Sandoval, and the PRD mayor of Tlajomulco, Alberto Uribe. This effort further reinforced the pattern of intergovernmental cooperation between the federal and state PAN governments, regardless of the partisan composition at the municipal level. The collaboration resulted in the more successful control of the criminal backlash and subsequent narco-blockades of major avenues in the city (Guerrero 2012). As one of the country's top recipients of security federal transfers, Guadalajara was able to strengthen the city's crime prevention efforts.

While intergovernmental cooperation helped federal, state, and municipal authorities deactivate the violence epidemics in Guadalajara for a few years, peace was not sustainable over the long-term. As in Baja California, in Jalisco evidence of potential collusion of the state's secretary of public security with the cartels was suppressed by state authorities and ignored by federal authorities (Proceso 2008 and Mural 2010) to maintain intergovernmental cohesion and to avoid a public opinion backlash and electoral punishment. This meant that linkages between subnational authorities and drug cartels in the gray zone of criminality persisted. Violence came under control in the short-run, but the conditions that would allow violence to reemerge in the future were not eradicated.

Guanajuato – Coroneo and the Southern Region

The central state of Guanajuato has been a PAN stronghold since 1991. Although the state has not historically been a major drug cultivation area or a major drug trafficking zone, it became a contested territory when the Gulf Cartel and its private militia, the Zetas, decided to contest the

Sinaloans' control over the state of Michoacán, Guanajuato's southern neighbor. In coalition with La Familia Michoacana, the Zetas removed the Sinaloans from Michoacán. Following this move, the outbreak of a major conflict between the former allies over the control of drug trafficking routes led the Zetas to use the southern tip of Guanajuato, including the municipality of Coroneo, as a military base from which to attack La Familia. Violence in Michoacán and in the southern tip of Guanajuato rapidly increased in the mid-2000s.[9]

When President Calderón launched his first military campaign as part of the War on Drugs and deployed the military to Michoacán in 2006, inter-cartel competition and violence between La Familia and the Zetas skyrocketed in Michoacán and quickly spread into the southern tip of Guanajuato. Although Calderón did not adopt a full-blown military campaign for Guanajuato, the evidence shows that the military was deployed and actively engaged in combat against cartels in the state.[10]

In containing the criminal backlash in Guanajuato, President Calderón worked closely with Governor Juan Manuel Oliva (PAN), who had been elected the same year as Calderón. Federal- and state-level authorities had collaborated from December 2006, when the army was deployed in the neighboring state of Michoacán. As drug-related murders continued to rise, a new "inter-institutional security group" – involving the army and federal, state, and municipal police forces – was set up in early 2008 to seal Guanajuato's southern border (Escalante 2008). Governor Oliva appointed a military zone commander as state secretary of public security, and the latter's office became the focal point of coordination between federal and state authorities and the army.

In 2011, state authorities in close coordination with the federal government began a purge of the municipal forces in southern Guanajuato. Coroneo, a PAN stronghold, was one of six municipalities that underwent major internal revisions.[11] The director of the municipal police of

---

[9] As we describe in the following section, the first military intervention by the federal government took place in Michoacán as criminal threats were on the rise in 2006. By 2007 the southern region of Guanajuato experienced twice as many organized crime-related murders (22) as the rest of the municipalities in the state (11) (CVM Database; other sources confirm the same ratio of homicides between both regions in Guanajuato state).

[10] For specific military operations, see Escalante (2008), *Reforma* (2008a, 2008b), and Proceso (2009). For quantitative data on military combat, see Atuesta et al. (2018).

[11] The six municipalities under investigation were: Acámbaro (PRD), Tarandacuao (PAN), Coroneo (PAN), Jerécuaro (PAN), Moroleón (PRI), and Uriangato (PRI). For more information on the police purge in Guanajuato, see Espinosa (2011).

Coroneo, Rafael González Escobedo, confessed to being on the payroll of La Familia Michoacana. However, the investigation was stalled, and González Escobedo did not face judicial prosecution. Coroneo's mayor, José Enrique Velazquez Pérez, did not face trial either, despite accusations of collusion with La Familia. The low profile of the purge and the decision not to prosecute PAN local officials revealed President Calderón's political strategy to protect his subnational co-partisans in a historical PAN electoral stronghold.

The tight coordination of federal and state authorities in Guanajuato and their strategic decision to purge corrupt co-partisans in the shadows without pursuing judicial prosecution – carefully preventing these cases from becoming major media scandals – contributed to the alignment of co-partisan authorities at all levels of government in Guanajuato. Such coordination allowed the federal government and the state governor to contain – at least for a few years – the spread of a major epidemic of violence. Although homicides continued to grow, they did not increase at the same rate as in neighboring Michoacán. And intergovernmental coordination was able to reduce kidnapping for ransom (see Aguilar 2011). Beyond the deactivation of the crisis, failure to undo the emerging gray zone of criminality in the southern state of Guanajuato enabled the preservation of conditions for the rise of violence in the future. The Zetas and other cartels engaged in a major struggle for the control of the oil pipelines that cut across different states (including Guanajuato) to connect the eastern and western parts of Mexico.

PARTISAN FRAGMENTATION AND INTERGOVERNMENTAL CONFLICT

Michoacán – Apatzingán and the Tierra Caliente Region

The case of Michoacán on the Mexican Pacific coast and the city of Apatzingán – the center of economic and political activity in the southern part of the state – illustrates how intergovernmental partisan conflict between federal (conservative) and (leftist) subnational authorities and the partisan use of law enforcement by the federal government led to previously unknown levels of criminal violence. It also facilitated the rise of the Knights Templar – formerly known as La Familia Michoacana – to become the de facto authority in a large swath of the state.

As discussed in Chapter 3, inter-cartel wars in Michoacán began after the first (leftist) opposition victory in the state in 2002, when the Gulf Cartel and its private army, the Zetas, ventured into Michoacán to contest the drug trafficking monopoly of the Valencia brothers,[12] the local allies of the Sinaloa Cartel. After the Zetas and their local allies, La Familia Michoacana, defeated the Valencia brothers and forced them out of the state, La Familia and the Zetas went to war with each other for the state's criminal hegemony (Guerrero 2011a). Between 2005 and 2006, violence escalated to new levels, and Apatzingán and its surrounding areas – the Apatzingán Valley and the Tierra Caliente region – became the epicenter of major turf wars.

The first federal intervention of President Calderón's administration occurred at the request of leftist Governor Lázaro Cárdenas Batel in December 2006.[13] This shows that despite political rivalries, PRD subnational officials did not hesitate to demand federal assistance when they faced major criminal threats. In fact, cooperation between the federal government and Governor Cárdenas (and later with his leftist successor, Governor Leonel Godoy) facilitated an initial military success. The joint military/police effort weakened the Zetas – many of whose members had to return to the northeastern state of Tamaulipas to defend their own territory from another military intervention – and undermined key players in La Familia's extensive drug production and distribution networks (Guerrero 2011b).

After the initial military success, however, La Familia launched a major counteroffensive and in 2008, they carried out a terrorist attack against the civilian population gathered in downtown Morelia – the state's capital – during the Independence Day celebrations and then blamed it on the Zetas. Even though Governor Godoy had had a good working relationship with President Calderón throughout 2007 and even though he and former Governor Cárdenas Batel had shared with the president their concern that 10 percent of the state's municipal authorities were on La Familia's payroll,[14] intergovernmental cooperation broke down after the terrorist attack. From that point on, the federal government did not share any security information with the state government, and the military did not coordinate security actions with state or municipal police forces.[15] Not

---

[12] Interview with Lázaro Cárdenas Batel, governor of Michoacán (2002–2008).   [13] Ibid.
[14] Interview with Leonel Godoy, governor of Michoacán (2008–2012).
[15] Interview with Guillermo Valdés, former director of Mexico's secret service agency (CISEN) under President Calderón.

only did the federal government fail to launch any joint economic or social intervention in the state, it actually significantly reduced the state's budget.[16]

Intergovernmental conflict reached a peak when the federal government unilaterally launched a mega arrest of 12 mayors from the three main political parties (most of them from the Apatzingán Valley and the Tierra Caliente regions) and 23 top- and mid-level officials of Governor Godoy's security cabinet in May 2009, just one month before the midterm federal election. The arrested officials were charged with protecting La Familia. Governor Godoy did not find out about the operation until federal police forces were breaking into the state's capitol. Following the arrest, the PAN launched a national electoral campaign emphasizing the president's commitment to fighting crime and framing the Left, by contrast, as corrupt and inept. A year later, however, all but one of the allegedly corrupt officials had been liberated, and a report by the National Human Rights Commission (CNDH) concluded that most of the arrests had been illegal and had violated due process.[17]

Security officials argue that the federal government did not inform Governor Godoy because they knew his half-brother was on La Familia's payroll and had facilitated the cartel's infiltration of state and local authorities.[18] The investigations behind this operation took place throughout 2008 and by January 2009, federal authorities were ready to conduct the arrest, but President Calderón asked them to wait until they were sure that the cases rested on sound judicial grounds. Federal authorities claim that every case was backed by solid evidence but that corrupt judges let all but one of the indicted officers go free.[19]

After the mega arrest, intergovernmental cooperation between the armed forces, the federal police, and the state and municipal authorities broke down completely, and federal and subnational authorities entered into an era of bitter conflict. The federal intervention against criminal violence in the Apatzingán Valley and Tierra Caliente was no longer a joint effort. According to national officials, the federal government decided not to cooperate at all with corrupt subnational authorities who had been liberated by a corrupt judicial system.[20] As reported by Governor Godoy, after the mega arrest the relationship with the federal

---

[16] Ibid.
[17] Recommendation 72/2009 by the Comisión Nacional de Derechos Humanos.
[18] Anonymous interview with a federal security official.   [19] Interview with Valdés.
[20] Ibid.

government was marked by distrust, personal animosity, and political rivalry.[21]

Genaro Guizar, the leftist mayor of Apatzingán – one of the 12 mayors arrested in 2009 – bitterly bewailed the absence of any intergovernmental cooperation after his return from prison: "When a major kidnapping occurred in the city, [the military and the federal police] took charge of the situation and didn't bother informing me" (Animal Político 2011). His recollection of the military occupation of Apatzingán in December 2010, when the federal government allegedly killed Nazario Moreno, La Familia's top leader, is harshly critical. He claimed that "The federal police raped young girls and violated human rights" (Ferrer and Martínez 2010). Without proper local information, the federal government believed – and announced on national television – that they had killed Nazario Moreno, while Michoacán government officials questioned their claim (Reforma 2011a, 2011b). In fact, the drug lord had survived the attack, gone underground, and revamped La Familia under a new name, the Knights Templar (Baranda 2014). In addition, two cells from La Familia, Los Incorregibles and La Empresa, emerged as new criminal groups and became heavily involved in extortion, kidnapping, and vehicle theft in the state (Guerrero 2011b).

Following the mega arrest, and amid the growing tensions between the federal security forces and leftist subnational authorities, the Knights Templar took advantage of the increasing vulnerability of mayors in the Apatzingán Valley and the Tierra Caliente region. As we will show in Chapter 7, the Knights Templar sought to capture local governments through lethal coercion in order to establish new forms of criminal governance in the cities – seizing control of municipalities and their local budgets, taking control of local businesses (e.g., lime and avocado producers), and intimidating citizens via extortion and kidnapping. From 2009 onward the state plunged into a wave of criminal attacks against local authorities that reached an unprecedented level of 40 attacks during the 2011 state elections.[22]

During the contested 2011 gubernatorial and municipal elections, in which Luisa María Calderón, the president's sister, ran for gubernatorial office, polarization between federal and leftist state authorities became particularly acute. The PRD and PRI candidates blamed the PAN's

---

[21] Interview with Godoy.
[22] Information from the Criminal Attacks against Political Actors in Mexico (CAPAM), analyzed and discussed in Chapters 6 and 7.

strategy for the rising violence, while the PAN candidate blamed the leftist state administration. The Knights Templar took advantage of inter-governmental partisan conflict and, through coercion and the assassina-tion of political candidates and party activists, tried to influence the election campaigns and the election outcome in favor of PRI candidates. After the election, the Knights were able to capture the state government and a large number of the state's municipalities; they looted municipal coffers, expanded criminal taxation to businesses and local citizens, and demanded social obedience. When leftist mayors who did not want to surrender their budgets to the Knights Templar requested federal protec-tion, national authorities simply did not respond. One striking case is that of Ygnacio López, a respected town doctor, social activist, and leftist mayor of Santa Ana Maya in the northern tip of Michoacán. He was killed after he went on a hunger strike to protest the bankruptcy of his municipality.[23]

The breakdown of intergovernmental cooperation meant that fed-eral authorities no longer had access to local information, and the bitter conflict and smear campaign meant that local authorities no longer had proper federal protection against criminal attacks. La Familia and the Knights Templar capitalized on these conflicts and rapidly moved to take over local governments and populations via lethal violence.

In Baja California, tight intergovernmental coordination allowed the federal government to deactivate the violence epidemics, partially recover the state's monopoly on violence, and reestablish order in the short run. But in Michoacán, the punishment strategy the federal government used against leftist subnational authorities opened the way for the Knights Templar to capture state and municipal powers and become the state's de facto rulers. In contrast to Baja California and Guanajuato, where federal authorities strategically protected local co-partisans suspected of collusion with organized crime, in Michoacán they opted for the public prosecution of local government officials and then blamed them for the growing violence. By making public charges against leftist subnational authorities, the federal government sent a clear signal to the criminal underworld – not only are leftist states and subnational authorities unpro-tected, but their municipalities are open terrain for violent contestation. Between 2008 and 2011, drug-related murders in the Tierra Caliente

---

[23] Anonymous interview with López's close collaborators. See also *Reforma* (2013).

region increased by 187 percent. By 2011, homicides in Apatzingán accounted for 40 percent of the total murders in this region.[24]

Additional Cases

Michoacán is not a unique case of partisan fragmentation, intergovernmental conflict, and growing inter-cartel violence. Subnational authorities in the leftist states of Guerrero and Zacatecas also experienced bitter confrontations with the PAN federal government after the federal War on Drugs resulted in major spikes of violence in their states. We highlight the cases of the state of Guerrero, with emphasis on the port of Acapulco (PRD mayor: 2006–2008; PRI mayor: 2009–2012), and the state of Zacatecas, with emphasis on the city of Zacatecas (PAN mayor: 2007–2009; PRI mayor: 2010–2013).

Guerrero – Acapulco

As noted in Chapter 3, the leftist candidate Zeferino Torreblanca was the first opposition governor elected in Guerrero following 75 years of uninterrupted PRI rule. After Torreblanca took office in 2005 and appointed new officials to head the state security apparatus, the breakdown of criminal protections forged under the PRI opened opportunities for the Zetas to contest the traditional control of the Sinaloa Cartel in the state. As our statistical analysis showed in Chapter 3, following party alternation, the Zetas and the Beltrán Leyva brothers – the Sinaloans' armed branch – engaged in bloody wars over the control of the tourist port of Acapulco and the rest of the state.

As part of the War on Drugs, President Calderón deployed the armed forces to Acapulco in January 2007, just a few days after the military deployment in Tijuana. But in Acapulco, unlike the federal intervention in Tijuana, federal forces did not coordinate their actions with the state and municipal security forces of Guerrero and Acapulco (Guerrero 2007). In fact, the leftist mayor of Acapulco, Félix Salgado Macedonio, was not informed of the federal government's military operation (Flores 2007). After the bitter 2006 presidential election, Salgado Macedonio refused to recognize Felipe Calderón's electoral victory and declared, instead, his allegiance to Andrés Manuel López Obrador, the defeated leftist presidential candidate, as "Mexico's legitimate president" (Flores 2006a, 2006b).

---

[24] Estimates are based on government data retrieved from the CIDE-PPD Database. See Atuesta et al. (2018).

Barely a month after the deployment of the armed forces in Guerrero, the federal intervention became politicized. When the leftist mayor of Acapulco requested federal assistance after receiving death threats from the cartels (Herrera 2007a), federal authorities accused him on national television of protecting organized crime (Reforma 2007). Although the federal government publicly retracted this accusation two weeks later (Herrera 2007b), Salgado Macedonio and his leftist successors and collaborators became vulnerable to criminal attacks. By running a smear campaign against the mayor, the federal government sent a loud and clear message to the criminal underworld: Mr. Salgado Macedonio was a politically unprotected mayor and Acapulco was open for violent contestation. The myriad of breakaway criminal organizations that resulted from the federal government's successful decapitation of the Beltrán Leyva organization rapidly moved into Acapulco to contest the open territory. Between 2007 and 2010, Acapulco's criminal landscape went from one to ten organized criminal groups, and drug-related murders increased by 510 percent between 2009 and 2011, turning the port into one of Mexico's most violent cities (Guerrero 2012).

Zacatecas – Zacatecas City

The northern state of Zacatecas, ruled by leftist governor Amalia García, experienced a similarly uncooperative strategy from the federal government when facing the spillover effect from the epidemics of violence that resulted from the major conflicts between the Gulf Cartel and their former armed branch, the Zetas, in the neighboring states of Coahuila, Nuevo León, and Tamaulipas.

In May 2009, 53 prisoners linked to the Zetas escaped from one of the state prisons, located in the city of Zacatecas. Governor García had bitterly complained that the federal government had transferred large numbers of criminals facing federal charges to state prisons without providing any additional federal assistance,[25] even though the Zetas' uncommon military power and lethality presented a serious challenge to Zacatecas or to any state. A few hours after the Zetas had left the prison en masse without bloodshed, the federal government released videos of the escape (Barajas 2009) and blamed Governor García's administration.[26] In contrast to Baja California or Guanajuato, where federal authorities worked closely together with PAN governors to avoid a media scandal in cases of local co-partisan corruption, in the midst of the 2009 midterm

---

[25] Interview with Amalia García, governor of Zacatecas (2004–2010).   [26] Ibid.

electoral campaign the federal government linked the cases of Michoacán and Zacatecas to portray the Left as both inept and corrupt. On the ground, the signal to the criminal underworld was that the leftist governor was unprotected. In subsequent years the Zetas easily gained control over significant parts of the state. In these years Zacatecas became the state with the greatest number of anonymous phone denunciations about criminal threats (Proceso 2010b).

PARTISAN FRAGMENTATION WITH CONTINGENT COOPERATION

Chihuahua – Ciudad Juárez

The federal intervention in the northern state of Chihuahua (PRI) in Ciudad Juárez (PRI) illustrates a case of contingent cooperation.[27] Exceptional circumstances drove the PAN federal government to collaborate with the PRI, but without adopting a strategy to punish PRI subnational authorities – as occurred against the Left in Michoacán. This case also shows that contingent intergovernmental cooperation helped to reduce an epidemic of criminal violence to pre-crisis levels in Juárez.

After the PAN's gubernatorial victory in Chihuahua in 1992, the PRI returned to power and controlled the governorship for three consecutive periods (1998–2016). Throughout these years, cartel alliances shifted substantially, with the Juárez and Sinaloa cartels violently confronting each other. By 2008 criminal violence had spiked in Ciudad Juárez, leading Governor José Reyes Baeza and Juárez's Mayor José Reyes Ferriz to request federal intervention (Zubía García 2008). In March 2008, the federal government, together with the governor and the mayor, jointly presented the new military deployment strategy (Arroyo 2008). As in other parts of the country, however, the federal intervention led to a major criminal backlash and to the unprecedented escalation of criminal violence that turned Juárez into "the world's murder capital" (Grillo 2011). Federal and subnational authorities blamed the escalation of violence on each other, and the initial intergovernmental cooperation quickly broke down (Castañón 2008; González 2008). Nine months after the deployment of the military in Chihuahua, Governor Baeza publicly acknowledged that the federal and subnational security forces did not

---

[27] For more information on state fragmentation in Ciudad Juárez, Chihuahua, see Durán-Martínez (2018).

share information and that their actions were not coordinated (Hernández 2008).

The crisis of insecurity reached its peak in January 2010, when 15 high school teenagers were tragically killed by hit men from La Línea – the Juárez Cartel's private militia – who had confused them with a rival gang. The federal government mishandled the civilian massacre. President Calderón publicly criminalized the students (Proceso 2010a), triggering a wave of civil outrage that forced him to refashion the federal intervention (Aziz Nassif 2012).

Facing state and municipal elections in the next months, the federal government quickly presented "Todos Somos Juárez" (We Are All Juárez), a key social intervention that involved a major expansion of public infrastructure, transportation, day care centers, and cultural opportunities for young students. This program brought in a varied and rich array of local civic groups, from medical committees to human rights organizations and business elites (Conger 2014). The president initially bypassed state and municipal governments in developing the early stages of this program (Salmón and Chávez 2010). However, mounting pressure from civil society participating in this initiative forced the federal government to cooperate with the PRI subnational authorities in the implementation of the program.[28]

Even though the national attorney had gathered important evidence that Governor Reyes Baeza and his state attorney had provided protection to the Juárez Cartel (Lagunas 2012), the federal government strategically declined to prosecute them or leak information to the media. In contrast to what it did in Michoacán, Guerrero, and Zacatecas, it decided instead to cooperate with the incoming PRI state governor – as it did in Baja California, Jalisco, and Guanajuato. In this new scheme of cooperation, federal authorities were instrumental in persuading Héctor Murguía, the new PRI mayor of Juárez, to appoint Colonel Julián Leyzaola – the former Tijuana police chief – as head of the Juárez police force (Castañón and Gallegos 2011). After a rough start in which Murguía, his security staff, and Leyzaola survived separate physical attacks from federal forces (Luján 2011) and the municipality's federal transfers for security reform were suspended (Morales and Cruz 2011), the federal government eventually supported Leyzaola's effort to purge the local police. It worked with city and state authorities to overcome the crime epidemic through a

---

[28] Anonymous interviews with two leading social activists in Juárez, July 2012.

combination of iron-fist policies, police reforms, and an extensive social intervention.

The case of Leyzaola is noteworthy. The fact that the same security official had smooth relations with the federal authorities when he was working for the president's party in Tijuana, Baja California, but relations became rocky when he started working for an opposition party in Ciudad Juárez, Chihuahua, provides strong indication of the president's willingness to work with his co-partisans and his reluctance to cooperate with opposition subnational governments. But, as we have insisted, not all opposition parties were the same.

While a major wave of civilian mobilization played an important role in demanding intergovernmental coordination, cooperation between federal and subnational authorities took place because it involved governors and mayors from the PRI. The PRI did not question President Calderón's election, it enabled his inauguration ceremony, and it was a likely legislative partner for the president's agenda of market-oriented reforms – rather than the leftist PRD.

This contingent cooperation paid off. The intelligence information shared between reformed local police forces and the military and federal police facilitated the decapitation of cartels and private militias, and the seizures of drug shipments and weapons. And the adoption of an extensive program of public goods provision contributed to depletion of the cartel's private militias. These actions weakened the Juárez and Sinaloa cartels and empowered local governments to resist violent attempts to capture local governments and civil society – as the Knights Templar succeeded in doing in Michoacán. Between 2009 and 2011, drug-related murders in Ciudad Juárez underwent a 24 percent reduction (Guerrero 2011b).

It must be said, however, that although the contingent cooperation between PAN and PRI authorities brought the epidemic of violence to an end in Juárez, the city remained a relatively violent place for the same reasons that Tijuana remained a conflictive urban center. In other words, Juárez continued to be a key gateway for the provision of illicit drugs to insatiable US consumers; assault weapons from the United States continued to flow into Mexico's northern border municipalities (Dube, Dube, and García-Ponce 2013); and the Juárez Cartel, the Sinaloans, and their private armies continued to enjoy some amount of state-level protection from units that the federal and state governments left unpurged in order to avoid a major political scandal.

Additional Case

A contingent cooperation between PAN federal authorities and PRI subnational officials, similar to the one that contributed to the de-escalation of an epidemic of violence in Ciudad Juárez, also took place in the northern state of Nuevo León. The experience of Monterrey, the state's capital, is informative about the dynamics of contingent cooperation between PAN and PRI.

Nuevo León – Monterrey

As we discussed in Chapter 3, after six decades of uninterrupted PRI rule in Nuevo León the PAN's victory in the state gubernatorial election of 1997 led to the breakdown of protection for the Gulf Cartel and to the onset of major inter-cartel disputes for control over Monterrey, home of the Gulf's families. To defend their turf against a major attack from the Sinaloa Cartel and their private militia, led by the Beltrán Leyva brothers, the Gulf Cartel created their own private militia, the Zetas, Mexico's most lethal private army. After six years of inter-cartel wars, the PRI returned to power in Nuevo León in 2003 and ruled for two consecutive periods. Following the arrest of Osiel Cárdenas, the Gulf's boss, the Zetas grew increasingly independent until they became a separate organization (Grillo 2011; Correa-Cabrera 2017). The breakup was not peaceful, however, and conflicts among the Gulf, the Zetas, and the private armies from the Sinaloa Cartel led to a major spike of violence in Mexico's northeastern region (Guerrero 2011b). Upon the request of the governors of Nuevo León and neighboring Tamaulipas, President Calderón made a major military deployment to both states in 2007 (Michel and Vicenteño 2007).

From the outset, Nuevo León's PRI governor complained that intergovernmental coordination with the federal government in the deployment of the army was practically nonexistent (García 2008). The absence of intergovernmental coordination continued during the first years of the newly elected PRI governor, Rodrigo Medina (García 2010a), in addition to ongoing friction between the governor and the PAN mayor, Fernando Larrazabal (García 2010b). However, in late 2010 President Calderón sent his own security adviser, Jorge Tello Peón, to work with state and municipal authorities to develop a joint security strategy, and cooperation improved considerably thereafter (García 2010c; Conger 2014).

Monterrey's civil society played a crucial role in transforming intergovernmental conflict into contingent cooperation. On multiple occasions the city's powerful business elite urged authorities across all levels of government to cooperate with each other and coordinate their actions (Martínez 2007; García 2010b; Herrera 2011). The close relationship between Monterrey's business leaders and President Calderón facilitated communication and collaboration with the state government. In fact, the purge of corrupt elements of the state judicial police and the creation of a new police force, Fuerza Civil, was possible thanks to the leadership of Monterrey's powerful business community.[29] President Calderón encouraged business involvement and persuaded Governor Medina to allow business leaders to participate in the creation of the new state police.[30] Under the supervision of the city's business elite, the federal government subsequently provided Fuerza Civil with specialized training in intelligence and crime analysis at no cost to the state government (Ramírez and Ruiz 2016). To facilitate coordination, Governor Medina appointed a high-ranking military officer as head of the state's public security police. Intergovernmental coordination allowed federal and subnational authorities to contain violence, even when the federal forces actively engaged in leadership decapitation of OCGs in the state. Between the second semester of 2012 and the first quarter of 2013, murders associated with inter-cartel and state–cartel wars decreased by 16.6 percent (Guerrero 2013).

In contrast to Michoacán and despite profound disagreements between the federal government and Governor Medina, President Calderón showed clear signs of willingness to collaborate by sending his security adviser to work hand-in-hand with Nuevo León's state government. As in Ciudad Juárez, civil society in Monterrey prompted federal and PRI subnational authorities to cooperate in controlling violence after the 2011 outbreak (Guerrero 2012). Civil society pressure was effective because the state governor was from the PRI and not from the PRD.

Summary

Table 5.1 summarizes the main information reported in the case studies. As the information reveals, in the War on Drugs the federal government launched military campaigns or deployed the military in combat across all cities. In all cases the federal forces succeeded in decapitating important organized criminal groups – from cartels to private militias to gangs. In all cases there was an initial backlash: inter-cartel and state–cartel violence

---

[29] See Conger (2014) and Ley and Guzmán (2019) for further details on the creation of Fuerza Civil and the participation of Nuevo León's business elite.
[30] Anonymous interview with a business leader in Monterrey, January 2016.

TABLE 5.1 *Federal Intervention in the War on Drugs – Summary of Case Studies*

	BC (Tijuana)	Jalisco (Guad.)	Gto. (Coroneo)	Chih. (Juárez)	N.L. (Mont.)	Mich. (Apatz.)	Gro. (Acap.)	Zac. (Zac.)
Partisan vertical power	PAN PAN PAN	PAN PAN PAN	PAN PAN PAN	PAN PRI PRI	PAN PRI PRI	PAN PRD PRD	PAN PRD PRD	PAN PRD PRD
Military intervention								
Military campaign or military active in combat	☑	☑*	☑*	☑	☑	☑	☑	☑*
Removal of leaders	☑	☑	☑		☑	☑	☑	☑
Logistic coordination								
Intergov. cooperation (info sharing, planning, joint actions)	☑	☑	☑	☒ (Initially) ☑ (After civ. soc. mob.)	☒ (Initially) ☑ (After civ. soc. mob.)	☒	☒	☒
Police/judicial intervention								
Fed. judicial prosecution vs. subnational authorities & smear campaign	☒	☒	☒	☒	☒	☑	☑	☑
Local police purges	☑	☒	☑	☑	☑	☒	☒	☒
Top recipients of federal subsidies for local police[α] (2008–2012)	☑	☑	NA	☑	☑	☒	☒	☒
Social intervention								
Targeted social/econ. policy intervention	☑	☒	☒	☑	☒	☒	☒	☒
Outcome								
Deactivation of violence epidemics	YES	YES	YES	YES	YES	NO	NO	NO

Note: Ordering of political parties: president (top), governor (middle), and mayor (bottom). PAN = Right; PRI = Center; PRD = Left; * = although there was no formal military campaign in this state, the military was heavily involved in combat; α = SUBSEMUN (Federal security subsidy for municipalities in large urban centers); NA = not applicable for Coroneo – a mid-size city.

swelled. But, in line with the statistical findings reported in Chapter 4, the case study material shows that the ability of the federal government to contain conflict and deactivate the epidemics of drug violence varied across different layers of partisan vertical fragmentation. As the table summarizes, the federal intervention varied widely across cases on several dimensions.

In states and municipalities where the president's conservative party ruled (PAN-PAN-PAN), federal authorities, governors, and mayors maintained close communication about objectives, strategies, targets, and timing of military/police interventions. The federal government assisted the mayors in purging their municipal police, and they all received important federal transfers to either reform their police forces or to launch crime prevention strategies. The federal government assisted and politically protected the president's co-partisans, even when there was evidence of corruption or collusion with organized crime – PAN local officials were silently removed without judicial prosecution or media scandal. In some cases, the federal government devised economic and social interventions for crime prevention purposes. Coordination and cooperation in these cases empowered subnational authorities to weaken the cartels and deterred OCGs in neighboring states from engaging in competition for turf following the decapitation of local cartels.

In contrast, as Table 5.1 summarizes, the federal intervention in leftist states with leftist mayors (PAN-PRD-PRD) did not contain the epidemics of violence but actually contributed to swelling murder rates. In these cases, the military intervention was unilateral and there was no intergovernmental information sharing of any kind. Quite the opposite: the national attorney prosecuted subnational authorities and/or ran smear campaigns to discredit leftist subnational authorities. Mayors received no meaningful federal support to purge or reform their police forces, and there were no targeted socio-economic programs for crime prevention.

Unlike leftist states, in PRI states (PAN-PRI-PRI) powerful civil society mobilizations forced federal authorities to cooperate with governors and mayors after an initial period of intergovernmental conflict. Violence in these cities was also contained. As the different dimensions of the interventions reported in Table 5.1 reveal, the interventions in these cases of contingent cooperation more closely resembled the co-partisan model than the conservative versus leftist punishment regime.

WARTIME TRANSFORMATIONS: THE NEW INDUSTRIAL
ORGANIZATION OF CRIME

Federal intervention in the War on Drugs not only shaped the uneven geography of violence in Mexico but also transformed the industrial organization of crime. It fragmented the criminal underworld, stimulated fierce competition for multiple criminal markets, and opened opportunities for the cartels to compete for turf in politically unprotected (leftist) subnational regions. Not only did violence skyrocket during the first six years of the War on Drugs, but cartels and their criminal associates and the gray zone of criminality changed in fundamental ways.

To understand this historic transformation of Mexico's criminal underworld, we need to look at the broader picture of the intervention and assess two of its most important strategies: (1) the decapitation of the cartels (the military strategy); and (2) the politicization of the intervention to attribute any reduction of criminal violence to the president's co-partisans and to blame the leftist opposition for any escalation of violence (the political strategy). In pursuing these joint strategies, Mexico's militaristic and politicized federal intervention had a dramatic impact on the gray zone of criminality and on the criminal underworld. Although the focus of this chapter has been on the second objective, to truly understand the impact of the federal intervention on the industrial organization of crime, we need to jointly assess the military and political faces of the intervention.

First, as noted by several scholars, the leadership decapitation strategy resulted in the fragmentation of the cartels into multiple criminal organizations (Guerrero 2011a). For purposes of illustration, consider the hypothetical case shown in Figures 5.I.a, b, and c. In this case, if the government succeeded in decapitating a cartel (Figure 5.I.a), the policy "success" would result in the mutation of the cartels' private militias into newly independent criminal organizations. The industry would then transform from one major cartel (N = 1) into three major criminal organizations (N = 3) (Figure 5.I.b). If the government succeeded in decapitating the leaders of these three new organizations, the industry would have nine criminal organizations (N = 9) led by the former plaza chiefs of the cartels' private militias (Figure 5.I.c). If the government persisted in pursuing these decapitation policies, the removal of the plaza chiefs would result in the rise of 27 street gangs as independent criminal organizations (N = 27) (Figure 5.I.c). To the extent that the government succeeds in decapitating some cartels but not others, a major transformation in the

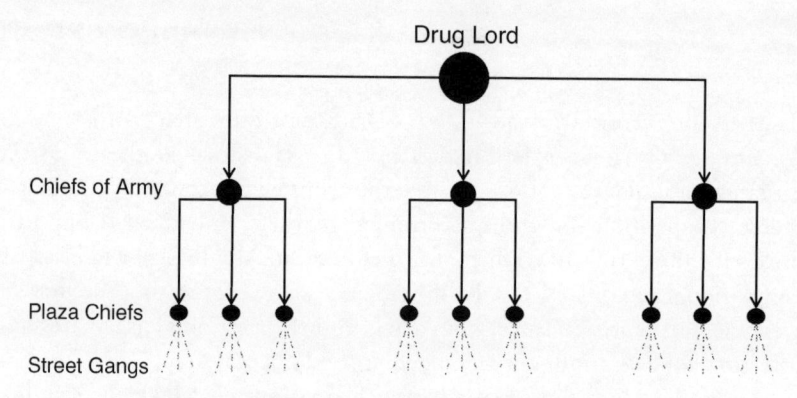

FIGURE 5.I.a Prototypical Drug Cartel Structure, 2006

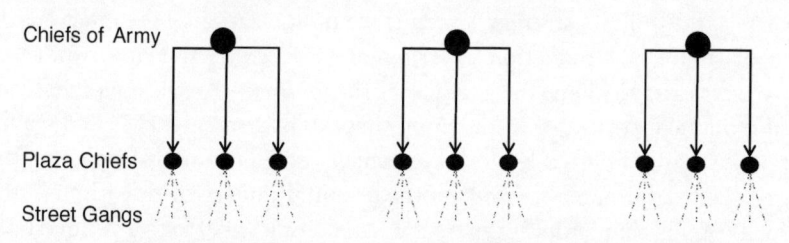

FIGURE 5.I.b New Criminal Organizations after Decapitation of Cartels, 2007–2012

FIGURE 5.I.c New Criminal Organizations after Decapitation of Private Militias, 2007–2012

criminal underworld is the development of a criminal industry with multiple criminal organizations of widely different sizes, operating at different territorial levels – national, state, municipal, and neighborhood.

As Guerrero's (2011a, 2011b) detailed analysis of the Mexican criminal industry shows, the decapitation policy followed by President Calderón in the War on Drugs did result in a major fragmentation of Mexico's criminal underworld. First, at the beginning of the Calderón administration, in 2006, there were five cartels and their private militias. However, by the end of his term, in 2012, there were more than 100 organized criminal groups. As the number of cartels and other criminal actors increased, competition for drug trafficking routes and other criminal markets became correspondingly intense. Several scholars have provided compelling evidence showing that fragmentation and competition led to a dramatic increase in inter-cartel violence (Guerrero 2011b; Dickenson 2014; Calderón et al. 2015; Phillips 2015).

Second, the intensification of wars for the control of drug trafficking routes led drug cartels and other criminal organizations to expand their activities into new illegal industries, particularly into the illegal extraction of human wealth – via extortion, kidnapping for ransom, and human smuggling[31] – and the illegal extraction of natural resources – the looting of forestry, mines, oil and fuel (Correa-Cabrera 2017). The resources from these alternative industries allowed them to finance their wars for the control of drug trafficking routes. In capturing and operating these new industries, criminal organizations sometimes engaged in fierce wars and at other times reached cooperation agreements. For example, cartels outsourced local extortion and kidnapping to street gangs, as happened in Acapulco (Guerrero 2011b). As we discuss in Chapters 6 and 7, cartels and other organized criminal groups were able to expand their markets into extractivist criminal industries in subnational leftist regions.

Third, as cartels and their criminal associates expanded their illegal activities to human extraction, civilian victimization and gross human rights violations became a reality of Mexico's War on Drugs. Whereas between 1990 and 2006 victims of inter-cartel wars were mainly members of cartels and their private militias, after 2006 organized criminal groups began targeting civilians and local government officials. Previously, they primarily fought to control drug trafficking routes, but after 2006 cartels and their criminal associates used violence to become de facto tax collectors and extract wealth from municipal governments, local businesses, churches, and families. As we discuss in Chapters 6 and 7, these patterns of violation were particularly extensive in leftist subnational regions.

Fourth, in unprotected subnational regions drug cartels and their criminal associates sought to take control over local governments, populations, and territories and to establish criminal governance regimes. As we will discuss in Chapters 6 and 7, drug lords and their associates took the unusual step of murdering mayors and local party candidates to gain de facto control over municipal government structures, including the police. This marked a radical transformation in the War on Drugs.

---

[31] See Open Society Justice Initiative (2016) and Aguayo et al. (2016).

Whereas in the past drug cartels were purely economic actors concerned only with controlling drug trafficking routes, after six years of the War on Drugs drug lords became interested in becoming de facto local rulers, controlling local populations, governments, and subnational territories.

CONCLUSION

While dominant explanations of criminal violence in Mexico suggest that the government's military intervention and its strategy of leadership decapitation of the cartels account for the dramatic increase in violence following the launching of the War on Drugs, in this chapter we have provided extensive evidence showing that, besides a faulty military strategy, the *politicization* of the federal intervention is a crucial factor in the escalation of criminal violence. In fact, as we have shown, it was the combination of the military and political biases of the federal intervention that stimulated the dramatic increase in criminal violence. This increase, as we have argued, was more intense in municipalities from leftist states, not because leftist subnational authorities were less competent than others or disinclined to cooperate with a conservative federal government. Rather, the conspicuous leftist bias resulted from the federal government's deliberate strategy of leaving leftist subnational authorities unprotected, and, after the swell in violence, accusing them of collusion with organized crime. Drug cartels and their criminal associates quickly learned about the opportunities to contest or conquer rival criminal markets in these vulnerable leftist subnational regions, where inter-cartel wars and violence became more intense.

The findings of this chapter highlight important lessons for our understanding of Mexico's drug wars and of the perils associated with the politicization of law enforcement in contexts marked by political polarization and war.

The first lesson is that a government attempt to contain criminal epidemics can trigger a major backlash on multiple fronts when the political punishment of electoral enemies becomes the driving motive of a militarized intervention. Because postauthoritarian Mexican elites failed to democratize the military, the security sector, and the judiciary, and the president continued to have a tight control over these institutions, President Calderón was able to politicize the federal intervention of the War on Drugs. As our case studies show, a politicized intervention distorts efficacy along several dimensions.

On the military dimension, the unilateral military/police interventions in states such as Michoacán and Guerrero were ineffective because the federal government's decision to bypass subnational authorities left federal forces without access to local intelligence information. Without proper information and following a military logic that dated from the anti-insurgency policies used by the Mexican armed forces during the country's Dirty War in the 1970s, the military/police intervention resulted in bitter battles with the cartels. This resulted in widespread extrajudicial executions, high levels of civilian victimization, and gross human rights violations.[32]

On the judicial dimension, the politicization of law enforcement to judicially harass leftist subnational authorities and to run smear campaigns accusing them of collusion with drug cartels left mayors and their municipal populations vulnerable to criminal attacks. Knowing that the federal government had purposefully left subnational regions ruled by the president's enemies unprotected, drug cartels and their criminal associates used their private armies to contest control over criminal markets in these open territories. Not only did inter-cartel violence skyrocket in these regions, but civilians became a primary target – a source of additional resources to finance the increasingly bitter drug wars.

The second lesson is that although drug cartels and their criminal associates are primarily interested in economic profits, the evidence from the case studies suggests that they are perfectly aware of the impact that major political changes may have on the power dynamics within the gray zone of criminality. In Chapters 2 and 3 we showed that subnational partisan alternation and the breakdown of one-party rule in Mexico had a major impact on the balance of power of the criminal underworld, forcing cartels to create their own private militias to defend their turf. In this chapter we have shown that intergovernmental partisan conflict between Right and Left in Mexico's illiberal democracy opened opportunities for cartels to contest controls over criminal markets. This means that in making crucial business and military decisions, cartels and their private militias do take cues from the political environment, including patterns of intergovernmental partisan conflict and cooperation.

Finally, the case study evidence presented in this chapter reveals that while intergovernmental partisan coordination can be crucial for containing violence epidemics, if unchecked it can be a recipe for long-term failure. As the experiences of Baja California and Guanajuato – and

---

[32] See Pérez Correa et al. (2015) and Open Society Justice Initiative (2016).

several other unexplored cases such as Morelos – show, when coordination goes beyond policy alignment and information sharing, and leads to federal authorities covering up subnational co-partisans' involvement in corrupt practices, coordination may bring short-term positive results but its long-lasting effects are limited. Intergovernmental partisan coordination allowed the federal and subnational conservative governments to deactivate a violence epidemic; but the unpunished corrupt practices that were swept under the rug to avoid a major political scandal contributed to the survival of the gray zone of criminality and facilitated the outbreak of new waves of criminal violence a few years later.

Up to this point we have provided extensive evidence of different pathways by which the dynamics of political change in Mexico's illiberal democracy created turbulence in the gray zone of criminality, changing the criminal balance of power and giving rise to powerful incentives for violence. In the following section we will address how, in the course of nearly two decades of intense inter-cartel and state–cartel conflicts, drug lords and their criminal associates slowly developed political ambitions and decided to redesign Mexico's local political orders by murdering subnational authorities and local political candidates. To be sure, these are not ambitions for holding national office; rather, they are ambitions for de facto political control over local governments, populations, and territories. This is the world of criminal governance – an uncharted territory to which we now turn.

PART IV

THE RISE OF CRIMINAL GOVERNANCE: SUBVERTING LOCAL DEMOCRACY IN WAR

6

Why Cartels Murder Mayors and Local Party Candidates

Subnational Political Vulnerability and Political Opportunities to Become Local Rulers

At the onset of Mexico's War on Drugs, drug cartels and their criminal associates took the unprecedented strategic decision to begin targeting local elected officials and party candidates for assassination. After 16 years of inter-cartel wars (1990–2006) in which drug trafficking organizations had rarely targeted any active government authority or politician, drug lords launched a series of systematic lethal attacks against subnational officials and local political leaders from 2006 onwards. Between 2007 and 2012, drug cartels murdered 15 state government officials, 64 mayors, 45 municipal government officials, 7 party candidates, and 25 party activists. If we add assassination attempts, public death threats, and kidnappings, Mexico experienced 311 lethal criminal attacks – affecting 9.6 percent of the country's 2,457 municipalities and 29 percent of the Mexican population who live in them. Over 80 percent of these attacks were directed at municipal authorities and municipal party candidates.

Why would organized criminal groups (OCGs) commit high-profile attacks against local rulers? Scholars of large-scale criminal violence suggest that the dynamics of inter-cartel and state–cartel wars can prompt drug lords to take the unusual decision to attack government authorities. Lessing (2017) argues that drug cartels attack state agents only when states declare war on the cartels and launch fierce unconditional attacks against them. Others argue that in the context of intense turf wars, competition for criminal markets leads cartels to murder subnational authorities who fail to provide them with effective protection or who protect their rivals (Ríos 2012).

If cartels are motivated to attack state officials who unconditionally attack them in the first place, why did drug lords target mayors and municipal officials when the War on Drugs had been launched by federal authorities? If their objective is to gain government protection, why did drug lords attack mayors and municipal authorities when the latters' involvement in the informal provision of government protection had been marginal? As we showed in Chapter 2, it was state-level officials linked to the state attorneys' offices and the state judicial police who had been at the center of protection networks.

High-profile criminal attacks are generally puzzling because they bring unnecessary attention to the criminal underworld. But this wave of attacks is even more surprising because those who became the main target of attacks had only played a marginal role in two decades of inter-cartel wars and in the War on Drugs.

Building on extant explanations and on new theoretical developments in the organized crime literature (Arias 2017) and on studies of civil war (Kalyvas 2006; Arjona 2016), we develop a new account: the criminal governance hypothesis. We argue that in the context of dual war, in which cartels were fighting other cartels (Ríos 2012) and the state (Lessing 2017), Mexican drug lords and their criminal associates were more likely to use targeted lethal violence against municipal officials and political candidates. Their aim was to subdue local governments and local populations and gain de facto territorial control over clusters of municipalities where they would develop subnational criminal governance regimes. Establishing de facto political control over several adjacent local jurisdictions would provide cartels with valuable resources which they could use to dominate the criminal underworld and also to monopolize violence and taxation, and take control over key local activities in the economic, social, and political spheres.

If cartels use high-profile criminal attacks to develop subnational regimes of criminal governance, the central question is about the conditions that allow them to launch such attacks on subnational political authorities. Following our findings in Chapter 5, which revealed that drug lords and their criminal associates take political cues from changes in political structures, we focus on *political opportunities* for criminal attacks. Cartels are interested in targeting local governments and populations where they are most likely to succeed in establishing control. Thus, we build on our arguments from Chapter 5 to argue that drug lords and their private militias launch attacks against subnational government officials and political leaders who are politically and militarily unprotected by central authorities. Because cartels want to colonize local government structures, we suggest that they launch attacks during local election cycles when local governments are elected, and incoming mayors define their cabinets and make new administrative appointments. Finally, cartels want to establish subnational territorial regimes of criminal governance, so we expect them to target officials and politicians from clusters of neighboring municipalities, rather than launch isolated attacks.

We test the criminal governance hypothesis alongside alternative explanations using information from the Criminal Attacks against Politicians in Mexico (CAPAM) Dataset – an original databank of public death threats, kidnappings, disappearances, assassination attempts against, and murder of, government authorities, political candidates, and party activists.[1] Records from 311 attacks show that over 80 percent of such attacks are waged against *municipal-level* authorities and party candidates – that is, attacks are primarily a local phenomenon.

Our statistical models for the 2007–2012 period show that while high-profile attacks were more common in municipalities where cartels were engaged in major wars against rival cartels and the state, and where mayors had access to greater local fiscal revenues, *political opportunities* for establishing subnational criminal governance regimes had a large and independent effect on the pattern of attacks. In the context of acute political polarization between Left and Right that Mexico experienced after the bitterly contested 2006 presidential election, attacks were 4.3 *times* more likely in opposition municipalities from leftist states. In these states, the conservative federal government did not provide sufficient political and military protection to mayors in conflictive regions. Attacks increased by 64 percent during subnational election cycles, when state and municipal power was transferred to new administrations and new appointments were made. They were regionally clustered – for every additional attack among adjacent geographic neighbors, a municipality became 41 percent more likely to experience another the following year.

To test whether political opportunities have a causal effect on attacks, we present two natural experiments conducted along the multiple state borders of the western state of Michoacán. First, focusing on Tierra Caliente, an extensive homogeneous region that cuts across the state

---

[1] Information in the CAPAM Dataset is drawn from a systematic review of the Mexican press. We used the national daily *Reforma* – the most specialized source on drug trafficking in Mexico – as our primary source and supplemented this with information from seven other national newspapers, 18 subnational newspapers, and two weekly magazines (*Proceso* and *Zeta de Tijuana*). See Appendix B for explanation of the data-generation process.

boundaries of Michoacán and its eastern neighbor, Guerrero, we assess the dynamics of criminal violence against government authorities and party candidates during subnational election cycles. Although municipalities on both sides of state borders are nearly identical in most respects, we take advantage of the fact that states in Mexico have staggered elections. Our evidence shows a large and unambiguous effect of election calendars on high-profile criminal attacks. Second, focusing on the border region between Michoacán and its northern neighbor, Guanajuato, we compare the impact of party fragmentation on attacks in municipalities in this otherwise homogeneous region. The comparison is possible because Michoacán was ruled by a leftist governor and Guanajuato by a conservative governor. Results confirm that attacks were significantly greater in municipalities from the leftist state.

This chapter establishes the causal association between political opportunities and violence; the connection between attacks and the development of subnational criminal governance regimes will be the subject of Chapter 7. Building on the statistical results from this current chapter, in Chapter 7 we use case studies to flesh out how cartels and their criminal associates capitalized on political opportunities to develop de facto local political power and to subvert local democracy.

This chapter is structured in five sections. We first discuss the extant explanations of high-profile criminal violence and use data from CAPAM to assess their explanatory power. In the second section we develop our criminal governance hypothesis. In the third section we present the statistical tests, and in the fourth section we discuss the findings from the natural experiments. In the conclusion, we discuss how the use of targeted political violence to establish subnational criminal governance regimes forces us to rethink some of our most fundamental assumptions about the alleged apolitical nature of organized crime. This opens a new area of research about the uncommon political ambitions that drug lords develop through the course of war and the unusual "politics" that criminal organizations play.

EXTANT EXPLANATIONS FOR HIGH-PROFILE ATTACKS

The assassination of local government officials and party candidates by OCGs is not an exclusively Mexican phenomenon. Journalists and scholars of organized crime have documented major waves of criminal attacks against local government officials and politicians in a wide variety of countries in Latin America, including Brazil (Albarracín 2018), Guatemala (Corcoran 2011), and Honduras (Spring 2013). Albarracín's pioneering work in Brazil reveals a surprising wave of hundreds of criminal assaults against local government authorities – mayors and municipal city councilors – in Rio de Janeiro. The shocking assassination of Marielle Franco, a social activist and Rio municipal councilor, was an instance of this dramatic wave (Marreiro and Hermida 2018). Students of the Italian mafia have also documented waves of violence against subnational government officials (Oliveri and Sberna 2014), and analysts of Colombia's civil war have documented the murders of hundreds of local officials perpetrated by armed rebel groups and paramilitary forces (López 2010).

The literatures on criminal and political violence offer three explanations: repression, competition, and rent-seeking.

The Repression Hypothesis

In his influential book on the logics of violence in criminal wars in Latin America, Lessing (2017) distinguishes two types of wars that drug cartels fight: wars against the state and wars against rival cartels. While Lessing suggests that inter-cartel wars can be easily explained by the inability of drug lords to reach credible commitments to divide up desirable territories, he finds state–cartel conflict puzzling. If cartels do not seek to topple the government and seize formal power and if they can use bribes or threats to elicit the informal cooperation of government authorities, he asks, why would they launch lethal attacks that would only "bring down additional heat" on them and jeopardize their illegal activities?

Lessing suggests that drug cartels engage in off-the-path equilibrium behavior in self-defense – that is, they attack state authorities when, regardless of the cartels' use of violent strategies, government officials order unconditional repression or crackdowns against them. This is a logic of war retaliation for purposes of self-preservation. Although Lessing is not explicit about which state officials are targeted, we can presume that the elected officials who ordered the crackdowns would be the targets. Because drug lords – as we have argued – are close observers of political dynamics and take cues from changes in political structures, it is not unrealistic to assume that they can easily attribute responsibilities for the ordering of attacks against them and their criminal associates.

The Competition Hypothesis

In her study of assassinations of mayors in Mexico's drug wars, Ríos (2012) suggests that cartels are more likely to attack local elected officials in municipalities experiencing inter-cartel competition and violence. In a separate independent study, using states as units of analysis, Blume (2017) shows that murders are more likely in states with greater cartel fragmentation and competition.

While Ríos provides empirical evidence showing a strong association between violent cartel competition and the murder of mayors, there is no explicit explanation for the motivations driving these killings. In a context of turf wars, in which cartels are fighting for the control of plazas, we can presume that drug lords will use lethal coercion to punish mayors who offer protection to their rivals or to coerce future authorities for protection. In this interpretation, cartels seek to influence political structures in order to prevail in turf wars and recover control over drug trafficking routes. But they are not interested in taking over local governments and populations.

The Rent-Seeking Hypothesis

Students of armed conflict observe that after Colombia created thousands of municipal governments in the 1980s, and gradually increased municipal transfers from 1991 until 2002, armed groups engaged in targeted violence to capture local government resources (Sánchez and del Mar Palau 2006; Eaton 2010; Chacón 2018). Chacón argues that in civil conflicts, non-state armed actors are reliant on rents in their fight against state authorities and rival armed groups. He provides compelling quantitative evidence showing that after the introduction of an ambitious fiscal decentralization reform, armed groups in Colombia launched major attacks against local officials and politicians in municipalities that received the largest fiscal transfers and that did not have the policing capacity to resist the armed violence.

In this interpretation the rent-seeking behavior of cartels is motivated by the desire to prevail in war. Armed groups seize fiscal transfers because they need resources for their ongoing conflicts – to buy weapons and acquire new resources to finance the living expenses of their foot soldiers. But there is no clear connection between assassinations and the desire of armed groups to gain de facto local political power.

Despite their differences, there is a common underlying logic to these three accounts: the *needs* that result from protracted wars drive cartels and armed groups to engage in high-profile assaults. They target state authorities in self-defense, in search of protection, or in search of rents to enable them to prevail in war.

Using original data from CAPAM, we next assess the extent to which these accounts may explain the dynamics of high-profile murders in Mexico.

Evaluating Extant Explanations

As we explained in Chapters 2 and 3, after Mexico's four main cartels – Tijuana, Juárez, Sinaloa, and Gulf – rose to international prominence in the 1980s, the drug trafficking industry enjoyed a period of peaceful coexistence under the PRI's one-party rule (Astorga 2005).[2] However, the first opposition victories in state-level politics and the alternation of political parties in state gubernatorial office throughout the 1990s led to the breakdown of informal government protection networks for cartels and to the outbreak of inter-cartel wars. As we explained in Chapters 4 and 5, after 16 years of inter-cartel conflict, and following a fiercely contested election in 2006, President Calderón declared a War on Drugs and deployed the military throughout the country's most conflictive regions to break up the cartels. Mexico experienced a five-fold increase in drug-related murders and the outbreak of new forms of violence, including high-profile attacks, in the following years – the wave of 311 incidents reported by CAPAM.

To understand whether high-profile assaults are random events or whether there are systematic patterns, we focus our initial descriptive analysis on the timing, targets, and geography of murders, assassination attempts, and kidnappings of government officials, party candidates, and party activists. We use these descriptive statistics as a baseline test of extant explanations.

Timing

As we have observed, one of the most conspicuous aspects of Mexico's inter-cartel wars is that drug cartels did not launch any systematic attacks against government officials and party candidates for more than a decade of turf wars.[3] As Figure 6.1 shows, between 1995 and 2005 there were

---

[2] Note that La Familia Michoacana came to prominence in the late 1990s and early 2000s.
[3] We exclude attacks against security forces – police and army officers – from the analysis because these follow a different logic. Unlike mayors and party candidates, security forces are (a) engaged in direct military confrontation with the cartels and (b) do not take policy decisions. We are interested in analyzing criminal attacks against incumbent and future policymakers because these actions are more directly linked to the cartels' desire to colonize local governments.

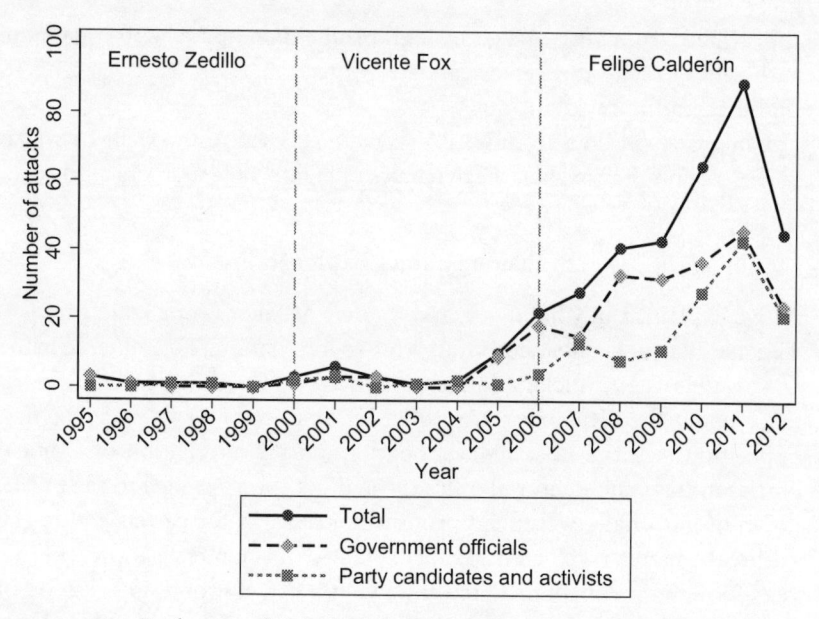

FIGURE 6.1 Evolution of Criminal Attacks against Government Officials and Party Members, 1995–2012 (counts)

only a few high-profile criminal attacks. Even though the country's main cartels were involved in violent competition for turf and the death toll of inter-cartel wars reached on average 270 battle deaths per year (Trejo and Ley 2018), during these years drug lords refrained from attacking government officials and politicians. In a context in which the federal government was not attacking the cartels, drug lords relied on bribery to negotiate local informal protection because it was cheaper to buy off subnational officials, getting them to look the other way, than murder them – which would have attracted unwanted federal attention (Lessing 2017). But, as Figure 6.1 shows, the wave of high-profile criminal violence began after 2006, when the federal government deployed the military to attack the cartels. This strategy led drug lords to expand their activities to illegal industries of human resource extraction (e.g., the extortion of local businesses and kidnapping for ransom) and natural resource extraction (e.g., forests, mines, and oil) to finance war.

The information in Figure 6.1 reveals that the competition hypothesis overpredicts the extent of violence – it fails to explain why, although cartels were at war for more than a decade, their militias did not murder subnational officials and politicians during this time. In contrast, and in line with the repression hypothesis, Figure 6.1 shows the outbreak of a wave of attacks after the federal government launched an unconditional war against all cartels as part of President Calderón's War on Drugs. There is an uptick of attacks in 2005–2006 when President Vicente Fox (2000–2006) deployed the army to several conflictive regions, particularly in the northeast of the country, to contain drug violence (Lessing 2017). But, as we explained in Chapters 4 and 5, the deployment of the military to practically all conflictive regions took place under the command of President Calderón (2006–2012).

Targets

One of the key features of the outbreak of high-profile criminal assaults in Mexico is that *local* government officials and party candidates were the primary target. As Figure 6.2 shows, almost 84 percent of attacks against government officials involved municipal authorities and 85 percent of attacks against party members involved municipal party candidates and activists.

The information in Figure 6.2 reveals that the repression hypothesis underpredicts violence against subnational officials. Following a repression logic, we would expect that after the federal government deployed the armed forces and the police to unconditionally destroy all

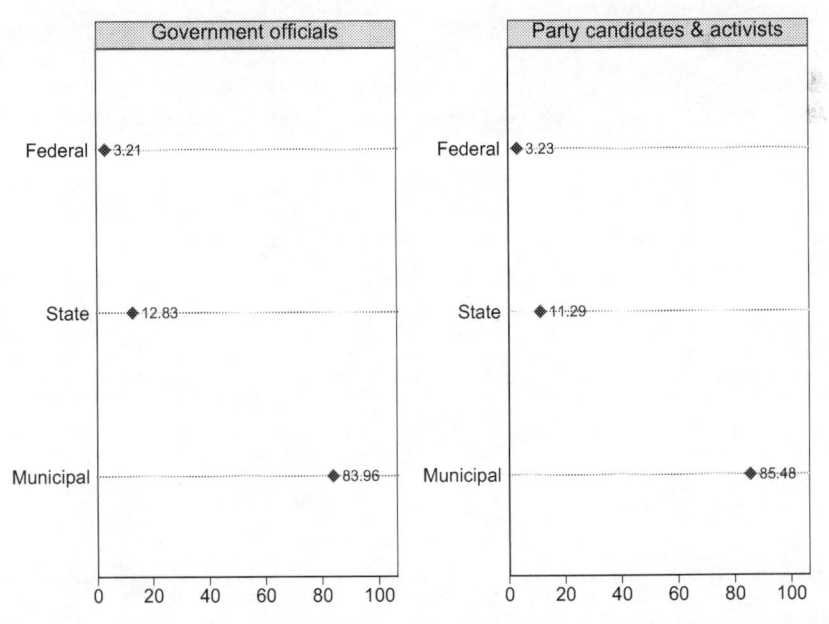

FIGURE 6.2 Criminal Attacks by Target and Level of Government, 2007–2012 (%)

cartels, drug lords would order their armies to attack federal incumbent officials. Targets would include personnel from the Office of the President, the secretariats of interior and public security, the secret service, and the attorney general's office – or even subnational officials in the governor's office working in coordination with federal forces to launch the attacks. As Figure 6.2 shows, however, fewer than 5 percent involved federal elected officials and party candidates and fewer than 15 percent involved state-level officials and party candidates. This means that while the repression hypothesis helps us explain when the wave of attacks began, it cannot explain why cartels overwhelmingly targeted officials and politicians who had *not* ordered the attacks on them and who played only a minor role in the state's War on Drugs.

A surprising feature of the wave of violence is that if we distinguish victims by partisan identity, it is evident that cartels had a partisan bias against subnational *opposition* authorities and party candidates, particularly those from the Left. As Figure 6.3 illustrates, in absolute terms most attacks against authorities involved government officials from the centrist opposition Institutional Revolutionary Party (PRI) and most attacks against party candidates involved politicians from the leftist coalition

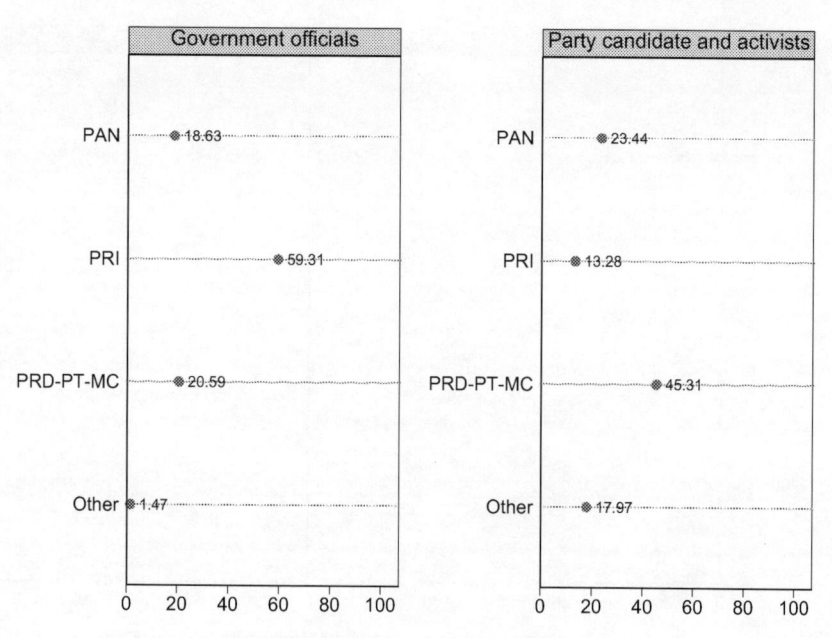

FIGURE 6.3 Criminal Attacks by Target and Party, 2007–2012 (%)

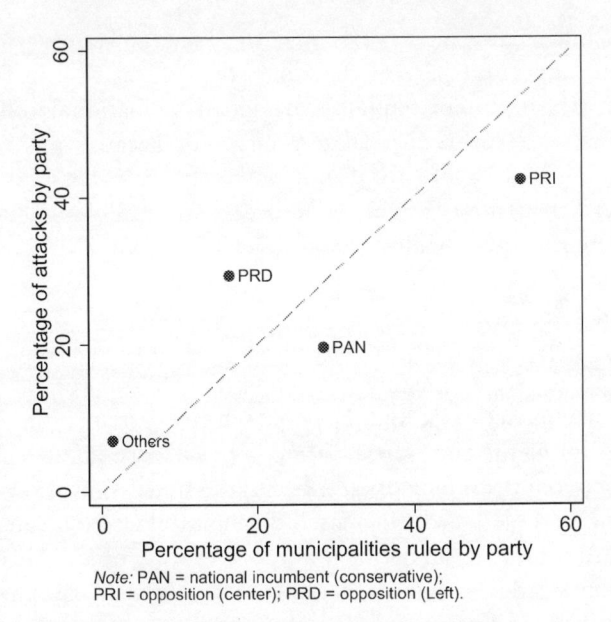

Note: PAN = national incumbent (conservative);
PRI = opposition (center); PRD = opposition (Left).

FIGURE 6.4 Municipalities Ruled by Political Party Compared to Targeted Government Officials and Party Members, 2007–2012

PRD-PT-MC. In relative terms, however, local officials and party candidates linked to the Left were disproportionately punished. Figure 6.4 plots assaults against different targets by party affiliation and the proportion of municipalities under the control of different parties. If they are politically unbiased, all parties would be placed along or near the 45-degree line – that is, the attacks would be proportional to their positions in office. A positive bias would place the party above the 45-degree line and a negative bias would situate it below the line. As Figure 6.4 shows, the only party above the diagonal was the leftist Party of the Democratic Revolution (PRD). As the data reveal, the Left governed 16 percent of the country's municipalities but experienced 29 percent of the attacks.

Although the repression hypothesis only speaks about cartels counterattacking national state officials who launched an unconditional war against them, a plausible implication of this hypothesis is that in federal systems, cartels would attack these officials' subnational co-partisans. Yet subnational authorities and local politicians from the president's party were not the main targets; on the contrary, most of the violence was directed against local opposition officials and candidates, particularly those from the Left – the president's main rival party. While Figure 6.1 reveals that the logic of state–cartel retaliation is an important part of the story, the information in Figure 6.4 suggests that it cannot explain why leftist subnational officials and politicians were disproportionately targeted. Because many of these leftist municipalities are rural and poor, this partisan bias suggests, moreover, that there might be more than purely financial (rent-seeking) motivations behind these attacks.

Geography

The geography of violence by state reveals a surprising electoral connection. Figure 6.5 shows the time-series of attacks for four of the states that we have examined throughout the book, which experienced more than 20 incidents during the 2006–2012 period. The evidence shows a close association between the timing of attacks and the states' subnational election cycles: high-profile attacks increased during local election campaigns or shortly after the new subnational authorities took office. This electoral connection strongly suggests that cartels are particularly interested in influencing the government succession process.

The geography of violence by municipality shows a logic of territorial control. As Map 6.1 shows, drug cartels and their criminal associates do not simply target one municipality at a time, but entire regions. The map

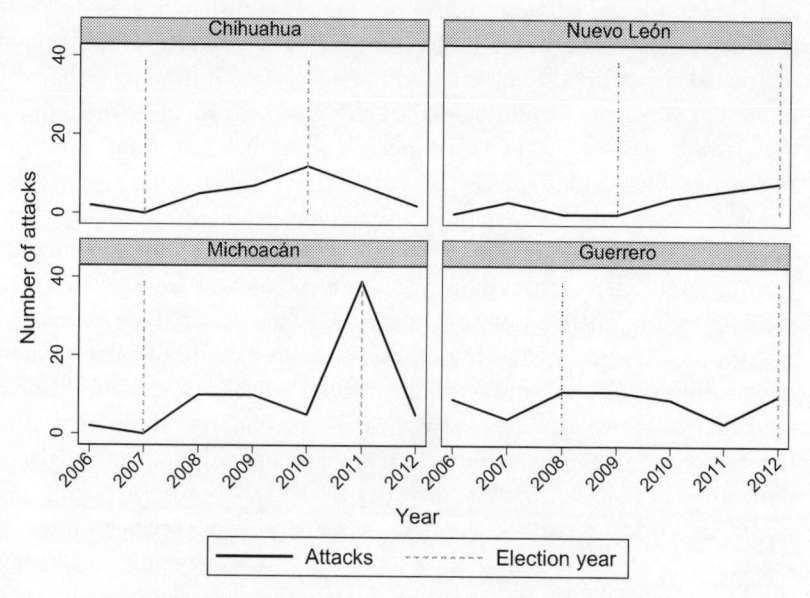

FIGURE 6.5 Criminal Attacks and Subnational Election Cycles

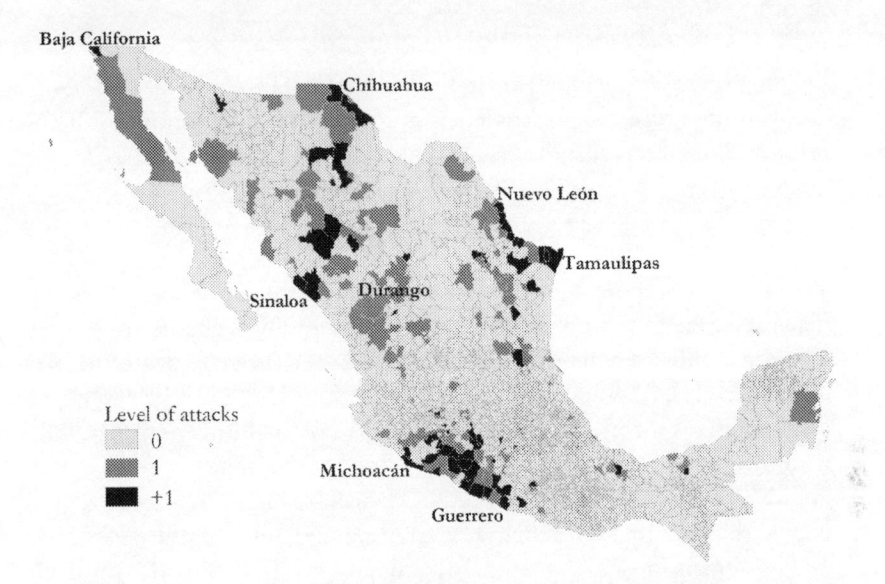

MAP 6.1 Geography of Criminal Attacks against Government Officials and Party Members, 2007–2012

identifies three clusters of criminal attacks: (1) northwest in the states of Baja California, Chihuahua, Sinaloa, and Durango; (2) northeast in the states of Nuevo León and Tamaulipas; and (3) southwest in the states of Michoacán and Guerrero on the Pacific coast. Recall that these sub-national regions have been the sites of major inter-cartel wars for the control of drug trafficking routes since the 1990s (see Chapter 3, Panel 3.I). We take the geographic clustering of attacks as a significant indication that cartels moved beyond a desire to simply control drug trafficking routes and sought to control adjacent municipalities and politically defined jurisdictions.

In sum, a descriptive analysis of the targets, timing, and geography of incidents suggests that extant explanations focused mainly on the cartels' war needs only partially account for the dynamics of high-profile criminal violence in Mexico. This could be the result of an important omission. While cartels may launch attacks for the purposes of self-survival in a context of increasingly competitive turf wars, the leftist bias, the election timing, and the geographic clustering of the attacks may be important indications that cartels have moved beyond interest-group logics of influencing local politicians through bribery and coercion, and have taken governance into their own hands.

A NEW EXPLANATION: THE LOGIC OF CRIMINAL GOVERNANCE

Building on new developments in the study of organized crime and in the civil war literature, we present a new account of the motivations for high-profile criminal attacks: the criminal governance hypothesis.

What Is Criminal Governance?

The concept of *criminal governance* was first introduced by students of the mafia. Gambetta (1996) defines the mafia as an OCG that monopolizes violence within a small territorial domain where it provides protection for illegal markets. As Varese (2010) and Skarbek (2014) have succinctly put it, the mafia is a form of governance of the criminal underworld. While mafiosi may use their governance infrastructure to influence formal economic activities (e.g., the construction business) or politics (e.g., engaging in vote-buying to favor their preferred candidate), for the most part mafias' operations are geared toward governing the world of illicit markets.

Moving beyond a focus on the criminal underworld, Arias's pioneering work on criminal governance in Brazil (2006a) and in the developing world (2017) demonstrates that in establishing controls over illicit markets, OCGs often develop criminal governance regimes that attempt to control different dimensions of local organization, including the political, economic, and social life of neighborhoods and districts in urban areas. OCGs are interested in controlling not only criminal markets but also the political and social domains in which they operate.[4]

At a political level, OCGs attempt to influence electoral processes through several mechanisms. Criminal groups may use bribes to influence the selection of their preferred political candidates to local office and use violence against voters to influence electoral outcomes (Ley 2018). Gaining political control allows OCGs to influence a wide range of public policies, from security to the distribution of public resources. Security policies affect OCGs' ability to operate and the possibility of capturing public resources offers a new source of rents. But economic controls may extend beyond the mere capture of public rents and include criminal taxation (in the form of protection fees), control over public development programs, and the operation of specific legal and illegal markets. The

---

[4] Arias's study of criminal governance speaks in important ways to Arjona's (2016) study of rebel governance.

setup of local political and economic controls necessarily involves inter-actions between OCGs and the local citizenry. Social controls are, there-fore, part of the logic of criminal governance. Criminal lords seek local allies that provide them with fine-grained information about individual behaviors that affect their activities (Magaloni et al. 2019) and also attempt to monitor, regulate, and punish individual or collective actions that could put them at risk (Arias 2017).

The use of coercion and corruption to influence local electoral pro-cesses, the local provision of security, the allocation of public resources, taxation, and the degree of civilian participation in everyday forms of economic and political life turn criminal organizations into *territorial* groups. It is important to note, however, that the presence of *any* form of political, economic, or social control is sufficient to indicate some degree of criminal governance. In fact, criminal governance regimes are quite varied, both in terms of the controls that OCGs exert and the degree of violence they use. Arias (2017) suggests that as OCGs become more consolidated and more engaged with state authorities, criminal govern-ance regimes are likely to fully exert the three types of controls and be less violent. Magaloni et al. (2019) further suggest that in a context of criminal monopoly, OCGs may even provide goods and services to the local population, possibly resulting in a relatively cooperative relationship between organized crime and civil society. In both accounts, contested criminal territories are likely to lead to more predatory behavior.

Our central claim is that when drug cartels are engaged in intense and protracted military conflicts against the state and rival OCGs, drug lords will have incentives to launch attacks against local government officials and political actors not only to gain protection or capture public rents but, more fundamentally, to gain control over local government structures and, thence, over local populations and territories.

As the civil war literature has shown, over the course of intense and protracted conflicts, armed actors seek to develop controls over popula-tions (Arjona 2016), territories (Kalyvas 2006), and natural resources (Ross 2004). Similarly, in intense and protracted *criminal wars* over the control of drug trafficking routes, to remain competitive, cartels often expand their range of illicit activities. These can range from drug traffick-ing into the illicit exploitation of human wealth – via extortion, kidnap-ping for ransom and human smuggling – and natural wealth – via the looting of mines or forests.

Municipalities become crucial in this expansion beyond the drug traf-ficking industry. Whether municipalities are large and urban or small and rural, they represent attractive sources of fresh resources and information. Through high-profile attacks, cartels seek to gain control over key municipal governmental appointments that will give them access to information, resources, and the local security apparatus. Imposing appointments in key positions related to the local property registry, local taxation, the allocation of public contracts, the regulation of the local service sector (including hotels, restaurants, bars, taxis, and public transportation), and the local police, gives criminal lords access to unique sources of financial and security information. This information enables them to engage in dual taxation: to capture government revenues and to impose informal criminal taxes on local businesses and populations. By controlling the municipal police, the cartels are able to use the police force and their own private militias to force citizens and businesses to pay criminal taxes and to influence elections. Gaining control over local governments, populations, and territories provides cartels with the economic resources, information, and geographic controls to more effectively confront the state and rival groups and to monopolize all illicit markets, including drug trafficking routes.

The decision to go beyond simply controlling drug trafficking routes and develop interests in controlling local governments, populations, and territories moves cartels squarely into the realm of politics. While drug lords do not directly compete for office, they do use high-profile violence to influence the formal electoral process, the functioning of local government, and the behavior of citizens – as voters and as consumers or producers. Through the use of targeted lethal violence, OCGs seek to recreate local political orders in which they aim to play the role of de facto political rulers.[5]

War Needs

In developing our criminal governance explanation, we recognize that intense and protracted drug wars do give rise to all sorts of needs for cartels and their criminal associates. Whether in search of self-defense, protection, or financial resources, as wars become more intense cartels are

---

[5] Although we emphasize the cartels' use of coercive power to establish criminal governance through high-profile assassinations, we recognize that in developing criminal governance regimes OCGs can combine coercion with clientelism or less coercive forms of civilian collaboration when their members have dense local ties (Berg and Carranza 2018) or monopolistic controls (Magaloni et al. 2019).

more likely to use violence against subnational authorities to remain competitive in the struggle over the control of drug trafficking routes. We thus expect that:

H.1. Local officials and politicians are more likely to become targets of criminal attacks in municipalities experiencing the most intense levels of state–cartel and inter-cartel violence.

Political Vulnerability

Because we assume that cartels are not only interested in gaining protection or capturing rents but, more fundamentally, they want to take over local government structures and control local populations and territories, we suggest that drug lords order attacks against local officials and politicians when they identify opportunities to succeed in establishing subnational criminal governance regimes. Following Iqbal and Zorn's (2006) important work on high-profile political assassinations, we assume that opportunities for attacks are intimately associated with how political power is distributed in society and with the timing of power successions.

In the context of large-scale criminal wars, subnational authorities need protection from national governments to confront powerful armed groups. As we discussed in Chapter 4, mayors in Mexico have neither the legal instruments nor the policing power to confront drug cartels and their private militias. In the face of major criminal threats, mayors need the federal assistance of the national authorities. But, as scholars of security in federations have recently shown, the national government's decision whether to provide protection for subnational authorities is not simply a technical issue. Following students of fiscal federalism, who suggest that partisanship plays a crucial role in the distribution of fiscal transfers from the center to the periphery (Weingast 2014), scholars in conflict studies have suggested that policing decisions in polarized societies are often guided by electoral incentives (Wilkinson 2004; Auyero 2006).

As we argued in Chapters 4 and 5, in the politically polarized context between Left and Right that characterized Mexico during the 2007–2012 period, inter-cartel violence was more intense in leftist subnational regions, where a conservative federal administration refused to provide effective protection for its leftist subnational political rivals and then blamed the resulting escalation of violence on them. In contrast, drug violence was relatively contained in subnational regions where the president provided effective protection for his co-partisans and took credit for the resulting lower levels of attacks.

We build on these arguments about electoral influence on policing decisions to suggest that Mexico's partisan intergovernmental conflict between Left and Right rendered mayors, local government officials, and party candidates vulnerable to criminal attacks and opened opportunities for cartels to establish criminal governance regimes through targeted lethal violence. We suggest that incentives for high-profile criminal assaults are greater in subnational regions where local elected officials are politically unprotected and therefore *vulnerable*. Cartels take cues from the political environment and attack subnational authorities that are purposefully left unprotected. We expect that in a polarized political context:

H.2. Local government officials are more likely to become targets of criminal attacks in subnational regions where political power is more vertically fragmented – that is, where subnational officials belong to a party that is an ideological rival of the president.

Political Opportunities

Scholars of contentious politics and civil war have shown that different forms of collective action, from peaceful mobilization (Trejo 2014) to armed insurgency (Staniland 2012) and violence in civil war (Steele 2011), are intimately associated with election cycles. Students of organized crime have suggested that election cycles can be a magnet for violence too. As Albarracín's study of Brazil (2018) suggests, politicians sometimes subcontract OCGs to eliminate their enemies or to coerce voters during elections. Alternatively, as Alesina, Piccolo, and Pinotti's (2019) study of Italy concludes, the mafia uses violence during the election campaign to influence voters' behavior and shortly after the election to influence policy choice.

Building on these arguments about criminal–electoral cycles, we suggest that as drug cartels become interested in colonizing municipal governments, subnational election cycles – when new governments come in and new administrative appointments are made – present an ideal *opportunity* to achieve this goal. Drug lords can use lethal violence against political candidates to eliminate potentially unfriendly officials and to co-opt likely winners and influence government appointments. Because cartels are not interested in taking over the national government but rather in developing subnational criminal governance regimes, we would expect attacks to take place in times of local elections. Thus:

H.3. Local government officials and politicians are likely to become targets of criminal attacks during subnational election cycles.

Subnational Territorial Controls

Following a logic of de facto *territorial governance*, as described by Arias (2017), drug lords no longer limit their ambitions to simply controlling the local airports, ports, bus stations, highways and roads that constitute drug trafficking corridors but seek to control governments and economic and political life in adjacent local administrative jurisdictions as well. In the Mexican case, after the federal intervention in the War on Drugs and the decapitation of cartels and private militias (see Chapter 5), plaza chiefs and gangs reconstituted themselves into new OCGs whose interest shifted from controlling drug trafficking routes to developing local controls in clusters of municipalities. This marks a dramatic transformation in the cartels' understanding of the territorial boundaries of their domains. Their new interest in formal administrative jurisdictions brings the gray zone of criminality within the boundaries of formal political power. As cartels seek to expand their domain into new criminal markets and into formal structures of local power, we would expect that:

H.4. High-profile attacks are more likely as the number of attacks in neighboring municipalities increases.

Figure 6.6 summarizes our main theoretical claims and helps us illustrate our research strategy. Following the figure, in the remainder of this chapter we statistically assess the association between our key independent variables (turf wars, vertical partisan fragmentation, and subnational election cycles) and our output variable (attacks). Focusing on election cycles and the distribution of political power along Mexico's federation, we will seek to establish the causal link between opportunities for criminal governance and violence. In Chapter 7, we present qualitative evidence from the states of Michoacán and Guerrero to establish the connection between our output variable (attacks) and the process outcome (criminal governance). That is, we will use case studies to understand how cartels capitalized on high-profile attacks to gain control over local governments,

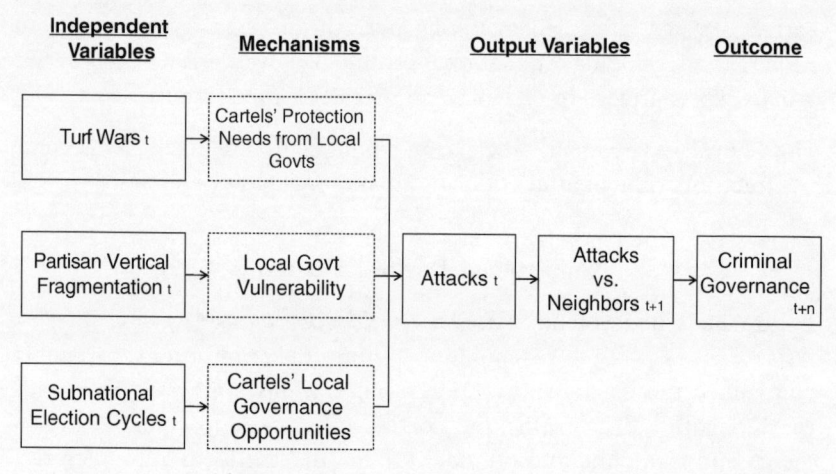

FIGURE 6.6 Explanatory Model of the Criminal Governance Hypothesis

populations, and territories. Note that in our explanatory model, the quantitative test and the case studies are truly complementary. Because we cannot directly measure criminal governance in our statistical analysis, we take criminal governance to be the latent motivation behind high-profile attacks. We use the case studies to show that these were the conduit by which drug cartels and their criminal associates developed subnational criminal governance regimes.

QUANTITATIVE EVIDENCE I: MULTIVARIATE REGRESSION MODELS

We draw on information from the CAPAM dataset to test the criminal governance hypothesis. We use the municipality as our spatial unit of analysis because: (1) the drug trafficking industry is a global chain of *local* operations; (2) drug cartels fight turf wars to control municipal sites (or plazas); (3) municipal governments become a crucial instrument to help cartels expand their illegal domain into the extraction of human and natural-resource wealth; and (4) 85 percent of attacks are linked to municipal politics.[6] We assess the annual

---

[6] For a study of political murders using Mexican states as units of analysis, see Blume (2017).

evolution of violence across 2,119[7] municipalities during the 2007–2012 period, when the Mexican federal government launched a war against drug cartels.[8]

The total count of criminal attacks against government officials and political candidates is our key dependent variable. CA_{it} expresses the count of attacks in municipality i in year t. We define "lethal attacks" as four types:[9] kidnapping, public death threats, assassination attempts, and murders; we examine 311 such attacks.[10] Two-thirds involve murders and assassination attempts.

Note that our dependent variable has two important innovations. First, unlike other studies that look exclusively at attacks against mayors (Ríos 2012), we extend the focus to government officials, political candidates, and party activists as well. This is important because drug cartels seek to influence the actions not only of incumbent authorities (e.g., mayors and their associates) but also of future political leaders (candidates) and their political associates (activists). Our data show that an exclusive focus on mayors would miss out two-thirds of the attacks. Because most of these are against government officials and party candidates, for convenience we do not always refer to party activists.

Second, whereas most studies only consider murders, we collected data on a wide variety of attacks, ranging from kidnappings, public death threats, and assassination *attempts* to murder. An exclusive focus on murders yields two sources of bias: it underestimates the extent of violence by assuming that murders are the only means of coercion available to OCGs; it also excludes cases in which criminal groups' assassination

---

[7] We exclude Mexico's Federal District and municipalities elected under indigenous customary law in Oaxaca (where the state law bans political parties from competing for office).

[8] Our analysis begins in 2007 because the War on Drugs was launched in December 2006, and we use calendar years as our temporal unit of analysis.

[9] CAPAM only includes attacks against government authorities and politicians that have been attributed to cartels in the newspaper reports. When none of the 19 local sources that CAPAM uses reported a name of a cartel in the incident, we included it in the database only if there was evidence of the cartels' modus operandi: the use of assault weapons, signs of torture and brutal violence (e.g., bodies wrapped in a rug or mutilated), or written messages left on the bodies.

[10] There are two types of threats: private and public. Because it is nearly impossible to measure and confirm the veracity of private threats, we only included *public* threats that resulted in (a) candidates withdrawing from the election, (b) parties being unable to put forth candidates, or (c) public authorities resigning to protect their lives. See Appendix B for a detailed discussion.

attempts are unsuccessful. Our data show that an exclusive focus on murders would miss out on one half of the attacks.

To test for the cartels' incentives to launch high-profile attacks in contexts of turf wars against the state and rival cartels (H.1), we use battle deaths in state–cartel and inter-cartel conflicts. Note that state–cartel conflicts involve battle deaths in wars between cartels and members of the armed forces and the police; this information *does not* contain targeted attacks against elected officials or party candidates (our dependent variable). Inter-cartel conflicts include battle deaths in wars between rival criminal organizations. We rely on two different information sources: (1) the Criminal Violence in Mexico (CVM) Dataset; (2) a dataset collected by the Office of the President on drug-related homicides. Based on a systematic review of the Mexican daily *Reforma*, CVM aggregates murders committed by OCGs, both as a result of state–cartel and inter-cartel conflicts, 2007–2012. We transform the count of murders into *Drug-related murder rate per 1,000 population (CVM)*.[11] The government database records battle deaths attributed to state–cartel and inter-cartel conflicts, 2007–2011.[12]

To test whether cartels launched attacks against politically and militarily unprotected subnational officials and political candidates (H.2), in line with the statistical analysis reported in Chapter 4 we use vertical political fragmentation (or juxtaposition) as our indicator of vulnerability. Recall that Mexico's party system has three major political parties (PAN, PRI, and PRD), which compete for office at three levels of government (federal, state, and municipal).[13] During the 2007–2012 period, the conservative PAN held the presidency but gubernatorial and municipal powers were dispersed across the three major parties, including the center opposition (PRI) and the Left opposition (PRD). As in Chapter 4, we test for nine different combinations of power fragmentation.[14] Thus the party identified on the first row in brackets is the party in presidential power, the second is the party in the state gubernatorial office, and the third is the party ruling the municipality. For the purposes of statistical analysis we

---

[11] We use a population base of 1,000 instead of the conventional 100,000 base because our universe of municipalities includes many municipalities with small populations under 10,000.

[12] For this dataset, see Atuesta et al. (2018).

[13] Because small parties fielded candidates for office in coalition with the three big parties, we subsumed the small parties into the three major ones (e.g., the Green Party under the PRI and the Workers' Party under the PRD).

[14] CIDAC: http://cidac.org/base-de-datos-electoral/. Accessed May 10, 2017.

use unified governance (PAN-PAN-PAN) as the reference category. We alternatively create a *Juxtaposition index* in which we rank the different combinations in one single metric from zero (PAN-PAN-PAN) to eight (PAN-PRD-PRD). This index reflects the polarization between Right and Left.

To assess whether drug cartels are interested in colonizing local governments and developing subnational criminal governance regimes, we test for the association of attacks with different election cycles (H.3). We use a dummy variable to identify the years of gubernatorial and municipal elections, *Subnational election cycles*, and a dummy variable to identify years of national legislative and presidential elections, *Federal election cycles*. Mexican states define their own election calendars and therefore subnational elections are staggered.

To assess whether cartels seek to establish subnational criminal governance regimes in territories that go beyond a single municipal space, we test for a one-year lag of criminal attacks against local government officials in neighboring municipalities, *Attacks in adjacent neighborhoods (t–1)*. We define neighboring municipalities as the most immediate adjacent neighbors that share geographic borders. Our assumption is that attacks are sequential, rather than simultaneous, events – that is, cartels target one municipality and then expand their rule over neighboring municipalities.

We control for three features of the state: (1) *Fiscal revenue*, which measures the percentage of the municipality's total income that comes from local taxes;[15] (2) *Federal security funds*, as calculated in Chapter 4; and (3) the municipal number of *Public prosecutor offices per 1,000 population*,[16] which is a proxy for state capacity. We also control for political variables that have been shown in the drug violence literature to be important drivers of criminal violence, including *Municipal* and *State alternation* of political parties in office (Trejo and Ley 2018) and *Municipal* and *State electoral competition* (Dube, Dube, and García-Ponce 2013). Finally, we control for seven geographic regions: *North*, *North-Center*, *Center*, *Pacific*, *Gulf*, *South*, and *Southeast*. We do not control for poverty and population size because both are highly correlated with *Fiscal revenue*.

As in previous analyses, we use negative binomial regression models which are the most appropriate technique for count data, particularly

---

[15] INEGI-SIMBAD, http://sc.inegi.org.mx/cobdem/. Accessed February 24, 2014.
[16] We did not include police per capita, because official data on municipal police are incomplete.

when observations are non-independent and over-dispersed – as is the case with the count of criminal attacks. We rely on random effects models instead of fixed effects models, because some of our key political variables (e.g., the juxtaposition variables) remain unchanged for a number of years and because the time-series is relatively short (T = 6) compared to the number of municipalities (N = 2,119). We cluster the standard errors by municipality. Because a significantly large number of municipalities did not experience attacks, the dataset contains a large number of zeros. To confront potential biases, we ran logit and rare event logit models using a binary transformation of the dependent variable (0, 1), and the main results remained unchanged (see Appendix F).

Results

Consistent with H.1, the results in Table 6.1 show that local government officials and party candidates were more commonly attacked in municipalities where cartels were involved in dual wars against the state and rival groups. Using data from newspaper records (CVM) and from government statistics (Gov.), the results in Models 1 and 2 show that public officials and party candidates were significantly more likely to become targets of criminal attacks in contexts of greater drug-related violence, where cartels were fighting fierce wars against both the state armed forces and rival criminal groups. As Model 1 shows, for every additional murder per 1,000 of population resulting from drug wars, as measured by CVM, the odds of high-profile criminal attacks increase by 33.3 percent (IRR = 1.333). Using the government data, Model 2 shows that the odds increase by 50.9 percent (IRR = 1.509).

The results in Models 1 and 2 show that high-profile criminal attacks were motivated not only by war dynamics but also by the cartels' ambition for rents. Incidents were more common in municipalities in which mayors enjoyed greater fiscal autonomy and cartels could extract more rents: for every additional percentage point of a municipality's total income that comes from local tax revenues, the probability of high-profile attacks increases by a percentage between 4.7 (IRR = 1.047) and 5.5 (IRR = 1.055). At the same time, both models also show that increasing levels of ear-tagged federal transfers for public security were associated with a lower incidence of attacks. This is consistent with our findings in Chapter 4. Not only did these funds help subnational authorities prevent or contain inter-cartel violence, but they also helped mayors to protect themselves from criminal attacks. But beyond the cartels' war needs and

TABLE 6.1 *Turf Wars and High-Profile Criminal Attacks, 2007–2012 (Random Effects Negative Binomial Models)*

	Model 1		Model 2	
	Coeff.	IRR	Coeff.	IRR
Turf wars				
Drug-related murder rate CVM^	0.287***	1.333		
	[0.073]			
Drug-related murder rate Gov.^			0.412***	1.509
			[0.075]	
Controls				
Fiscal Revenue	0.046***	1.047	0.053***	1.055
	[0.012]		[0.013]	
Federal security funds	−0.612**	0.542	−0.676**	0.509
	[0.247]		[0.263]	
Prosecutor offices^	0.542	1.720	−0.227	0.797
	[1.284]		[1.387]	
Mun. Alternation	−0.005	0.995	−0.009	0.991
	[0.152]		[0.160]	
St. Alternation	−0.092	0.912	0.033	1.034
	[0.191]		[0.201]	
Mun. Electoral competition	−0.382***	0.682	−0.464***	0.629
	[0.128]		[0.136]	
St. Electoral competition	0.731***	2.076	0.928***	2.529
	[0.271]		[0.286]	
Geographic regions	YES		YES	
Constant	7.080**		7.889**	
	[3.582]		[3.801]	
Observations	9,854		8,960	
Number of municipalities	1,995		1,995	
Log-likelihood	−1,090.960		−987.029	
BIC	2,338.246		2,128.767	

*** $p<0.01$, ** $p<0.05$, * $p<0.10$.
^ per 1,000 inhabitants.
Clustered standard errors in brackets.

their search for rents, the results in Table 6.2 show that cartels attacked local government officials and political candidates where they saw *opportunities* to establish criminal governance regimes.

TABLE 6.2 *Governance Opportunities and High-Profile Criminal Attacks, 2007–2012 (Random Effects Negative Binomial Models)*

	Model 1		Model 2	
	Coeff.	IRR	Coeff.	IRR
Turf wars				
Drug-related murder rate CVM^	0.244***	1.277	0.252***	1.287
	[0.068]		[0.070]	
Vertical partisan fragmentation				
PAN-PAN-PRI	0.384	1.468		
	[0.460]			
PAN-PAN-PRD	−0.153	0.858		
	[1.083]			
PAN-PRI-PAN	0.399	1.490		
	[0.417]			
PAN-PRI-PRI	0.642*	1.901		
	[0.383]			
PAN-PRI-PRD	0.334	1.397		
	[0.515]			
PAN-PRD-PAN	1.290**	3.633		
	[0.535]			
PAN-PRD-PRI	1.635***	5.128		
	[0.438]			
PAN-PRD-PRD	1.724***	5.609		
	[0.436]			
Juxtaposition index			0.210***	1.234
			[0.048]	
Election cycles				
Subnational elections	0.484***	1.623	0.464***	1.590
	[0.142]		[0.142]	
Federal election	−0.457*	0.633	−0.540**	0.583
	[0.245]		[0.254]	
Territorial ambition				
Attacks in adjacent neighbors t−1	0.342***	1.407	0.342***	1.408
	[0.069]		[0.070]	
Controls				
Fiscal Revenue	0.048***	1.049	0.050***	1.052
	[0.012]		[0.012]	

(continued)

TABLE 6.2 *(continued)*

	Model 1		Model 2	
	Coeff.	IRR	Coeff.	IRR
Federal security funds	−0.122	0.885	−0.138	0.871
	[0.266]		[0.265]	
Prosecutor offices^	0.519	1.681	0.518	1.678
	[1.287]		[1.297]	
Mun. Alternation	0.049	1.051	0.021	1.021
	[0.155]		[0.151]	
St. Alternation	−0.058	0.944	−0.038	0.963
	[0.196]		[0.195]	
Mun. Electoral competition	−0.303**	0.739	−0.329**	0.719
	[0.129]		[0.130]	
St. Electoral competition	0.132	1.141	0.234	1.263
	[0.322]		[0.311]	
Geographic regions	YES		YES	
Constant	−0.647		−0.533	
	[3.843]		[3.806]	
Observations	9,854		9,704	
Number of municipalities	1,995		1,991	
Log-likelihood	−1,058.418		−1,049.84	
BIC	2,374.313		2,292.466	

*** $p<0.01$, ** $p<0.05$, * $p<0.10$.
^ per 1,000 inhabitants. Clustered standard errors in brackets.
The party in the first cell is the president's; the second is the governor's; and the third is the mayor's. PAN-PAN-PAN is the reference category. PAN = national incumbent (conservative); PRI = opposition (center); PRD = opposition (Left).

Consistent with H.2, the results in Table 6.2, Model 1, show that cartels conducted high-profile attacks in politically neglected states where mayors presumably could not count on federal protection. The results strongly suggest that the governor's party affiliation is the main distinguishing factor across cases. Compared to a situation of unified vertical governance in which the president's conservative co-partisans ruled at the gubernatorial and municipal levels (PAN-PAN-PAN), local officials and politicians were significantly more exposed to criminal attacks in states ruled by opposition governors, particularly by the leftist PRD – perceived by the president as his greatest political threat. If we focus on municipalities from leftist states (where the PRD appears as the second category), results show that local opposition government authorities and party candidates were 412 percent and 461 percent (IRR = 5.128 and 5.609) more likely to become targets than local officials in states where the president's co-partisans ruled. But the results also show that, although the odds were lower (IRR = 3.633), conservative PANista mayors in leftist states were also at risk.

To facilitate the substantive interpretation of these results, Figure 6.7 provides a graphic representation of the model's main findings. Recall that variables are statistically significant when the confidence interval does not cross the zero line. These findings provide a strong indication that the partisan intergovernmental conflict between a conservative president and leftist state governors affected all mayors and local party candidates, who became likely targets of attacks because murder became a relatively cheaper alternative mechanism of criminal control than bribes.

As the results in Figure 6.7 show, there is nothing unique about leftist municipalities – no probable shared attribute – that would make them more vulnerable to criminal attacks. In comparison to a situation of unified governance (PAN-PAN-PAN), leftist mayors and local

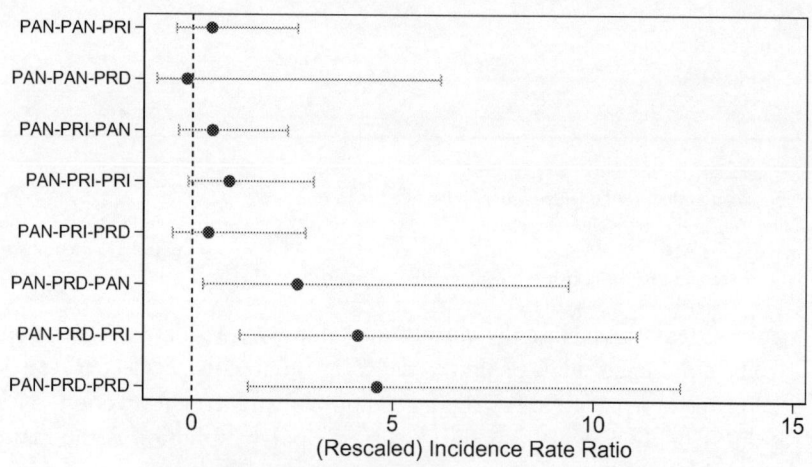

Incidence Rate Ratios (IRR) from Model 1 in Table 6.2 were rescaled for purposes of interpretation.
Original IRRs were subtracted one unit to show the direct impact of juxtaposition on criminal attacks.
PAN = Incumbent party in presidential power (conservative);
PRI = Opposition party (center); PRD = Opposition party (left).
Note that the party in the first cell is the president's, the second one is the governor's, and the third is the mayor's. PAN-PAN-PAN is the reference category.

FIGURE 6.7 Impact of Vertical Fragmentation of Power on Criminal Attacks in Mexico, 2007–2012

candidates in conservative states (PAN-PAN-**PRD**) and in states with PRI governors (PAN-PRI-**PRD**) were no more likely to experience criminal attacks, but leftist mayors in leftist states (PAN-PRD-**PRD**) were. If leftist municipalities or leftist politicians had a shared attribute that made them likely targets of attacks, *all* configurations of partisan vertical fragmentation with PRD mayors would be statistically significant. And this is not the case. In fact, the raw data show that PRD municipalities experienced one attack in PAN states, eight attacks in PRI states, and 49 attacks in PRD states. It is highly unlikely that leftist PRD governors would have purposefully rendered their local co-partisans vulnerable to attacks; rather, these results are consistent with the logic of intergovernmental partisan conflict in a context of extreme polarization between Left and Right.

The results from the *Juxtaposition index* in Table 6.2, Model 2, confirm the greater vulnerability to attack of mayors in opposition-ruled states, particularly those ruled by the Left: For every additional layer away from unified governance (PAN-PAN-PAN), the odds increased by 23.4 percent (IRR = 1.234). This means that at the highest level of juxtaposition, a leftist mayor from a leftist state was 187.2 percent more likely to suffer an attack (23.4 × 8) than a conservative mayor from a conservative state. The raw data confirm these patterns. While Mexicali (PAN), the capital city of the northwestern state of Baja California (PAN), experienced no attacks between 2007 and 2012, Chilpancingo (PRD), the capital city of the southern state of Guerrero (PRD), experienced three. Overall, Baja California experienced six attacks while Guerrero experienced 57.

As predicted in H.3, the results in Models 1 and 2 also show not only that cartels targeted municipal authorities and party candidates in politically vulnerable states but also that they did so at predictable times – during local election cycles. The results show that municipalities were at least 59 percent (IRR = 1.623 and 1.590) more likely to experience a high-profile attack during a subnational election cycle. We take this as a strong indication that cartels used violence to try to influence local election campaigns, outcomes, and administrative appointments in the incoming governments. The fact that violent incidents decreased by as much as 41.7 percent during federal election cycles (IRR = 0.633 and 0.583) is also an indication that cartels were probably not interested in contesting national power.

Finally, in line with H.4, the results in Model 1 are consistent with a logic of subnational territorial control: For every attack experienced by a municipality in year t, the likelihood of an attack among adjacent neighbors increased by 41 percent in $t+1$ (IRR = 1.407 and 1.408). This strikingly high odds ratio speaks about spillover effects and economies of scale on attacks – once cartels targeted local government officials or party candidates in one municipality and penetrated the municipal government structures, they would use this as a base to target its neighbors. This dynamic suggests that cartels were probably focused not on controlling single towns but on establishing subnational criminal governance regimes in clusters of adjacent municipalities.

QUANTITATIVE EVIDENCE II: NATURAL EXPERIMENTS

Up to this point we have firmly argued that the political vulnerability of subnational authorities in leftist states and the political opportunities afforded by subnational election cycles drive high-profile criminal attacks. But is it possible that they actually shape political opportunities rather than the other way around? Or is it possible that there are unobservable factors that may explain both opportunities and attacks? We use the multiple borders of the western state of Michoacán – a leftist state that experienced multiple incidents – along with other states – ruled by the PAN, PRI, and PRD – to address challenges of endogeneity. We focus on the two variables that we use to measure political opportunities for attacks: subnational election cycles and partisan vertical fragmentation.

Subnational Election Cycles

A comparison of the Tierra Caliente region, which cuts across the leftist state of Michoacán and its eastern Guerrero neighbor, as shown in Map 6.2, allows us to assess in a quasi-experimental setting whether local election cycles opened opportunities for high-profile violence and had an independent causal effect on criminal attacks. Map 6.2 highlights the neighboring municipalities from the Tierra Caliente region that we compare and shows the number of attacks per municipality.[17] Although separated by state borders, these municipalities share many geographic, sociodemographic, cultural, economic, and political features (see Appendix G and Table G.1 for detailed information and a discussion about the relevance and validity

---

[17] We use a two-degree neighborhood criterion, as in Chapter 4.

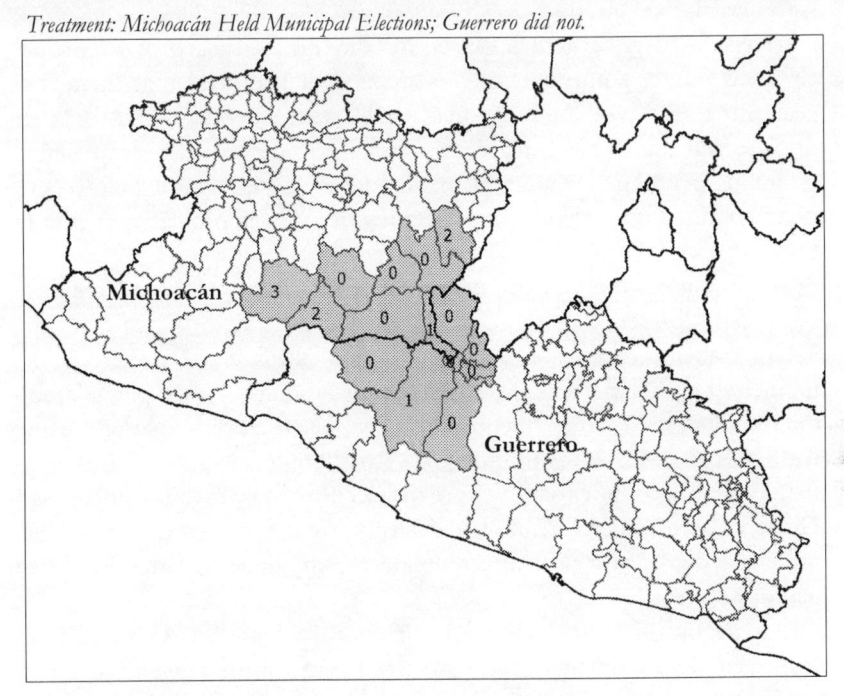

MAP 6.2 Criminal Attacks against Government Officials and Party Members in Neighboring Municipalities of Michoacán and Guerrero, 2011

of this comparison).[18] In terms of criminal markets, as we explained in Chapter 5, Tierra Caliente in Michoacán was the bastion of La Familia Michoacana, the state's leading cartel in the 2000s. La Familia extended its grip to include the Tierra Caliente region of Guerrero after 2005, when the PRI lost power after seven decades of one-party rule and a leftist governor was elected (see Chapters 2 and 3). In both regions La Familia was immersed in deadly turf wars and sought to establish criminal governance regimes through high-profile attacks between 2007 and 2012.

An important difference between the two regions is that Guerrero and Michoacán hold state legislative and municipal elections at different times. In 2011, Michoacán simultaneously held gubernatorial elections,

---

[18] In Appendix G we address four potential challenges: (1) imbalance of predictors and contextual factors between groups of municipalities; (2) lack of independent effect of treatment; (3) unidentified intervening variables; and (4) 'self-selection' of municipalities across states.

state legislative elections, and *municipal elections*. That same year, Guerrero held gubernatorial elections but no legislative or municipal elections. For the purposes of our analysis, it is crucial that municipal elections in the two states are held in different calendar years. Because drug cartels and their criminal associates are interested in establishing criminal governance regimes at the municipal level, including clusters of municipalities, municipal elections represent the key political opportunity for drug cartels.

As shown in Map 6.2, another important distinction is that there were significant differences in targeted violence across state borders: while the Tierra Caliente region of Michoacán experienced eight attacks against municipal authorities and municipal party candidates (or 5 per 100,000 inhabitants), the Tierra Caliente region in Guerrero only experienced one (or 0.55 per 100,000 inhabitants). We attribute this eight-fold difference in the absolute number of attacks to the election cycle. In other words, had Guerrero experienced a municipal election cycle in 2011, high-profile attacks would have been approximately eight times greater than they actually were.

It is important for our claim that state borders between Michoacán and Guerrero were defined in the nineteenth century for reasons that had nothing to do with inter-cartel wars – these broke out 150 years after the states' boundaries were outlined.

It is also crucial for our argument that subnational election cycles are defined by state constitutions on fixed dates – that is, election cycles are an exogenous feature. This means that there is no risk of reverse causality: the municipal election cycle of Michoacán opened opportunities for attacks, rather than attacks leading to new election cycles. It also means that there is no risk of omitted variable bias: because election calendars are fixed, no other omitted factor may influence the occurrence of elections.

Partisan Vertical Fragmentation

A comparison of the northern municipalities of Michoacán with the southern municipalities of the state of Guanajuato, as shown in Map 6.3, allows us to confirm that partisan vertical fragmentation and inter-governmental conflict between a conservative federal government and a leftist governor rendered municipalities in leftist states more vulnerable to criminal violence and had an independent causal effect on attacks. Both regions share important geographic, sociodemographic, cultural, and economic similarities (see Appendix G and Table G.2 for detailed

Treatment: A Leftist Governor Ruled in Michoacán; a Conservative Governor in Guanajuato.

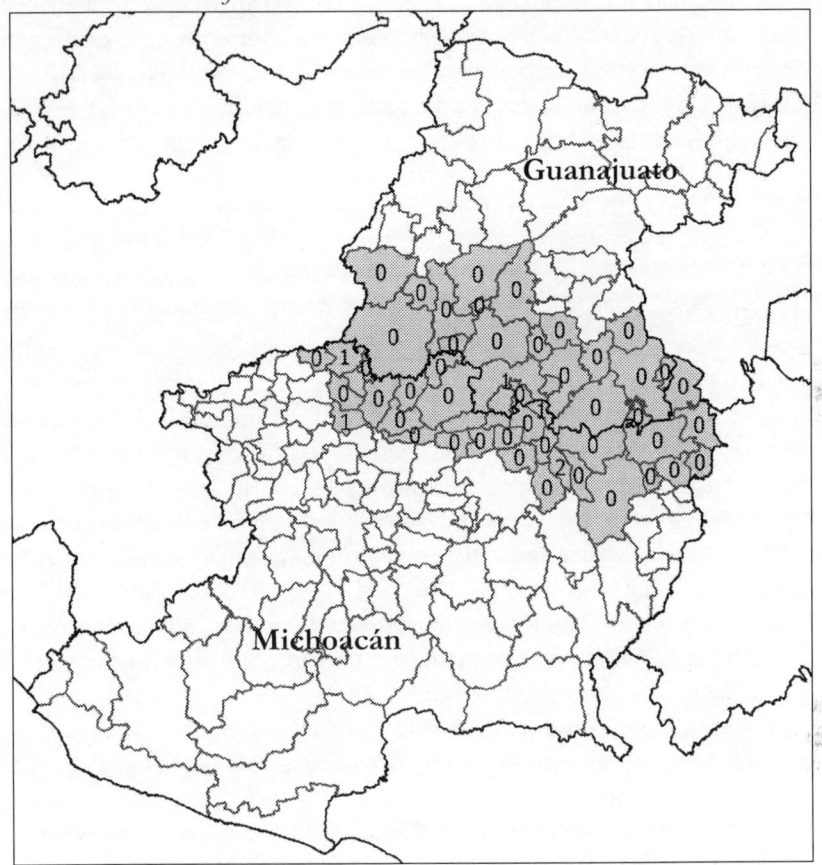

MAP 6.3 Criminal Attacks against Government Officials and Party Members in Neighboring Municipalities of Michoacán and Guanajuato, 2008–2011

information and a discussion on the relevance of this comparison).[19] As we discussed in Chapter 5, La Familia made decisive inroads into Guanajuato in their battles against the Zetas, who used the southern tip of Guanajuato as an area of refuge from which to launch attacks and then retreat. This was a region that became a battlefield between La Familia and the Zetas, and La Familia actively sought to penetrate local governments and police forces to establish criminal governance regimes.

[19] Ibid.

An important difference between municipalities in northern Michoacán and their neighbors in southern Guanajuato is that a leftist governor ruled Michoacán and a conservative governor ruled Guanajuato. As we described in Chapter 5, in confronting the escalation of drug violence in Guanajuato, President Calderón worked closely with his PAN co-partisan. He devised a federal intervention that closely aligned the actions of the military, the governor and the state security apparatus (headed by a general), and the mayors of the state's southern region.[20] With full federal support the governor, in coordination with municipal authorities, was able to dismantle multiple police forces infiltrated by the cartels.[21] This coordinated support provided protection for the mayors, deterring La Familia from attempting high-profile attacks in order to take over.[22] In contrast, as we explained in Chapter 5, President Calderón and the leftist Governor, Leonel Godoy, were engaged in a bitter intergovernmental partisan conflict that prevented any meaningful cooperation and that led Calderón to adopt a punishment regime against the governor and his team. The military intervention in Michoacán was unilateral and bypassed the state's judicial and police forces. The federal government pursued an aggressive judicial campaign to arrest key members of the governor's team and dozens of mayors for alleged collusion with the cartels; it launched a major smear campaign to portray subnational leftist authorities in Michoacán as inept and corrupt; and it withheld federal financial assistance for Michoacán.

Another important difference between the two regions was the differing patterns of high-profile criminal violence. As shown in Map 6.3, between 2008 and 2011[23] there was one attack in the southern municipalities of Guanajuato (or 0.05 attacks per 100,000 population), whereas during the same period there were five attacks in northern Michoacán (or 0.89 per 100,000 population). We attribute the five-fold difference in the absolute number of attacks between these two regions to partisan intergovernmental conflict between Left and Right. In the context of acute political polarization, had Guanajuato had a leftist state government then federal authorities under President Calderón would have most likely left

---

[20] See Univisión (2009) and Álvarez (2011).

[21] See Álvarez (2011) and El Sol del Bajío (2011).

[22] Similar patterns of PAN-PAN-PAN cooperation in Baja California resulted in a limited number of high-profile attacks. For a detailed discussion, see Trejo and Ley (2016) and Durán-Martínez (2018).

[23] This is the time period in which a left-wing governor ruled in Michoacán and a right-wing governor ruled in Guanajuato.

subnational authorities unprotected and high-profile attacks in the southern region would have been five times greater. Like the eastern borders of Michoacán, it is worth stressing that the state's northern borders were also defined in the nineteenth century for reasons entirely unrelated to twenty-first-century narco wars.

It is also crucial for our claim that the Left ruled in Michoacán and the Right in Guanajuato for reasons unrelated to the drug violence. The governor of Guanajuato was elected prior to the War on Drugs (2006) and the governor of Michoacán was elected just as the War was starting (2007). This should dispel concerns about reverse causality. Moreover, within the states, both northern Michoacán and southern Guanajuato are small enough to render it unlikely that voting in these municipalities could determine the outcome of the gubernatorial elections. It is therefore safe to consider the fact that one region had a leftist governor and the other a conservative governor as an exogenous factor that led the two regions into different trajectories of violence.

CONCLUSION

One of the most dramatic developments in protracted civil conflicts – including civil wars and criminal wars – is the outbreak of multiple forms of violence against a multiplicity of targets. In this chapter we analyzed a surprising wave of over 300 lethal attacks against municipal government authorities and party candidates. It is a surprising wave, as we suggested in the opening remarks of the chapter, because local authorities had not played a leading role in the provision of informal government protection for the cartels since their rise to international prominence in the 1980s and because the federal government, rather than local authorities, launched the War on Drugs in 2006.

Although the scholarly literature suggests that in the context of turf wars cartels target local officials and politicians to force their successors to provide them with protection or to capture rents to finance wars, we have shown the limitations of looking exclusively at arguments based on war needs. We have offered extensive evidence showing that Mexican cartels took advantage of political vulnerability and governance opportunities, afforded by politically unprotected municipalities and local election cycles, to attack mayors and party candidates. We have conjectured that the ultimate goal of these assaults was to gain control over local governments, populations, and territories and establish subnational criminal governance regimes.

The causal connections between political vulnerability, opportunities for criminal governance, and the cartels' high-profile attacks unveiled by our statistical analyses and natural experiments suggest important lessons for the study of organized crime and large-scale criminal violence in democracies.

First, our findings have important implications for the study of the political rationality of organized criminal behavior. Attacks against Mexican subnational officials and party candidates, as we have shown, are not random events but outcomes that have clearly discernible logics. One of them is the logic of political opportunities. In line with Iqbal and Zorn's (2006) finding about political factors driving the assassinations of 52 heads of state, our research shows that the distribution of partisan power and the dynamics of power succession during elections defined the incentives for assassinations of subnational officials and politicians in Mexico's drug wars. Looking at lethal attacks by an allegedly *apolitical* actor – drug cartels – our study reveals that drug lords likewise sought to "topple ... incumbent government[s], retard [their] policy imperatives, and bring about political change" (Iqbal and Zorn 2006, p. 491). In our case, however, drug lords did not seek to become national rulers but to subdue local governments and populations and establish de facto subnational criminal governance regimes.

Second, although Mexican cartels do not want to topple the federal government or become a national political force, it would be misleading to continue defining them simply as illicit economic enterprises that exclusively seek to monopolize the criminal underworld or as violent interest groups that use coercion simply to influence public policy in their favor. Our findings suggest that the organized crime literature has to recognize that drug cartels can develop informal "political" ambitions. These ambitions lead them to use targeted lethal violence as a means to establishing subnational criminal governance regimes. While this does not turn them into armed rebel groups who seek to topple national institutions, their de facto political ambition distinguishes them from mafias and prison gangs who only want to govern the criminal underworld. After two decades of war, drug cartels in Mexico have become "political" actors with subnational governance ambitions. Recognizing the peculiar nature of the politicization of OCGs is crucial for a more subtle understanding of the changing motives and goals of criminal lords in protracted conflicts.

Third, although the political ambitions of drug lords and their criminal associates do not belong to the realm of de jure power but to the sphere of de facto politics, the statistical results and natural experiments suggest that the outcomes of formal electoral processes – subnational elections cycles – and the formal distribution of power – partisan vertical fragmentation – do inform their de facto political ambitions. This means that politics enter the gray zone of criminality in two fundamental ways: by informing OCGs' ambitions and the strategies by which they achieve their ends.

To gain a more effective understanding of how drug lords and their criminal associates capitalize on the dynamics of political change and intergovernmental partisan conflict, in Chapter 7 we use strategically selected case studies to take a closer look at the rise, development, and the dynamics of criminal governance in three Mexican states.

7

Seizing Local Power

Developing Subnational Criminal Governance Regimes

In the course of protracted conflicts, including civil wars and criminal wars, armed groups and/or organized criminal groups (OCGs) may take the radical step of developing de facto local governance regimes. Scholars of civil wars have recognized and extensively analyzed the phenomenon of rebel governance – or *rebelocracy*, in Arjona's (2016) effective formulation. Students of mafias (Gambetta 1996; Varese 2011) and organized crime have studied for decades the de facto governance structure of criminal markets and prisons (Skarbek 2014; Lessing and Willis 2019) but have only recently begun to explore the phenomenon of criminal governance in society (Arias 2006a, 2017) – that is, when OCGs seek to control local governments, populations, and territories. The development of de facto local governance regimes marks an inflection point in criminal wars. OCGs step outside the criminal underworld and, in consequence, the weakest layer of government – mayors in the Mexican case – becomes the target of attacks and civilians become a new source of resources to finance drug wars. As taxpayers and owners of private property and local businesses, civilians become victims of extortion, kidnapping for ransom, or human smuggling.[1]

As we discussed in Chapter 6, the Mexican drug trafficking industry and the criminal underworld experienced a major transformation, following the federal government's War on Drugs in 2006, when drug cartels launched a wave of lethal attacks against mayors and party candidates in

---

[1] The systematic study of these phenomena in Mexico is still in its early phases. For extortion, see Magaloni et al. (2019) and for a pioneering study of kidnapping for ransom, see Ochoa (2019).

10 percent of Mexico's municipalities and sought to take de facto control over subnational governance.[2] As we have argued, drug lords and their criminal associates aimed to develop subnational criminal governance regimes in regions experiencing fierce turf wars and in areas where subnational authorities were purposefully left politically and militarily unprotected by the federal government. In the localities in which drug cartels and their criminal associates have become de facto rulers, civilian victimization and gross human rights violations are widespread. Under these new local orders, life, to quote Hobbes (1651/1968) again, is "nasty, brutish and short."[3]

Drawing on extensive in-depth interviews with national government officials, governors, former mayors, social, religious, and business leaders, and human rights defenders, this chapter seeks to explain how drug cartels used targeted lethal violence against mayors and local party candidates to develop subnational criminal governance regimes. We explore how drug lords capitalized on these high-profile attacks to seize local electoral processes and gain control over the municipal police forces and key financial and regulatory offices in municipal governments. We also explore how they used these positions of coercive and administrative power, and their own private militias, to gain the monopoly over violence and taxation, control key economic activities, and control the outer boundaries of clusters of municipalities where they developed subnational criminal governance regimes. Our emphasis is on (1) the sequence of events that facilitated the criminal appropriation of political, social, and economic life in these towns and municipalities; and (2) the mechanics of conquest – that is, the process by which the power dynamics of the gray zone of criminality came to dominate formal social, economic, and political relations beyond the criminal underworld.

Our analysis focuses on municipalities from three different states – Michoacán, Guerrero, and Baja California. Michoacán and Guerrero are two leftist states where intergovernmental partisan conflict between

---

[2] Cartels and other OCGs may establish subnational criminal governance regimes via different paths than the high-profile assassination of local authority and political elites. Hence a larger percentage of Mexican municipalities may in fact experience criminal governance.

[3] Following Arias (2017), we recognize that when OCGs gain control over specific territories they develop less coercive criminal governance arrangements in which criminal lords engage in clientelistic relationships and can even mediate in the provision of social services. There is little evidence of the systematic mix of coercion with clientelism in Mexico. For evidence on clientelistic relations and potential civilian collaboration with OCGs in Mexico, see Magaloni et al. (2019).

a conservative federal government and leftist subnational authorities rendered mayors and local party candidates vulnerable to attack. These are cases that score high values on one of our key explanatory factors (partisan vertical fragmentation with leftist subnational presence) and on our dependent variable (the existence of criminal governance). In contrast, Baja California, a conservative bastion, represents a case of partisan alignment where Mexico's conservative president worked closely with the governor and mayors and where high-profile attacks were few and cartels failed to develop criminal governance regimes. This is a case that scores low on partisan fragmentation and criminal de facto power. The analysis of an outlier – the indigenous communities in the eastern part of the leftist state of Guerrero, where high-profile attacks are conspicuously low and criminal governance is non-existent – allows us to explore alternative explanations, particularly the likely importance of societal coordination in preventing narco rule.

The chapter is divided into four sections. We first discuss the literature on criminal and rebel governance to outline the basic conceptual terminology used throughout the chapter. In the second section we discuss the "positive" case studies, where the cartels succeeded in developing subnational criminal governance regimes (Michoacán and Guerrero). In the third section we focus on the "negative" cases, where the cartels did not succeed in becoming local de facto rulers (Baja California and the eastern highlands of Guerrero). In the conclusion, we highlight theoretical lessons from the cases studies for our understanding of how drug cartels change over the course of protracted wars and develop interests in reinventing local social orders beyond an exclusive focus on controlling drug trafficking routes.

THE DIFFERENT DIMENSIONS OF CRIMINAL GOVERNANCE

The initial analysis of criminal governance was confined to the governance of illicit markets. However, since the pioneering work of Arias (2017), the study of criminal governance has moved beyond the control that mafias and other OCGs establish in the criminal underworld and now analyzes de facto control over social, economic and political spheres. Arias's influential studies of drug trafficking in Brazil (2006a), Jamaica, and Colombia (2017) demonstrate that drug cartels are interested in governing not only the criminal underworld but also the world of formal social interactions and institutions in their neighborhoods of residence. Arias describes OCGs as *territorial* armed groups that use coercion and corruption to influence local electoral processes, the local provision of security, the allocation of public resources, and participation in civil society organizations. Control over formal social and political processes enables them to secure control over the criminal underworld.

While we follow Arias's understanding of criminal governance, our focus is not on small and medium-sized gangs operating in poor urban neighborhoods, but on OCGs that operate in larger subnational units and have powerful private militias to protect their turf through large-scale criminal violence. Thus, we analyze criminal governance on a larger territorial scale, where drug cartels and their criminal associates aspire to rule several contiguous subnational jurisdictions. This brings our analysis closer to the phenomenon of rebel governance described by Arjona (2016), in which armed groups use their military power to establish economic, political, judicial, and social controls over multiple communities and villages and develop subnational regimes of rebel rule. A crucial difference, however, is that unlike rebel groups, who aspire to eventual de jure rule nationwide, OCGs harbor no ambitions to become formally established political authorities.

In our definition, drug cartels and their criminal associates create subnational regimes of criminal governance when they establish a diverse set of controls over local governments, populations, and territories. Although formally elected authorities and governments operate de jure within their jurisdiction, OCGs can develop a de facto monopoly of violence, control key appointments within municipal governments and systems of local taxation, define the rules of economic, social, and political transactions, and establish informal controls over the territorial boundaries of this domain.

In Chapter 6, we suggested that drug cartels and their criminal associates seek to establish criminal governance regimes in subnational territories where fierce competition over the control of drug trafficking routes pushes them to seek informal government protection or government rents through high-profile attacks. They also target regions where subnational authorities have been left politically and militarily unprotected and there are opportunities for conquest. Focusing on the political/military vulnerability argument, in the next section we explore how cartels have capitalized on intergovernmental partisan conflict and the vulnerability of subnational authorities to establish criminal governance regimes in selected Mexican subnational regions. Although we focus only on a few prototypical cases, bear in mind that between 2006 and 2012 one-tenth of Mexico's municipalities – where one-third of Mexico's population lives –

experienced at least one high-profile criminal attack. These municipalities are therefore likely to have developed some form of subnational criminal governance regime.

ESTABLISHING CRIMINAL GOVERNANCE

Michoacán

Ruled by leftist governors and by mayors from the three leading parties, the western state of Michoacán provides multiple examples of vertical political fragmentation and political vulnerability, where municipal authorities and party candidates were between 2.6 and 4.6 times more likely to experience attacks than mayors and candidates from states ruled by the president's conservative party. Focusing on cities and towns from the Tierra Caliente and northern regions of the state identified in Map 7.1, we analyze municipalities that score high values both on vertical fragmentation and on attacks, where cartels were more likely to establish criminal governance regimes.

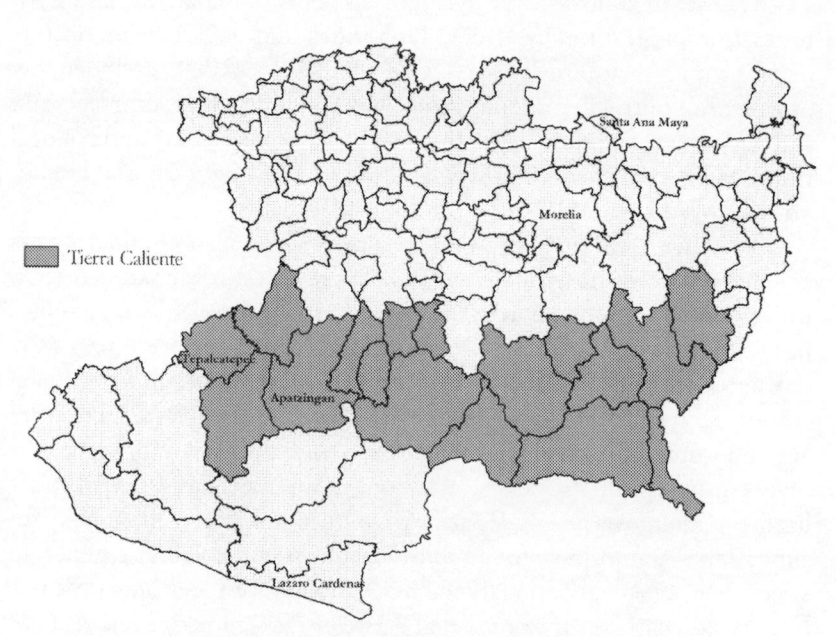

MAP 7.1 Selected Regions and Municipalities in Michoacán

The Federal Intervention and the Transformation
of Criminal Industries

As we analyzed in Chapters 3 and 6, inter-cartel wars in Michoacán broke out when the Gulf Cartel deployed the Zetas, their private army, to the Pacific coast to challenge the southern empire of the Sinaloa Cartel. Allied with La Familia Michoacana, a local self-defense group, the Zetas were able to remove the Valencia Cartel – the local representatives of the Sinaloans – from the state. The strategic partnership between La Familia and the Zetas, however, quickly came under severe stress when the Zeta leaders decided to take control over the state's main drug trafficking routes and relegate La Familia to a secondary role. Between 2003 and 2006, this conflict led to an unprecedented level of violence and brutality in the state, including the rolling of decapitated bodies and human heads in public spaces (Grillo 2011).

When President Calderón declared the War on Drugs in the midst of the 2006 post-electoral crisis, he accepted the request of leftist Governor Lázaro Cárdenas Batel to deploy a military operation to Michoacán – Calderón's home state but a leftist bastion – as the first federal campaign to curb inter-cartel violence.[4]

This federal intervention initially brought levels of violence under control. It rapidly became evident, however, that the initial deployment of the army had only led the Zetas and La Familia to hide, regroup, rearm, and prepare for a multiple-front, protracted war against the state and against each other. From 2008, the murder rate skyrocketed, together with other forms of victimization, as both La Familia and the Zetas quickly engaged in fierce battles over the control of new illicit markets. Practices included the extortion of local businesses in the rural and service sectors, kidnapping for ransom, the control of the Lázaro Cárdenas port (where most pirate goods from Asia entered the Mexican market), and the looting of natural resources (particularly mining in the western part of the state and forests in the northwestern region). Seizing de facto control over local municipal governments became crucial in these new conflicts. Between 2008 and 2011, Michoacán experienced one of Mexico's most lethal criminal wars, in which municipal governments, local government officials, and local party candidates became key criminal targets.

---

[4] Interviews with Governors Lázaro Cárdenas Batel and Leonel Godoy, August and September 2014.

Intergovernmental Partisan Conflict: Opening Opportunities for Attacks

Although the initial deployment in 2006–2007 was made under close cooperation between the incoming conservative president and an outgoing leftist governor, intergovernmental relations deteriorated sharply after the federal intervention resulted in a major spike in violence starting in 2008. Bitter partisan strife between the new PRD governor, Leonel Godoy, and the federal government made the state and all mayors and local politicians vulnerable to attack. Reflecting on the expansion of the narcos in the state, Guillermo Valencia, the PRI mayor of Tepalcatepec in the Tierra Caliente region, did not hesitate to identify a major cause: "the conflict between the leftist governor Leonel Godoy and President Calderón" (Padgett 2014).

Facing a dramatic violent backlash from the cartels against the federal intervention, President Calderón sought to blame the escalation of violence on the opposition, particularly the leftist PRD – the party that did not accept his victory in the 2006 presidential election. In contrast to the tight coordination between the president and his conservative subnational co-partisans in such places as Baja California and Guanajuato, in leftist states the federal intervention became a unilateral action in which local authorities were never informed or consulted before the army or the federal police made an assault in their municipalities.[5]

As the turf wars between La Familia Michoacana and their former allies the Zetas escalated to unprecedented levels in Michoacán, President Calderón took a revealing radical step. A few hours before the beginning of the 2009 midterm national legislative campaign, his attorney general conducted a large-scale arrest of 23 top- and mid-level officials of Governor Godoy's security cabinet and 12 of the state's mayors (mostly from the PRI and the PRD). Although all but one of the arrested officials were released a year later, this mass arrest allowed the federal government to launch a major smear campaign against the leftist state government and prime the electorate to view leftists as partners of organized crime.

After the mega arrest, intergovernmental cooperation between the armed forces, the federal police, and state and local authorities broke down completely in Michoacán.[6] In this context of bitter partisan

---

[5] Although they disagreed on the motivations behind the federal intervention, in separate interviews Guillermo Valdés, head of Mexico's national intelligence agency under President Calderón, and the leftist Governor Leonel Godoy confirmed to us the unilateral nature of the intervention. Personal interviews, August 2014.

[6] Ibid.

intergovernmental conflict, and facing a two-front war against the Zetas and the federal government, La Familia began using high-profile criminal attacks to gain control over local populations and local governments in 2009. Leftist mayors who received death threats did not hesitate to reach out to the federal government, but there was no response. Ricardo Baptista, the director of the Association of Local Authorities in Mexico (AALMAC), a network of leftist mayors, eloquently portrayed the mayors' political vulnerability: "[President Calderón] was perfectly aware of the death threats that mayors ... were receiving, but he was never willing to meet with us when we asked for help" (SinEmbargo 2013a).

As partisan intergovernmental conflict became more severe, La Familia, which by 2011 had been rebranded as the Knights Templar, decided to capitalize on this window of opportunity and launched an unprecedented wave of high-profile attacks during the 2011 local election cycle.

Seizing Local Electoral Processes

The 2011 election cycle in Michoacán – in which the state elected a new governor, 40 state legislators, and 113 mayors – was one of the most violent election periods in recent Mexican history. The Templars and their associates were clear in their intent: they asked the electorate to vote for the PRI and demanded that local party candidates from the leftist PRD (the party of the incumbent state governor) and the conservative PAN (the party of the incumbent national president) step down.[7] Michoacán experienced 39 attacks during the 2011 elections, most of which were aimed at candidates from the cross-party coalitions led by the PRD. As a result of these attacks, and of public death threats, 46 mayoral candidates and 5 congressional candidates stepped down (García 2011).

But government officials and party candidates were not the only targets of the Templars and their criminal associates; they used coercion threats to influence voters directly. A criminal cell working for the Templars used recorded phone conversations to coerce voters to vote for PRI candidates (Univisión 2011). On election day an anonymous message appeared in the local newspaper, *La Piedad*, spelling out the rules of the game: "[As you go to the voting stations], don't wear T-shirts with propaganda in favor of the PAN because we don't want any confusion; we don't want to kill

---

[7] Cartels in Mexico do not have well-defined ideological preferences. Whether they support one party or another in local elections depends on changing political opportunities.

innocent people" (Reforma 2011c, p. 1). Unknown individuals distributed flyers to voters with very specific threats: "Mr. Felipe Calderón [Mexico's president]: If you intervene in this election and the PAN wins, there will be war and executions" (Reforma 2011d, p. 17).

After 12 years in opposition, the PRI returned to gubernatorial power in Michoacán in 2011 and several PRI candidates won surprising victories in the Tierra Caliente region – a leftist bastion and an epicenter of high-profile attacks. It is likely that in the absence of this lethal wave of criminal attacks and intimidation, the PRI would not have won the governorship nor recovered many municipalities from Tierra Caliente (Becerra and Meza 2015). The wave of attacks and the election results showed Michoacán's citizenry and the newly elected local governments "who called the shots" in the state.

Colonizing Municipal Governments

A number of former municipal officials from governments elected in Michoacán during the state's violent 2011 election cycle anonymously reported to us that after they assumed office, the Templars – which had by then become the hegemonic cartel – abducted most of the states' mayors for 24 hours and took them to their stronghold in the state's southern mountains to personally hand them the instructions on how to pay their monthly fees.[8]

Guillermo Valencia, a PRI mayor from Tepalcatepec elected in 2011, is explicit about the dynamics of looting: "Under life threat, I was forced to surrender 10 percent of my budget to the Templars ... You simply couldn't say 'no' to them ... Paying the criminal fee was my life insurance" (Calderón and Chouza 2014). Valencia's neighboring mayors from the Tierra Caliente region confirmed that they were coerced by threats into paying criminal fees and surrendering their budgets for public works (Calderón and Chouza 2014; Maerker 2014). In the main, these mayors are from municipalities with a history of assassination attempts and murders of local officials: Coalcomán (one), Parácuaro (three), Tingüindín (none), Chinicuila (three), Aquila (four), and Uruapan (one).

Mayors were told to pay criminal fees and keep silent.[9] As Valencia put it, "if you went to the public prosecutor's office to report a criminal threat, the Templars would kill you; there is a lengthy list of murdered mayors ... whose main sin was to publicly denounce extortions" (Padgett 2014). The

---

[8] Two former state-level government officials from previous leftist administrations validated this information. Anonymous interviews.

[9] Interview with Ricardo Baptista, August 2014.

case of Ygnacio López, the leftist mayor of Santa Ana Maya in the northern part of the state, is an example of the Templars' modus operandi. After nearly two years of paying criminal fees, Santa Ana Maya went bankrupt. López organized a hunger strike in the Senate in Mexico City to demand new federal resources, which he received. However, when the mayor returned home and declined to pay 10 percent of the new federal transfers to the Templars, he was brutally murdered on a double count: for publicly reporting extortion and for refusing to pay criminal fees (Redacción AN 2013).

Controlling the Municipal Security Apparatus

Although the municipal police in Mexico are relatively weak, municipal security forces can play a key role in the development of criminal governance regimes. Under the cartels' control, municipal police officers serve as informants and enforcers of the cartels' decisions in the localities. In contrast to the battlefield situation, where they simply seek to eliminate police officers, cartels use targeted attacks against mayors and municipal security deputies to subdue the municipality's security personnel and take control over the security apparatus "from above."

Rafael García, mayor of Coalcomán, a municipality in Michoacán from the Tierra Caliente region, was explicit about the Templars' use of the police. García took office after the 2011 election and he described the state of his security apparatus thus: "My police force was totally subdued; I was not in charge. In fact, [the Templars] controlled me through the municipal police commanders. But I could not resist; those who did were eliminated" (Maerker 2014). Former government associates of Ygnacio López, the murdered mayor of Santa Ana Maya, also reported that the Templars took over the municipal police.[10]

Controlling Local Economies

Not only do drug cartels target local authorities to extract resources from the municipal coffers or to commandeer the police; they also seek to infiltrate the government and gain access to privileged administrative positions and information, which will enable them to control local economies and loot local businesses and households. Access to the property tax registry, the municipal treasury, or local units regulating local economic activities provides them with privileged information to more effectively conduct extortion and kidnapping for ransom activities. After

---

[10] Anonymous interviews, August 2014.

establishing their hegemony in Michoacán in 2011, the Templars turned their attention to the state's producers of limes and avocados.

The Templars took control over the six lime-producing municipalities in the Tierra Caliente region and selectively mounted a number of attacks against local officials: Aguililla (zero), Apatzingán (zero), Buenavista (two), Múgija (two), Parácuaro (two), and Tepalcatepec (zero). Attacks in neighboring municipalities led the mayors of Aguililla and Apatzingán to become more amenable to the cartel's orders. Rather than simply imposing a criminal tax on producers in the region, the Templars decided to regulate the market. The price of limes was too low, so they reduced the supply by forcing local producers to harvest on a limited schedule, while the cartel's own farms harvested freely and sold at a higher market price (García-Ponce and Lajous 2014).[11]

North of Tierra Caliente the Templars likewise used violence to gain control over Michoacán's avocado-producing region. The municipality of Tancítaro is an emblematic case. The Templars forced the resignation of Mayor José Trinidad Meza, his deputies, and the municipality's alderman in 2009 by issuing public death threats and then murdering the interim mayor, Gustavo Sánchez, thereby establishing their rule in Tancítaro. Avocado growers did not resist when the Templars imposed a criminal quota per cultivated hectare and forced them to schedule the cropping seasons according to the cartel's needs (Reforma 2013).

Extortion affected both rural producers and service providers in the state's urban areas. According to data from the 2014 National Business Victimization Survey (ENVE), 22 percent of Michoacán's small- and medium-sized enterprises reported having been victims of criminal extortion in 2013.

Establishing Territorial Controls

Building subnational regimes of criminal governance in strategic regions of Michoacán allowed the Templars to militarily defeat and expel the Zetas from the state and to bring their war against the federal government to a stalemate. They not only controlled key formal economic sectors but also expanded their reach to monopolize the state's criminal underworld (Maerker 2014).

Despite their hegemonic control, the Templars could not become a lawful political actor. Unlike armed guerrilla groups that, following a peace agreement, can become lawful political forces and compete for office, cartels and other OCGs cannot. A drug lord or his family members

---

[11] This was confirmed to us by a local producer. Anonymous interview, September 2014.

might perhaps join a political party, but cartels cannot become lawful political forces. Without a long-term horizon, and facing a permanent threat from the federal government, the Templars continued plundering local governments and citizens. They continued to pray, also, because the plaza chiefs of the Templars were outsiders – that is, they were not local residents of the communities where they were plundering (LeCour Graindmason 2016; Pansters 2018). It would take a tax revolt by lime producers, followed by a popular uprising assisted by the federal government in 2014, to dethrone the Templars from de facto power in Michoacán (García-Ponce and Lajous 2014; Maerker 2014).

Guerrero

To explore in greater detail the causal chain that connects intergovernmental partisan conflict, subnational election cycles, and high-profile attacks, we focus on municipalities in the southern state of Guerrero. This leftist state experienced a major spike in inter-cartel violence between 2005 and 2012, when dozens of mayors and party candidates, mainly from the centrist PRI and the leftist PRD, became targets of lethal criminal attacks, which took place in municipalities with high inter-cartel violence and high partisan fragmentation (PAN-PRD-PRI or PAN-PRD-PRD cases). In these areas, cartels and their criminal associates were more likely to use targeted lethal violence against local government officials and party candidates in order to capture the new financial resources required to remain competitive in the turf wars. Targeted criminal attacks were possible in a state ruled by the Left, such as Guerrero, because municipal authorities and local party candidates were left purposefully unprotected by a conservative federal government that used security policy to punish their subnational (leftist) political rivals. Our analysis centers mainly on the tourist resort of Acapulco and on rural municipalities in the western Tierra Caliente region, as shown in Map 7.2.

The Federal Intervention and the Transformation of Criminal Industries

For much of the 1990s and into the early 2000s the drug production and trafficking industries in Guerrero, a major producer of marijuana and poppy, were under the monopolistic control of the Sinaloa Cartel and its private militia led by the Beltrán Leyva brothers. After the PRI lost the state's gubernatorial seat in 2005 and the Sinaloans temporarily lost access to the informal protection they had enjoyed from state authorities,

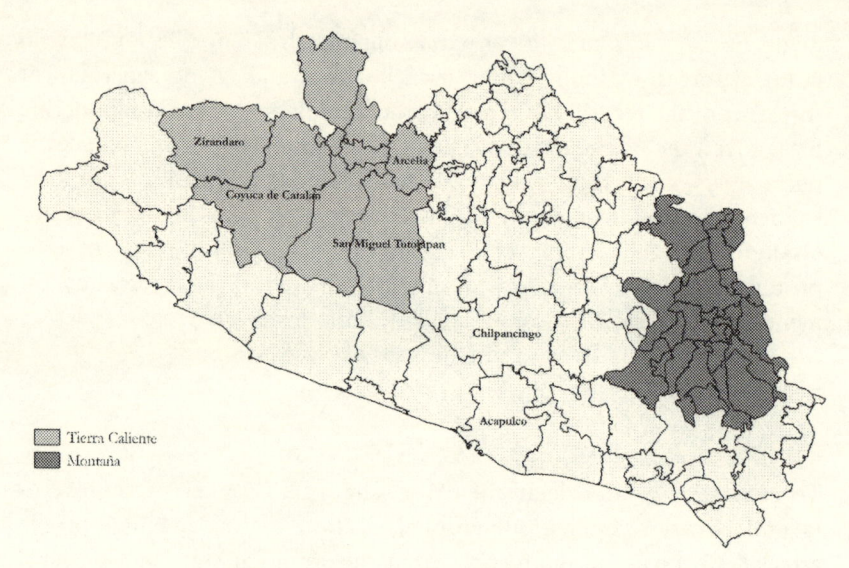

MAP 7.2 Selected Regions and Municipalities in Guerrero

the rival Gulf Cartel sought to capitalize on this opportunity by sending their powerful private militia, the Zetas, to Guerrero to challenge the Sinaloans' control over Guerro (Trejo and Ley 2018). The breakdown of the Sinaloa Cartel's drug monopoly in Guerrero led to the outbreak of fierce turf wars between the Beltrán Leyva brothers (the armed branch of the Sinaloans) and the Zetas (the armed branch of the Gulf Cartel).

Although inter-cartel wars in Guerrero broke out in 2005, it was only after the 2006–2007 federal intervention that the state experienced a dramatic increase in drug violence and a major transformation in the drug industry.

The federal policy of cartel decapitation pursued throughout the country had a dramatic impact in Guerrero. The state plunged into a major inter-cartel war when one of the Beltrán Leyva brothers was arrested and another was murdered. Suspicions that the leaders of the Sinaloa Cartel had facilitated Alfredo Beltrán Leyva's arrest first led the Beltrán Leyva Organization (BLO) to break from the Sinaloans. And Arturo Beltrán Leyva's subsequent murder led to the fragmentation of the BLO. Many of the BLO local plaza chiefs – the BLO commanders who controlled specific cities or towns – created their own independent criminal organizations and engaged in fierce wars for control of Guerrero's criminal underworld (Kyle 2015). Security experts estimate that by 2016, 25 different organized criminal groups – from large drug cartels to regional criminal organizations to local gangs – operated in the state (Guerrero 2016).

The decapitation of cartels and their criminal associates resulted in two important transformations in the criminal underworld. First, following the arrest or assassination of a major drug lord, paramilitary groups and private militias such as the BLO, which had operated as the security arms of the Gulf and Sinaloa cartels, became independent and transformed themselves into new drug cartels. Second, the government's success in decapitating cartels and arresting or killing the chiefs of private militias weakened internal controls in these criminal organizations. This allowed a significant number of their plaza chiefs and street gangs – whose members had worked as foot soldiers for private militias – to become relatively independent. A local observer of crime in Acapulco, Guerrero's largest city and a major tourist destination, effectively captured this dynamic: "After Arturo Beltrán Leyva [head of the BLO] was killed in December 2009, inter-cartel violence skyrocketed in Acapulco and new local leaders heading a multiplicity of criminal groups emerged in the region. These groups specialized in criminal activities hitherto unknown in the state, including extortion, car robbery, and kidnapping for ransom" (Gurrea 2013, n.p.).

As Guerrero's criminal underworld moved from criminal monopoly to dyadic conflict to multiple-front wars, the drive for new financial resources to fight these wars led OCGs to expand into new criminal markets, particularly extortion and kidnapping for ransom. Initially, OCGs developed extortion and kidnapping rings in Guerrero's main urban centers, including Chilpancingo – the state capital – and Acapulco. They subcontracted local gangs to gain local territorial control in peripheral impoverished neighborhoods and used these places as bases of operation (Kyle 2015). Although they first targeted wealthy businesses (e.g., hotels and construction companies), from 2008 they added small enterprises (e.g., restaurants, tortilla retail shops, and pharmacies) and social service providers (e.g., teachers, doctors, and priests). OCGs also rapidly expanded from the state's main urban centers to the countryside, particularly the state's east–west mountain chain. In these regions they worked with local caciques (Kyle 2015) to gain control over Guerrero's rich natural resources, minerals and forests, and over drug production – particularly marijuana and poppy – as well as drug trafficking routes connecting the Pacific Ocean with central and northern Mexico.

The proliferation and independence of multiple criminal groups in Guerrero's criminal underworld resulted in the development of new illegal markets to finance turf wars.[12] One of the most surprising outcomes of this transformation is that as cartels expanded into new illegal activities beyond drug trafficking, municipal governments became crucial instruments in the cartels' pursuit of new resources to finance their turf wars.

Intergovernmental Partisan Conflict: Opening Opportunities for Attacks

Although the federal intervention and the policy of leadership decapitation of the cartels triggered a major escalation of drug violence in Guerrero and a major diversification of the cartels into new criminal markets where both local governments and populations became targets of criminal attacks, federal assistance to the leftist state of Guerrero did not flow as rapidly and effectively as it did in conservative states. Guerrero is a leftist bastion where hundreds of local political leaders and publicly elected authorities had refused to recognize President Calderón's victory in the contested 2006 presidential election and had expressed their allegiance to Andrés Manuel López Obrador. Nonetheless, they did not hesitate to demand federal protection after receiving death threats from OCGs. But the federal response, as was the case in Michoacán and other leftist states such as Zacatecas, was a poorly coordinated federal program, combined with direct smear campaigns orchestrated by the federal government against the state's leftist subnational authorities.[13]

The case of the leftist government in the tourist resort of Acapulco – the state's economic hub and largest city – is an emblematic example of the federal punishment regime directed against the president's political enemies.

After receiving several death threats from OCGs throughout 2006, including a decapitated human head in his office, the leftist mayor of Acapulco, Félix Salgado, demanded federal protection for himself and federal intervention to confront a major wave of criminal violence in his city (Flores and Guerrero 2006; Herrera 2007a; La Jornada Guerrero 2007). As we explained in Chapter 5, although the federal government did deploy the military to Acapulco, President Calderón's Secretary of Public Security, instead of offering protection to Mayor Salgado, launched a smear campaign against the mayor for alleged collusion with the cartels. A few weeks after the first tendentious accusations, the secretary retracted. But the mayor and his team had been exposed as vulnerable targets of

---

[12] On the proliferation of criminal groups throughout the country, see Guerrero (2011b) and Atuesta and Ponce (2017).

[13] Interview with Amalia García, former governor of Zacatecas, August 2014.

criminal attacks. According to local leftist leaders, the fact that Salgado had denounced Calderón's election as fraudulent explained the reluctance of federal authorities to protect the mayor's life (La Jornada Guerrero 2007).

Over the next six years, cartels and breakaway OCGs took advantage of partisan intergovernmental conflicts between the federal government and the Left in Guerrero to coerce local authorities and to expand their illegal actions into extortion and kidnapping among a wide range of social and economic groups in Acapulco. After Michoacán, Guerrero became Mexico's second most lethal state for mayors and local political leaders.

Leftist and PRI mayors and local government officials from the municipalities in Tierra Caliente experienced a similar political disdain from the federal government to that experienced by the leftist mayor of Acapulco. After the federal intervention in the neighboring state of Michoacán led to the relocation of cells from La Familia Michoacana to the western municipalities of Guerrero, inter-cartel violence skyrocketed in this region. Fighting over the control of the cultivation of poppy for heroin production, La Familia cells engaged in bitter inter-cartel conflicts with breakaway OCGs from the BLO. Seeking protection from municipal authorities and access to fresh financial resources to remain competitive in the struggle for control over poppy cultivation and heroin production and traffic, OCGs launched a wave of attacks against local government officials and party candidates. As Map 6.1 in Chapter 6 illustrates, between 2007 and 2012 the municipalities of western Guerrero, including Coyuca de Catalán and Zirándaro, became the most dangerous places for local authorities and party candidates in Mexico. Despite these attacks, federal assistance never came to this leftist bastion.

Seizing Local Electoral Processes

During the 2008 and 2012 municipal election cycles in the state of Guerrero, seven candidates and 15 party activists were targets of criminal attacks. As in Michoacán, the cartels and their criminal associates sought to penetrate the political campaigns, condition the behavior of candidates and future authorities, and shape the citizens' electoral behavior. In the region of Tierra Caliente in the western part of the state – one of the most contested regions in Mexico, where associates from the Sinaloa Cartel and the Zetas were at war for most of the 2000s – running election campaigns can be a matter of life and death. After campaigning in the village of El Naranjo in Coyuca de Catalán, Catalino Duarte, the leftist candidate for the state legislative chamber, was the target of an assassination attempt. A former Zirándaro mayor, Duarte was blunt about the risks involved in campaigning: "I fear for my life," he stated after surviving the attack (Guerrero 2008, p. 19). During election days, cartels and their criminal associates targeted voters. In the 2009 federal election the cartels ordered "halcones" (hawks) – local informants – to intimidate voters as they went to the polls. In Coyuca de Catalán an armed commando attacked a polling station, while yelling "You know who to vote for!" And in nearby Coyuca, an inhabitant of the municipality of Arcelia reported that he had been threatened by a group who told him that he would regret it if he was seen casting his ballot on election day (Jiménez 2009). But the most dramatic event took place in the municipality of Coahuayutla, next to Coyutla and Zirándaro, where 12 leftist party activists were massacred on Election Day (Guerrero 2009).

Colonizing Municipal Governments

As municipalities became a primary source of new revenues for the cartels' criminal ambitions, mayors and local party candidates in Guerrero became primary targets of criminal attacks. Cartels and their criminal associates used targeted coercive violence to extract two types of resources: the municipalities' local revenues and information about private property.

Cartels and their criminal associates used death threats against local government officials to secure access to municipal resources and murdered them when they resisted or failed to pay "protection" fees. As an AALMAC (Association of Local Authorities in Mexico) representative put it, "After criminal organizations gain access to the municipality's annual budget, they demand that mayors divert a significant proportion of their budget for public works to pay criminal fees and sometimes even ask that companies on their payroll become contractors" (SinEmbargo 2013b). A former mayor from AALMAC thus described this process: "The cartel's plaza chiefs ask mayors to pay a 'security fee' if they want to be safe and left alone. Mayors from small municipalities are asked to pay monthly fees of up to [8,000 dollars] while medium and large municipalities have to make monthly payments of up to [16,000 dollars]."[14] Mayors have little choice about whether to resist. As Robell Urióstegui, a leftist mayor of Teloloapan in northern Guerrero, put it: "They first harass you and then schedule a meeting for you to meet with the narco bosses. If you don't go, they kill one of your relatives. And if you go, you become a delinquent" (García Orozco 2015).

---

[14] Personal interview.

In the region of Tierra Caliente in the western part of Guerrero mayors have reported being coerced into paying criminal fees to different cartels. With a long history of attacks since 2006, local officials from Coyuca de Catalán (six attacks), Arcelia (one attack), and Pungarabato (one attack) reported that, because of the lack of protection from the federal government, they have been forced for several years to surrender part of their budget to the drug lords. Moreover, these local officials report great difficulty resisting the cartels' demand that they appoint cartel members as directors of the municipal treasury (Herrera and López 2016; Aristegui Noticias 2015). While these municipalities' own history of high-profile attacks shapes mayors' and local candidates' behavior, attacks in neighboring municipalities and in the region also influence their actions. When mayors from Coyuca, Arcelia, and Pungarabato describe the pressure from cartels and their criminal associates, they also have in mind the long history of violence in other municipalities in the region, including San Miguel Totolapan (one attack) and Zirándaro (three attacks). As the statistical results reported in Chapter 6 reveal, an attack in one municipality increases the odds of attacks in a neighboring municipality by 41 percent.

Controlling the Municipal Security Apparatus

The municipal police forces of Acapulco, Chilapancingo (the state capital), and most of the Tierra Caliente municipalities are known to have been infiltrated by cartels and their criminal associates. As José Villanueva, the state's spokesman put it, criminal dynamics in Michoacán have heavily influenced the Tierra Caliente region in Guerrero and there have been criminal spillover effects that have led La Familia Michoacana to take control of the police in Arcelia, Totolapan, Pungarabato, Coyuca de Catalán, and Zirándaro and other municipalities (Esteban 2014). Beyond this western region, evidence of criminal control of the local police became evident in Acapulco, when Lieutenant José Manuel Rodríguez, then secretary of security of Acapulco, declared that a significant proportion of the police under his command worked as "halcones" (informants) for local gangs and the multiple breakaway organizations that operated in the city (*El Informador* 2012). A month after Rodríguez's denunciation the newly elected leftist mayor, Luis Walton, confirmed the Lieutenant's statement and demanded federal support to confront the challenge of organized crime, particularly in cities where new mayors could not work with a police force that was under criminal control (Contreras 2012).

Controlling Local Economies

Cartels and their criminal associates targeted local government officials not only to extract resources from the municipal coffers but also to infiltrate local governments and gain access to the privileged administrative positions and information that allowed them to gain control over the local economies and loot local businesses and households. The case of the tourist resort of Acapulco, on Guerrero's Pacific Coast, is typical of the criminals' demands for local information. A few weeks after taking office in Acapulco in 2012, leftist municipal authorities faced a wave of death threats from local criminal groups. Local gangs, which had become racketeers since the assassination of Arturo Beltrán Leyva, the head of the BLO, demanded that the new authorities give them access to the municipal property tax registry, where they knew they could find detailed information about thousands of home owners, hotels, restaurants, retail stores, and other local businesses. Their goal was to become more efficient in levying criminal taxes and conducting kidnapping for ransom. Because local officials resisted, two municipal officials from the property tax office were murdered within weeks of the new government administration (Reforma 2012). Following these murders, the property office director[15] resigned and the position remained vacant for the rest of the administration.

Having access to accurate local information is absolutely crucial for criminal organizations seeking new resources through extortion and kidnapping for ransom. As a prominent Catholic priest from Acapulco puts it, "Criminal organizations want to infiltrate municipal institutions such as the property tax office or the local business regulatory office because they want access to Acapulco's largest and most important databases. [With this information they are able to charge criminal fees to] restaurant, hotel and shop-owners ... but also to private health clinics, law and accounting firms" (Gurrea 2013). Data from the 2014 National Business Victimization Survey (ENVE)[16] substantiate the clergyman's description: In 2013, 30 percent of Guerrero's small and medium enterprises – from tortilla retail stores, to restaurants, and pharmacies – reported having been victims of criminal extortion in the previous year. Largely as a result of such rising insecurity, more than 300 small and

---

[15] Dirección del Catastro e Impuesto Predial.

[16] This is a large-scale survey on the victimization of Mexican business owners, which has been conducted by the National Institute of Statistics and Geography (INEGI) on a biannual basis since 2012.

medium-sized bars and restaurants closed down operations in Acapulco (Juárez 2016).

But extortion is not only an urban phenomenon or an illicit business affecting wealthy municipalities such as the tourist resort of Acapulco. In the Tierra Caliente region in the western part of Guerrero, La Familia developed a network of 50 young hit men who worked as racketeers to impose criminal taxes on rural households. In the municipality of Coyuca de Catalán, 20 of La Familia's hit men operated a racket to extort local businesses in the city of Coyuca, the municipal head town (Dávila 2014). Rackets linked to La Familia and other breakaway cartels have also targeted the mining companies in the region and have imposed criminal taxes on national and international corporations working in the area.

Controlling Local Populations and Territories

Besides seizing control over local governments and economies, drug cartels and their criminal associates also seek to control local populations – their places of residence and movements in and out of the communities. As La Familia gained contingent control over the Tierra Caliente region of western Guerrero in 2011, drug lords increasingly approached rural producers with a simple dictum: "You join us or you leave or you die" (Araujo 2013). It was during these years that the municipalities of Coyuca de Catalán, Coahuayutla, Pungarabato, and San Miguel Totolapan experienced the highest rates of internal population displacement in Mexico (Díaz 2011; Rubio and Pérez 2016). Cartels became particularly interested in taking control over the region's natural resources – mining and forests – and its fertile lands for poppy cultivation. As a result, rural families, who had little access to federal protection due to intergovernmental partisan conflict, were either coerced into joining the narcos or displaced from their homes, leaving their land plots under the control of the drug cartels (Araujo 2013). Between 2012 and 2014, one-fifth of all reported cases of mass displacement in Mexico occurred in Guerrero, particularly in the Tierra Caliente region (Rubio 2015).

From Attacks to Criminal Governance

Figure 7.1 summarizes the pathway from high-profile criminal attacks to the development of criminal governance in Michoacán and Guerrero. In Mexico's War on Drugs, cartels seized on the political vulnerability of mayors due to intergovernmental partisan conflict and the opportunities afforded by subnational election cycles to target municipal authority

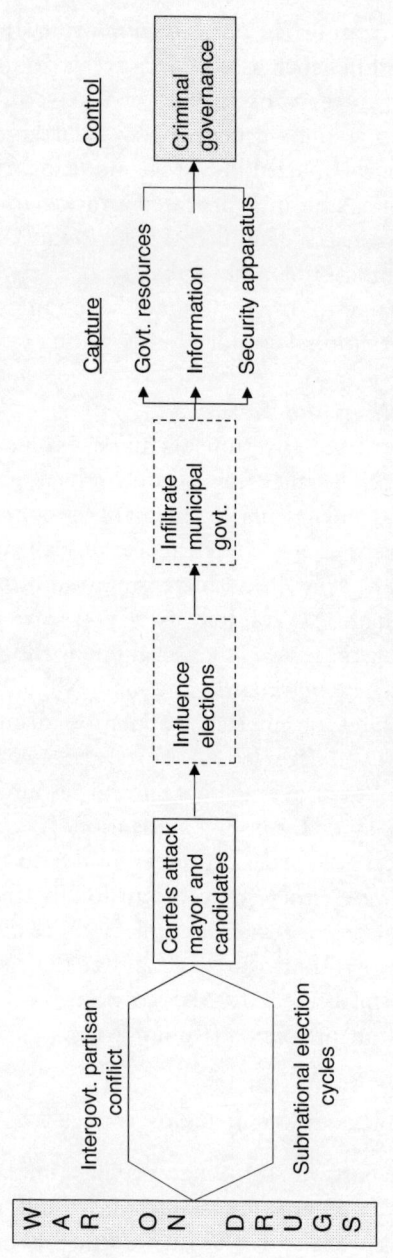

FIGURE 7.1 The Pathway from High-Profile Criminal Attacks to Criminal Governance

figures and party candidates. These high-profile criminal assaults allowed them to influence local elections and eventually to penetrate the new municipal governments in key areas. Here, they would capture an important share of the municipal government budget, access key information such as the property tax registry, and gain control over the municipal police. Access to these government structures and resources, together with the cartels' own internal military and financial resources, enabled drug lords and their criminal associates to develop de facto control over local governments, populations, and territories. This trajectory reflects the pathway toward criminal governance of such states as Michoacán and Guerrero; while the sequencing may be a little different for other states, the outcome is ultimately the same: cartels' use of targeted violence to develop subnational regimes of criminal governance.[17]

AVERTING CRIMINAL GOVERNANCE

Baja California

Intergovernmental Coordination and State Cohesion
In contrast to the experiences of local authorities in the leftist states of Guerrero and Michoacán, in states such as Guanajuato, Jalisco, and Baja California – where the PAN had held the gubernatorial seat since 1989 – the federal intervention against the drug cartels was designed to assist, cooperate with, and protect mayors, especially those affiliated with the PAN, the president's party (Sabet 2012).

The city of Mexicali, in the northwestern state of Baja California – where PANista federal, state, and municipal authorities worked together to reduce levels of violence associated with major turf wars between the Tijuana Cartel and the Sinaloa Cartel – is emblematic of partisan cooperation. Despite experiencing levels of inter-cartel violence similar to those in Guerrero's largest cities (e.g., Acapulco) in 2007, Mexicali did not suffer a single criminal attack against local government officials during the Calderón administration (2006–2012).[18] As we described in Chapter 5,

---

[17] Note, again, that there might be other pathways leading to the development of criminal governance that do not necessarily involve the assassination of local government officials and party candidates. For a wider range of options, see (Arias 2017).

[18] The city of Tijuana, home of the Tijuana Cartel and also ruled by the PAN, experienced a major outbreak of inter-cartel conflict in 2008, but intergovernmental cooperation, as we explained in Chapter 5, allowed local authorities to contain the violence. Although Tijuana did experience five attacks against municipal authorities and party candidates

the federal government designed a comprehensive federal intervention for Baja California – particularly for the city of Tijuana. The federal, state, and local governments worked closely to facilitate an effective military and social intervention in the city and also worked in a coordinated fashion to purge the local police force. This intervention was extended to Mexicali, where the PAN mayor, Rodolfo Valdez, cooperated closely with the state's attorney and the federal authorities. Although serious accusations were made that Mexicali's police force provided protection to the narcos, PAN co-partisans at Mexico's three levels of government worked together to avoid a public scandal – they purged the Mexicali police (Corpus 2008), and Mexicali became one of Mexico's top recipients of federal resources to develop crime prevention strategies and programs of police evaluation, training, and professional development. These coordinated actions helped to contain violence and prevent high-profile attacks in Mexicali (Sabet 2012; Trejo and Ley 2016; Durán-Martínez 2018).

While intergovernmental coordination was neither automatic nor unproblematic in Mexicali and Tijuana,[19] shared electoral incentives motivated co-partisans from different levels of government to work together effectively and to recover the state's authority over territories previously controlled by drug cartels. In contrast to leftist Guerrero and Michoacán, aligned partisan incentives in Baja California led conservative national and subnational authorities to collaborate. Consequently, their coordinated and cohesive government actions discouraged the cartels from attacking local government officials and party candidates.

The Eastern Indigenous Highlands of Guerrero: An Outlier

Societal Coordination

The case of 11 indigenous municipalities in the eastern highlands of Guerrero, La Montaña/Costa Chica region, presents an intriguing outlier. Despite being part of a leftist state in which a conservative federal government systematically ignored demands for federal assistance from

between 2006 and 2012, intergovernmental cooperation empowered subnational authorities to prevent the development of criminal governance regimes – as happened in cities of similar size and development, for instance Acapulco in Guerrero.

[19] The federal intervention in Baja California experienced an initial crisis when high-ranking military officials deployed in the state accused PAN local officials of corruption and collusion with criminal organizations. See Trejo and Ley (2016) for a detailed discussion of this case.

leftist subnational authorities and even used smear campaigns to discredit them, these 11 municipalities only experienced one high-profile attack between 2006 and 2012. To be sure, this is a highly valued region, with enormous potential for the cultivation of poppy and with rich natural resources. Cartels and breakaway OCGs operating in the central part of Guerrero have long tried to take control over eastern Guerrero.

As Ley, Mattiace, and Trejo (2019) note, what set these communities apart was the creation of a powerful network of community police (PC) forces and a parallel judicial system (CRAC) built in the 1990s. These de facto indigenous institutions coexisted with the formal state and municipal police and the public prosecutors' offices. Building on indigenous customary laws and traditions and on trans-local networks developed after decades of mobilization for land and ethnic rights, these communities created a powerful parallel police force and a justice system to confront crime. Members of the police force and prosecutors were elected by community assemblies and were accountable to them. This made it particularly hard for the narcos to corrupt the community police and their justice system, which meant that the primary condition for the existence of the gray zone of criminality – the collusion between state agents and criminals – was not there to enable organized crime to flourish. But as Ley, Mattiace, and Trejo (2019) explain, these mechanisms of internal societal control could be effective only because they were supported by trans-local networks developed through years of mobilization for land and ethnic rights. When threatened by powerful cartels, PC and CRAC officials could come together with other village forces to confront the narcos. In fact, as Ley, Mattiace, and Trejo's ethnographic interviews show, it was strength in numbers – the ability of villagers to call hundreds or even thousands of villagers connected through the CRAC-PC system – that allowed them to deter the cartels from entering their territories and prevented organized criminals from launching high-profile attacks to take control over local governments and populations – as happened in the Tierra Caliente region in western Guerrero.

On the basis of the cases of Ciudad Juárez (Chihuahua) and Monterrey (Nuevo León) (see Chapter 5), we have argued that societal coordination can be a powerful mechanism forcing federal and state authorities to overcome their differences and work together to contain epidemics of violence. Although the federal government did not cooperate with indigenous communities in eastern Guerrero, what this case shows is that *societal coordination* can create conditions of self-governance, by which formal authorities are bypassed and new forms of de facto societal governance are used to prevent the development of narco rule. The experience of the indigenous eastern highlands of Guerrero shows the power of societal coordination: even in a context in which the federal government left municipal authorities unprotected in confronting the narcos, indigenous municipalities that were part of societal networks built over decades of shared mobilization were able to contain the drug cartels.

CONCLUSION

After two decades of inter-cartel and state–cartel wars in Mexico, in which changes in political structures continually upset the balance of power in the gray zone of criminality, drug cartels and their criminal associates took the historic decision to remake local political orders through the use of lethal violence. Rather than merely reacting to political developments insofar as they affected crime, OCGs in Mexico decided to take the upper hand and proactively affect subnational political structures. As the evidence reported in Chapters 6 and 7 shows, drug lords took the uncommon decision to attack municipal authorities and local party candidates to gain de facto control over local governments, populations, and territories. The cartels' decision to create subnational criminal governance regimes had crucial implications not only for the drug trafficking industry but also for Mexico's municipal governments and for the country's civilian population. In expanding their menu of illicit activities far beyond drug trafficking activities and into the illicit extraction of human wealth – via extortion and kidnapping for ransom – and the illicit exploitation of natural resource wealth – mines, forests, and oil – OCGs sought to develop tight controls over local governments and civilians, who became new targets of criminal attacks. The emergence of subnational criminal governance regimes in Mexico's protracted drug wars raises important lessons for the evolution of Mexico's criminal markets and for our general theoretical understanding of the transformation of OCGs and the gray zone of criminality in protracted conflicts.

First, the Mexican experience shows that during protracted criminal wars, drug cartels and other OCGs can develop political interests. Cartels are axiomatically considered to be illicit economic enterprises, whose entrepreneurs are assumed to be *apolitical* actors. However, in Chapters 6 and 7 we have shown that the intensification of turf wars and partisan intergovernmental conflict opened opportunities for cartels to establish control over local governments, populations, and territories in order to remain competitive in the drug business. Through lethal violence, cartels took control over elections and key local government offices, including finance, property tax registries, economic regulation and public works, and the police. Building on these controls and on the coercive power of their own private militias, drug lords and their criminal associates were able to subdue civilian populations in multiple capacities – as voters, taxpayers, and producers. Not only did they influence how citizens voted and to whom they paid taxes but also, and more dramatically, their local economic activities and places of residence – whether they could stay to work their land or were displaced. This meant that in establishing criminal governance regimes, cartels influenced the gray zone of criminality, the civilian population, and the formal political, economic, and social structures where the gray zone was territorially located.

Second, although cartels and their criminal associates seek to reinvent local social orders and, in many cases, have become de facto local rulers, their interest in formal power does not scale up to the national level. For the most part, cartels seek to indirectly control municipalities and have increasingly put forward their own candidates in places with long histories of high-profile violence where one cartel has become a hegemonic force. While there are cases, such as Michoacán in 2011, in which cartels were able to penetrate state gubernatorial power, the norm has been for them to control clusters of municipalities where they exercise de facto power. Perhaps this self-imposed constraint reflects the structural legacy of the drug trafficking industry – a global chain of local operations. Or perhaps they stay subnational – local – because they know that they cannot defeat the state – the Mexican armed forces and the federal police – in the same way, say, that an armed insurgency can depose a government and its security forces and rule nationally. Whatever the reason, the fact is that cartels and their criminal associates in Mexico, like similar organizations elsewhere, have limited their ambitions to taking control and reinventing political power at the local level.

Finally, as the case studies of criminal governance in this chapter attest, in reinventing local social orders drug cartels and their criminal associates turned civilians into a target not only for control but also for gross human rights violations. In a context of state–cartel wars, in which the military continued to use iron-fist policies to eliminate cartels and other OCGs and in which inter-cartel wars continued to expand, civilians became a primary target. Over the course of the six-year War on Drugs, not only were 311 local government officials and party candidates attacked, but civilian victimization also grew dramatically – more than 20,000 people went missing, thousands of mass graves were found across the country, and more than a quarter of a million people were displaced from their homes. Understanding the extent to which the development of sub-national criminal governance regimes explains the expansion of civilian victimization is a key agenda for future research.

Conclusion

One of the most puzzling aspects about transitions from authoritarian rule to democracy in Latin America in the past half century is the outbreak of criminal wars and large-scale criminal violence in several new democracies. In this book we have sought to explain three phenomena. First, why cartels went to war in Mexico as the country transitioned from authoritarian rule to multiparty democracy in the 1990s. Second, why drug violence dramatically escalated after the Mexican federal government declared war on the cartels in the 2000s. And third, why after two decades of inter-cartel and state–cartel wars drug lords and their criminal associates became political-territorial actors who developed subnational criminal governance regimes to de facto control local populations, municipal governments, and territories through force. More generally, our goal was to explain why Mexico's new democracy was from its inception intimately intertwined with the production of drug violence – that is, why electoral competition, party alternation, and the decentralization and territorial fragmentation of political power inadvertently became catalysts of large-scale criminal violence from the early stages of the transition.

In responding to these questions, the book offers a new understanding of organized crime and develops a series of new theoretical propositions about the association between political change and the prospects for peace versus eruptions of violence from the criminal underworld. Challenging over a century of research in the social sciences that has consistently perceived organized criminal groups (OCGs) as non-state apolitical actors, whose main objective is to control illicit markets, we conceptualize OCGs as illicit networks that emerge in a gray zone of criminality in which corrupt state security agents and criminals coexist. In our formulation,

OCGs are not simply criminals organized as private enterprises to mono-polize illicit markets but, crucially, criminals with access to informal state protection. We suggest that gray zones of criminality, where OCGs breathe and grow, often emerge in authoritarian regimes, in which auto-crats secure the loyalty of state security forces – members of the armed forces, the police and pro-government militias and death squads – charged with repressing political dissidents by allowing them to transform their political impunity to kill into criminal impunity to run illicit markets. When countries transition from authoritarian rule to democracy without reforming the security sector – through the democratization of the military and the police or through transitional justice processes to expose and punish repressive actors – the dynamics of electoral competition and political change introduce a great degree of uncertainty into the gray zone of criminality and quickly become catalysts for the breakdown of peace in the criminal underworld, leading to the outbreak of violence. We suggest that Mexico experienced a major outbreak of criminal violence because the country transitioned from authoritarian rule to democracy without establishing the foundations for a democratic rule of law. The armed forces, the police, and the judicial system continued to operate as authoritarian enclaves while the country moved into a new era of multi-party competition.

Based on a wide variety of statistical analyses and case studies, the book systematically analyzes the intimate connection between political-electoral change in Mexico's illiberal democracy and the outbreak and escalation of criminal wars. Our findings have important implications for (1) empirically unraveling the dynamics of peace and violence in one of Mexico's most tumultuous historical periods, (2) theoretically rethinking the political foundations of organized crime and large-scale criminal violence, and (3) reassessing security policy in new democracies. We assess each of these contributions in turn.

REASSESSING MEXICO'S DRUG WARS: POLITICS, THE STATE, AND CRIMINAL ACTORS

The Outbreak and Early Phase of Inter-cartel Wars (1990–2006)

The book provides extensive evidence showing that after a decade of peaceful coexistence under one-party rule, drug cartels in Mexico went to war when opposition parties conquered state gubernatorial power and appointed new personnel in the state attorney's office and the state police, compromising the stability of the informal government protection networks that had allowed drug cartels to thrive and coexist with minimal inter-cartel confrontation. We show that without immediate access to informal state protection, cartels developed their own private militias to defend their turf against incoming opposition governments and rival cartels. After securing their drug trafficking routes, drug lords used their private militias to challenge rival cartels in states experiencing party alternation, where the gray zone of criminality lost its protective networks. They engaged in wars of conquest that would lead to the outbreak of multiple dyads of conflict in Mexico's "wild west," the Pacific coast, and the northeastern states.

While most studies of drug violence in Mexico focus on the post-2006 period, after the Mexican state declared war on the cartels, we have provided extensive evidence of the outbreak of multiple inter-cartel conflicts over the control of drug trafficking routes and of their intimate connection with the dynamics of party alternation and the breakdown of subnational protection networks forged in the era of one-party rule. Recognizing this often-neglected history of inter-cartel wars should not be used as a defense of Mexican President Felipe Calderón's decision to go to war against the cartels. Rather, it should be used to understand why ignoring the long history of these conflicts, the political drivers of peace and conflict in the gray zone of criminality, and the organizational complexity of the cartels and their private militias led to flawed policy decisions that have cost hundreds of thousands of lives in Mexico.

The State's War on Drugs and the Escalation of Violence (2006–2012)

The book argues that after more than a decade of inter-cartel wars, the federal government's surprising War on Drugs against the cartels led to a dramatic intensification of violence partly because partisanship led the federal intervention in the states. While several scholars have shown that the deployment of the military to Mexico's most conflictive regions, and the use of the "kingpin" strategy to decapitate the cartels, contributed to the escalation of violence, our analysis reveals that the politicization of the War on Drugs was a major driver of the intensification of violence. We provide evidence showing that, in a context of acute political polarization between Right and Left, the federal government devised effective and coordinated military, judicial, and economic interventions in states ruled by the president's conservative co-partisans, where intergovernmental cooperation facilitated the deactivation of major spirals of violence. In contrast, we show that the federal government devised poor unilateral interventions in states ruled by the Left – the president's main rival party – in which intergovernmental partisan conflict and the vulnerability of leftist subnational authorities opened opportunities for cartels to compete for turf through war.

We argue that after two decades of inter-cartel and state–cartel wars, drug cartels expanded their range of criminal activities into the illegal extraction of human wealth (via extortion or kidnapping for ransom) and of natural resource wealth (via the looting of forests, mines, and oil pipes) to remain competitive in these protracted wars for control of drug trafficking routes. In seeking to control these new markets, drug lords and their criminal associates discovered the strategic importance of municipal governments and sought to develop subnational criminal governance regimes in which they gained de facto local control over municipalities and their populations and territories. We maintain that cartels murdered municipal authorities and local party candidates as a means to gain local governance controls. Our analysis reveals that cartels were able to murder local officials and party candidates – and establish criminal governance regimes – in leftist states (where the conservative federal government left subnational authorities purposefully unprotected), during subnational election cycles (when newly elected governments made new appointments), and in geographically adjacent municipalities (where they sought to control multiple subnational jurisdictions). In developing these subnational de facto criminal governance regimes, cartels subverted local democracy in one-tenth of Mexico's territory, where one-third of the country's population lives.

Our in-depth study of the outbreak, intensification, and transformation of Mexican drug wars, from 1990 to 2012, provides a new explanatory narrative for students of drug violence in Mexico. This narrative helps to identify the causal impact of political change on the outbreak and intensification of criminal violence in a country that transitioned from authoritarian rule to (thin) electoral democracy without reforming the authoritarian security sector or dismantling the intimate connection between authoritarian specialists in violence and criminal organizations. It shows that cartels and their criminal associates can become de facto local political actors and seek to transform local social orders through violence.

The Multiplication of Criminal Wars and Civilian Victimization
(2012–2018)

Although the book's empirical analysis ends in 2012, our theoretical framework and empirical findings provide the building blocks for understanding the proliferation of criminal wars and the dramatic escalation in civilian victimization that took place under the administration of President Enrique Peña Nieto (2012–2018), when the Institutional Revolutionary Party (PRI) returned to presidential power after 12 years in opposition. A deep assessment of this period would require a new book. Our purpose here is simply to highlight how the political logics that we have identified as drivers of criminal violence would take us a long way in accounting for the proliferation of criminal violence during the Peña Nieto presidency.

Between 2012 and 2018, some of the key political and policy factors identified as drivers of the intensification of violence during the administration of Felipe Calderón did not change under Peña Nieto.

Mexico continued to be an illiberal democracy because the armed forces, the police, and the justice system did not undergo any fundamental democratic transformation and continued to operate as authoritarian enclaves. Rather than become more transparent and accountable to internal and external controls, the armed forces – particularly the military – expanded their economic and political power and autonomy with the continuation of the War on Drugs. And while the federal police force underwent important changes, it did not become less militarized and accountable; rather, in the context of the War on Drugs, it became increasingly militarized and unaccountable (Open Society Justice Initiative 2016; International Crisis Group 2018). State and municipal police forces remained unchanged across states and municipalities, and only a few exceptional cities experienced reforms. Morover, the president continued to exercise direct political control over the attorney general's office. Although Mexico completed the transition from an inquisitorial to an adversarial (or oral) justice system during the Peña Nieto years, the fact that the different police forces did not develop any meaningful investigative capacities rendered judicial reform largely ineffective and even contributed to the intensification of criminal violence in the states that pioneered the transition to the new system (Ruiz-González 2018).

The Peña Nieto administration continued with the same security policies emblematically encapsulated in the War on Drugs against the cartels. The federal government increased the number of military campaigns to attack the cartels and deployed the military to more places than its predecessor. The kingpin strategy continued to dominate the federal intervention, leading to more leadership decapitations of the cartels. As a result, the number of cartels and OCGs increased from 60 to over 200, increasing the intensity of criminal competition and war (Lantia Intelligence 2019b). Because the president continued to have tight control over the attorney general's office and over the security sector, the War on Drugs and the increasing number of atrocities committed by the armed forces and the federal police were kept under the shadow of impunity (Open Society Justice Initiative 2016; International Crisis Group 2018). Governors continued to have strict control over their state attorney generals and the state judicial and state security police forces. As President Calderón did with his co-partisans, Peña Nieto protected his co-partisan PRI governors and granted them political impunity and criminal immunity as long as they cooperated with the president's agenda (McDonnell 2017; International Crisis Group 2018). Several PRI governors and their judicial and police authorities used these exceptional powers to regulate and profit from the criminal underworld in ways that were unforeseen in previous years (Fregoso 2017). Some of the cartels and OCGs under their protection launched aggressive attacks against local political elites to gain control over local populations, governments, and territories, thus expanding the landscape of criminal governance.

In the face of continuity in security policies and the persistence of authoritarian institutional enclaves, it is no surprise that between 2012 and 2018 Mexico's War on Drugs yielded 80,000 homicides associated with criminal wars, including state–cartel and inter-cartel wars (Lantia Intelligence 2019a). If we add the 70,000 murders previously experienced under the Calderón administration to this new number, this means that over the course of 12 years Mexico experienced a total of 150,000 murders – that is, nine times the median death toll of all civil wars of the second half of the twentieth century. If we add the number of victims of other types of violence, Mexico's victimization landscape more closely resembles the mass atrocities that characterize civil wars. For example, during the Peña Nieto administration the number of missing people more than doubled, reaching a staggering number of over 40,000 (Animal Político 2019). As happens in protracted civil wars, journalists and families of victims began uncovering the existence of thousands of clandestine mass graves. By 2018, the most accurate study estimated the existence of nearly 2,000 of these (Guillén, Torres, and Turati 2018).

The deepening of the illiberal traits of Mexico's democracy took place while the country continued to organize elections at all levels of government with clockwork precision. The country continued to experience increasing electoral competition at all levels of government, party alternation in state and municipal governments, and political decentralization and partisan fragmentation along its federal structure. It is highly plausible, in light of the quantitative and qualitative evidence presented in this book for the 1990–2006 period, that these political-electoral mechanisms, that are a fundamental institutional feature of democracy, continued to be catalysts of large-scale criminal violence (see Guerrero 2018). In 2018, Mexico attested to the disturbing indication of the continued association between electoral mechanisms and different forms of criminal violence. In a year with the greatest number of state and municipal elections in contemporary Mexican history, drug cartels and their criminal associates committed the greatest number of murders of municipal authorities and party candidates (International Crisis Group 2018). In line with this book's findings, it is plausible that in many of these cases OCGs went on to establish subnational criminal governance regimes.

THEORETICAL IMPLICATIONS

Beyond Mexico, our findings have important theoretical implications for the way we think about cartels and OCGs, the state, criminal wars, and regime change and about policies to reduce large-scale criminal violence. Highlighting these general implications can help students of organized crime and large-scale criminal violence to test our arguments beyond Mexico and guide policymakers to connect scholarly research with policy practice.

Drug Cartels as Political Actors

One of the longest-standing assumptions in the field of criminology is that OCGs are non-state, apolitical actors (Reuter 2009). This assumption has informed the study of organized crime and criminal violence and has influenced public security policies devised by government officials who typically view drug violence as either a socioeconomic or a judicial problem, or one that results from a global prohibitionist regulatory regime. But in this book, we have claimed that OCGs are political actors. To be sure, we do not claim that they are political partisans – cartels as such (unlike professional politicians, social activists or rebels) do not have political ideologies or party-political loyalties. But they are affected by national and subnational politics. In fact, politics conditions their behavior and strategy. Political change may confront them with threats or present them with opportunities, or both. They may have vested interests in certain political outcomes, and expedience may motivate them to intervene in political processes (even to the extent of setting up their own de facto local governance regimes).

Contrary to the widely held conceptualization of OCGs as apolitical actors, our examination of two decades of drug wars in Mexico revealed that drug trafficking is a deeply political arena and that political regimes and electoral politics can be major determinants of peace and violence in the criminal underworld. As our analysis has shown, the system of governance of Mexico's one-party rule was inextricably intertwined with the development of Mexican cartels as major players in the global drug trafficking industry, and the subsequent dynamics of political competition and conflict became a decisive factor in whether peace or war prevailed in the gray zone of criminality. As we showed in Chapters 2 and 3, Mexico's *pax mafiosa* emerged under one-party rule, and the spread of subnational multiparty competition caused the breakdown of informal government protection networks and motivated cartels to go to war. In democracy, in the context of acute political polarization between Right and Left, partisan vertical fragmentation and intergovernmental partisan conflict between a conservative president and leftist governors opened opportunities for cartels to contest rival territory in areas where leftist subnational authorities were unprotected. In seeking to develop subnational controls through the assassination of local government officials and party candidates, cartels took cues from the political environment: they targeted these politically unprotected individuals in leftist states, and launched attacks during subnational election cycles and in geographically adjacent municipalities.

Our analysis reveals not only that politics shaped cartels' incentives for peace or violence but also that, after a prolonged period of intense conflict, cartels eventually took an active role in shaping local political processes. Decades into war, Mexican drug lords and their criminal associates decided to move beyond behaving merely as violent interest groups – using coercion or bribery to influence policy – and attempted to gain control over municipal governments, local populations, and territories. This mutation turned them into de facto political actors. As we extensively described in Chapter 7, drug lords used political assassination to influence subnational electoral processes and colonize municipal governments. Gaining control over municipal structures allowed them to seize control over formal and criminal taxation, monopolize violence, regulate major economic activities, and control the flow of information and populations across subnational jurisdictions. By becoming de facto governance units, cartels and their criminal associates became political-territorial armed actors.

The fact that cartels and their criminal associates are motivated to seek subnational political power and remake local social orders by their need to remain competitive in the struggle for the control of illicit markets should not be taken as proof that they are exclusively economic agents. Instead, what our analysis reveals is that politics and the economic profits in illegal markets are endogenously intertwined – the dynamics of political change affect criminal markets and developments in criminal markets shape political processes. Rather than uphold the misleading assumption that cartels are fundamentally economic apolitical actors, we need to gain a better understanding of the logics of this dynamic relation of economic and political drivers in the gray zone of criminality.

Outlining the different goals of political parties, armed rebel groups and drug cartels may help identify the singular way in which OCGs become political actors. Armed rebels and political parties want national control and formal recognition as legitimate power holders and are politically motivated by policy goals and ideologies. In contrast, OCGs and drug cartels want local controls and de facto illegal power without holding any aspirations for formal recognition and legitimacy and are economically motivated by the drive to maximize profits in illegal markets. To be sure, these are important differences. But they do not justify the drawing of strict boundaries in which OCGs and drug cartels have no place in politics. Cartels and OCGs are de facto "political" actors.

State Agents as Political-Criminal Actors

Another widely held assumption in the field of criminology is that state security agents and OCGs operate from separate, mutually exclusive, and opposing spheres: law enforcement versus crime (Skaperdas 2001). Relations between the state and criminals are held to be zero sum. Building on this, scholars in criminology have long assumed that security decisions to confront cartels and other OCGs are primarily driven by technical (apolitical) considerations, particularly the goal of establishing a monopoly of the legitimate use of violence within a given territory (Weber 1918/1994).

In contrast to these established assumptions, this book's findings reveal the existence of multifaceted states, in which some state agents do act as law enforcement agents who fight cartels (often adopting iron-fist militarized policies) but many others develop informal networks of government protection for cartels and still others defect from the state to lead the cartels' private militias. Recognizing these multiple faces of the state is crucial to developing a new understanding of OCGs as networks of state–criminal collusion. As the Mexican experience showed, members of the military led the informal provision of government protection for cartels in the 1980s (Chapter 2); elite members of the military defected to create the Zetas, the powerful private militia of the Gulf Cartel in the late 1990s (Chapter 3); and military battalions played a leading role in the federal government's War on Drugs in the late 2000s (Chapter 5). Failing to recognize these multiple faces of the state – in this case of the military – can lead to an oversimplified understanding of criminal markets and of the key actors involved in fighting criminal wars. This failure can be particularly damaging when policymakers themselves fail to recognize that the state is a heterogeneous, not a homogeneous, multifaceted actor.

While policymakers have incentives to portray themselves as Weberian state actors who seek to establish the monopoly of violence throughout a country's territory, our evidence from Chapters 4, 5, 6, and 7 reveals that partisanship, rather than technical efficiency, was a key driver of the military strategy in the War on Drugs. Recognizing the important scholarly research which has shown that the militarization of the federal intervention (Flores-Macías 2018) and the use of the kingpin strategy (Guerrero 2011b; Calderón et al. 2015; Phillips 2015) to decapitate the cartels have resulted in major violence escalations, we provide extensive evidence showing that the politicization of the intervention is another crucial factor explaining (1) the escalation of violence and (2) why the escalation was subnationally uneven. These findings suggest that in a context in which newly elected democratic elites fail to reform the authoritarian institutional infrastructure that empowers presidents to discretionarily use the military and the police for partisan purposes, the dynamics of electoral competition and electoral incentives can motivate national authorities to politicize law enforcement and leave subnational political enemies strategically unprotected and blame the corresponding increase in violence on them.

Both the multifaceted nature of the state and the recognition of electoral incentives as motivators of law enforcement show that the standard Weberian definition of the state cannot always be used as an empirical descriptor of what states actually are or of what state agents aspire the state to actually be. A major implication of recognizing the multiple faces of the state is that the sweeping claim that cartels and OCGs exist where the state has no presence loses theoretical and empirical ground. Instead of state absence, our analysis has suggested looking into state–criminal networks that enable the existence of the gray zone of criminality and of OCGs. Another implication is that in the case of those state agents who do not collude but fight crime, our analysis has suggested that we should no longer assume their actions will be based on grounds of technical efficiency and the goal of monopolizing violence. As this book has made clear, we need to explore the political motivations that guide law enforcement, particularly in times of political polarization.

Democratic Transitions and the Gray Zone of Criminality

Most of what is considered common knowledge in the social sciences about transitions from authoritarian rule to democracy (O'Donnell and Schmitter 1986; Przeworski 1991) ignores the potential impact of regime change on the gray zone of criminality and on OCGs. By distinguishing between hardliners and reformists, students of democratic transitions have recognized the importance of the security sector – particularly the armed forces – in the negotiation of regime change. However, they have not recognized the leading role that these authoritarian state specialists in violence can play in the workings of the criminal underworld. Ignoring the repression–criminal nexus can be a major omission, particularly because some of the leading scholars of democratic transitions have become strong advocates of granting amnesty laws to authoritarian state specialists in violence as a way to dissuade them from becoming democratic spoilers.

One of the key takeaways from this book is that when postauthoritarian elites lead "thin" transitions to democracy – in which countries simply adopt multiparty electoral competition as a mechanism to select political leaders, without transforming authoritarian security and judicial institutions and practices – they enable authoritarian state specialists in violence to continue playing a key role in the criminal underworld and to become key actors in the production of violence in democracy. "Electoralism" – as Karl (1986, 2000) famously described El Salvador's "thin" electoral transition – or illiberal democracy can pave the way for the intimate association of democratic elections with criminal violence. As the Mexican case attests, failing to recognize the dual role of authoritarian state specialists in violence as repressors and leading criminal actors – and failing to adopt anti-impunity policies to expose and punish them – can have devastating consequences for the development of peaceful democratic societies. While amnesty laws can offer political stability to countries transitioning from authoritarian rule to democracy, by providing impunity to authoritarian state specialists in violence, these measures can facilitate the mutation of political violence (in autocracy) into criminal violence (in democracy).

Criminal Wars are not Civil Wars

Despite Collier's (2000) influential proposition that armed rebellions should be seen as quasi-criminal activities, scholars of civil wars in the past two decades have forcefully argued in favor of distinguishing between armed rebel groups and OCGs, and of treating civil wars and criminal wars as distinct phenomena (Kalyvas 2015). Our in-depth study of Mexican cartels has suggested that, compared to armed rebel groups, OCGs have different objectives, face different constraints, and often adopt different governance strategies.

Whereas armed rebel groups fighting civil wars have well-defined political ideologies and seek to topple the national government and become national political rulers (Kalyvas 2006; Arjona 2016), cartels and OCGs do not have putative ideologies and generally seek to establish monopolistic controls over illicit markets. When conflicts for criminal markets become too intense, cartels and OCGs may expand their horizons – as the Mexican case attests – and seek to gain de facto subnational political power to further their economic aims. However, the political ambitions of armed revolutionary actors and criminal actors are different for structural reasons. Armed rebel groups fight wars in which all actors are potentially constrained by the laws of war and they often participate in peace agreements and become lawful political organizations in post-conflict scenarios. In contrast, drug cartels and OCGs and their private militias fight turf wars in which international norms do not apply, and cartels and their criminal associates cannot become formal political parties with parliamentary representation. This means – as the case of the Knights Templar in Michoacán showed – that drug cartels and OCGs generally have shorter time horizons than rebels and rarely become stationary bandits and public goods providers.[1] With shorter time horizons, cartels and OCGs tend to be more predatory than rebels, even when they have monopolistic controls over violence within a given territory.

Our findings have also suggested that the roles that states and civilians play in criminal wars are significantly different from the roles they play in civil wars. On the one hand, states and armed rebel groups in civil wars are opposing actors involved in zero-sum relations – that is, whatever the rebels gain is at the expense of the state (Kalyvas 2006). In the case of criminal wars, as we have emphatically argued, OCGs need some level of informal state protection, even while at the same time they may be equipping themselves to fight zero-sum battles against other state agents. On the other hand, while civilian support represents a fundamental resource for armed rebel groups fighting asymmetric guerrilla warfare (Kalyvas and Balcells 2010), it is not a factor for OCGs fighting criminal wars. In fact, state protection, rather than civilian support, is the main source of criminal power in the gray zone of criminality. When OCGs seek to develop subnational criminal governance regimes, gaining protection from some state agents is crucial in order to fight "clean" law enforcement agents and to subdue civilian populations.

A Political Science of Organized Crime and Large-Scale Criminal Violence

In this book we have made the strong claim that organized criminal groups can only exist and thrive to the extent that they have access to some level of state protection – particularly to state specialists in violence. Because political regimes define how state power is distributed and how state coercion is used, politics is a key determinant of the rise of organized crime and a key driver of peace or war in the gray zone of criminality. Scholars of organized crime in Latin America have in the past decade forcefully argued for the need to recognize the different forms of engagement between state agents and OCGs (Arias 2006a, 2017; Snyder and Durán-Martínez 2009; Barnes 2017; Lessing 2017; Bergman 2018; Durán-Martínez 2018; Yashar 2018). But in this book, we have tried to go one step further by assessing how political regimes, regime transitions,

---

[1] Keep in mind that Olson's (2000) influential discussion of criminals becoming stationary bandits and public goods providers with long-term horizons and "encompassing interests" in the communities where they live is based on a criminal *metaphor*, not on the realities of organized crime.

and electoral politics can influence the balance of power in the gray zone of criminality and define the prospects for peace or violence in the criminal underworld.

By ignoring the political foundations of organized crime and large-scale criminal violence, which this book has tried to show, scholars are likely to introduce a major source of bias in their explanations of criminal war and peace. To be sure, we are not advocating for a mono-causal (political) explanation of criminal wars. Rather, we are advocating for the development of a theoretical and empirical corpus that will lead to the systematic testing of the likely impact of political regimes, political change, and electoral politics on large-scale criminal violence. While sociologists have succeeded in showing that changes in community cohesion can be a major driver of criminal violence and economists have shown that changes in opportunity cost and in law enforcement can motivate individuals to engage in criminal behavior, in political science we are in the early stages of establishing the key role that changes in political-electoral conditions can have on delimiting the contours of peace and violence in the criminal underworld.[2] Through a systematic analysis of the outbreak and escalation of drug violence in Mexico during the transition from one-party rule to multiparty illiberal democracy, this book has sought to contribute to the development of a new political science of organized crime and large-scale criminal violence.

POLICY IMPLICATIONS

How Can a Political Science of Organized Crime Inform a Democratic Security Policy?

Developing a political science of organized crime and large-scale criminal violence can have important policy implications for the development of alternative public security policies in democracy. Let us explore three such implications.

A crucial policy implication that follows from a political understanding of OCGs as networks of state–criminal collusion is that in combating organized crime, or in seeking to abate drug violence in

---

[2] See, among others: Snyder and Durán-Martínez (2009); Dube, Dube, and García-Ponce (2013); Oliveri and Sberna (2014); Osorio (2015); Alesina, Piccolo and Pinoti (2019); Trejo and Ley (2016); Atuesta and Ponce (2017); Ley (2017); Durán-Martínez (2018); Trejo and Ley (2018); Albarracín (2018); Trejo and Ley (2019).

countries such as Mexico, governments should focus on dismantling these networks through intelligence and judicial action, rather than through militarized iron-first policies and open military combat.[3] As our findings would suggest, rather than focus on criminal bosses, democratic elites should focus on identifying and removing authoritarian specialists in violence who are at the center of state–criminal networks. These are members of the military or the police who use their positions of power to provide informal government protection, or they are defectors who become leading actors in the development of private militias to fight turf wars. By exposing and punishing these authoritarian state specialists in violence for gross human rights violations, democratic elites can weaken OCGs and reduce the size of the gray zone of criminality – even if criminal collusion is not fully proven.

A second important implication is that in devising public policies to contain criminal wars and large-scale criminal violence, policymakers should focus on creating institutional reforms that prevent presidents and executive authorities from making a partisan use of security agencies – including the armed forces and the police – and the judiciary. As the Mexican experience shows, a key element of this reform would be to depoliticize law enforcement while at the same time making security forces more transparent and subject to civilian oversight. When President Calderón took office, the institutional mechanisms of authoritarian control that had empowered presidents to control the military, the police, and the judiciary during the era of one-party rule remained intact. This persisting concentration of control in the president's hands enabled Calderón to politicize the War on Drugs. As the cross-national experience shows, democratically elected presidents do not easily surrender these powers; it is through the active mobilization of opposition forces, civil society organizations, and families of victims of military and police brutality that these powers are placed under effective checks and balances.

Finally, the outbreak of criminal wars and the dramatic escalation of drug violence as Mexico transitioned from one-party rule to multiparty democracy leave us with a sobering lesson: When new democratic elites fail to reform authoritarian sources of state coercive power and leave a long history of state impunity for gross human rights violations intact –

---

[3] The International Commission Against Impunity in Guatemala (CICIG) has championed this approach in Guatemala since 2007 with remarkable success. For an in-depth discussion of this approach, see Beltrán (2008).

as Mexican political elites did in 2000 – democratic institutions are likely to become intimately intertwined with organized crime and key democratic practices such as electoral competition, party alternation, and the decentralization and fragmentation of political power can become triggers of criminal wars and large-scale criminal violence. While recognizing that improving economic conditions and enhancing community cohesion can go a long way in reducing the prospects of large-scale criminal violence in new democracies, this book has tried to emphatically show that regulating the use of coercive power by state specialists in violence can be equally important in developing peaceful democracies.

APPENDIX A

Criminal Violence in Mexico Database (CVM)

GENERAL DESCRIPTION

The Criminal Violence in Mexico Database (CVM) is an original newspaper-based databank of murders and other violent events (kidnappings, murder attempts, and death threats) that can be attributed to conflicts in Mexico's drug trafficking industry and that took place between December 1994 and December 2012. For the most part, these events involve inter-cartel and state–cartel conflicts. Note that we use the more generic category of criminal violence because – as we explain in this book – between 2006 and 2012 drug cartels broke into a number of related criminal organizations that extended the range of their illicit activities beyond drug trafficking.

CVM provides a count of murders that can be attributed to organized criminal groups (OCGs) in Mexico during the presidential administrations of Ernesto Zedillo (December 1994–December 2000), Vicente Fox (December 2000–December 2006), and Felipe Calderón (December 2006–December 2012).

Although the Mexican government produces reliable data on homicides, official statistics do not distinguish homicides committed by common criminals from those committed by OCGs. Because we are interested in analyzing organized criminal violence, we relied on a systematic review of Mexico's leading newspapers to document violence resulting from conflicts that involve OCGs. To be sure, *this is not a census* that measures the universe of murders associated with criminal organizations but a data collection that uses Mexico's leading national newspapers to approximate the *intensity* of violence across geographic regions while minimizing different sources of biases. Because the intensity of violence varied significantly across presidential administrations, we separated the data collection into two time periods (1994–2006 and 2007–2012) and followed different data gathering strategies.

For the 1994–2006 period, CVM contains information on 4,257 murders associated with inter-cartel and state–cartel conflicts reported in three Mexican daily newspapers: *Reforma* (1994–2006), *El Universal* (1994–2006), and *El Financiero* (1997–2006). Based in Mexico City and Monterrey, and with extensive coverage of central and northern Mexico, *Reforma* is the most specialized source of daily information on drug trafficking in Mexico (Shirk and Wallman 2015). *El Universal* offers good coverage of central Mexico and the Pacific and Gulf coasts, and *El Financiero* covers the central region. The three newspapers together provide a fair coverage of the south. Although the CVM does not provide a census of drug-related violence during this period, it minimizes any significant geographic bias.

The data collection strategy relied on human coders and took place in 2009 and 2010. Trejo and Ley devised a basic format for coders to record specific information about every report on drug and organized crime-related violence. Ley trained the coders and oversaw the data collection process, which was conducted by Ley herself (a native Spanish speaker) and two native Spanish-speaking political science undergraduate students (at that time): Mario Moreno (Duke University) and Valeria Ramírez (CIDE). Most of the data collection took place in Mexico City and the team was in permanent communication.

For the 2007–2012 period, CVM contains information on 21,815 murders associated with inter-cartel and state–cartel conflicts reported in *Reforma*. Given the significant increase in violence and the corresponding increase in newspaper reports, it was practically impossible to extend the data collection using the three newspapers we had covered for the earlier period and relying exclusively on human coding. We decided to opt for *Reforma* as our main source because it is the newspaper with the widest national coverage and the one that developed specialized teams of reporters to cover the War on Drugs and its effects during the administration of President Calderón. We also decided to continue using human coders – in contrast to automated identification of event data – for two main reasons: (1) to be consistent throughout our data collection process and (2) to fully understand the ongoing changes in news coverage strategies as a result of the dramatic increase in drug violence, as described below.

The data collection took place in Mexico City between 2011 and 2012. Trejo and Ley oversaw the data collection, which was conducted by Ley, Ramírez and two new coders: Francisco Orta and Alejandro Sanders, both of them Spanish speakers and by then undergraduate political science students at CIDE and ITAM, respectively.

Despite *Reforma*'s wide and specialized coverage, as the War on Drugs unfolded editors and reporters became targets of death threats. To be sure, this was not exclusive to *Reforma*, but a more generalized phenomenon that affected the Mexican press and turned Mexico into one of the most dangerous countries for journalism during this period (CPJ 2017). Editors followed different strategies to deal with violence. Some stopped covering drug violence while others, like *Reforma*, continued to report but made anonymous bylines, provided fewer details and avoided reporting the names of criminals or organizations, or gave less visibility to the reports by moving them from the newspaper's front page to the interior pages (Ramírez 2011). At the height of the violence, around 2011, however, *Reforma* significantly reduced the number of reports for a number of months. Then, in 2012, as the presidential election approached, it also shifted its focus to campaign-related events. Still, our data collection process allowed us to measure the intensity of violence across geographic regions, which is the book's focus.

Because there are reasons to believe that violence against journalists might have affected *Reforma*'s coverage for a few months, we supplemented our analysis for the Calderón period using an official dataset produced by the Office of the President covering all murders associated with inter-cartel and state–cartel conflicts from 2006 until 2011. Drawing on military and police information, the government created this unique instrument, which was only made publicly available by the end of the Calderón administration. A more complete version of this dataset was obtained by researchers from CIDE and made publicly available in December 2018 (Atuesta, Sordia, and Madrazo 2018).

To check our statistical results based on data from CVM for the 2006–2012 period, we ran every test using the dataset from the Office of the President. Most results – and practically all the results that tested our hypotheses – remained unchanged.

CLASSIFICATION CRITERIA

Determining whether a violent event could be classified as one associated with drug or organized criminal violence was relatively straightforward when the newspaper report provided detailed information about the name of the organization involved and important contextual information about the event. This was generally the case for the 1994–2006 period and for the early years of the drug war. As the conflict escalated – and presumably, as journalists and reporters began to receive death threats – the information became more encrypted and thus it became more challenging to correctly classify events.

When the newspaper report did not clearly attribute responsibility of a violent event to a specific criminal organization or to conflicts of state forces against criminal organizations, we classified the event as part of drug violence or OCG violence if the attack showed at least two of the following characteristics:

a. use of assault weapons
b. multiple gunshot wounds
c. coup de grâce
d. signs of torture
e. decapitation or other signs of mutilation
f. message left on or next to the body.

APPENDIX B

Criminal Attacks Against Political Actors in Mexico (CAPAM) Database

The Criminal Attacks against Political Actors in Mexico (CAPAM) Database is an original newspaper-based databank of criminal attacks against government authorities, political candidates, and party activists perpetrated between 1995 and 2012, which we created. Information from CAPAM is drawn from a systematic analysis of eight national daily newspapers, 18 subnational daily newspapers, and two weekly magazines specializing in drug trafficking and organized crime, as listed in Table B.1.

Unlike other datasets on political violence that focus exclusively on the murder of mayors, CAPAM measures lethal attacks against government authorities, political candidates, and party activists. Also, unlike other datasets that measure only murders, CAPAM provides detailed information about a wide range of attacks, including murder and murder attempts, public death threats, and kidnapping.

We followed strict criteria that allowed us to verify the involvement of organized criminal groups (OCGs) in such events. First, we attributed an attack to organized crime when at least two sources (*Reforma* and another national or local source) named a specific OCG as the perpetrator.

Second, in the case of murders, when news reports did not include the name of the OCG involved, we relied on three indicators associated with the modus operandi of drug cartels and their criminal associates to include the event in the dataset: (a) the use of assault weapons for killing; (b) signs of torture and brutal violence (e.g., bodies wrapped in a rug or mutilated); and (c) written messages left on the bodies. The type of assault weapon used was also an important indicator for the inclusion of an attack in our dataset.

TABLE B.1 *National and Subnational Newspapers for Data Collection*

Type	State	Source
National		*Reforma***
		El Universal
		La Jornada
		*Proceso**
		Milenio
		Excelsior
		Crónica
		El Economista
		El Sol
Local	Baja California	*Zeta de Tijuana**
	Campeche	*La Tribuna de Campeche*
	Coahuila	*El Siglo de Torreón*
		El Zócalo
		Vanguardia
	Chihuahua	*El Heraldo de Chihuahua*
		El Norte de Ciudad Juárez
		El Diario
	Durango	*La Voz de Durango*
		El Siglo de Durango
	Guerrero	*La Jornada Guerrero*
		El Sur de Acapulco
	Jalisco	*La Jornada Jalisco*
	Michoacán	*Cambio de Michoacán*
		La Jornada de Michoacán
	Sinaloa	*Noroeste*
	Sonora	*El Imparcial*
	Tabasco	*Tabasco Hoy*
		Diario Avance de Tabasco

** Main source.
* Weekly magazines specializing in reporting on drug trafficking and organized crime. Note that *Zeta de Tijuana* offers extensive coverage of crime in the state of Baja California, but it also publishes news from the rest of the country.

Third, in the case of public death threats, we only included the event in our dataset if a publicized threat by OCGs against public authorities or party candidates resulted in one of three actions: (1) candidates were forced to leave the electoral competition; (2) political parties explicitly recognized they had been unable to place candidates for a specific position; and (3) public authorities were subsequently forced to resign or move out of their municipality. When threats did not meet these criteria, we did not include them in our dataset.

Note that, as we explain in Chapter 6, there are two types of threat that OCGs make against government authorities and political candidates: private and public. Private threats are very hard to measure and, even though newspapers do report some of them, we decided not to include them in our dataset to avoid a potentially important source of measurement error. When a mayor or a political candidate colludes with OCGs, s/he would have incentives to say that s/he did it under threat. If there is no public evidence of such a threat, it would be very hard to actually corroborate whether the threat ever existed. In contrast, public threats are more likely to be corroborated because OCGs have incentives to publicize their threats through messages left on victims (e.g., wrapped bodies are left with a message) or by hanging banners with their message on public places (e.g., bridges). Despite the publicity, as we explain above, we restricted the case of public threats to those that actually led to the withdrawal of local government officials or party candidates from their professional activities.

Based on these criteria, our coders adhered to the following routine as part of the data generation process. The routine began with the review of the eight national daily newspapers to make an initial count of lethal attacks directed against politicians. The systematic evaluation was conducted using *Infolatina*. When these reports did not provide enough information, we used subnational newspapers, which often provided extensive follow-ups in the case of attacks against local politicians. These follow-ups were published a few months after the attack and sometimes included information from the state prosecutors' investigations. When we found inconsistencies between two sources, we looked for further information that allowed us to clearly determine the involvement of organized crime in the attacks. If we did not find enough detailed information to cross-verify one source of information, we excluded the event.

In the case of high-profile attacks against government authorities and party candidates, biases in the data due to self-censorship in the coverage of these events among the Mexican press was not a major concern. Attacks against government authorities and party candidates hardly go unnoticed and are often made public due to the political implications. As noted, we were able to find and use extensive follow-ups in subnational newspapers to complement or verify information.

Overall, the use of multiple sources of information – national and subnational – maximizes the precision of our measure of high-profile criminal attacks, while at the same time minimizing sources of geographic bias.

Trejo and Ley devised a format for data gathering and Ley coordinated the data collection. The data collection took place during 2014 and 2015. Ley collected some of the data and trained two undergraduate students to participate in this process: Magdalena Guzmán (by then an undergraduate political science student at the University of Notre Dame) and Elizabeth Orozco (by then an undergraduate human rights student at Claustro de Sor Juana in Mexico City).

APPENDIX C

Chapter 2. Multivariate Regression Models (Robustness Checks)

Available online at: www.cambridge.org/VotesDrugsandViolence

CONTENTS

APPENDIX D

Chapter 4. Multivariate Regression Models (Robustness Checks)

Available online at: www.cambridge.org/VotesDrugsandViolence

CONTENTS

Chapter 4. Natural Experiment (Additional Information)

MICHOACÁN AND JALISCO

As shown in Map 4.2 in Chapter 4, we use municipalities located across the state borders of Michoacán and Jalisco to isolate the likely impact of vertical party fragmentation on criminal violence. Table E.1 reports information about these two regions on multiple dimensions. The data reveal that the municipalities across the state borders share multiple similarities and constitute a homogeneous region that happens to be separated by state borders. Note, again, that the table reports information that may not be directly relevant to the study of inter-cartel violence but that nonetheless helps us make the point that we are comparing municipalities that constitute a self-contained region due to a number of geographic, sociodemographic, cultural, and economic similarities.

The western region of Tierra Caliente (in Michoacán) and southeast Jalisco constitute a homogeneous region with deep roots in the Cristero Movement – the Catholic rural militias that fought against the anticlerical laws resulting from the 1910 Mexican Revolution and the 1917 constitution (Meyer 1976). As shown in Table E.1, this is a relatively elevated area and municipalities in both regions are relatively proximate to their states' capitals. While municipalities in Michoacán are more populated than in Jalisco, almost half of the population on both sides of the border lives in rural localities and is predominantly Catholic. Approximately two-fifths of the population on both sides of the border is employed in agricultural activities and the rest participates in service-related activities. One-third of the population on both sides lives under

TABLE E.I *Comparison of Border Municipalities of Michoacán and Jalisco*

	Michoacán Tierra Caliente (border municipalities)	Jalisco Southeastern Region (border municipalities)
Geographic		
Altitude* Measured in meters above sea level (masl) Source: INEGI	965.71	1,012.86
Distance from state capital* Linear distance (km)	166.64	130.30
Distance from state capital* Driving distance (km)	227.51	177.96
Sociodemographic		
Municipal population, 2010* Source: INEGI, 2010 Population Census	30,325.86	20,341.15
% indigenous population, 2010* Source: INEGI, 2010 Population Census	1.03	0.20
% youth, aged 15–34, 2010* Source: INEGI, 2010 Population Census	55.47	51.55
% mono-parental households, 2010* Source: INEGI, 2010 Population Census	21.09	23.03
Sex ratio, 2010* Source: INEGI, 2010 Population Census	99.44	97.70
% international migrants, 2010* Mexicans who were international migrants in 2005, but counted in 2010 Census Source: INEGI, 2010 Population Census	2.74	3.31
% population living in rural localities, 2010* Localities with 2,500 inhabitants or fewer Source: INEGI, 2010 Population Census	40.96	49.09

(continued)

TABLE E.I *(continued)*

	Michoacán Tierra Caliente (border municipalities)	Jalisco Southeastern Region (border municipalities)
% Catholic, 2010 Source: INEGI, 2010 Population Census	94.65	96.51

Economic

Poverty, 2010* Source: Conapo, 2011 Marginality Index, Rescaled 0–100	29.90	28.52
Gini index of inequality, 2010* Source: Coneval, 2012	0.41	0.40
% population employed in agriculture, 2010* Source: INEGI, 2010 Population Census	37.44	40.93
% municipal income from local taxes, 2007–2011* Source: INEGI, Public Finance Statistics	2.20	4.26

Political

Governor's party	PRD (2007–2011)	PAN (2006–2011)
% PRD municipalities from sample** Source: State Electoral Institutes	2005–2007: 42.86 2008–2011: 85.71 **Average: 64.28**	2007–2009: 0 2010–2012: 0 **Average: 0**
% PRI municipalities from sample** Source: State Electoral Institutes	2005–2007: 28.57 2008–2011: 14.28 **Average: 21.42**	2007–2009: 42.86 2010–2012: 57.14 **Average: 50**
% PAN municipalities from sample** Source: State Electoral Institutes	2005–2007: 28.57 2008–2011: 0 **Average: 14.28**	2007–2009: 57.14 2010–2012: 42.86 **Average: 50**

Narco activity

Cartel presence & inter-cartel conflict	La Familia Michoacana Sinaloa Cartel	Sinaloa Cartel Zetas
Drug trafficking region	YES	YES

(continued)

TABLE E.1 *(continued)*

	Michoacán Tierra Caliente (border municipalities)	Jalisco Southeastern Region (border municipalities)
Marijuana crop eradication, 2007–2010 (hectares)* Source: Sedena, 2015	189.65	53.71
Poppy crop eradication, 2007–2010 (hectares)* Source: Sedena, 2015	1.43	0.003
Drug-related murders 2008–2011 Source: CVM Dataset	77	40

* Regional mean (includes only the municipalities under analysis).
** The sample includes the municipalities under analysis shown in Map 4.1 in this book.

conditions of poverty and levels of inequality in both regions are practically identical. Municipalities from southeast Jalisco collect more fiscal revenues than municipalities in western Michoacán, but both regions are largely dependent on federal fiscal transfers.

La Familia Michoacana had been the dominant cartel on the Michoacán side of the border and the Sinaloa Cartel, first, and later breakaways from the Sinaloans dominated the Jalisco side of the border (Grillo 2011; Guerrero 2012). By 2010, however, municipalities from both sides of the state border were immersed in major turf wars: La Familia Michoacana against the Sinaloa Cartel on the Michoacán side and the breakaways of the Sinaloa Cartel against the Zetas on the Jalisco side.

As the data in Table E.1 show, these two regions are marijuana producers, but marijuana cultivation is considerably greater in the Michoacán municipalities than in Jalisco. This should not be a major concern because a significant share of the marijuana produced in the Tierra Caliente region of Michoacán was trafficked through Jalisco on its way to Tijuana, which we would expect to generate more inter-cartel violence on the Jalisco side.

Politically, one major difference between both regions is that from 2008 until 2011 municipalities from western Tierra Caliente in Michoacán were under the rule of a leftist PRD governor while southeastern Jalisco municipalities were under the rule of a PAN conservative governor. As shown in Table E.1, the political landscape in the municipalities was another important political difference. While in Michoacán, the PRD (64.28 percent) and the PRI (21.42 percent) were the dominant political forces and the PAN had a limited presence (14.28 percent), in Jalisco the PAN (50 percent) and the PRI (50 percent) were the two main forces, while the PRD had null presence (0 percent). Using the categories of party layering that we employ in this book, this means that most municipalities in Michoacán belonged to the PAN-PRD-PRD and PAN-PRD-PRI layers. In contrast, all cases in Jalisco belonged to the PAN-PAN-PAN and PAN-PAN-PRI layers.

In terms of criminal violence, a major difference between regions is that between 2008 and 2011 municipalities from western Michoacán experienced a significantly larger number of drug-related murders than their neighboring municipalities of Jalisco. As we discuss in this book, after isolating partisan vertical fragmentation as an important distinguishing factor of otherwise nearly identical municipalities separated by state borders, we attributed differences in attacks to different patterns of partisan fragmentation. First, despite multiple similarities, municipalities from this region belonged to states with different governors. Michoacán municipalities belonged to a state where a conservative federal government was engaged in a major political conflict with a leftist governor and, as a result, inter-cartel violence increased significantly. In contrast, Jalisco municipalities belonged to a state where a conservative federal government and a conservative governor closely cooperated to control inter-cartel violence (Mural 2010). Second, consistent with our statistical findings, the micro comparison across borders confirms that within leftist states, leftist PRD and PRI municipalities experienced a higher probability of attacks than PAN municipalities.

A natural experiment requires that we carefully identify possible alternative mechanisms that may have influenced the divergent outcomes in the Jalisco and Michoacán municipalities. Following Dunning (2008), McCauley and Posner (2015), and Kocher and Monteiro (2016), we address four major challenges to the causal claim we make based on our natural experiment: (1) an imbalance of variables that could possibly explain the difference in the average intensity of violence across our two groups of municipalities; (2) lack of an independent effect of treatment effect (partisanship, in our analysis); (3) the existence of other possibly unrelated intervening variables that could have led to the differences in violence that we observe in western Michoacán and southern Jalisco; and (4) the occurrence of self-selection processes in PAN (control) and PRD (treatment) states.

To confront the first challenge, building on the statistical evidence we presented in Table 4.2 in the main text, and in Appendix D (online), in Table E.1, we list an extensive number of potential factors giving rise to criminal violence that are both theoretically and empirically grounded. As Stokes (2014) suggests, rather than try to seek to control (or balance) for an infinite number of variables, we should pay attention to factors that have proven to be of relevance in accounting for variation in our outcome variable (criminal violence) in a wide variety of studies. The information reported in Table E.1 systematically reveals that municipalities on both sides of the state border share multiple social and economic characteristics that have been shown to be crucial drivers of criminal violence in the literature. While balancing is important, as Stokes (2014) and Kocher and Monteiro (2016) suggest, we must look beyond the heterogeneity of our two groups of municipalities and focus instead on the nature of the treatment.

To address the second challenge, we need to assess whether the partisanship of the governors during our period under study did indeed have an independent effect on criminal violence. As noted in Chapter 3, PAN won Jalisco's gubernatorial office for the first time in 1995, while the PRD won Michoacán's governorship for the first time in 2002. Both victories meant that the PRI lost the governorships in these states for the first time in half a century. One potential challenge to the independent effect of partisanship on violence could be the time of tenure of the PAN and the PRD in the gubernatorial seat. Is it possible, we must ask, that the contrasting levels of violence across the bordering municipalities of Jalisco and Michoacán result from different lengths in tenure in the gubernatorial seat instead of their governors' partisan identification? Specifically, did the longer tenure of the PAN in Jalisco's gubernatorial seat result in a relatively more stable criminal market and therefore reduce levels of violence, compared to Michoacán, where the PRD had governed for just four years before the federal military intervention?

The evidence we reported in Chapter 3 showed that after PAN Governor Alberto Cárdenas took office in 1995, Jalisco plunged into multiple inter-cartel wars, as the Tijuana Cartel first and subsequently the Juárez Cartel challenged the hegemony of the Sinaloa Cartel in the state over the next decade. We also showed in Chapter 3 that the Gulf Cartel sought to challenge the Sinaloans' hegemony in Michoacán when they deployed the Zetas in the state after the 2002 victory of PRD

Governor Lázaro Cárdenas Batel. The Zetas sought to take control over southern Michoacán and use the Michoacán–Jalisco municipalities as an entry point to penetrate Jalisco – the state of residence of the Sinaloans' families. By 2006, when President Calderón deployed the army to Mexico's most conflicted regions, the hegemony of the Sinaloa Cartel in both Jalisco and Michoacán was under violent dispute. Over the course of his administration, the Zetas, war against the Sinaloans in Michoacán spilled over the Jalisco–Michoacán border. As we show in Chapter 5, the key difference in the different trajectories of violence across municipalities is that, when criminal violence began to rise, President Calderón worked closely with Jalisco's Governor Emilio González Márquez, his PAN co-partisan, while he purposefully entered into a bitter conflict, failed to cooperate with, and punished leftist authorities in Michoacán.

To address the third challenge about the existence of other intervening variables we may have failed to recognize, we can think of the nature of the military intervention in Jalisco and in Michoacán. While in Jalisco President Calderón did not launch a formal military campaign to confront the cartels, in Michoacán the federal government launched the first military campaign. Is it possible that this difference may explain the distinct levels of violence in the bordering municipalities of Jalisco and Michoacán? As noted by Merino (2011), Espinosa and Rubin (2015), and Flores-Macías (2018), military interventions are associated with increases in violence. However, as we show in Chapter 5, while not part of a formal military campaign, the federal government did make an important deployment of the army and the federal police in Jalisco to arrest the cartels' leaders and the leaders of their private militias. As we also show, the nature of the intervention in each state differed precisely because of the governors' partisanship. In Jalisco, the federal and the state PAN government authorities held weekly "security coordination meetings" to align the goals and actions of the intervention among security forces and to share information. In contrast, in Michoacán, the federal government did not share any security information with the PRD state government, and the military did not coordinate security actions with state or municipal police forces. Therefore, the different levels of violence in the bordering municipalities of Michoacán and Jalisco are not explained by the presence (or absence) of a formal military campaign but by its nature (whether the federal government cooperated or not with subnational authorities), which was in fact dictated by the partisan affiliation of the president and the governors.

A final challenge is whether each set of municipalities could have "self-selected" themselves into PAN and PRD states respectively. However, as we discussed in the main text, inter-state borders in Mexico were defined in the nineteenth century for reasons entirely unrelated to the twenty-first-century narco wars. Also, numbers of voters on each side of the state borders are relatively small and would not be able to weigh heavily in the gubernatorial election outcome. Therefore, the election of PAN and PRD governors on each side of the border is exogenous to the particular social dynamics within these municipalities.

In sum, following Kocher and Monteiro's (2016) advice, our reconstruction of the process through which partisanship affected violence in the western bordering municipalities in Michoacán and the southern bordering municipalities in Jalisco validates the independent causal effect of the governors' partisanship on criminal violence, as well as the mechanisms through which our key explanatory variable operates (see Chapter 5 for further elaboration).

APPENDIX F

Chapter 6. Multivariate Regression Models (Robustness Checks)

Available online at: www.cambridge.org/VotesDrugsandViolence

CONTENTS

APPENDIX G

Chapter 6. Natural Experiments (Additional Information)

As shown in Map 6.2, in Chapter 6, we use municipalities from the Tierra Caliente region located across the state borders of Michoacán and Guerrero to isolate the potential impact of subnational election cycles on criminal attacks against local authorities, party candidates, and party activists. Table G.1 reports detailed information about these two regions. The comparison reveals that this is a set of remarkably similar municipalities that happen to be separated by state borders. Note that the table includes information that may not be directly relevant for the study of criminal attacks (e.g., % Catholics per municipality) but that nonetheless helps us substantiate that on average the sample of Tierra Caliente municipalities from Michoacán shares multiple characteristics with the sample of Tierra Caliente municipalities from Guerrero. In other words, in terms of geography and key sociodemographic, cultural, economic and political features this is a self-contained region split by a state border.

Situated in the basin of the Balsas River, the Tierra Caliente municipalities comprise a low-level region that is fairly distant from the Michoacán and Guerrero state capitals. Predominantly rural and Catholic, this is a region where over one-third to one-half of the population are employed in agricultural activities, and the rest participate in mining and service-related activities. Municipalities on both sides of the border have the same level of poverty (almost half the population living in conditions of destitution), and levels of income inequality are practically identical. Municipalities on both sides of the border also have very weak

TABLE G.1 *Comparison of Border Municipalities of Michoacán and Guerrero*

	Michoacán Tierra Caliente (border municipalities)	Guerrero Tierra Caliente (border municipalities)
Geographic		
Altitude* Measured in meters above sea level (masl) Source: INEGI	435	265.71
Distance from state capital* Linear distance (km)	103.20	149.41
Distance from state capital* Driving distance (km)	177.48	218.45
Sociodemographic		
Municipal population, 2010* Source: INEGI, 2010 Population Census	22,398	27,260
% indigenous population, 2010* Source: INEGI, 2010 Population Census	0.36	0.16
% youth, aged 15–39, 2010* Source: INEGI, 2010 Population Census	17.99	17.71
% international migrants, 2010* Mexicans who were international migrants in 2005 but counted in 2010 Census Source: INEGI, 2010 Population Census	0.01	0.01
% population living in rural localities, 2010* Localities with 2,500 inhabitants or fewer Source: INEGI, 2010 Population Census	65.79	61.19
% Catholic, 2010 Source: INEGI, 2010 Population Census	92.24	87.45
Economic		
Poverty, 2010* Source: Conapo, 2010 Marginality Index, Rescaled 0–100	47.99	48.27
Gini index of inequality, 2010* Source: Coneval, 2012	0.46	0.46
% population employed in agriculture, 2010* Source: INEGI, 2010 Population Census	47.52	35.93

(continued)

TABLE G.1 *(continued)*

	Michoacán Tierra Caliente (border municipalities)	Guerrero Tierra Caliente (border municipalities)
% municipal income from local taxes, 2007–2011* Source: INEGI, Public Finance Statistics	0.58	1.05
Political		
Leftist governor	YES (2007–2011)	YES (2005–2011)
% PRD municipalities from sample** Source: State Electoral Institutes	2008–2011: 12.50	2009–2012: 14.29
% PRI municipalities from sample** Source: State Electoral Institutes	2008–2011: 75.00	2009–2012: 71.43
% PAN municipalities from sample** Source: State Electoral Institutes	2008–2011: 12.50	2009–2012: 14.29
Subnational election cycle (2011)	• Governor • 40 State legislators • 113 Mayors	• Governor
Narco activity		
Cartel presence & inter-cartel conflict	• La Familia Michoacana • Sinaloa Cartel	• La Familia Michoacana • Sinaloa Cartel
Drug-related murder rate per 10,000 pop., 2007–2011* Source: CVM Dataset	4.65	9.11
Drug trafficking region	YES	YES
Marijuana crop eradication by federal govt, 2007–2010 (hectares)* Source: Sedena, 2015	221.83	30.35
Poppy crop eradication by federal govt, 2007–2010 (hectares)* Source: Sedena, 2015	1.43	416.91
High-profile criminal attacks, 2007–2010 Source: CAPAM Dataset	7	9
High-profile criminal attacks, 2011 Source: CAPAM Dataset	8	1

* Regional mean (includes only the municipalities under analysis).
** The sample includes the municipalities under analysis shown in Map 6.2. in the main text.

taxing capacities and are by default equally dependent on fiscal transfers from the federal government. Politically, both states have a long leftist tradition, and in 2011 both were ruled by governors from the leftist PRD. At a more local level, Tierra Caliente municipalities on both sides of the border have been ruled by elected officials from the PRI and the PRD, and the conservative PAN has had a very limited presence.

Tierra Caliente is known as a violent region that became a focal point for drug production (marijuana and poppy), drug trafficking (marijuana and poppy), and deadly inter-cartel wars in the 2000s (Zepeda 2018). La Familia Michoacana had been the dominant cartel on the Michoacán side of the border, and the Sinaloa Cartel first and, later, breakaways from the Sinaloans dominated the Guerrero side of the border (Grillo 2011). By 2010, however, municipalities from both sides of the state border were immersed in major turf wars: La Familia Michoacana against the Sinaloa Cartel on the Michoacán side and La Familia against breakaways from the Sinaloans on the Guerrero side (Kyle 2015). As the evidence from CVM reported in Table G.1 reveals, inter-cartel violence has been more intense among the Tierra Caliente municipalities of Guerrero, but evidence from CAPAM shows that prior to 2011, municipalities from both sides of the state borders had similar histories of criminal attacks against local government authorities and party candidates. Taking a national view, this was one of Mexico's deadliest regions for mayors and local party candidates.

Despite multiple similarities, Tierra Caliente municipalities from the two states had one significant difference: in 2011 Michoacán had a full subnational election cycle (governor, state legislature, and mayors), while Guerrero had a partial cycle (governor). Although there was a long history of criminal attacks against municipal authorities and local party candidates in both regions, in 2011 the Michoacán municipalities experienced eight times more attacks than their Guerrero counterparts. As Table G.1 shows, this gap remains significantly large even if we weight the number of attacks by population size. As we argue in Chapter 6, we attribute this gap in attacks to the opportunities that a full subnational election cycle opened in Michoacán in 2011 – including the election of 113 new mayors – but not in Guerrero.

Note that although peasants and OCGs on both sides of the state borders are engaged in marijuana and poppy cultivation, the evidence from crop eradication reported in Table G.1 could be considered as a partial indication that poppy cultivation is significantly greater in the Guerrero municipalities than in Michoacán. To be sure, only some parts of the territory of three of the municipalities in our sample (Coyuca de Catalán, Pungarabato, and Ajuchitlán) are part of the "opium pentagon" – a major mountainous area of poppy cultivation in the western and central part of Guerrero (Témeris and Espino 2015). This difference in poppy cultivation across regions should not be a major concern for two reasons. First, a significant share of the poppy produced in the Guerrero municipalities is processed into heroin in the Tierra Caliente region of Michoacán and subsequently shipped into the US. Since both regions are involved in the production of heroin – one cultivating the plant and the other processing it into an illegal drug – differences between both regions become less salient. Second, due to the heavy involvement of the three Guerrero municipalities in the cultivation of poppy – a much more profitable illicit crop than marijuana – we would expect to see more, not fewer, attacks at any time on the Guerrero side than on the Michoacán side. And yet, in 2011 due to differences in the subnational election cycles, we saw exactly the opposite: a significantly higher number of attacks in Michoacán.

Following the discussion about the four challenges to a natural experiment outlined in Appendix E, we need to address how this natural experiment confronts potential problems of unbalanced factors; discard the lack of an independent effect of our treatment; evaluate the existence of additional intervening variables; and assess challenges of self-selection.

First, as we described above, municipalities in the Tierra Caliente region on both sides of the Michoacán–Guerrero border are largely balanced on different dimensions that may be affecting the display of high-profile violence, including the partisan affiliation of subnational authorities – a crucial explanatory factor in our analysis. In fact, both states experienced the end of PRI hegemony and party alternation (leftist governors were elected) with only a three-year difference. Second, because election calendars are fixed, and such electoral cycles are not dictated by the dynamics of violence, we can claim that the local election in Michoacán had an independent effect on the number of attacks experienced in the state's Tierra Caliente municipalities. Relatedly, because municipalities cannot autonomously define their electoral calendars, we can disregard possible concerns about self-selection processes of the municipalities under study in the Tierra Caliente region that could have affected the timing of high-profile attacks on each side of the border. In other words, parties and candidates in Tierra Caliente municipalities in

Guerrero were unable to manipulate electoral calendars to prevent attacks.

MICHOACÁN AND GUANAJUATO

As shown in Map 6.3, Chapter 6, we use municipalities located across the state borders of Michoacán and Guanajuato to isolate the likely impact of vertical party fragmentation on criminal attacks against local government officials, party candidates, and party activists. Table G.2 reports detailed information about these two regions. The data reveal that the municipalities across the state borders share multiple similarities and constitute a homogeneous region that happens to be separated by state borders. Note, again, that the table reports information that may not be directly relevant to the study of criminal attacks but that nonetheless helps us make the point that we are comparing municipalities that constitute a self-contained region due to a number of geographic, sociodemographic, cultural, and economic similarities.

Northern Michoacán and southern Guanajuato are part of the Bajío region and share multiple characteristics, including their deep engagement in the Cristero Movement – the Catholic rural militias that fought against the anti-clerical laws that resulted from the 1910 Mexican Revolution and the 1917 constitution (Meyer 1976). As shown in Table G.2, municipalities in both regions have a high elevation and are located at a relatively short distance to their states' capitals. While municipalities in Guanajuato are more populated than in Michoacán, there is a similar distribution of rural population and a majority of Catholics on both sides of the state border. Roughly one-quarter of the population in both northern Michoacán and southern Guanajuato are employed in agriculture. Approximately one-quarter of the population on both sides of the border live under conditions of poverty. Inequality, as measured by the Gini index, is practically identical in both regions. Taxing capacities among municipalities from northern Michoacán and southern Guanajuato are weak and are (roughly) equally dependent on federal fiscal transfers.

Although La Familia Michoacana's main bastions were in southern Michoacán, particularly in the Tierra Caliente region, the cartel had a strong presence in the state's northern municipalities and had made important inroads into southern Guanajuato starting in 2005. In the context of the main battles between La Familia and the Zetas – the private militia of the Gulf Cartel that became an independent cartel – for the control over Michoacán (Grillo 2011), the municipalities of northern

Appendix G

TABLE G.2 *Comparison of Border Municipalities of Michoacán and Guanajuato*

	Michoacán Northern Region (border municipalities)	Guanajuato Southern Region (border municipalities)
Geographic		
Altitude* Measured in meters above sea level (masl) Source: INEGI	1,938.12	1,792.73
Distance from state capital* Linear distance (km)	64.97	86.12
Distance from state capital* Driving distance (km)	94.73	124.45
Sociodemographic		
Municipal population, 2010* Source: INEGI, 2010 Population Census	28,057	88,754
% indigenous population, 2010* Source: INEGI, 2010 Population Census	0.23	0.15
% youth, aged 15–39, 2010* Source: INEGI, 2010 Population Census	17.51	17.45
% international migrants, 2010* Mexicans who were international migrants in 2005 but counted in 2010 Census Source: INEGI, 2010 Population Census	0.03	0.01
% population living in rural localities, 2010* Localities with 2,500 inhabitants or fewer Source: INEGI, 2010 Population Census	59.44	45.84
% Catholic, 2010 Source: INEGI, 2010 Population Census	95.57	94.70

(continued)

TABLE G.2 *(continued)*

	Michoacán Northern Region (border municipalities)	Guanajuato Southern Region (border municipalities)
Economic		
Poverty, 2010* Source: Conapo, 2011 Marginality Index, Rescaled 0–100	29.97	26.31
Gini index of inequality, 2010* Source: Coneval, 2012	0.40	0.41
% population employed in agriculture, 2010* Source: INEGI, 2010 Population Census	29.56	21.76
% municipal income from local taxes, 2007–2011* Source: INEGI, Public Finance Statistics	2.71	5.05
Political		
Governor's party	PRD (2007–2011)	PAN (2006–2011)
% PRD municipalities from sample** Source: State Electoral Institutes	2005–2007: 46.87 2008–2011: 59.37 **Average: 53.12**	2007–2009: 4.50 2010–2012: 13.64 **Average: 9.07**
% PRI municipalities from sample** Source: State Electoral Institutes	2005–2007: 46.87 2008–2011: 25.00 **Average: 35.94**	2007–2009: 27.27 2010–2012: 36.36 **Average: 31.82**
% PAN municipalities from sample** Source: State Electoral Institutes	2005–2007: 6.25 2008–2011: 15.62 **Average: 10.93**	2007–2009: 68.18 2010–2012: 50 **Average: 59.09**
Narco activity		
Cartel presence & inter-cartel conflict	La Familia Michoacana Zetas	La Familia Michoacana Zetas
Drug-related murder rate per 10,000 pop., 2007–2011* Source: CVM Dataset	0.76	0.51
Drug trafficking region	YES	YES
Marijuana crop eradication, 2007–2010 (hectares)* Source: Sedena, 2015	3.49	0.17

(continued)

TABLE G.2 *(continued)*

	Michoacán Northern Region (border municipalities)	Guanajuato Southern Region (border municipalities)
Poppy crop eradication, 2007–2010 (hectares)* Source: Sedena, 2015	0.02	0
High-profile criminal attacks, 2008–2011 Source: CAPAM Dataset	5	1

* Regional mean (includes only the municipalities under analysis).
** The sample includes the municipalities under analysis shown in Map 6.3 in the main text.

Michoacán and southern Guanajuato represented the front door to La Familia's domain and both cartels fought fierce battles to control this strategic entry point (Álvarez 2009; Espinosa 2012). As the data in Table G.2 show, these were not drug cultivation regions but drug trafficking corridors. Between 2008 and 2011, inter-cartel and state–cartel violence across state borders were equally intense – although not nearly as intense as in the Tierra Caliente region.

Politically, one major difference between both regions is that from 2008 until 2011 municipalities from northern Michoacán were under the rule of a leftist PRD governor, while southern Guanajuato municipalities were under the rule of a PAN conservative governor. As shown in Table G.2, the political landscape in the municipalities was another important difference. While in Michoacán, the PRD (53 percent) and the PRI (35 percent) were the dominant political forces and the PAN had a limited presence (11 percent), in Guanajuato the PAN (59 percent) and the PRI (32 percent) were the leading forces and the PRD had a limited presence (9 percent). Using the categories of party layering proposed in Chapters 4 and 6, this means that most municipalities in Michoacán belonged to the PAN-PRD-PRD and PAN-PRD-PRI layers. In contrast, most cases in Guanajuato belonged to the PAN-PAN-PAN and PAN-PAN-PRI layers.

In terms of criminal violence, a major difference between regions is that between 2008 and 2011, municipalities from northern Michoacán experienced a significantly larger number of high-profile attacks than their neighboring municipalities of Guanajuato. This gap remains equally large whether we use absolute numbers or per capita numbers of attacks. As we discussed in Chapter 6, after isolating partisan vertical fragmentation as an important difference across otherwise nearly identical municipalities separated by state borders, we attributed differences in attacks to different patterns of partisan fragmentation. First, despite multiple similarities, municipalities from this region belonged to states with different governors. Michoacán municipalities belonged to a state where a conservative federal government was engaged in a major political conflict with a leftist governor and as a result local officials facing criminal threats were left unprotected by the federation (see the Michoacán case study in Chapter 7). In contrast, Guanajuato municipalities belonged to a state where a conservative federal government and a conservative governor closely cooperated to deter high-profile criminal attacks (Univisión 2009; Álvarez 2011; El Sol del Bajío 2011; Excélsior 2011). Second, consistent with our statistical findings reported in Chapter 6, the micro comparison across borders confirms that within leftist states, leftist PRD and PRI municipalities experienced a higher probability of attacks than PAN municipalities.

As we discussed in Appendix E, a natural experiment design must identify possible alternative mechanisms that may have intervened in the divergent outcomes in each control and treatment group. In this case, we must make sure that other intervening variables or processes – related or unrelated to our key explanatory variable, the governor's partisanship – do not lead to the differences in high-profile attacks that we observe in northern Michoacán and southern Guanajuato.

The state of Guanajuato has been governed by the PAN since 1991, while the PRD won Michoacán's gubernatorial seat in 2002. However, the divergent tenures of the ruling parties in each state are not the underlying cause behind the contrasting number of attacks among the two groups of bordering municipalities under analysis. More specifically, the PAN's longer tenure in Guanajuato did not result in more stable criminal markets than in Michoacán. As noted in Chapter 5, it is important to consider that although Guanajuato was not a major drug trafficking zone in the 1990s, it became a contested territory when the Zetas, in alliance with La Familia Michoacana, went to war against the Sinaloans over the control of the state of Michoacán, Guanajuato's southern neighbor. Violence in Michoacán and in the southern tip of Guanajuato grew exponentially in the mid-2000s, as the Zetas broke their initial alliance with La Familia Michoacana. By 2007, the southern region of Guanajuato experienced twice as many organized crime-related murders (22) as the rest of the municipalities in the state (11).[1] Therefore, we can exclude the possibility that the longer tenure of the PAN in Guanajuato's gubernatorial seat resulted in a relatively more stable criminal market and therefore a lower number of high-profile attacks, compared to Michoacán, where the PRD had governed for just six years before our study period here (2008–2011).

An additional potential challenge we need to address is the role of military interventions in each state. During the Calderón administration, there were eight main military campaigns, one of which was deployed in the state of Michoacán. Although Calderón did not adopt a full-blown military campaign for Guanajuato, as we show in Chapter 5, the military was deployed and actively engaged in combat against cartels in Guanajuato's southern border (Escalante 2008). Therefore, both states experienced a military intervention, but what was different was the nature of these interventions. While the army and federal, state, and municipal police forces were highly coordinated in Guanajuato, the federal government did not share any security information with Michoacán's PRD state government. We attribute this to the politicized (partisan) nature of the military intervention, rather than to the presence (or absence) of a military campaign. Such politicization significantly increased high-profile attacks in Michoacán, but not in Guanajuato. Finally, we find no evidence of self-selection: the relatively small size of the electorate from the selected municipalities on each side of the state borders could not define the gubernatorial election outcome. Therefore, the election of a PAN governor in Guanajuato and a PRD governor in Michoacán is exogenous to the particular social processes within these municipalities. In sum, we can safely conclude that the partisanship of the governors in Michoacán and Guanajuato had an independent causal effect on high-profile attacks in their neighboring municipalities.

---

[1] Data are derived from the CVM Database, but other sources confirm the same ratio of homicides between both regions in Guanajuato state.

References

Abadie, Alberto, Alexis Diamond, and Jens Hainmueller. 2015. "Comparative Politics and the Synthetic Control Method," *American Journal of Political Science* 59(2): 495–510.

Acemoglu, Daron, James A. Robinson, and Rafael J. Santos. 2013. "The Monopoly of Violence: Evidence from Colombia," *Journal of the European Economic Association* 11(1): 5–44.

Aguayo, Sergio, Delia Sánchez, Manuel Pérez, and Jacobo Dayán. 2016. *En el Desamparo: Los Zetas, el Estado, la sociedad y las víctimas de San Fernando, Tamaulipas (2010) y Allende, Coahuila (2011)*. Mexico City: El Colegio de México and CEAV.

Aguilar, Andro. 2011. "Militarizan mandos policiales ... y nada," *Reforma*, April 7.

Aguilar, Rubén and Jorge Castañeda. 2009. *El Narco: La Guerra Fallida*. Mexico City: Punto de Lectura.

Albarracín, Juan. 2018. "Criminalized Electoral Politics. The Socio-Political Foundations of Electoral Coercion in Democratic Brazil," Ph.D. Thesis, University of Notre Dame.

Albertus, Michael. 2015. *Autocracy and Redistribution: The Politics of Land Reform*. Cambridge: Cambridge University Press.

Alegre, Luis. 2004. "Exige Fox sustentar acusaciones ante PGR," *Reforma*, April 16.

Alesina, Alberto, Salvatore Piccolo, and Paolo Pinotti. 2019. "Organized Crime, Violence, and Politics," *The Review of Economic Studies* 86(2): 457–499.

Allum, Felia, Rosella Merlino, and Alessandro Colletti. 2019. "Facilitating the Italian Mafia: The Grey Zone of Complicity and Collusion," *South European Society and Politics* 24(1): 79–101.

Álvarez, Xóchitl. 2009. "Violencia en Guanajuato por venganza de narcos," *El Universal*, November 23.

Álvarez, Xóchitl. 2011. "Guanajuato investiga a 66 agentes por narco," *El Universal*, May 13.

Animal Político. 2011. "Los medios están satanizando a Apatzingán: Genaro Guizar, alcalde," *Animal Político*, August 5, www.animalpolitico.com/2011/o 8/%E2%80%9Clos-medios-estan-satanizando-a-apatzingan%E2%80%9D-g enaro-guizar-alcalde/. Accessed December 4, 2019.

Animal Político. 2019. "Hay más de 40 mil desaparecidos y 36 mil muertos sin identificar en México, reconoce Gobernación," *Animal Político*, 17 January, www.animalpolitico.com/2019/01/40-mil-desaparecidos-mexico-victimas-sin-identificar/. Accessed December 4, 2019.

Aparicio, Javier. 2009. "Análisis estadístico de la elección presidencial de 2006: ¿Fraude o errores aleatorios?" *Política y Gobierno*, Special Issue: 225–243.

Aranda, Jesús. 2002. "Sabía alto mando de los ilícitos de Quirós," *La Jornada*, August 12, www.jornada.com.mx/2002/08/12/012n1pol.php?print ver=o. Accessed December 4, 2019.

Araujo, Brisa. 2013. "Te sumas al narco, te vas, o te mueres: desplazados en Guerrero," desinformémonos, July 28, https://desinformemonos.org/te-sumas-al-narco-te-vas-o-te-mueres-desplazados-en-guerrero/. Accessed December 4, 2019.

Arellano, Alberto. 2011. "Los gobiernos panistas en Jalisco," *Espacios Públicos* 14(30): 138–154.

Arias, Enrique Desmond. 2006a. "The Dynamics of Criminal Governance: Networks and Social Order in Rio de Janeiro," *Journal of Latin American Studies* 38(2): 293–325.

Arias, Enrique Desmond. 2006b. "Faith in Our Neighbors: Networks and Social Order in Three Brazilian Favelas," *Latin American Politics and Society* 46(1): 1–38.

Arias, Enrique Desmond. 2009. "Dispatches from the Field: Milícias and Police Corruption in Rio de Janeiro," *Americas Quarterly* 3(2): 90–93.

Arias, Enrique Desmond. 2017. *Criminal Enterprises and Governance in Latin America and the Caribbean*. New York: Cambridge University Press.

Arias, Enrique D. and Daniel Goldstein. 2010. *Violent Democracies in Latin America*. Durham, NC: Duke University Press.

Arjona, Ana. 2016. *Rebelocracy: Social Order in the Colombian Civil War*. Cambridge: Cambridge University Press.

Arjona, Ana, Nelson Kasfir, and Zachariah Mampilly (eds.). 2015. *Rebel Governance in Civil War*. Cambridge: Cambridge University Press.

Arroyo, Javier. 2008. "Complace respuesta de la Federación," *El Diario*, March 28.

Aristegui Noticias. 2015. "Gobierno federal simula seguridad en la Tierra Caliente de Guerrero," Aristegui Noticias, December 3, http://aristeguinoticias .com/0312/mexico/gobierno-federal-simula-seguridad-en-la-tierra-caliente-de-guerrero-parte-i/. Accessed December 17, 2019.

Astorga, Luis. 2005. *El Siglo de las Drogas: El Narcotráfico, del Porfiriato al Nuevo Milenio*. Mexico City: Plaza y Janés.

Astorga, Luis and David A. Shirk. 2010. "Drug trafficking organizations and counter-drug strategies in the U.S.–Mexican context," *Mexico Institute of the Woodrow Wilson International Center*, Working Paper Series, January 2010.

Atuesta, Laura. 2017. "Militarización de la lucha contra el narcotráfico: los operativos militares como estrategia para el combate al crimen organizado," in Laura Atuesta and Alejandro Madrazo Lajous (eds.), *Las violencias: en busca de la política pública detrás de la guerra contra las drogas*. Mexico City: Editorial CIDE Coyuntura y Ensayo.

Atuesta, Laura H. and Aldo F. Ponce. 2017. "Meet the Narco: Increased Competition among Criminal Organisations and the Explosion of Violence in Mexico," *Global Crime* 18(4): 375–402.

Atuesta, Laura, Oscar Sordia, and Alejandro Madrazo. 2018. "The War on Drugs in Mexico: (Official) Dataset of Events between December 2006 and November 2011," *Journal of Conflict Resolution* (December 25): 1–25.

Auyero, Javier. 2006. "The Political Makings of the 2001 Lootings in Argentina," *Journal of Latin American Studies* 38(2): 241–265.

Aviña, Alexander. 2018. "A War Against Poor People: Dirty Wars and Drug Wars in 1970s Mexico," in Jaime M. Pensado and Enrique C. Ochoa (eds.), *Mexico Beyond 1968*. Palo Alto, CA: Stanford University Press.

Aziz Nassif, Alberto. 2012. "Violencias en el Norte de México: el caso de Ciudad Juárez," *Revista Iberoamericana* 12(48): 143–155.

Bagley, Bruce. 2011. "Carteles de la Droga: De Medellín a Sinaloa," *Criterios* 4 (1): 233–247.

Bagley, Bruce. 2012. *Drug-trafficking and Organized Crime in the Americas*. Washington, DC: Woodrow Wilson Center Update on the Americas.

Bailey, John and Matthew M. Taylor. 2009. "Evade, Corrupt, or Confront? Organized Crime and the State in Brazil and Mexico," *Journal of Politics in Latin America* 1(2): 3–29.

Barajas, Abel. 2009. "Indaga PGR fuga … ¡de video!," *Reforma*, May 23.

Baranda, Antonio. 2014. "Eliminan (ahora sí) al 'Chayo'," *Reforma*, March 9.

Barnes, Nicholas. 2017. "Criminal Politics: An Integrated Approach to the Study of Organized Crime, Politics, and Violence," *Perspectives on Politics* 15(4): 967–987.

Becerra, Lorena and Mariana Meza. 2015. "Violencia y votos: el caso de Michoacán," *Animal Político*, June 3, www.animalpolitico.com/tanque-pensante/violencia-y-votos-el-caso-de-michoacan/. Accessed December 4, 2019.

Becerra, Ricardo, Pedro Salazar, and José Woldenberg. 2001. *La mecánica del cambio político en México*. Mexico City: Cal y Arena.

Becker, Gary S. 1968. "Crime and Punishment: An Economic Approach," *Journal of Political Economy* 76(2): 169–217.

Beer, Caroline. 2003. *Electoral Competition and Institutional Change in Mexico*. Notre Dame, IN: University of Notre Dame Press.

Beltrán, Adriana. 2008. "The captive state: organized crime and human rights in Latin America," *WOLA*, February 28.

Berg, Louis-Alexandre and Marlon Carranza. 2018. "Organized Criminal Violence and Territorial Control: Evidence from Northern Honduras," *Journal of Peace Research* 55(5): 566–581.

Bergman, Marcelo. 2018. *More Money, More Crime: Prosperity and Rising Crime in Latin America*. Oxford: Oxford University Press.

Blancornelas, Jesús. 2002. *El Cártel. Los Arellano Félix, la mafia más poderosa en la historia de América Latina*. Mexico City: DeBolsillo.

Blaydes, Lisa. 2010. *Elections and Distributive Politics in Mubarak's Egypt.* Cambridge: Cambridge University Press.

Blume, Laura. 2017. "The Old Rules No Longer Apply: Explaining Narco-Assassinations of Mexican Politicians," *Journal of Politics in Latin America* 9(1): 59–90.

Braga, Anthony, Rod Brunson, and Kevin Drakulich. 2019. "Race, Place, and Effective Policing," *Annual Review of Sociology* 45: 535–555.

Bravo Regidor, Carlos. 2011. "La 'guerra' en el discurso presidencial," *La Razón,* January 31.

Brenneman, Robert. 2013. *Homies and Hermanos: God and Gangs in Central America.* Oxford: Oxford University Press.

Bruhn, Kathleen and Kenneth Greene. 2007. "Elite Polarization Meets Mass Moderation in Mexico's 2006 Elections," *PS: Political Science and Politics* 40 (1): 33–38.

Buchanan, James M. 1973. "A Defense of Organized Crime?," in Simon Rottenberg (ed.), *The Economics of Crime and Punishment.* Washington, DC: American Enterprise Institute for Public Policy Research.

Burt, Jo-Marie. 2009. "Guilty as Charged: The Trial of Former Peruvian President Alberto Fujimori for Human Rights Violations," *International Journal of Transitional Justice* 3(1): 384–405.

Caldeira, Teresa and James Holston. 1999. "Democracy and Violence in Brazil," *Comparative Studies in Society and History* 41(4): 691–729.

Calderón, Gabriela, Gustavo Robles, Alberto Díaz-Cayeros, and Beatriz Magaloni. 2015. "The Beheading of Criminal Organizations and the Dynamics of Violence in Mexico," *Journal of Conflict Resolution* 59(8): 1455–1485.

Calderón, Verónica and Paula Chouza. 2014. "El narco cobraba el 10% del dinero federal enviado a Michoacán," *El País,* March 14, https://elpais.com/internacional/2014/03/14/actualidad/1394762409_823220.html. Accessed April 7, 2020.

Camp, Roderic Ai. 2005. *Mexico's Military on the Democratic Stage.* Westport, CT: Greenwood Publishing Group.

Carey, Sabine C., Michael P. Colaresi, and Neil J. Mitchell. 2015. "Governments, Informal Links to Militias, and Accountability," *Journal of Conflict Resolution* 59(5): 850–876.

Carrizales, David. 1996. "Renunció Rizzo García en NL," *La Jornada,* April 18, www.jornada.com.mx/1996/04/18/rizzo.html. Accessed December 4, 2019.

Castañón, Araly. 2008. "Acciones del Operativo son deficientes: alcalde," *El Diario,* August 20.

Castañón, Araly and Rocío Gallegos. 2011. "Dejaron huella en Juárez," *El Diario,* November 12.

Castillo García, Gustavo. 2002. "Acosta y Quirós ordenaron asesinar más de 1,500, dice testigo protegido," *La Jornada,* November 18, www.jornada.com.mx/2002/11/18/012n1pol.php?printver=1. Accessed December 17, 2019.

Cedillo, Adela. 2019. "Intersections Between the Dirty War and the War on Drugs in Northwestern Mexico (1969–1985)," Ph.D. Dissertation, University of Wisconsin-Madison.

Centro de Derechos Humanos Fray Francisco de Vitoria, *Paz y Justicia*, multiple years, 1988–1998.

Cervantes, Miguel. 2007. "Designan a military en Policía de BC," *Reforma*, December 6.

Chacón, Mario. 2018. "In the line of fire: political violence and decentralization in Colombia," *NYU–Abu Dhabi*, Working Paper, July, 2018, https://papers .ssrn.com/sol3/papers.cfm?abstract_id=2386667. Accessed December 4, 2019.

Clunan, Anne and Harold Trinkunas. 2010. *Ungoverned Spaces? Territorial Statehood, Contested Authority, and Softened Sovereignty*. Stanford, CA: Stanford University Press.

Collier, Paul. 2000. "Rebellion as a Quasi-Criminal Activity," *Journal of Conflict Resolution* 44(6): 839–853.

Comisión Nacional de Derechos Humanos (CNDH). 2009. Recommendation 72/ 2009, CNDH, October 30, www.cndh.org.mx/sites/default/files/doc/Recomen daciones/2009/REC_2009_072.pdf. Accessed December 4, 2019.

Committee to Protect Journalists (CPJ). 2017. "No excuse: Mexico must break cycle of impunity in journalists' murders," May 3, https://cpj.org/x/6c82. Accessed December 4, 2019.

Conger, Lucy. 2014. "The private sector and public security: the cases of Ciudad Juárez and Monterrey," *Wilson Center-University of San Diego*, Working Paper Series on Civic Engagement and Public Security in Mexico, March 2014.

Consejo Nacional de Evaluación de la Política de Desarrollo Social (CONEVAL). 2012. Informe de pobreza y evaluación de las entidades federativas 2010–2012. CONEVAL, www.coneval.org.mx/coordinacion/entidades/Paginas/Informes-de-pobreza-y-evaluación-2010–2012.aspx. Accessed December 18, 2019.

Consejo Nacional de Población (CONAPO). 2010. Índice de marginación de CONAPO. 2010. CONAPO, www.conapo.gob.mx/es/CONAPO/Indices_de_Ma rginacion_2010_por_entidad_federativa_y_municipio. Accessed December 18, 2019.

Contreras, Karina. 2012. "Todos sabemos lo de los halcones porque es cierto: Walton," *El Sur*, August 3.

Corchado, Alfredo and Ricardo Sandoval. 2004. "Gang linked to serial killing," *The Dallas Morning News*, May 2, www.google.com/amp/s/www.sun-sentinel.com/news/fl-xpm-2004-05-02-0405010393-story,amp.html. Accessed December 17, 2019.

Corcoran, Patrick. 2011. "Guatemalan mayoral candidate killed," InSight Crime: Organized Crime in the Americas, June.

Córdova, Abby. 2019. "Living in Gang-Controlled Neighborhoods: Impacts on Electoral and Nonelectoral Participation in El Salvador," *Latin American Research Review* 54(1): 201–221.

Cornelius, Wayne A. and David A. Shirk (eds.). 2007. *Reforming the Administration of Justice in Mexico*. La Jolla and Notre Dame: Center for US–Mexican Studies and Notre Dame University Press.

Corpus, Aline. 2008. "Dimite funcionaria acusada por Aponte," *Reforma*, May 8.

Correa-Cabrera, Guadalupe. 2017. *The Zetas Inc.: Criminal Corporations, Energy, and Civil War in Mexico*. Austin, TX: The University of Texas Press.

Cox, Gary W. and Mathew D. McCubbins. 1986. "Electoral Politics as a Redistributive Game," *Journal of Politics* 48(2): 370–389.

Cribb, Robert. 2009. "Introduction: Parapolitics, Shadow Governance and Criminal Sovereignty," in Eric Wilson and Tim Lindsey (eds.), *Government of the Shadows. Parapolitics and Criminal Sovereignty.* New York: Pluto Press.

Crónica. 2002. "Asume Cárdenas Batel como Gobernador de Michoacán," *Crónica*, February 15, www.cronica.com.mx/notas/2002/5376.html. Accessed December 4, 2019.

Cruz, José Miguel. 2011. "Criminal Violence and Democratization in Central America: The Survival of the Violent State," *Latin American Politics and Society* 53(4): 1–33.

Dal Bó, Ernesto, Pedro Dal Bó, and Rafael Di Tella. 2006. "Plata o Plomo?: Bribe and Punishment in a Theory of Political Influence," *American Political Science Review* 100(1): 41–53.

Data Cívica. 2017. "Personas Desaparecidas," Data Cívica, http://personasdesaparecidas.mx/db/db. Accessed December 4, 2019.

Dávila, Patricia. 2014. "Un mapa criminal de todos conocido," *Proceso*, November 1. www.proceso.com.mx/386442/un-mapa-criminal-de-todos-conocido. Accessed December 19, 2019.

Davis, Diane. 2006. "Undermining the Rule of Law: Democratization and the Dark Side of Police Reform in Mexico," *Latin American Politics and Society* 48 (1): 55–86.

Daxecker, Ursula E. and Brandon C. Prins. 2016. "The Politicization of Crime: Electoral Competition and the Supply of Maritime Piracy in Indonesia," *Public Choice* 169: 375–393.

de Castro, Rodrigo and Juan Gasparini. 2000. *La delgada línea blanca.* Buenos Aires: Ediciones B.

de Loza, Isaak. 2010. "Realiza PGR operativos en Guadalajara," *El Informador*, May 2010.

Díaz, Leticia. 2011. "Guerrero: Las comunidades se quedan solas," *Proceso*, June 24.

Díaz-Cayeros, Alberto. 2006. *Federalism, Fiscal Authority, and Centralization in Latin America.* Cambridge: Cambridge University Press.

Dickenson, Matthew. 2014. "The Impact of Leadership Removal on Mexican Drug Trafficking Organizations," *Journal of Quantitative Criminology* 30(4): 651–676.

Díez, Jordi. 2008. "Legislative Oversight of the Armed Forces in Mexico," *Mexican Studies* 24(1): 113–145.

Díez, Jordi. 2012. "Civil–Military Relations in Mexico: The Unfinished Transition," in Roderic Ai Camp (ed.), *The Oxford Handbook of Mexican Politics.* New York: Oxford University Press.

Dube, Arindrajit, Oeindrila Dube, and Omar García-Ponce. 2013. "Cross-border Spillover: US Gun Laws and Violence in Mexico," *American Political Science Review* 107(3): 397–417.

Dunning, Thad. 2008. "Improving Causal Inference: Strengths and Limitations of Natural Experiments," *Political Research Quarterly* 61(2): 282–293.

Durán-Martínez, Angélica. 2018. *The Politics of Drug Violence: Criminals, Cops and Politicians in Colombia and Mexico*. Oxford: Oxford University Press.

Durkheim, Emile. [1893] 1964. *The Division of Labor in Society*. New York, NY: Free Press.

Eaton, Kent. 2010. "The Downside of Decentralization: Armed Clientelism in Colombia," *Security Studies* 15(4): 533–562.

Eleazar, Daniel. 1997. "Contrasting Unitary and Federal Systems," *International Political Science Review* 18(3): 237–251.

El Informador. 2012. "Policía de Acapulco reconoce 'posible' infiltración del crimen," *El Informador*, August 1, www.informador.mx/Mexico/Poli cia-de-Acapulco-reconoceposible-infiltracion-del-crimen-20120801–0134.h tml. Accessed December 18, 2019.

El Norte. 1997a. "De Regios," *El Norte*, September 30.

El Norte. 1997b. "Los peros del gabinete," *El Norte*, September 30.

El Sol del Bajío. 2011. "Deslindan al alcalde de Tarandacuao del narco," *El Sol del Bajío*, May 2.

Enciso, Froylán. 2015. *Nuestra historia narcótica: Pasajes para (re) legalizar las drogas en México*. Mexico City: Debate.

English, T. J. 2007. *The Havana Mob: Gangsters, Gamblers, Showgirls and Revolutionaries in 1950s Cuba*. Edinburgh and London: Mainstream Publishing.

Escalante, Jorge. 2008. "Integran a Ejército en operativos," *Mural*, March 25.

Espinosa, Valeria and Donald Rubin. 2015. "Did the Military Interventions in the Mexican Drug War Increase Violence?," *The American Statistician* 69(1): 17–27.

Espinosa, Verónica. 2011. "El 'guanajuatazo'," *Proceso*, July 2.

Espinosa, Verónica. 2012. "Operan en Guanajuato cinco cárteles: Procuraduría," *Proceso*, March 16.

Esteban, Rogelio. 2014. "Infiltrada por el crimen la policía de 11 municipios de Guerrero," *Milenio*, October 6.

Excélsior. 2011. "Detienen a 130 policías de Acámbaro por nexos con el Narco," *Excélsior*, May 4.

Fajnzylber, Pablo, Daniel Lederman, and Norman Loayza. 2002. "Inequality and Violent Crime," *Journal of Law and Economics* 45(1): 1–40.

Fearon, James. 1995. "Rationalist Explanations for War," *International Organization* 49(3): 379–414.

Fearon, James D. and David D. Laitin. 2003. "Ethnicity, Insurgency, and Civil War," *American Political Science Review* 97(1): 75–90.

Ferrer, Eduardo and Ernesto Martínez. 2010. "Oleada de Asaltos en Apatzingán mientras la policía se ubicaba," *La Jornada*, December 14, www .jornada.com.mx/2010/12/14/politica/005n1pol. Accessed April 7, 2020.

Financial Times. 2005. "Mexico's own goal: prosecuting the capital city's mayor will damage democracy," *The Financial Times*, April 7.

Fiorentini, Gianluca and Sam Peltzman (eds.). 1995. *The Economics of Organized Crime*. Cambridge: Cambridge University Press.

Flávia, Marreiro y Xosé Hermida. 2018. "Conmoción en Brasil por el asesinato de Marielle Franco, concejal y activista de Río," *El País*, March 2018, https://elpais.com/internacional/2018/03/15/actualidad/15210 80376_531337.html. Accessed December 18, 2019.

Flom, Hernán. 2019. "State Regulation of Organized Crime: Politicians, Police, and Drug Trafficking in Argentina." *Latin American Politics and Society* 6(3): 104–128.

Flores, Ezequiel. 2018. "Con René Juárez Cisneros el narco sentó sus reales en Guerrero," *Proceso*, May 3, www.proceso.com.mx/532715/con-rene-juarez-cisneros-el-narco-sento-sus-reales-en-guerrero. Accessed December 4, 2019.

Flores, Sergio. 2006a. "Desconoce Salgado Macedonio a Calderón," *Reforma*, September 8.

Flores, Sergio. 2006b. "Pretende Salgado coordinarse con AMLO," *Reforma*, September 21.

Flores, Sergio. 2007. "Desconoce Salgado operativo en Acapulco," *Reforma*, January 10.

Flores, Sergio and J. Guerrero. 2006. "No soy 'Rambo', revira Salgado," *Reforma*, July 1.

Flores-Macías, Gustavo A. 2018. "The Consequences of Militarizing Anti-Drug Efforts for State Capacity in Latin America: Evidence from Mexico," *Comparative Politics* 51(1): 1–20

Fox, Sean R. and Kristian Hoelscher. 2012. "Political Order, Development and Social Violence," *Journal of Peace Research* 49(3): 431–444.

Frantz, Erica. 2018. "The Legacy of Military Dictatorship: Explaining Violent Crime in Democracies," *International Political Science Review* 40(3): 1–15.

Fregoso, Juliana. 2017. "México: 16 ex gobernadores investigados por corrupción y la pregunta por la ruta del dinero," Infobae, 22 April, www.infobae.com/am erica/mexico/2017/04/22/mexico-16-ex-gobernadores-investigados-por-corrup cion-y-la-pregunta-por-la-ruta-del-dinero/. Accessed December 18, 2019.

Gambetta, Diego. 1996. *The Sicilian Mafia: The Business of Private Protection.* Cambridge, MA: Harvard University Press.

Gandhi, Jennifer and Adam Przeworski. 2007. "Authoritarian Institutions and the Survival of Autocrats," *Comparative Political Studies* 40(11): 1279–1301.

García, Adán. 2011. "Dejan contiendas 51 en Michoacán," *Reforma*, October 17.

García, Carola and Leonardo Figueiras. 2006. *Medios de comunicación y campañas electorales (1988–2000).* Mexico City: Plaza y Valdés.

García, Dennis. 2013. "El amor por Sara Cristina Cosío llevó a prisión al Narco de narcos," *Crónica*, August 10, www.cronica.com.mx/notas/2013/774736.html. Accessed December 4, 2019.

García, José. 2008. "Defiende Nati el Operativo NL," *El Norte*, February 18.

García, José. 2010a. "Urge cambiar lucha anticrimen … federal," *El Norte*, June 30.

García, José. 2010b. "Sostienen reunión Medina y Larrazabal," *El Norte*, August 18.

García, José. 2010c. "Asesora Tello Peón a NL," *El Norte*, October 8.

García-Ponce, Omar and Andrés Lajous. 2014. "¿Por qué tardaron tanto en leventarse las autodefensas?," *Nexos: Blog de la redacción*, May 22, https://re daccion.nexos.com.mx/?p=6272. Accessed December 18, 2019.

García Orozco, Rosario. 2015. "Presidentes municipales de Guerrero viven inseguridad: Robell Urióstegui Patiño," *El Financiero*, November 8, www .elfinanciero.com.mx/nacional/presidentes-municipales-de-guerrero-viven-inse guridad-robell-uriostegui-patino. Accessed December 18, 2019.

Garzón, Juan Carlos. 2012. *Mafia & Co.: The Criminal Networks in Mexico, Brazil, and Colombia*. Washington, DC: Woodrow Wilson Center.

Gil, Melina and Julio Pérez. 2012. "Promete Calderón dar apoyo por ataque," *Mural*, March 12.

Gillies, Allan. 2018. "Theorising State–Narco Relations in Bolivia's Nascent Democracy (1982–1993): Governance, Order and Political Transition," *Third World Quarterly* 39(4): 727–746.

Giraudy, Agustina, Eduardo Moncada, and Richard Snyder (eds.). 2019. *Inside Countries: Subnational Research in Comparative Politics*. Cambridge: Cambridge University Press.

Gleditsch, Nils Petter, Havard Strand, Mikael Eriksson, Margareta Sollenberg, and Peter Wallensteen. 2001. "Armed Conflict 1945–99: A New Dataset," *Journal of Peace Research* 39(5): 615–637.

Goertz, Gary. 2017. *Multimethods Research, Causal Mechanisms, and Case Studies: An Integrated Approach*. Princeton, NJ: Princeton University Press.

Golden, Tim. 1993. "Cardinal in Mexico killed in a shooting tied to drug battle," *The New York Times*, May 25, www.nytimes.com/1993/05/25/world/cardinal-in-mexico-killed-in-a-shooting-tied-to-drug-battle.html. Accessed December 4, 2019.

González, Féliz. 2008. "Estado a la Federación: hay que esclarecer ejecuciones," *Norte de Ciudad Juárez*, August 19.

Greene, Kenneth F. 2007. *Why Dominant Parties Lose: Mexico's Democratization in Comparative Perspective*. Cambridge: Cambridge University Press.

Greene, Kenneth F. 2010. "The Political Economy of Authoritarian Single-Party Dominance," *Comparative Political Studies* 43(7): 807–834.

Greitens, Sheena. 2016. *Dictators and their Secret Police: Coercive Institutions and State Violence*. Cambridge: Cambridge University Press.

Grillo, Ioan. 2011. *El Narco: Inside Mexico's Criminal Insurgency*. New York: Bloomsbury Publishing.

Guerrero, Eduardo. 2010. "Pandillas y cárteles: La gran alianza," *Nexos*, June 1, www.nexos.com.mx/?p=13690. Accessed December 4, 2019.

Guerrero, Eduardo. 2011a. "La raíz de la violencia," *Nexos*, June 1, www.nexos.com.mx/?p=14318. Accessed December 4, 2019.

Guerrero, Eduardo. 2011b. *Security, Drugs, and Violence in Mexico: A Survey*. 7th North American Forum. Mexico City: Lantia Consultores.

Guerrero, Eduardo. 2012. "Epidemias de violencia," *Nexos*, July 1.

Guerrero, Eduardo. 2016. "La inseguridad 2013–2015," *Nexos*, January 1.

Guerrero, Eduardo. 2018. "La segunda ola de violencia," *Nexos*, April 1.

Guerrero, Jesús. 2007. "Critican en Guerrero el operativo antinarco," *Reforma*, February 11.

Guerrero, Jesús. 2008. "Denuncia amenazas candidato en Guerrero," *Reforma*, October 1.

Guerrero, Jesús. 2009. "Denuncia el PRD 13 ejecuciones," *Reforma*, July 6.

Guillén, Alejandra, Mago Torres, and Marcela Turati. 2018. "El país de las dos mil fosas," Quinto Elemento Lab. https://quintoelab.org/project/el-pais-de-las-2-mil-fosas. Accessed December 18, 2019.

Gurrea, José Antonio. 2013. "Acapulco tiene miedo; hasta las autoridades renuncian," *El Financiero*, March 11. www.elfinanciero.com.mx/archivo/acapulco-tiene-miedo-hasta-las-autoridades-renuncian. Accessed December 18, 2019.

Gutiérrez, Maribel. 1997. "Caso Aguas Blancas: juicio inconcluso," *La Jornada*, June 29.

Heinle, Kimberly, Octavio Rodríguez Ferreira, and David A. Shirk. 2014. "Drug violence in Mexico. Data and analysis through 2013," Justice in Mexico Project: Special Report, University of San Diego, https://justiceinmexico.org/wp-content/uploads/2014/09/2014_DVM.pdf. Accessed December 4, 2019.

Hernández, Carlos. 2008. "Cambian de estrategia anticrimen," *El Diario*, November 25.

Herrera, Rolando. 2007a. "Enfrenta Salgado amenazas del narco," *Reforma*, January 24.

Herrera, Rolando. 2007b. "Revelan disculpa de la SSP a Félix," *Reforma*, February 17.

Herrera, Rolando. 2011. "Exhiben pleito Medina-Larrazabal y fallas de Calderón en coordinación," *Reforma*, January 13.

Herrera, Rolando and Mayolo López. 2016. "Pidieron a Alcalde hasta apagar la luz," *Reforma*, July 27.

Hidalgo, Jorge Arturo. 2001. "Anuncian megamarcha contra Reforma Fiscal," *Reforma*, September 9.

Hobbes, Thomas. [1651] 1968. *Leviathan*. Baltimore: Penguin Books.

InSight Crime. 2018. "Venezuela: A Mafia State? Venezuela has become a hub of organized crime in the region," InSight Crime, https://es.insightcrime.org/wp-content/uploads/2018/05/Venezuela-a-Mafia-State-InSight-Crime-2018.pdf. Accessed December 4, 2019.

International Crisis Group. 2018. "Building peace in Mexico: dilemmas facing the López Obrador government," Report no. 69/Latin America & Caribbean, October 11. www.crisisgroup.org/latin-america-caribbean/mexico/69-building-peace-mexico-dilemmas-facing-lopez-obrador-government. Accessed December 18, 2019

Iqbal, Zaryab and Christopher Zorn. 2006. "Sic Semper Tyrannis? Power, Repression, and Assassination since the Second World War," *Journal of Politics* 68(3): 489–501.

Jaffe, Rivke. 2013. "The Hybrid State: Crime and Citizenship in Urban Jamaica," *American Ethnologist* 40(4): 734–748.

Jensen, Nathan and Guillermo Rosas. 2007. "Foreign Direct Investment and Income Inequality in Mexico, 1990–2000," *International Organization* 61(03): 467–487.

Jentzsch, Corina, Stathis N. Kalyvas and Livia I. Schubiger. 2015. "Militias in Civil Wars," *Journal of Conflict Resolution* 59(5): 755–769.

Jiménez, Benito. 2009. "Estaban cazando a quien votaba y los intimidaban," *Reforma*, July 6.

Jiménez, Benito and Miguel Cervantes. 2008. "Promete José Osuna depuración," *Reforma*, April 25.

Jones, Nathan. 2013. "The Unintended Consequences of Kingpin Strategies: Kidnap Rates and the Arellano-Félix Organization," *Trends in Organized Crime* 16(2): 156–176.

Juárez, Alfonso. 2016. "Cierran restaurantes en Acapulco por crimen," *Reforma*, March 29.

Kalyvas, Stathis. 2006. *The Logic of Violence in Civil War*. New York: Cambridge University Press.

Kalyvas, Stathis. 2015. "How Civil Wars Help Explain Organized Crime – and How They Do Not," *Journal of Conflict Resolution* 59(8): 1517–1540.

Kalyvas, Stathis and Laia Balcells. 2010. "International System and Technologies of Rebellion: How the End of the Cold War Shaped Internal Conflict," *American Political Science Review* 104(3): 415–429.

Karl, Terry L. 1986. "Imposing Consent: Electoralism Versus Democratization in El Salvador," in Paul Drake and Eduardo Silva (eds.), *Elections in Latin America*. San Diego: University of California Press, pp. 9–36.

Karl, Terry L. 2000. "Electoralism: Why Elections are not Democracy," in Richard Rose (ed.), *The International Encyclopedia of Elections*. Washington, DC: Congressional Quarterly Books.

Klesner, Joseph 2005. "Electoral Competition and the New Party System in Mexico," *Latin American Politics and Society* 47(2): 103–142.

Kocher, Matthew A. and Nuno P. Monteiro. 2016. "Lines of Demarcation: Causation, Design-Based Inference, and Historical Research," *Perspectives on Politics* 14(4): 952–975.

Koonings, Kees and Dirk Kruijt (eds.). 2004. *Organized Violence and State Failure in Latin America*. London: Zed Books.

Kyle, Chris. 2015. "Violence and Insecurity in Guerrero," in *Building Resilient Communities in Mexico: Civic Responses to Crime and Violence*. Briefing Paper Series, Woodrow Wilson Center.

La Jornada Guerrero. 2007. "Diputados perredistas critican amenazas de muerte contra Salgado Macedonio," *La Jornada Guerrero*, February 11.

Lagunas, Icela. 2012. "Otro gobernador en la mira," *Reporte Índigo*, July 30.

Langston, Joy. 2007. "The PRI's 2006 Electoral Debacle," *PS: Political Science and Politics* 40(1): 21–25.

Langston, Joy. 2018. *Democratization and Authoritarian Party Survival: Mexico's PRI*. Oxford: Oxford University Press.

Lantia Intelligence. 2019a. "Total de ejecuciones anuales," November 14. https://bit.ly/2utkPNl. Accessed January 7, 2020.

Lantia Intelligence. 2019b. "Mapa criminal," November 16. https://bit.ly/2T1yd Ta. Accessed January 7, 2020.

Lawson, Chappell. 2000. "Mexico's Unfinished Transition: Democratization and Authoritarian Enclaves in Mexico," *Mexican Studies/Estudios Mexicanos* 16 (2): 267–287.

LeCour Graindmason, Romain. 2016. "Vigilar y limpiar: Identification and Self-Help Justice-Making in Michoacán, Mexico," *Politix* 3(115): 103–125.

Lessing, Benjamin. 2015. "Logics of Violence in Criminal War," *Journal of Conflict Resolution* 59(8): 1486–1516.

Lessing, Benjamin. 2017. *Making Peace in Drug Wars: Crackdowns and Cartels in Latin America*. Cambridge: Cambridge University Press.

Lessing, Benjamin and Graham Denyer Willis. 2019. "Legitimate Criminals: How to Build a Drug Empire from Behind Bars," *American Political Science Review* 113(2): 584–606.

Levitt, Steven. 2004. "Understanding Why Crime Fell in the 1990s: Four Factors that Explain the Decline and Six that Do Not," *Journal of Economic Perspectives* 18(1): 163–190.

Ley, Sandra. 2017. "Security and Crime Issue Voting: Electoral Accountability in the Midst of Violence," *Latin American Politics and Society* 59(1): 3–27.

Ley, Sandra. 2018. "To Vote or Not to Vote: How Criminal Violence Shapes Electoral Participation," *Journal of Conflict Resolution* 62(9): 1963–1990.

Ley, Sandra and Magdalena Guzmán. 2019. "Doing Business in the Context of Criminal Violence in Mexico," in Deborah Avant, Marie Berrie, Erica Chenoweth, Rachel Epstein, Cullen Hendrix, Oliver Kaplan, and Timothy Sisk (eds.), *Civil Action and the Dynamics of Violence*, Oxford: Oxford University Press.

Ley, Sandra, Shannan Mattiace, and Guillermo Trejo. 2019. "Indigenous Resistance to Criminal Governance: Why Regional Ethnic Autonomy Institutions Protect Communities from Narco Rule," *Latin American Research Review* 54(1): 181–200.

Lieberman, Evan. 2005. "Nested Analysis as a Mixed-Method Strategy for Comparative Research," *American Political Science Review* 99(3): 435–452.

López, Claudia. 2010. *y refundaron la patria ... De cómo mafiosos y políticos reconfiguraron el Estado colombiano*. Bogotá: Nuevo Arcoiris.

Lucardi, Adrián. 2017. "Building Support from Below? Subnational Elections, Diffusion Effects, and the Growth of the Opposition in Mexico, 1984–2000," *Comparative Political Studies* 49(14): 1855–1895.

Luján, Francisco. 2011. "Ataque a Leyzaola rompe relación Municipio-Federal," *Norte de Ciudad Juárez*, July 27.

Lupsha, Peter A. 1991. "Drug Lords and Narco-Corruption: The Players Change but the Game Continues," *Crime, Law and Social Change* 16, 41–58.

Maerker, Denise. 2014. "Auxilio: ¿Dónde está el Estado?," *Nexos*, April 1, www .nexos.com.mx/?p=20052. Accessed April 7, 2020.

Magaloni, Beatriz. 2006. *Voting for Autocracy: Hegemonic Party Survival and its Demise in Mexico*. Cambridge: Cambridge University Press.

Magaloni, Beatriz. 2008. "Credible Power-Sharing and the Longevity of Authoritarian Rule," *Comparative Political Studies* 41(4–5): 715–741.

Magaloni, Beatriz, Aila M. Gustavo Robles, Alberto Díaz-Cayeros Matanock, and Vidal Romero. 2019. "Living in Fear: The Dynamics of Extortion in Mexico's Drug War," *Comparative Political Studies*. 53(7): 1124–1174.

Mainwaring, Scott. 2012. "From Representative Democracy to Participatory Competitive Autocracy: Hugo Chávez and Venezuelan Politics," *Perspectives on Politics* 10(4): 955–967.

Maldonado, Salvador. 2012. "Drogas, Violencia y Militarización en el México Rural. El caso de Michoacán," *Revista Mexicana de Sociología* 74(1): 5–39.

Mann, Michael. 1984. "The Autonomous Power of the State: Its origins, mechanisms, and results," *European Journal of Sociology* 25(2): 185–213.

Martínez, Fernando. 2007. "Exige la IP a Nati reorientar agenda," *El Norte*, April 14.

Martínez, Julieta. 2008. "Carta íntegra del Comandante Sergio Aponte Polito," *El Universal*, April 23.

McCauley, John F. and Daniel N. Posner. 2015. "African Borders as Sources of Natural Experiments Promise and Pitfalls," *Political Science Research and Methods* 3(2): 409–418.

McDonnell, Patrick. 2017. "The sordid record of former Mexican governors: 3 in prison, 3 under investigation and 4 wanted by authorities," *Los Angeles Times*, March 31, www.latimes.com/world/mexico-americas/la-fg-mexico-governors-20170331-story.html. Accessed December 18, 2019.

Medellín Mendoza, Laura N. 2006. "La travesía de la liberalización política de Nuevo León," *Espiral, Estudios sobre Estado y Sociedad* 12(35): 65–91.

Melgar, Ivonne. 2002. "Define Fox derechos desde la concepción," *Reforma*, May 11.

Mendez, Patricia. 2002. "Divide al Congreso la reforma eléctrica," *Reforma*, December 10.

Mendoza Rockwell, Natalia. 2012. "Crónica de la cartelización," *Nexos*, June 1, www.nexos.com.mx/?p=14846. Accessed December 18, 2019.

Merino, José. 2011. "Los operativos conjuntos y la tasa de homicidios: Una medición," *Nexos*, June 1. https://www.nexos.com.mx/?p=14319. Accessed December 18, 2019.

Merino, José, Jessica Zarkin, and Eduardo Fierro. 2013. "Marcado para morir," *Nexos*, July. https://www.nexos.com.mx/?p=15375. Accessed December 18, 2019.

Merino, Mauricio. 2003. *La transición votada: Crítica a la interpretación del cambio político en México*. Mexico City: FCE.

Meyer, Jean. 1976. *La Cristiada*. Mexico City: Siglo XXI.

Meyerson, Harold. 2005. "Greetings from Mexistan," *The Washington Post*, April 13.

Michel, Víctor Hugo and David Vicenteño. 2007. "Lanzan operativo antinarco en noreste," *Reforma*, February 18.

Mizrahi, Yemile. 1996. "¿Administrar o gobernar? El reto del gobierno panista en Chihuahua," *Frontera Norte* 8(16): 57–80.

Monarrez Fragoso, Julia Estela. 2000. "La cultura del feminicidio en Ciudad Juárez, 1993–1999," *Frontera Norte* 12(23): 87–117.

Monarrez Fragoso, Julia Estela. 2013. *Trama de una Injusticia: Feminicidio Sexual Sistémico en Ciudad Juárez*. Tijuana: El Colegio de la Frontera Norte.

Morales, Alberto y Juan Manuel Cruz. 2011. "Suspenden a Cd. Juárez subsidio para seguridad," *El Universal*, July 29.

Moran, Jon. 2011. *Crime and Corruption in New Democracies: The politics of (in)security*. New York: Palgrave Macmillan.

Moreno, Alejandro and Roberto Gutiérrez. 2005. "Prevén triunfo perredista," *Reforma*, May 30.

Mural. 2010. "Tiene Jalisco reunión de seguridad," *Mural*, June 19.

Neumayer, Eric. 2003. "Good Policy Can Lower Violent Crime: Evidence from a Cross-National Panel of Homicide Rates, 1980–97," *Journal of Peace Research* 40(6): 619–640.

New York Times. 2005. "Let Mexico's voters decide," *The New York Times*, April 7.

Oates, Wallace. 1972. *Fiscal Federalism*. New York: Harcourt.

Ochoa, Rolando. 2019. *Intimate Crimes: Kidnapping, Gangs, and Trust in Mexico City*. Oxford: Oxford University Press.

O'Donnell, Guillermo. 1993. "On the state, democratization, and some conceptual problems," *Kellogg*, Working Paper Series 192, April 1993.

O'Donnell, Guillermo and Philippe Schmitter. 1986. *Transitions from Authoritarian Rule: Tentative Conclusions about Uncertain Democracies*. Baltimore: Johns Hopkins University Press.

Oliveri, Elisabetta and Salvatore Sberna. 2014. "Set the night on fire! Mafia violence and elections in Italy," Paper presented at the Conference of the American Political Science Association, August 18.

Olson, Mancur. 2000. *Power and Prosperity: Outgrowing Communist and Capitalist Dictatorships*. New York: Basic Books.

O'Neil, Shannon K. 2009. "The Real War in Mexico," *Foreign Affairs* 88(4): 63–77.

Open Society Justice Initiative. 2016. *Atrocidades Innegables. Confrontando Crímenes de Lesa Humanidad en México*. New York: Open Society.

O'Shaughnessy, Hugh. 2000. *Pinochet: The Politics of Torture*. New York: New York University Press.

Osorio, Javier. 2015. "The Contagion of Drug Violence: Spatiotemporal Dynamics of Mexican War on Drugs," *Journal of Conflict Resolution* 59(8): 1403–1432.

Osorno, Diego Enrique. 2012. *La guerra de los Zetas*. Mexico City: Grijalbo.

Pachico, Elyssa. 2011. "Why violence could boil over in Guatemala elections," InSight Crime, June 20, www.insightcrime.org/news/analysis/why-violence-could-boil-over-in-guatemala-elections/. Accessed December 4, 2019.

Padgett, Humberto. 2014. "Imposible decirle 'no' a los Templarios," *SinEmbargo*, March 14, www.sinembargo.mx/14-03-2014/931679. Accessed April 7, 2020.

Pansters, Wil. 2018. "Drug Trafficking, the Informal Order, and Caciques. Reflections on the Crime–Governance Nexus in Mexico," *Global Crime* 19 (3–4): 315–338.

Parametría. 2005. "El desafuero de López Obrador," Parametría, www .parametria.com.mx/carta_parametrica.php?cp=81. Accessed December 4, 2019.

Patiño, Martín. 2010. "Capturan a líder del cártel de 'Los Valencia'," *El Informador*, May 10.

Peacock, Susan and Adriana Beltrán. 2003. *Hidden Powers: Illegal Armed Groups in Post-Conflict Guatemala and the Forces Behind Them*. Washington, DC: WOLA.

Pensamiento, Daniel, Claudia Salazar, and Carolina Pacón. 2004. "Prevé PRD rompimiento con el Ejecutivo," *Reforma*, April 16.

Petersen, Paul. 1995. *The Price of Federalism*. Washington, DC: The Brookings Institution.

Phillips, Brian J. 2015. "How Does Leadership Decapitation Affect Violence? The Case of Drug Trafficking Organizations in Mexico," *Journal of Politics* 77(2): 324–336.

Plascencia, Ángel. 2013. "El Oscuro Pasado del Director," *Reporte Índigo*, September 23, www.reporteindigo.com/reporte/el-oscuro-pasado-del-director/. Accessed December 4, 2019.

Ponce, Aldo. 2016. "Cárteles de Droga, Violencia y Competitividad Electoral a Nivel Local: Evidencia del Caso Mexicano," *Latin American Research Review (LAAR)* 51(4): 62–85.

Popper, Karl. 1962. *The Open Society and Its Enemies* (vol. I). Princeton: Princeton University Press

Prado, Henia. 2011. "Impulsan talleres de sensibilidad," *Reforma*, May 29.

Presidencia de la República. 2006. "Palabras al Pueblo de México desde el Auditorio Nacional," Presidencia de la República, December 1, http://calderon.presidencia.gob.mx/2006/12/palabras-al-pueblo-de-mexico-desde-el-auditorio-nacional. Accessed February 7, 2015.

Proceso. 1992a. "'No voy a renunciar,' decía Cosío, y al día siguiente se fue, su relevo, impugnado antes de llegar," *Proceso*, May 2, www.proceso.com.mx/159267/no-voy-a-renunciar-decia-cosio-y-al-dia-siguiente-se-fue-su-relevo-impugnado-antes-de-llegar. Accessed December 4, 2019.

Proceso. 1992b. "Al fondo a la investigación sobre Elías Ramírez, 'caiga quien caiga': Barrio," *Proceso*, October 17, www.proceso.com.mx/160309/al-fondo-en-la-investigacion-sobre-elias-ramirez-caiga-quien-caiga-barrio. Accessed December 19, 2019.

Proceso. 1994. "Acusaciones de corrupción, presunta responsabilidad de la tragedia de Guadalajara," *Proceso*, June 18, www.proceso.com.mx/165618/acusaciones-de-corrupcion-presunta-responsabilidad-de-la-tragedia-de-guadalajara. Accessed December 4, 2019.

Proceso. 1997. "Canales Clariond iniciará una nueva forma de gobierno, con 'un PRI como alma en pena'," *Proceso*, July 5, www.proceso.com.mx/175905/canales-clariond-iniciara-una-nueva-forma-de-gobierno-con-un-pri-como-alma-en-pena. Accessed December 4, 2019.

Proceso. 2004. "Narcogobierno en Chihuahua," *Proceso*, March 7, www.proceso.com.mx/191188/narcogobierno-en-chihuahua. Accessed December 19, 2019.

Proceso. 2006. "De paraíso a cubil de narcos," March 26, www.proceso.com.mx/97387/de-paraiso-a-cubil-de-narcos. Accessed December 4, 2019.

Proceso. 2008. "Jalisco: las entrañas de la narcopolicía," *Proceso*, September 27, www.proceso.com.mx/88882/jalisco-las-entranas-de-la-narcopolicia. Accessed December 4, 2019.

Proceso. 2009. "Guanajuato. La matazón, una historia maquillada," *Proceso*, July 6.

Proceso. 2010a. "Presenta Calderón plan para Juárez; se disculpa con padres masacrados," *Proceso*, February 11, www.proceso.com.mx/109865/presenta-calderon-plan-para-juarez-se-disculpa-con-padres-de-masacrados. Accessed December 4, 2019.

Proceso. 2010b. "Calderón y Amalia 'perdieron' Zacatecas," *Proceso*, August 22, www.proceso.com.mx/81075/81075-calderon-y-amalia-perdieron-zacatecas. Accessed December 4, 2019.

Proceso. 2010c. "Termina la tregua y Guadalajara vuelve a ensangrentarse," *Proceso*, May 30.

Przeworski, Adam. 1991. *Democracy and the Market*. Cambridge: Cambridge University Press.

Quiñones, Sam. 2015. *Dreamland: The True Tale of America's Opiate Epidemic*. New York: Bloomsbury Publishing.

Ramírez, Arturo and Reyes Ruiz. 2016. *Security Strategies: Experiences of the Mexican States of Chihuahua and Nuevo León*. Stanford: Hoover Institution Press.

Ramírez, Ignacio. 2002. "Surge Monterrey como nuevo asiento del narco," *El Universal*, January 6.

Ramírez, Valeria. 2011. "¿Silenciarse ante la violencia? La autocensura y la cobertura de narcoviolencia. Caso Reforma 2006–2009," B.A. Thesis, Centro de Investigación y Docencia Económicas (CIDE).

Rea, Daniela. 2011. "Lanzan ahora 'Convivir Mejor'," *Reforma*, September 18.

Redacción AN. 2013. "Matan a alcalde de Michoacán que denunciaba pagos de cuotas al 'narco'," *Aristegui Noticias*, November 8, https://aristeguinoti cias.com/0811/mexico/matan-a-alcalde-de-michoacan-que-denunciaba-al-na rco/. Accessed December 18, 2019.

Reforma. 2004. "Aprueban panistas programa político," *Reforma*, May 1.

Reforma. 2005. "Moviliza 'tropas' y regresa al GDF," *Reforma*, April 25.

Reforma. 2007. "Indaga SSP vínculos de Salgado con narco," *Reforma*, February 12.

Reforma. 2008a. "Respalda Gobernador de BC a Procurador," *Reforma*, April 23.

Reforma. 2008b. "Denuncia Aponte 'complot' en su contra," *Reforma*, August 3.

Reforma. 2011a. "No hay plena prueba sobre 'Chayo'. Godoy," *Reforma*, January 17.

Reforma. 2011b. "Legalmente, 'Chayo' no está muerto," *Reforma*, January 18.

Reforma. 2011c. "Amenazan a votantes," *Reforma*, November 13.

Reforma. 2011d. "Votan entre amenazas," *Reforma*, November 13.

Reforma. 2012. "Niega base de datos y crimen lo ejecuta," *Reforma*, October 30.

Reforma. 2013. "Pide Edil Ayuda y Lo Matan," *Reforma*, November 8.

Remes, Alain. 1999. "Gobiernos yuxtapuestos en México: Hacia un marco analítico para el estudio de las elecciones municipales," *Política y Gobierno* 6 (1): 225–253.

Reuter, Peter. 2009. "Systemic Violence in Drug Markets," *Crime, Law and Social Change* 52(3): 275–284.

Riker, William. 1964. *Federalism: Origins, Operations, and Significance*. Boston: Little Brown.

Riker, William H. 1975. "Federalism," in Fred I. Greenstein and Nelson W. Polsby (eds.), *Handbook of Political Science: Governmental Institutions and Processes*. Reading, MA: Addison-Wesley.

Riker, William H. and Ronald Schaps. 1957. "Disharmony in Federal Government," *Systems Research and Behavioral Science* 2(4): 276–290.

Ríos, Viridiana. 2012. "El asesinato de periodistas y alcaldes en México y su relación con el crimen organizado," in José Antonio Aguilar (ed.), *Las Bases Sociales del Crimen Organizado y la Violencia en México*. Mexico City: CIES-SSP.

Ríos, Viridiana. 2013. "Why Did Mexico Become So Violent? A Self-reinforcing Violent Equilibrium Caused by Competition and Enforcement," *Trends in Organized Crime* 16(2): 138–155.

Ríos, Viridiana. 2015. "How Government Coordination Controlled Organized Crime: The Case of Mexico's Cocaine Markets," *Journal of Conflict Resolution* 59(8): 1433–1454.

Ríos-Figueroa, Julio and Paloma Aguilar. 2018. "Justice Institutions in Autocracies: A Framework for Analysis," *Democratization* 25(1): 1–18.

Rivera, Mauricio. 2016. "The Sources of Social Violence in Latin America: An Empirical Analysis of Homicide Rates, 1980–2010," *Journal of Peace Research* 53(1): 84–99.

Ross, Michael. 2004. "How Does Natural Resource Wealth Influence Civil Wars? Evidence from Thirteen Cases," *International Organization* 58(1): 35–67.

Rubio, Laura. 2015. *Desplazamiento interno inducido por la violencia: Una experiencia global, realidad mexicana*. Mexico City: ITAM-CMPDH.

Rubio, Laura and Brenda Pérez. 2016. "Desplazados por violencia. La tragedia invisible," *Nexos*, January 1, www.nexos.com.mx/?p=27278. Accessed December 18, 2019.

Ruiz-González, Reyes. 2018. "Don't Rush to Judgment: Justice Reform and the Rise of Violence in Mexico," Ph.D. Thesis, University of Notre Dame.

Sáenz-Rovner, Eduardo. 2008. *The Cuban Connection: Drug Trafficking, Smuggling, and Gambling in Cuba from the 1920s to the Revolution*. Chapel Hill: University of North Carolina Press.

Sánchez, Fabio and María del Mar Palau. 2006. "Conflict, decentralization and local governance in Colombia, 1974–2004," *HiCN*, Working Paper 14, May 2006.

Sánchez Murillo, Luis Fernando and Francisco de Jesús Aceves González. 2008. "Campañas políticas y configuración del voto electoral en 2006. Encuestas electorales y publicidad política," *Revista Mexicana de Ciencias Políticas y Sociales* 50(202): 93–116.

Sabet, Daniel. 2012. *Police Reform in Mexico*. California: Stanford University Press.

Salazar, Claudia and Víctor Fuentes. 2002. "Reavivan PAN y PRD debate por aborto," *Reforma*, January 31.

Salmón, Alejandro and Orlando Chávez. 2010. "Truena Reyes Baeza contra Gabinete de Seguridad," *El Diario*, February 6.

Sambanis, Nicholas. 2004. "What is Civil War? Conceptual and Empirical Complexities of an Operational Definition," *Journal of Conflict Resolution* 48(6): 814–858.

Sampson, Robert. 1993. "The Community Context of Violent Crime," in William J. Wilson (ed.), *Sociology and the Public Agenda*. Newbury Park, CA: Sage.

Sampson, Robert and Byron Groves. 1989. "Community Structure and Crime: Testing Social-Disorganization Theory," *American Journal of Sociology* 94(4): 774–802.

Schatz, Sara. 2011. *Murder and Politics in Mexico: Political Killings in the Partido de la Revolución Democrática and Its Consequences*. Columbus, OH: Springer.

Schedler, Andreas. 2007. "The Mexican Standoff: The Mobilization of Distrust," *Journal of Democracy* 18(1): 88–102.

Schelling, Thomas C. 1971. "What is the Business of Organized Crime?," *The American Scholar* 40(4): 643–652.

Schumpeter, Joseph. 1943. *Capitalism, Socialism, and Democracy*. London: George Allen & Unwin Ltd.

Scott, Peter. 2009. "Drugs, Anti-Communism and Extra-Legal Repression in Mexico," in Eric Wilson and Tim Lindsey (eds.), *Government of the Shadows. Parapolitics and Criminal Sovereignty*. New York: Pluto Press.

Secretaría de la Defensa Nacional (Sedena). 2009. "Detención de Óscar Orlando Nava Valencia (a) 'EL LOBO,' líder de la Organización Delictiva 'LOS VALENCIA'," Sedena, October 30.

Secretaría de la Defensa Nacional (Sedena). 2015. Information request to Sedena regarding the number of marijuana and poppy plantations and hectares eradicated by municipality. *Sedena*. Request number: 0000700002215.

Secretariado Ejecutivo del Sistema Nacional de Seguridad Pública (SESNSP). 2011. "Reporte de los Programas y Proyectos de Prevención Social de la Violencia y la Delincuencia con Participación Ciudadana," SESNSP, October 19, www.secretariadoejecutivosnsp.gob.mx/work/models/Secretariad oEjecutivo/Resource/378/1/images/ProgramasXinstitucionesConsultoras_2.pd f. Accessed December 4, 2019.

Secretariado Ejecutivo del Sistema Nacional de Seguridad Pública (SESNSP). 2016. "Tasa por cada 100 mil habitantes 1997–2016," *SNSNSP*, February 20.

Shirk, David and Joel Wallman. 2015. "Understanding Mexico's Drug Violence," *Journal of Conflict Resolution* 59(8): 1348–1376.

Sierra, Jorge Luis. 2012. "Mexico's Anti-insurgency Policies in the 1970s and 1980s," in Fernando Herrera and Adela Cedillo (eds.), *Challenging Authoritarianism in Mexico: Revolutionary Struggles and the Dirty War, 1964–1982*. New York: Routledge.

SinEmbargo. 2013a. "FCH es oportunista, ahora tuitea pero ni nos recibió," *SinEmbargo*, November 8, www.sinembargo.mx/08-11-2013/808887. Accessed April 7, 2020.

SinEmbargo. 2013b. "La extorsión generalizada alcanza a los alcaldes; ya no es asunto de ciudadanos, comerciantes y agricultores," *SinEmbargo*, November 16.

Skaperdas, Stergios. 2001. "The Political Economy of Organized Crime: Providing Protection When the State Does Not," *Economics of Governance* 2 (3): 173–202.

Skarbek, David. 2014. *The Social Order of the Underworld: How Prison Gangs Govern the American Penal System*. Oxford: Oxford University Press.

Smith, Douglas A., Christy A. Visher, and Laura A. Davidson. 1984. "Equity and Discretionary Justice: The Influence of Race on Police Arrest Decisions," *Journal of Criminal Law and Criminology* 75(1): 234–249.

Snyder, Richard and Angélica Durán-Martínez. 2009. "Does Illegality Breed Violence? Drug Trafficking and State-Sponsored Protection Rackets," *Crime, Law and Social Change* 52(3): 253–273.

Sobering, Katherine and Javier Auyero. 2019. "Collusion and Cynicism at the Urban Margins," *Latin American Research Review* 54(1): 222–236.

Spring, Karen. 2013. "Context of the Honduran electoral process 2012–2013: incomplete list of killings and armed attacks related to political campaigning in Honduras," Rights Action, http://rightsaction.org/sites/def ault/files/Honduras-Violence-Political-Campaign.pdf. Accessed December 4, 2019.

Staniland, Paul. 2012. "States, Insurgents, and Wartime Political Orders," *Perspectives on Politics* 10(2): 243–264.

Steele, Abbey. 2011. "Electing Displacement: Political Cleansing in Apartadó, Colombia," *Journal of Conflict Resolution* 55(3): 423–445.

Stokes, Susan. 2014. "A Defense of Observational Research," in Dawn Teele (ed.), *Field Experiments and their Critics*. New Haven: Yale University Press.

Svolik, Milan W. 2012. *The Politics of Authoritarian Rule*. Cambridge: Cambridge University Press.

Tarrow, Sidney. 1998. *Power in Movement: Social Movements and Contentious Politics*. Cambridge: Cambridge University Press.

Témeris, Greco and David Espino. 2015. "Disputan 10 cárteles Mercado de amapola," *El Universal*, February 3.

Tiscornia, Lucía. 2019. "Who Calls the Shots? Police Reform and Criminal Violence in the Aftermath of Internal Armed Conflict," Ph.D. Thesis, University of Notre Dame.

Torres, Bernardo. 2019. "Escapa joven de campo de concentración en Guerrero; lo querían convertir en sicario," *Redes del Sur*, December 2, http://redesdelsur .com.mx/index.php/es/seguridadyjusticia-pag1/escapa-joven-de-campo-de-con centracion-en-guerrero-lo-querian-convertir-en-sicario. Accessed April 7, 2020.

Trejo, Guillermo. 2012. *Popular Movements in Autocracies: Religion, Repression, and Indigenous Collective Action in Mexico*. Cambridge: Cambridge University Press.

Trejo, Guillermo. 2014. "The Ballot and the Street: An Electoral Theory of Social Protest in Autocracies," *Perspectives on Politics* 12(2): 332–352.

Trejo, Guillermo and Sandra Ley. 2015. "Municipios bajo fuego (1995–2014)," *Nexos*, February, www.nexos.com.mx/?p=24024. Accessed December 4, 2019.

Trejo, Guillermo and Sandra Ley. 2016. "Federalism, Drugs, and Violence. Why Intergovernmental Partisan Conflict Stimulated Inter-Cartel Violence in Mexico," *Política y Gobierno* 23(1): 9–52.

Trejo, Guillermo and Sandra Ley. 2018. "Why Did Drug Cartels Go to War in Mexico? Subnational Party Alternation, the Breakdown of Criminal Protection, and the Onset of Large-Scale Violence," *Comparative Political Studies* 51(7): 900–937.

Trejo, Guillermo and Sandra Ley. 2019. "High-Profile Criminal Violence: Why Drug Cartels Murder Government Officials and Party Candidates in Mexico," *British Journal of Political Science*. http://dx.doi.org/10.1017/S0007123418000637

Trejo, Guillermo, Juan Albarracín, and Lucía Tiscornia. 2018. "Breaking State Impunity in Postauthoritarian Regimes: Why Transitional Justice Mechanisms Deter Criminal Violence in New Democracies," *Journal of Peace Research* 55 (6): 787–809.

Treviño Rangel, Javier. 2009. "Pánico moral en las campañas electorales de 2006: la elaboración del 'peligro para México'," *Foro Internacional* 49(3): 638–689.

Tunander, Ola. 2009. "Democratic State vs. Deep State: Approaching the Dual State of the West," in Eric Wilson and Tim Lindsey (eds.), *Government of the Shadows. Parapolitics and Criminal Sovereignty*. New York: Pluto Press.

United National Development Program. 2013. *Citizen Security with a Human Face*. New York: United Nations.

United Nations Office on Drugs and Crime (UNODC). 2008. *World Drug Report*. New York: UNODC.

United Nations Office on Drugs and Crime (UNODC). 2012. "Transnational Organized Crime in Central America and the Caribbean. A Threat Assessment," *UNODC*, www.unodc.org/documents/data-and-analysis/Studies/TOC_Central_America_and_the_Caribbean_english.pdf. Accessed December 4, 2019.

Univisión. 2009. "12 sicarios muertos tras enfrentarse con autoridades en Guanajuato," Univisión, June 26.

Univisión. 2011. "Denuncian que 'narcovoto' llegó a Michoacán," Univisión, November 22.

Urrusti Frenk, Sinaia. 2012. "La Violencia como Consecuencia de la Falta de Coordinación Política," in José Antonio Aguilar (coord.), *Las Bases Sociales del Crimen Organizado y la Violencia en México*. Mexico City: Secretaría de Seguridad Pública.

Valdés, Guillermo. 2013. *Historia del narcotráfico en México*. Mexico City: Aguilar.

Varese, Federico. 2001. *The Russian Mafia. Private Protection in a New Market Economy*. Oxford: Oxford University Press.

Varese, Federico. 2010. "What is Organized Crime?," in Federico Varese (ed.), *Organized Crime*. London: Routledge.

Varese, Federico. 2011. *Mafias on the Move: How Organized Crime Conquers New Territories*. Princeton, NJ: Princeton University Press.

Vargas, Robert. 2016. *Wounded City: Violent Turf Wars in a Chicago Barrio*. Oxford: Oxford University Press.

Villarreal, Andrés. 2002. "Political Competition and Violence in Mexico," *American Sociological Review* 67(4): 477–498.

Waldern, David. 2015. "What Makes Process Tracing Good? Causal Mechanisms, Causal Inference, and the Completeness Standard in Comparative Politics," in Andrew Bennett and Jeffrey Checkel (eds.), *Process Tracing: From Metaphor to Analytic Tool*. Cambridge: Cambridge University Press.

Weber, Max. [1918] 1994. "Politics as a Vocation," in Hans Heinrich Garth and Charles Wright Mills (eds.), *Essays in Sociology*. New York: Macmillan.

Weingast, Barry R. 2014. "Second Generation Fiscal Federalism: Political Aspects of Decentralization and Economic Development," *World Development* 53: 14–25.

Wilkinson, Steven I. 2004. *Votes and Violence: Electoral Competition and Ethnic Riots in India*. Cambridge: Cambridge University Press.

Wolf, Sonja. 2018. *Mano Dura: The Politics of Gang Control in El Salvador.* Austin, TX: University of Texas Press.

Wood, Elisabeth. 2011. "The Social Process of Civil War: The Wartime Transformation of Social Networks," *Annual Review of Political Science* 11: 539–561.

Yashar, Deborah. 2018. *Homicidal Ecologies: Illicit Economies and Complicit States in Latin America.* Cambridge: Cambridge University Press.

Zakaria, Fareed. 2003. *The Future of Freedom: Illiberal Democracy at Home and Abroad.* New York: W. W. Norton & Company Inc.

Zamarripa, Roberto. 2007. "Es un asunto de seguridad nacional," *Reforma*, December 16.

Zepeda, Guillermo. 2004. *Crimen sin castigo: Procuración de justicia penal y ministerio público en México.* Mexico City: CIDAC/FCE.

Zepeda, Raúl. 2018. "Violencia en Tierra Caliente: desigualdad, desarrollo y escolaridad en la guerra contra el narcotráfico," *Estudios Sociológicos* 36 (106): 125–159.

Zubía García, Ángel. 2008. "Confía Reyes Baeza en el apoyo federal," *Norte de Ciudad Juárez*, February 20.

Index